THE NEW TSARS

Russia Under Stalin's Heirs

Other Books by John Dornberg

THE OTHER GERMANY

SCHIZOPHRENIC GERMANY

JOHN DORNBERG

THE NEW TSARS
Russia Under Stalin's Heirs

Doubleday & Company, Inc.
Garden City, New York
1972

PHOTO CREDITS

A C E R, Paris: 5.
CBS News Special Report: "Voices from the Russian Underground": 6, 7.
John Dornberg: 3, 11, 12, 13, 14, 17, 18, 19, 20, 21, 23, 24, 26, 27, 28, 29, 30, 31, 32.
Stephan Dornberg: 22, 25.
Eastfoto: 16.
Eupra GmbH: 15.
Julius Telesin: 4
Observer/Transworld Feature: 8, 9.
UPI: 1, 2, 10.

Contents

PART FIVE

PART SIX

PART SEVEN

Preface

This is a book I once swore solemnly never to write.

When I accepted the assignment to go to Moscow I proceeded to amass a background and reference library of books on tsarist Russia and the Soviet Union. In no time it grew into such a huge collection that I concluded that no subject, no country has been as thoroughly examined and covered by so many authors. Just one more book on Russia, I felt, would not only be presumptuous but would require considerable justification. Yet, a year or so after my arrival in the U.S.S.R., the idea for this one began to germinate. Because it may seem temerarious to contribute more words to the millions already written, I must explain briefly why I decided, after all, to do so.

The decision was neither quick nor easy but rather the slow, inevitable result of my deepening involvement with all aspects of Soviet affairs, the metastasis of my personal attitude toward the U.S.S.R. and Russia, of my improving ability to break through the wall of isolation that surrounds all foreign correspondents in Moscow. It also grew out of my eventual realization that there were numerous developments and features of the Soviet Union that would interest a wide audience for which, however, the media of daily and weekly journalism would never provide an adequate forum because of their physical limitations and the requirement to keep pace with current events. But most important, I became aware that knowledge of the significant changes that have taken place in the U.S.S.R. since Nikita Khrushchev's fall is surprisingly limited.

It required about eight years after Khrushchev's famous speech denouncing Stalin in 1956 for the notion of a changed, more liberal, more open, less belligerent Soviet Union to become imbedded in the public consciousness of the West. By then the corpulent, outspoken, often irrational but comparably benevolent dictator had already been toppled from the pinnacle of power. In the seven years since his political demise hope has again faded in that tormented and unhappy land. But the fact of this retrogressive transformation has not really yet reached the West. Out of Russia on vacations, in talks and discussions with friends, acquaintances and strangers, in meetings with Western visitors to Moscow, while answering questions at lectures or during after-dinner conversations, I realized that the picture my interlocutors had of the U.S.S.R. was critically out of date.

It is largely to revise that picture that this book has been written.

It is not intended as a book for experts, for the Sovietologists and Kremlinologists who know what has transpired in the Soviet Union in recent years, although I hope that they too will find it useful, that it will provide them with the third-dimensional picture that only on-scene reporting, despite the obstacles raised by Soviet authorities, can produce from Moscow. But primarily it is a book—focusing largely on the nearly three-year period when I was in Moscow—that reflects my discovery that the U.S.S.R. is again a haunted land.

I claim no special qualifications that would entitle me to add yet another volume on the bending shelves of books about Russia. My Russian, learned on the job after arrival in Moscow, is imperfect. It was often complemented by the translation services of my patient wife, who is a far better linguist, in addition to being intuitive. I did not travel more extensively or more freely than other foreign correspondents in the U.S.S.R. Given the obstacles that Soviet authorities deliberately raise, my contacts and my insight were no better or worse than those of other newsmen. And even when I was expelled as a correspondent in October 1970, I was not unique—merely the fourth Western journalist to be ordered out of the U.S.S.R. that year, the eighteenth since pre-publication censorship was abolished in 1961. Thus I can offer only a book that I finally wanted very much to write because I felt that it needed to be written.

It could not have been written without the collective experience, advice and counsel of the journalistic colleagues who preceded me in Moscow and those who are still there working in a most difficult and trying situation. Nor could it have been written without the friendship extended and the insight accorded me by a large number of Soviet citizens whose trust and faith in me I hope this book, which they may never see, will justify. The repressive nature of the system under which they live has forced me to preserve the anonymity of most of them, just as I have changed the locales and identifying descriptions of some of those who are quoted in these pages.

I am grateful, also, to those experts and specialists on Soviet affairs, only some of whom are cited by name in the text, who gave freely of their time and their knowledge to contribute and enlarge mine.

The transliteration system for Russian words and names which I have used is intended for those readers who do not know Russian with the aim of approximating, as closely as possible, while still observing the rules of Russian spelling and grammar, the sound of the word in Russian. Exceptions are those words and names for which different spellings have come to be so widely accepted that deviations would only serve to confuse the reader. For example: Tchaikovsky, Khrushchev and Soviet as well as certain Christian and family names which exist in both Russian and English or Russian and other languages, such as Alexander, Edward and (Svyatoslav) Richter.

Most prices are given in rubles. And while there is considerable doubt concerning the ruble's real value, largely because it is not freely convertible, I recommend using the official exchange rate of $1.11 to 1 ruble. It is the rate at which Western tourists, diplomats, correspondents and businessmen must convert and the rate I have employed in those instances where dollar equivalents are used in the text.

Munich, September 1971   J.D.

I judge a country by the faces of its
inhabitants. Many Russians pass
through Lübeck. They have two
expressions. When they come here
on their way to Europe they have
a gay, free, happy air . . . The same
people on their return have a long,
gloomy, tormented look, a worried
face . . . A country which one leaves
with such joy and returns to with so
much regret must be a bad country.

A Lübeck innkeeper to
Astolphe Marquis de Custine
July 4, 1839

Prologue

Behind the Curtain

Two dozen passengers—most of them Soviet officials, a few German
and Austrian diplomats, some Western businessmen and journalists—
stood, sat and paced impatiently in the waiting room of Vienna's
Schwechat airport. They looked worried and gloomy. They had
already spent thirty uncomfortable minutes aboard the Moscow-
bound jet parked on the tarmac, only to be told to debark again
because departure had been delayed.

"A minor mechanical difficulty," grumbled an unkempt-looking
and tight-lipped crew member when pressed for information by the
Western passengers. The Russian travelers, patient, docile and accustomed to a life of delays over which they had no control, had not
even troubled to ask.

More than two hours after scheduled departure the plane taxied
noisily and unsteadily toward the runway. A plump, untidy stewardess in an ill-fitting, faded blue uniform, a beehive of peroxided

blond hair perched precariously atop her round head, her eyes framed by an excess of mascara, picked up a microphone in the galley.

"Aeroflot, the Soviet airline, welcomes you aboard our Soviet-made Tupolev-134 on its flight to Moscow, capital of the U.S.S.R., via Kiev," she said in heavily accented English. "On board you will find chess sets, dominoes and newspapers and magazines in many languages. Fasten your seat belts."

As she came down the aisle to ascertain whether her order had been followed, I asked her for a copy of the Paris *Herald Tribune* or Vienna's *Die Presse*.

"Nyet," she said gruffly in Russian. *"Tolko sovietskykh gazet i zhurnalov* (only Soviet newspapers and magazines)." Then, switching back into English, she added: "We have *Moscow News, Soviet Union* magazine and *The World Marxist Review.*"

With a sense of profound dismay I suddenly realized that I was in an isolation ward—not unlike that which I had experienced on many trips as a correspondent to the countries of Eastern Europe, only tighter, stricter and far more severe. As the plane lifted off the runway and the suburbs of Vienna began to shrink beneath us, I experienced for the first time a sensation that was to repeat itself whenever I returned to the Soviet Union from a trip abroad.

I felt that I was being hurtled onto an island of uncertainty from which there was no way back, that I was being locked up in a vast prison of sadness, escape from which could be barred momentarily and arbitrarily by a gargantuan, impersonal bureaucracy on whom I depended for travel permits and exit visas. If I felt this way as a privileged foreigner, theoretically entitled to leave at any time—provided I had passed the seemingly insuperable hurdles of bureaucracy—how must Soviet citizens feel, with a once-in-a-lifetime opportunity to travel abroad?

It was but the first of a jumble of impressions that was to cascade on me within the next few hours.

The plane—seemingly sturdy and more than adequately powered—reeked with the sweet, indefinable smell of a disinfectant endemic to all public places in the U.S.S.R. Moreover it was an interior decorator's nightmare: narrow, uncomfortable, spindly seats mounted on bases that appeared to be of cast iron; carpeting, in magenta with a pseudo-modern pattern of black crisscrosses and polka dots, that had been thrown down loosely so that each time a stewardess or a passenger walked down the aisle it bunched in lumps and humps; a heavy, white kitchen refrigerator displayed ostentatiously in the galley; loose screws in the ceiling paneling. And each time the craft left its cruising altitude to land, condensation water coagulated on the ceiling and dripped, like a medieval torture device, on the unfortunate passengers. "It is normal," said the beehived stewardess when I called this to her attention. Normality, I was to learn in the years to come, is a decidedly relative concept in the U.S.S.R.

Aeroflot's meal turned out to be the epitome of the contradictions that typify life in the Soviet Union: caviar; Crimean champagne; black bread; a slippery leg of cold, boiled chicken; lukewarm rice of a pasty consistency; two whole tomatoes; a wrinkled, battered apple; a stale cookie—all served on scratched and cracked utensils that looked as if they had been borrowed from an army mess hall. Only later was I to learn that this fare, except for the caviar and champagne, a specialty on international flights, is standard on all Aeroflot routes from Minsk to Tomsk, from Pinsk to Omsk.

Kiev, though southerly by Soviet standards, and despite the fact that it was March 8, was glaciated in a temperature of 14 degrees Fahrenheit, an adumbration of what the Russians mean by winter.

Smells, strange and difficult to identify, struck my nostrils as we hurried across the frozen tarmac to the desolate, nearly empty terminal building of Kiev's new international airport: poorly refined gasoline and jet fuels, disinfectant, cheap plastics and, inside, oriental tobaccos.

Customs and passport control took place in a sterile, deserted, steel-and-glass temple replete with white on red posters reading *"Slava KPSS* (glory to the CPSU)," oversized portraits of Lenin (usually looking upward and pointing forward in a dramatic gesture of leadership) and a small army of soporific and dour bureaucrats in wrinkled and badly tailored uniforms. They outnumbered the passengers by a ratio of two to one and scrutinized each passport and visa from cover to cover as if it were the traveler's life dossier.

The waiting room was virtually empty except for the handful of passengers. Several stolid, heavy-lidded young border guards— peasant boys, blond, crew-cut, with ruddy cheeks, who seemed to be bursting out of their olive tunics—stood around idly. A squad of rubber-booted and kerchiefed women indolently and haphazardly slopped dirty mops back and forth across a floor that in some sections of the hall consisted of a crazy quilt of broken tiles, in others of a synthetic type of linoleum that was pock-marked with holes and bubbles and undulated like a moonscape. Along one wall was a row of counters and kiosks which offered Russian and Ukrainian souvenirs, vodka and caviar—all for foreign currency—a random selection of cosmetics, cigarettes and tobacco, newspapers and magazines. There was no one to serve them and in front of each hung a penciled or stenciled sign reading: *"Zakrit* (closed)."

The pilot, a squat, corpulent, dark-haired Ukrainian in a soiled, wrinkled and washed-out uniform, came toward us, arms spread, and swept some of the diplomats, journalists and businessmen toward the abandoned bar at one end of the hall. "Set 'em up," he told the bosomy barmaid, "these are my friends." Out came five-inch-high water glasses for each of us, which she quickly filled with *khorilka s pertsem,* a fiery Ukrainian mixture of vodka brewed with three red peppers in each bottle. *"Do dna, do dna* (to the bottom, to the bottom)," said our pilot, spurring us on. "What about you?" I asked, nearly choking as I tried to swallow the volcanic concoction. *"Ya ne mogu,"* he replied, toasting us with a glass of mineral water, and flashing a smile that divulged a row of gleaming stainless steel teeth, "I can't. I'm driving."

Moscow, which we reached a little more than an hour later, was even colder—9 degrees Fahrenheit. Sheremetyevo, one of the capital's four airfields, boasts a squat, round, flying-saucer-shaped terminal building like one of those at New York's Kennedy International Airport. Nikita Khrushchev ordered a replica built in Moscow. But for years it proved unusable because Aeroflot had not installed the mobile covered gangways such a terminal requires. Thus the saucer sat empty, like a deflated spare tire, adjacent to the main administration building.

The customs and passport control room into which we were ushered instead was as dimly lighted, and as spartanly furnished, as the second-class waiting room of a provincial railway station. The inspection, the second since crossing the border, was even more laborious than at Kiev, no doubt because customs officials were baffled by my extraordinary amount of luggage—virtually all my clothing plus a steamer trunk with 160 overweight pounds of books and file folders which, fortunately, they did not peruse.

Time seems to move at half its normal speed in Moscow. So do officials, airport and Intourist employees, luggage porters and even the passengers. An hour after landing I cleared the quarantine area.

A young man, clutching a bouquet of three tulips wrapped in cellophane, stood just beyond the glass door, waiting for his wife or girl friend. March 8, I had been told in Kiev by our pilot, who presumed it was celebrated around the world, is International Women's Day, a legal holiday in the Soviet Union and the Communist countries, but unheard of elsewhere. The tulips, I was to learn shortly, had cost him $1.50 *each,* two hours' wages for an average industrial worker.

The road into Moscow, Leningrad Highway, was choked with an endless procession of trucks, buses and taxis nearly each of which leaned perilously either to the left or to the right—the result, I surmised, of either improper loading or broken springs.

Apartment houses, shops, public monuments, bridges, trams, buses, cars, taxis, trucks, pedestrians, traffic cops, housewives in grocery shop queues, children playing on the street—all seemed somehow gray, colorless, shabby, rusty, untidy, unkempt, flaked off, chipped off.

Gorky Street, Leningrad Highway's extension, and Moscow's Fifth Avenue, is not even a good Potemkin façade. Dark, forbidding, sparsely illuminated at night, gray and uniform in dusk, bizarre in its Victorian and Stalinist gingerbread face by day, it was in March 1968 the best the Soviet Union had to offer. And I thought: "Ugliness isn't even a word for it."

The Kremlin, ruby-red stars on its towers and spires illuminated, loomed out of the darkness at the foot of Gorky Street. Forbidding yet captivating, monstrous yet strangely beautiful, it is the center of Moscow and Russia—architecturally, historically, spiritually, ideologically and politically. As we neared and passed it names and images flashed through my mind: Ivan the Terrible, Boris Godunov, the Romanovs, Lenin, Stalin, Khrushchev, Brezhnev—a succession of tsars, crowned and uncrowned.

The National Hotel, where I was to spend the next month, is situated on Manege Square across from the Kremlin. A turn-of-the-century structure, it has changed little since the days when it was built and counted as Moscow's most exclusive hostelry. The same semi-nude, pseudo-Hellenic gods still support the ceiling in the lobby, though liveried bell captains and desk clerks have been replaced by seedy elderly peasants and corpulent, stern-faced, bespectacled matrons who eye each newly arrived guest with the skepticism of a veteran desk sergeant from behind a counter marked "Reception-Administration." The imitation oriental carpets and runners in the hall look as threadbare as if they had lain there since the grand opening. The original chandeliers have been replaced by flickering neon lights which, a Russian later explained to me, "are more modern and up-to-date." The only other apparent concessions to Soviet contemporaneity: doors that fit into their jambs like square pegs into round holes, bathroom tiles and fixtures that appear to have been laid and installed by an abstract artist, or a drunk.

The furnishings in my room could have been random selections from a *Kitsch* museum—a heavy oak Victorian wardrobe; imitation Empire bed and nightstands with lion's-head posters and lion's-paw feet; a bronze desk lamp with green glass shade; a bent-neck ceiling lamp (made in East Germany); a fire-engine-red telephone (made in Czechoslovakia); imitation oriental carpets and ocher-colored walls.

From my window, which faced the Kremlin and the History Museum, I could see in the distance the red granite Lenin Mausoleum and the fanciful spires of St. Basil's Cathedral, illuminated by floodlights. Outside I could hear the roar and scraping of snowplows as they cleared Marx Avenue and Manege Square of the snow that had fallen since my arrival. And at midnight, from the Kremlin's fifteenth-century Spasskiye Tower, I could hear the distinctive sounds of the Kremlin chimes.

These then were the impressions with which I fell asleep on my first night in Moscow.

Before arriving I had spent many years as a correspondent covering the so-called satellite countries of Eastern Europe, including that citadel of orthodoxy, East Germany. This experience, I and presumably my editors felt, was sufficient preparation for working in all Communist capitals, including Moscow. Moreover, I was encouraged by the much-touted winds of change and currents of liberalization, by the economic pragmatism and the hints of pluralism which had swept Eastern Europe in the wake of Nikita Khrushchev's campaign of de-Stalinization.

After all, just six weeks before arriving in Russia I had watched Alexander Dubcek and the Czechoslovak reformers come into office and take the first hesitant steps toward "Communism with a human face." East Germany, notwithstanding its political and ideological conformity, was a burgeoning economic and political reality with a solid niche among the world's ten greatest industrial powers. Romania was proudly flexing its muscles of diplomatic independence. Hungary had just inaugurated the Communist world's most daring experiment in economic reform. Poland, while neither free nor on the economic launching pad, was at least a country vibrant with nationalism and interesting ideas.

Where, I had wondered, is the Iron Curtain we have heard so much about? I found few signs of it in the Communist world I knew. I was to discover it soon after arriving in the U.S.S.R. It runs along the Soviet border.

It is not the ideological and geopolitical curtain of which Winston Churchill spoke at Fulton, Missouri, in 1946 and which came to symbolize the propaganda of the darkest Cold War days. Instead, it is a psychological, philosophical and sociological curtain woven and forged by centuries of Russian isolation from the mainstream of Western thought and development.

For foreigners in Moscow it is a curtain that obscures the truth about the Soviet Union. For newsmen and diplomats it is a reverse *cordon sanitaire* of police surveillance, crippling travel restrictions, bugged apartment walls, tapped telephones, obstacle courses of bureaucracy, secrecy and deliberate withholding of even the most innocuous and elementary information.

Several months after my arrival, across Red Square from the Kremlin, in the shadow of Moscow's mammoth new steel-and-glass Rossiya Hotel, workmen began faithfully restoring not only ancient churches but a strange relic from Russia's imperial past: the Anglisky Dvor, or Old English Court. Built during the reign of Ivan the Terrible, this squat, two-story stone building served in the days of the tsars to house English diplomats and merchants and provided them with a place to show their wares. More than that, it furnished Russia's rulers with an isolation ward in which to place potentially dangerous foreign visitors and prevent them from mixing with the people. Its refurbishment is sadly but fittingly symbolic of the xenophobia and penchant for secrecy which govern the modern Soviet Union as much as they did the Russia of yesteryear.

Foreigners in the U.S.S.R. today—diplomats, merchants, tourists and, of course, correspondents—are as suspect as the itinerant traders of Tsar Ivan's days who trekked the thousands of miles to old Muscovy to sell their rudimentary industrial goods in exchange for furs, hides and fish. And just as in Ivan's time—as well as centuries before and after—foreigners in Moscow are kept in almost total isolation: a segregation so tight that it drives many of them into self-isolation. In fact, thirty-two months of living and working in Moscow convinced me that Communism and technological progress have merely perfected the traditional means of quarantine beyond any tsar's wildest dreams.

The moat of isolation requires diplomats, correspondents and permanently accredited businessmen to live in fenced-off and guarded compounds where apartments are assigned them by the government, or in diplomatic residences and embassies which are just as vigilantly guarded. The only exceptions: several correspondents who have been in Moscow since the 1930s.

Militsionery (policemen) stand guard at the entranceways twenty-four hours daily, ostensibly to protect foreign property, though in reality they keep "unauthorized" Russians out and maintain an exact record of the movements of all residents. The sentry boxes from which they operate have telephones, which seem to ring incessantly, and are constructed in such a fashion that the militiamen can look out but nobody can look in. Periodically, security is tightened. Policemen and sentry boxes are added or relocated to provide the guards with a clearer view of who enters and who leaves.

"Authorized" Russians are all those who either have clearance to work in the "golden ghettos" or enter on official business, such as representatives of the Soviet Foreign Ministry, its service organizations and the press and propaganda organs. Ordinary citizens will be stopped, questioned, asked for their identity cards or internal passports, lectured on the dangers of consorting with foreigners, all of whom are considered potential spies, and turned away. Sometimes they are even arrested, as was the case with a Russian Jew who claimed (and subsequently was granted) American citizenship and was barred from entering the U. S. embassy. Periodically I heard the screams and protests of Russians being led away or arrested by the militiamen at the sentry hut just beneath our seventh-floor windows on Kutuzovsky Prospect. When Russian friends came to visit, they would call from a nearby phone booth, then my wife or I would go down to the street and escort them furtively past the sentry box and upstairs to our apartment. We never allowed them to leave alone but always accompanied them to a bus station or taxi rank or drove them out of the compound. It was the only safe procedure.

Official Soviet assertions that the police serve to protect foreigners and their property are sheer hypocrisy. The cases of vandalism of foreigners' cars, committed right under the militiamen's noses, are too frequent to recount. The perpetrators were always agents of the KGB, the secret police, or its hired thugs, and the attacks were always deliberate warnings to newsmen to desist from reporting certain developments, such as the dissent movement, or retaliatory for published articles or acts of vandalism committed against Soviet representatives abroad.

What could be more blatant, for example, than the willful damaging of Associated Press correspondent Mike Johnson's automobile in January 1971 as it was parked, near the sentry box on the lot at a foreign compound. This was a deliberate act of retaliation for the excesses of the Jewish Defense League against Soviet diplomats, correspondents and commercial representatives in the United States. Asked about it, the policeman on duty said he had not seen how the windows of Johnson's car were smashed, but suggested that he look inside. On the front seat was a note in Russian: "Watch out, snake. The next time will be worse." As he was reading the note Johnson heard another *militsioner* whisper sonorously: "If they are attacking our embassy in America, what do they expect?"

Naturally, telephones are tapped, diplomats and reporters are periodically tailed by the KGB and foreigners' living room, dining room, bedroom and bathroom walls, even their automobiles, are bugged. Like all newcomers I refused to believe this when I arrived in Moscow, but it did not take me long to realize that these tales were neither exaggerated nor the imaginary products of people who had read too many espionage stories and thrillers. I not only found evidence that my apartment was wired but discovered how to detect the presence of miniature transmitters in the walls by tuning in on their wave length with an FM radio, which immediately piped out the feedback effect.

Thus I learned to engage in "written conversations," a favorite Moscow technique that requires the use of scratch pads, pencils and the exchange of countless notes between the people "talking." The prudent "conversationalist" knows enough to burn the note paper and flush the ashes down the toilet afterward.

Of course, the mail of foreign residents is read. The envelopes are resealed in telltale fashion with thick Soviet glue. But to provide proof a Latin American diplomat once used the diplomatic pouch to instruct his former secretary back home to send him a passionate "love letter" via regular mail. He told her to say in the letter that she was enclosing one hair from her head as a token of her love but instructed her to be sure *not* to put the hair in the envelope. She did as told and when the letter arrived at the diplomat's apartment in Moscow, a hair was in it—not a black one, as his secretary's would have been, but a blond one, added by the censors or the KGB.

All correspondents' and diplomats' automobiles have special license plates—easily recognizable because they are black on white with Latin lettering instead of white on black with Cyrillic lettering, as is used on Soviet cars. Thus it is simple not only to maintain surveillance over the movements of foreigners but to prevent their driving beyond the circle that delimits the area, in a twenty-five-mile radius from the Kremlin, to which they are restricted. All access roads are guarded by stationary police patrols.

To go beyond the perimeter requires a special travel permit, written application for which must be made well in advance. No permission is granted, of course, unless a definite destination and route, the purpose of the journey and mode of travel are specified. Frequently such requests are denied and even when approval is forthcoming it will be delayed—either intentionally or because of the vast bureaucracy that pervades the Foreign Ministry and other Soviet institutions.

Only certain roads may be used by those who go by car, and stops en route, except at specified places, not even to picnic or to relieve oneself, are prohibited. Pity the diplomat or correspondent who has obtained approval to visit the Troitse-Sergeyeva Monastery in Zagorsk, about fifty miles from Moscow, and decides to stop in one of the lovely forests or glens along the roadside. A motorcycle policeman will be there in no time. Some diplomats have been followed by militia patrols in helicopters which set down on the highway if the car stops or pulls off to the side.

Millions of the Soviet Union's 8,674,172 square miles are closed to all foreigners, tourists included. Foreign residents of Moscow who want to visit the so-called "open" areas and cities must obtain advance permission and make travel arrangements either through Intourist or the Foreign Ministry's service department for the diplomatic corps. Most of these places may be reached only by train or plane and the regulations change frequently. Cities that were accessible only by train one day may be reachable only by plane the next. Towns that were "open" last week may be closed this week. One veteran diplomat has likened the endless revisions of the regulations to a game of roulette in which the rules keep changing but only the croupier knows what they are.

None of the restrictions on foreigners, however, are really innovations of the Soviet regime. Travelers, diplomats and merchants as long ago as the fifteeth century complained of them.

In his epic *Journey to the Muscovites,* based on his travels to Moscow in 1526, Baron Sigismund zu Herberstein, Emperor Maximilian I's ambassador, told trenchantly of the limitations placed on foreign emissaries to the court of the Grand Duke of Muscovy and the bureaucratic obstacles raised at the border. "The Russians," he wrote more than four hundred years ago, "ask whether someone has been in their country before, demand to know the names of all the legate's aides and servants accompanying him, their first names, their last names, their parents' names, in which countries they were born, which languages they speak and understand . . ." En route, he related, he and his entourage were closely guarded and isolated from the population by the Grand Duke's "escorts." As soon as they arrived in Moscow they were quarantined in a "golden ghetto" until their first audience with the tsar.

"When a foreign merchant arrives at the border," wrote Heinrich von Staden, a German who served in Ivan the Terrible's terroristic *oprichnina,* "he and his goods are dispatched by a stage to Moscow along with a *pristav* [escort] who sees that the goods are not taken from him. But actually he goes along with him to see that he does not poke into every corner and examine every town and city along the way."

Conditions had not improved much by the seventeenth century when Adam Olearius traveled to Moscow as secretary to the Duke of Holstein's ambassador. "Some foreign rulers maintain in Moscow legates, permanent consuls or residents who live in special compounds," he wrote in a book that became an international best seller in 1647. "The gates of the ambassadors' houses are posted with strong guards and, formerly, they strictly saw to it that none of an ambassador's suite went out and that no strangers entered." In fact, Olearius' party was the first ever to be allowed around the city without escorts.

And in the nineteenth century Astolphe Marquis de Custine, who by his own admission went to Russia in 1839 "in search of arguments against representative government" and "returned from Russia a partisan of constitutions," wrote:

> The diplomatic corps and Westerners in general have always been considered by this government, with its Byzantine spirit, and by Russia as a whole, as malevolent and jealous spies. They judge us by themselves . . . I am spied upon; every foreigner is . . . Here one can see nothing alone. A native of the country is always with you . . . One can see nothing here without ceremony and advance preparation. To go anywhere, no matter where, at the moment you have the desire is impossible. Russian hospitality, bristling with formalities, makes life difficult for the most favored foreigners; it is a polite pretext for hampering the movements of the traveler and for limiting his license to observe . . . As for unsponsored visitors, they see nothing at all. This country is organized in such a fashion that without the immediate intervention of government agents, no foreigner can travel freely or agreeably.

Today direct contact between foreigners and Soviet citizens is as proscribed as it was between Russians and Westerners in centuries past. I was made painfully aware of this during a visit to Tbilisi, the capital of Georgia. Georgian gregariousness and friendliness are legendary and we were exposed to these qualities the first evening. My wife, son and I were dining in the hotel restaurant, at a table "reserved for foreigners," when the waitress brought us a bottle of Crimean champagne and a heaped plate of sweets and chocolates— a gift from the couple at the neighboring table. I wanted to thank them and went over to propose a toast. They suggested we join them, which we did with alacrity. They were about our age and as the conversation developed, they said they had a boy a few years younger than ours and proposed that we meet the following day when the children could play together.

After a few minutes the restaurant manager approached and whispered into our host's ear. He turned red with anger and replied: "I have the right to invite anyone whom I want to my table." I attempted to question him about the incident but he waved me off and pursued our earlier conversation. Shortly, another man approached and asked our new acquaintance for his identity papers, which he refused to show. By then we decided that, to prevent more difficulties for them, it would be best to leave. We parted with the understanding that they would telephone us in the morning to arrange a meeting.

I never expected them to call. But at the time agreed upon, the phone in our hotel room rang. When I took the receiver off the hook, the phone was dead. I replaced it and it rang again. The same thing happened. It rang a third time with the same results. The KGB was at work digging an electronic moat between us. The incident was not an isolated one.

Officially, no correspondent is allowed to have any contact, for direct or indirect reporting purposes, with any Soviet citizen unless he first obtains permission from the Foreign Ministry's press department. Since permission of any kind is difficult to obtain, and under certain circumstances to seek it would endanger the source involved, most newsmen break the rules and risk expulsion—when it seems important enough—or grit their teeth with frustration.

This policy more often than not compels correspondents to accept the highly filtered version of what *Pravda* and *Izvestia* claim the public reaction and the mood to be. Because the Soviet press, by its own admission, disparages "bourgeois objectivity" and serves to indoctrinate and propagandize, not inform, that reaction will always be exactly what the men in the Kremlin would like it to be.

All interviews, no matter how seemingly innocuous or apolitical the subject, must be arranged and requested through the Foreign Ministry. The Ministry, as practice has shown, tends to shelve such requests for weeks, sometimes months and occasionally years. Until my departure, one colleague had spent two years in Moscow, unsuccessfully, trying to do a reportage on the Red October Chocolate and Candy factory.

Usually the only alternative is to approach Novosti Press Agency, a commercially oriented publicity arm of the Soviet state with close connections to the KGB. To open doors and arrange interviews Novosti generally charges a fee of $50 per day. And when it cannot, or does not want to deliver the interviewee, it offers to assign one of its own correspondents to the story—for a price, naturally: $30 per thousand words. Correspondents whose editors object to such "checkbook journalism" are simply out of luck. And even this high-powered organization is not omnipotent. Most of the time it asks: "Have you cleared that request through the Foreign Ministry? Well, we cannot act until you do."

Shortly after my arrival I was assigned a story on the future development of the Soviet space program. Not only did Novosti fail to provide me with the interviews I wanted, but it was unable to put one of its science writers on the project and either have him answer or speculate on the questions raised by my editors.

"Well, what should I do?" I asked Novosti's American-desk chief. "Do you have a good morgue on Soviet space science?" he asked. I replied that I had. "Use it," he suggested. Thus, my article on the future course of Soviet space research and exploration was based on a careful culling and meticulous examination of past Soviet press clippings in which that which is *not* said is sometimes more important than that which *is*. As my editor said, graciously paraphrasing my dilemma: "Trying to piece together a total picture of the U.S.S.R.'s space effort is similar to describing what a prehistoric man looked like, based on a few jawbone fragments."

The curtain of secrecy, particularly surrounding the space program, is so opaque that to date only four Westerners have ever seen the Soviet rocket and space exploration center at Baiknonur: French presidents Charles de Gaulle, Georges Pompidou and their respective foreign ministers. Pompidou and Robert Schumann were taken there in the fall of 1970, during their state visit to the U.S.S.R., in a special train whose windows were shut and blinds drawn tight, though it traveled by night, until it arrived at the site.

Contacts with politicians and responsible government officials are next to impossible or channeled along such restrictive guidelines that they become meaningless. Usually the Soviet leadership can be heard and viewed only on television or from a distance of scores of yards on Red Square. Interviews with high-ranking officials are rare exceptions. When they do occur they usually degenerate into rote recitation of standard Soviet propaganda or worn-out platitudes by the Russian being interviewed.

Moreover, interviews, attendance at public functions, not to mention group tours to remote areas of the country, are treated by Soviet officialdom as privileges and rewards to be dispensed for conformity and favorable reporting, for what the Foreign Ministry's press department considers "good behavior." A correspondent who derisively refers to political dissenters as "professional protesters" may find himself automatically the pool man in the Kremlin to cover the opening session of an important conference, or getting the news of a Soviet space shot an hour before his competition. A reporter whose dispatches (naturally the teletype and the telephone on which he transmits them are monitored) portray the Soviet Union in what the Foreign Ministry considers a favorable light will see his request to travel and to interview minor officials granted or granted more speedily. A magazine that confines its reporting to upbeat features on Soviet collective farm life, the achievements of the Revolution or Soviet gastronomy may suddenly discover its long-standing request to interview the premier approved, provided, of course, that the editors also agree to print his diatribes and propagandistic pronouncements verbatim. Radio and television correspondents (who operate under the narrowest limitations because they are usually required to use Soviet camera crews which have firm directives on what they may and may not film) know that if they say unfriendly things their future requests will be turned down, their film may be delayed in shipment until it loses its news value or the sound tract may simply be "lost" or confiscated.

The consequence of all this obfuscation is that foreign observers glean at least 80 per cent of their news from the Soviet press though they know it slants and distorts to confirm with whatever the Kremlin happens to be. Not even all of the press is available to foreigners, however. *Leningradskaya Pravda,* the party daily in the U.S.S.R.'s second largest city, is not on sale in Moscow and requests by foreign embassies and correspondents to subscribe to it are regularly refused. It is always a minor sensation in the foreign community when a diplomat or journalist has been to Leningrad and brought back a few issues of that paper.

Moreover the information disclosed by all Soviet papers is but a fraction of what Communist Party organs in Eastern Europe divulge. In Warsaw, Budapest, Bucharest and East Berlin, for example, the party organs print, if not always verbatim then at least in considerable detail, the reports delivered at their central committee plenary sessions. *Neues Deutschland,* the East German party daily, usually devotes forty to forty-eight columns to the speeches delivered at such meetings. In the U.S.S.R., on the other hand, reports of Central Committee meetings have been pared to the barest information: that the meeting was held, who presided, who spoke. Kremlin watchers are lucky even to find out what anyone spoke about. The leadership has apparently reverted to the Stalin-era practice of disseminating Central Committee minutes to the party's lower echelons by secret circular.

Even diplomats and correspondents from the Communist countries do not have much access. They live and work in the same compounds as Westerners and labor under the same restrictions. One of them confided to me not long after I arrived in Moscow: "We cannot obtain any more information than you. We enjoy only one advantage. Being Communists, we can read the 'code.' What *Pravda* says or does not say means more to us than to you." And the correspondent for New York's *Daily World* once lamented: "I know even *less* than you do. Being a member of the American Communist Party and representing its paper, I am not invited to the weekly briefings which the U.S. ambassador gives the American press corps."

The extent of all this deliberate concealment raises the obvious question of the reliability and accuracy of both diplomatic and journalistic reporting from Moscow. The conditions of secrecy, distrust and isolation under which diplomats and journalists work force the majority of them to spend most of their time reading the official press and interviewing each other in the hope of eliciting information which neither group has. They spend countless hours searching for hidden meanings in the party and government press, sifting truth from fiction out of the myriad rumors that circulate on the daily cocktail party circuit and evaluating the "leaks" planted by "semi-official" sources whose veracity and identity no one can check. It is generally assumed that these shadowy tipsters are agents of the KGB's infamous Department of Misinformation, but even that cannot be verified.

Analyses of developments and interpretation of Soviet positions are pregnant with error. To predict borders on the irresponsible. Anyone who tries it should remember that on the October morning in 1964 when Khrushchev returned to Moscow from his vacation retreat on the Black Sea not even he knew that by evening he would be a private citizen.

Proving anything in Moscow is next to impossible. Anyone who claims to know something with certainty is either lying to himself or trying to fool his editors or his government. At best he can say with reasonable certainty what he does *not* know. To this day, for example, no correspondent or diplomat knows how the Politburo divided on the question of invading Czechoslovakia or, for that matter, whether it was divided at all. It remains a matter of speculation.

On that March 8, 1968, when I arrived in Moscow, my predecessor, Robert Korengold, warned me: "All you can do in this place is record promotions and demotions and guess at the reasons why. You cannot predict and you cannot really know." Thirty-two months later I found it to be an understatement.

Reporting from Moscow became for me like trying to report what is happening in a jungle. One can merely observe the rustling in the underbrush, the half-visible movement in the branches overhead and hear the occasional cry of pain.

While the curtain of secrecy prevents foreigners from learning too much about the Soviet Union, it is even more effective in keeping the vast majority of Soviet citizens ignorant of developments abroad, and therefore *relatively* complacent. A widely whispered Soviet anecdote describes the situation pithily. Asked at one of his lectures whether it is true that Adam and Eve were the first real Soviet man and woman, a party propagandist replied: "In principle, yes. Adam and Eve dressed frugally, had very little to eat and did not have an apartment of their own. Nevertheless, they were convinced that they were living in paradise."

For centuries Russia's masses have been subjected to the paradisaical interpretation of their misery by their rulers—to an extent where xenophobia, voluntary isolation, "disdain for what they do not know" and the conviction that theirs is the best of all possible worlds have become a way of life and national characteristics.

The Soviet Communist Party's chief ideologist, Mikhail Suslov, epitomized these traits when he told Stalin's daughter, Svetlana Alliluyeva: "Why are you so anxious to go abroad? Take my family and my children—they never go abroad, don't even want to. Not interested."

André Gide, writing of his disillusionment and break with Communism following his visit to the U.S.S.R. in 1936, was equally astonished by Russian attitudes:

> They smile skeptically when I say that Paris, too, has a subway. Have we even got streetcars? Buses? One of them—and these were not children but educated workmen—asked whether we had schools, too, in France.
>
> In a circle of naval officers on board a battleship which had just been presented for our admiration, when I went so far as to say that I was afraid that people in the Soviet Union were less well-informed about what is doing in France than the people in France are about what is being done in the Soviet Union, a distinctly disapproving murmur arose.

Pravda, Gide was told, "gives us sufficient information about every-thing . . . In order to describe all the new and splendid and great things that are being done in the Soviet Union there would not be enough paper in the whole world."

Gide's encounter was similar to one my wife had more than thirty years later when, it could be assumed, a more enlightened Soviet generation had matured. Standing in front of a counter piled with chickens in a peasant market, she was approached by a Russian woman who gave her a quick appraisal, decided she was a foreigner and then asked, pointing to the chickens: "Do you have those where you come from?" My wife, astounded by the naïveté of the question, stuttered that we not only have chickens but that they cost about one third as much. The woman shook her head disbelievingly and stalked off in a huff.

Countless are the guides who either believed, or tried to convince me they believed, that the architectural monuments they showed me were the most beautiful, best preserved and most spectacular in the world, the factories we inspected the largest and most efficient, the kolkhoz we visited the most productive, the airplane or train on which we traveled the fastest and most comfortable, or the school or kin-dergarten we saw the most up-to-date in the world. And countless are the guides who reacted with hurt incredulity when I strove to correct their view of the world. After a while I gave up trying.

"Do you *really* mean that, that your jetliners are better than ours?" asked a skeptical Russian engineer who was my seat neighbor on a flight from Leningrad to Moscow once. I didn't know how to begin to explain the differences as we blew our noses, puffed our cheeks and massaged our splitting heads to counteract the poor depressuriza-tion on descent that is endemic to all Soviet aircraft.

Nor can I forget the Pyrrhonistic attitude of several elderly women in Moscow's Central Synagogue when they were introduced to my mother, visiting us in 1969, and were told that she is "also a pen-sioner." Fully convinced, by decades of Soviet propaganda, that the U.S.S.R. is the only country in the world with a social welfare and old age pension system, they became incredulously indignant when we calculated that on the basis of the official exchange rate my mother's benefits nearly tripled theirs and were probably worth four or five times as much in actual purchasing power.

Fully convinced that they are living in paradise, because they have no basis for comparison, Russians live in a world prescribed by

Pravda and the majority believe that it really means Truth. They measure their own well-being and progress by what the party tells them life was like before the Revolution. Their history is always told in the fashion of a fairy tale that could almost be paraphrased as "once upon a time there lived a bad man called the tsar. Along came a good man named Lenin who rallied the people around him, slew the tsar and all lived happily ever after."

Access to information from abroad is tightly restricted. The Russian and Soviet-language broadcasts of foreign radio stations such as the Voice of America and the British Broadcasting Corporation are jammed, at least in the large cities, and anyone wanting to hear them must make a special effort, go into the countryside or purchase the right kind of equipment.

The import of non-Communist foreign books is prohibited and censorship restrictions place innumerable obstacles in the way of translations. Ernest Hemingway's *For Whom the Bell Tolls,* for example, was not published in Russian translation until 1969 because it had not passed muster by the censors previously. Few foreign films are imported and then only those which the censors consider ideologically and politically neutral. And even the present quota, to judge from the editorials in the Soviet press which militate against the "insidious propaganda and ideological subversion on our cinema screens," is too great for some Soviet authorities.

Officially the U.S.S.R. can claim that it imports four Western bourgeois newspapers for public sale: the London *Times,* the Paris *Herald Tribune, Le Monde* and the *Neue Zürcher Zeitung.* In fact, only *sixty* copies of each paper arrive daily—for sale *only* in the large Intourist hotels of Moscow and Leningrad, where newsstand operators are under strict orders to keep the papers under the counter—like pornography—and never to sell them to Soviet citizens—only foreigners.

Sometimes, when their contents or opinions are at variance with Soviet official views, even foreign Communist newspapers such as Italy's *L'Unità,* France's *L'Humanité* and Britain's *Morning Star* are banned from public sale. And as a rule they are available only in the largest cities.

Major libraries, such as Moscow's Biblioteka Lenina, subscribe to thousands of foreign publications—Communist and non-Communist. But they are required to keep them under lock and key in restricted sections and on restricted shelves where they are available only to privileged readers with special passes or orders. When Soviet papers quote from the Western press it is usually in a highly selective and propagandistically slanted fashion.

The crassest case of outright misrepresentation occurred after the publication of the Pentagon Papers by the New York *Times,* Washington *Post* and others in June 1971. Yuri Zhukov, chief political commentator of *Pravda,* presented the battle between press and government to his Soviet readers as a charade which has nothing to do with freedom of the press. He portrayed the dispute as a contest between "powerful clans of big business" some of whom had grown tired of declining profits and were now fighting others. The press, he contended, was merely a "tool" of these powerful forces. An *Izvestia* contributor said: "The U.S. bourgeois press is invariably the mouthpiece of the monopolies. If one or another American newspaper or magazine 'allows' itself in individual instances to speak against government policy and against individual government agencies, this signifies that behind such criticism stand sufficiently impressive forces, in the interest of and by orders of which such statements are organized." *Literaturnaya Gazeta,* the weekly newspaper of the Soviet Writers' Union, even published a diagram purporting to show which newspapers are linked with which monopolies and with which sectors of the economy: the military-industrial complex, its "Vietnam sector" and "forty-three monopolies producing basically civilian products." It is with the latter, alleged *Literary Gazette,* that the papers which published documents from the "McNamara Report" are connected.

The degree of isolation, especially for people who professionally need contact with foreigners, is staggering.

In Kazan, four hundred miles east of Moscow, I once met a university English professor who told me that I was the first native speaker of the language whom he had encountered in more than a decade. He had acquired his excellent pronunciation by listening to the English-language broadcasts of the BBC and VOA. I could not be so callous as to tell him that I was born in Germany and that real natives probably would detect an accent in my English.

In Vinnitsa, a provincial town in the Ukraine, a graduate philology student, majoring in English, once told me that the only English-language publications available to him were *Moscow News, New Times* and *Soviet Union* magazine—all three published in Moscow for Soviet propaganda purposes. He considered it a memorable occasion when he could obtain a copy of London's *Morning Star* or the New York *Daily World*, official organs of the British and American Communist parties.

Isolation is of course far less complete than it was a few decades ago and a few decades ago it was less effective than several centuries ago. Russians *are* being exposed to the world gradually through their own mass media and through travel, though both remain constricted channels by Western standards. While more than 672,000 Western visitors came to the U.S.S.R. in 1969, it is doubtful whether even one tenth as many Soviet citizens were permitted to travel outside the Communist countries—and then invariably in groups and under conditions of severe regimentation and surveillance.

Only the most reliable, in the ideological and political sense, are permitted to join such groups (though even this does not seem to safeguard against a high rate of defections). Both tourists and group leaders are thoroughly indoctrinated in advance.

Group leaders have special instructions on how to organize their groups so that it "is one body, the same body that it was in the U.S.S.R.," so that it "does not really leave the U.S.S.R. but only goes to look at another country." They are taught to use black and white comparisons, bourgeois on one side, proletariat on the other, capitalist here, Communist there. The objective is to bring the group back more convinced of the benefits of life in the Soviet Union than before it left. As a result, tourists to the U.S.A., for example, are taken to Wall Street to see "the machinery of anonymous, imperialistic capital in operation"; to Madison Avenue to observe "the functioning of the apparatus for mass stupefication of the workers"; to Fifth Avenue to see "the portion of the working class which has sold out to the capitalists"; to Harlem to see "a typical section of the city inhabited by the American proletariat and the living conditions of average American workers." Solo excursions are tantamount to disloyalty.

One Moscow woman who guides Soviet group tours to England was ordered to tell her charges that the reason Marks and Spencer's store on London's Oxford Street is so empty (by comparison with Soviet shops, which are always bursting with customers battling for non-existent merchandise) is "because average English workers cannot afford to buy there."

A Soviet traveler abroad once told me that his journey included almost four hours of lectures and indoctrination by Soviet embassy officials each morning.

Soviet tourists who return with a more favorable or more balanced picture of what they saw should not publicize their impressions. They need merely recall the case of novelist Viktor Nekrasov, who was accused of "bourgeois objectivism" by Khrushchev and threatened with expulsion from the Communist Party in 1963 for the objective view of the United States that he presented in his travel book *Both Sides of the Ocean.*

Restrictions on travel abroad, to judge from such writers as Herberstein and Von Staden, predate even the time of Boris Godunov, an active and systematic Westernizer who sent thirty selected future leaders of Russia to study in Europe, only to have twenty-eight of them defect and elect to remain in the West.

Olearius drew attention to the difficulties Russians have traveling abroad in his seventeenth-century report and two hundred years later Custine said acrimoniously: "The difficulties one experiences getting into this country are annoying but not frightening. What impresses me more is the difficulty one might have getting out. It has been said, 'the doors leading into Russia are wide, those leading out are narrow.'"

The obstacles to leaving "paradise" mirror a strangely dichotomous, almost schizophrenic attitude toward the world and people abroad. It is, perhaps, a sublimated inferiority complex which manifests itself in a behavioral syndrome of superiority. As Guide put it: "Though they do take some interest in what is happening abroad, they are far more concerned about what the foreigner thinks of them. What really interests them is to know whether we admire them enough. What they are afraid of is that we should be ill-informed as to their merits. What they want from us is not information but praise."

Perhaps that is why I, like many other foreigners who have reported similar experiences, was frequently accosted by ordinary citizens and prevented from taking photographs of dirty but picturesque peasant markets, old, dilapidated but architecturally beautiful structures, scenes that depicted life as it is, not as *Pravda* and Novosti would like it to be.

"Why do you foreigners always take pictures of the old and ugly, never the new and the beautiful?" an angry *grazhdanin* (citizen) once asked as he physically and roughly deterred me from photographing a neglected baroque courtyard in Vilnius. Then, answering his own question, he said: "To make bad propaganda about us abroad."

He would not have understood had I told him that I could purchase pictures of the "new and beautiful" by the bushelful from Novosti and Tass; workers and peasants always photographed from an angle so that they look upward and forward confidently into a better future; streets and highways filled with cars, although only one in every hundred Russians owns one; façades of factories and apartment houses that are but incompleted shells; city scenes in the summer sun but never in winter or fall or the barren spring— seasons that account for nine of the twelve months—when nearly all places in the U.S.S.R. are genuinely gray and drab.

Perhaps this is also why today, as in centuries past, accidents and natural calamities are rarely reported in the press. This is news which, apparently, is not fit to print.

This curtain of secrecy that separates the Soviet Union from the rest of the world is as old as Russian civilization, just as many of the aspects of Soviet life that struck me as strange on arrival have their roots and origins not in the Bolshevik coup d'état of October 1917 but in patterns laid down in the tenth to thirteenth centuries when ancient Rus was first Christianized, then conquered and occupied by the Mongol hordes.

Russia inadvertently cut herself off from the rest of Europe when Prince Vladimir of Kiev opted for the Christianity of Constantinople instead of Rome. By the tenth century Byzantine Christianity had become a most conservative and anti-intellectual ethos. Moreover Kievan Russia accepted Orthodox Christianity's claim to have solved all basic problems of belief and worship more unquestioningly than Byzantium itself. *Pravoslaviye,* which in English means "right praising," became the name of the religion and the worship. There is more than just a semantic difference from the Greek word *orthodoxos,* which means "right in opinion or belief."

Because the Russian clergy was less educated and more isolated than the Greek, the early Russians were drawn to Orthodoxy more by its aesthetic appeal than the rationality of its theology. Concrete beauty, not abstractions, expressed the essence of Christianity to Kievan Rus. Man's role was not to analyze or explain but faithfully and with humility to enrich the established forms of praise and worship, thereby gaining a vague notion of the wonderful world to come after death.

The decline of Constantinople and the Tartar invasion with the fall of Kiev in 1240 merely served to strengthen Russian faith and cultivate Russian isolation. The retreat of central power and authority to the forests around Vladimir, Suzdal and Moscow from the banks of the Dnieper was a physical factor. Subjugation by and kowtowing to an Asian power whose rule lasted more than 250 years was a political factor. The eventual fall of Constantinople, which left the Russians as the last remaining state to profess the Orthodox faith, was an ideological factor.

"Russian" and "right belief" became synonymous and church and monarchy entered into a mutual dependency. Its most xenophobic symbols, perhaps, were the towel, soap and pitcher of water that the tsars kept visibly within reach of the throne to wash their hands after they had been kissed by such "non-believing" foreign emissaries as Herberstein or the Duke of Holstein's ambassador.

Yet the presence of these ambassadors reflected the serious contradictions that had been introduced into Russian culture by the mid-sixteenth and early seventeenth centuries. In theory, the entire culture was superior to others inasmuch as its foundation, the religion, was considered the true belief. On the other hand, tsars such as Godunov and the Romanovs, who soon followed him, realized the need for instruction and assistance from the West and actively sought it. Humiliating as this must have been, they succeeded in utilizing and, at the same time, containing it. By the middle of the seventeenth century they had gone so far as to convert Moscow's Western community, by then quite large, into a caste. Forbidden to wear Russian clothing, they were relegated to a physically segregated community, the *Nemetskaya Sloboda,* literally the German, or Foreign, Suburb.

Though the capital was removed to St. Petersburg some fifty years later this foreign enclave of Moscow continued to exist through the nineteenth century. Today's foreigners' compounds with their guards, sentry huts and fences are a revival of the idea.

Westernization was given its real impetus by Peter I and brought to its fruition by Catherine the Great, a German princess. But it was a relatively short-lived episode during which the imperial government looked like a Westernized court with a Westernized gentry but in fact remained true to the old Muscovite traditions and culture. At best it was a veneer of Westernization. Catherine's grandson, Nikolas I, stripped it away when he recognized and crushed the

Western influences that had fostered the Decembrist uprising, a mini-revolution of 1825, which nearly cost him his coronation.

True, there were brief periods of flirtation with the West following Nikolas' death in 1855, and again in the first years of this century. But the Bolshevik take-over, Lenin's decision to move the capital back to insular Moscow from Westward-looking Petrograd and the indignation at Western intervention following the Revolution all helped to set the signals for renewed insularity. Stalin, a Russophile perfected it by destroying the Western-oriented intelligentsia and the core of Old Bolsheviks during the Great Terror of the 1930s.

Of traditions and attitudes forged centuries ago, far more than the foreigners' compounds survive today.

Corruption, despotism and sycophancy—scourges of Soviet life—may well be rooted in the 250 years of Tartar rule which imbued the Russian national character with aspects it never lost. The Tartars left the Russian nobility intact, merely turning the princes into vassals. Not the Russian boyars but the khans in Sarai determined who became grand duke in Muscovy or prince in Vladimir or Kiev. And no one mounted any throne unless he had first obtained a letter of approval from the khan, for which he had to journey to Sarai and bow, his head touching the floor, before the Tartar lord. As Russian rulers learned humiliation, so they learned to humiliate others, their boyars and nobles, their warriors and servants. These in turn passed the pressures to those below them. Nor was servility the only tribute the khans and their courts demanded. Bribery was a way of life in Sarai, as it was soon to be in all the Russias.

Thus the boyars, once proud nobles, became quivering and spiteful toadies whom the tsar could whip, torture and pull by the hair. In turn they kicked and beat their deferential underlings. Life in Russia metamorphosed into a singular chain of cruel rulers and truckling ruled. The yoke of Tartar occupation was finally thrown off in 1480 and Central Russia never again had to recognize a foreign power as its overlord, but the 250 years of khanite rule left a permanent scar.

Like the Kiev Russians of the tenth century, twentieth-century Russians adopted a foreign belief, in this case a political philosophy born in the specific conditions of West European capitalism and believed, by its founder Karl Marx, to be totally unsuitable for Russia. Again, as a millennium before, they paid more attention to its form than its content.

Today the similarities between Soviet Communism and Russian Orthodoxy are more striking than their differences. "Right praising" has become the official policy, while rational analysis borders on heresy. Doubt is confined to asking whether this, that or the other policy or action is "along the right line." The line itself is never questioned. Man's role again is not to analyze or explain but faithfully and with humility to adhere to the proper forms of praise and worship.

Lenin's words are venerated like an apocalypse. The *vozhd* (leader), lying waxen in his glass cabinet in the mausoleum, has been apotheosized. On feast days, as in centuries past, the members of the hagiocracy appear to venerate him. Even the location of the festivities and ceremonies is the same as it was five centuries ago: Red Square.

Iconography is practiced today with almost the same blind faith and fanaticism as it was in the nearly thousand years preceding the October Revolution. Portraits of Lenin in the "red corner" of factories, stores, theaters, schools, public buildings and kolkhoz offices have replaced the icons of Christ and the Virgin in the "icon corner" of tsarist days. Pictures of the Soviet leaders, the members of the Politburo are today deployed in a prescribed order of importance on either side of a portrait of Lenin. They have replaced the old iconostasis, the screen of Russian Orthodox churches, in which saints were arranged in a fixed order to the left and right of Christ enthroned. Even the principle of the icon procession has been retained in May Day and Revolution Day parades through Red Square, where huge portraits of the leaders and Lenin are held aloft by the crowd.

And like the tsars and patriarchs, the princes and metropolitans, the boyars and bishops and priests of old, today's Communist rulers and ideologues believe, and propagate the view, that theirs is the only true faith. Miscreants are condemned to eternal damnation. Ritualistic observance of prescribed practices and devotions, not philosophic speculation or subtle contemplation, point the way to salvation. Rote recitation of meaningless slogans and platitudes that have long lost their meaning is a modern form of the ancient services which were committed to memory without benefit of prayer book.

Fear of foreign influences and heresies, the specter of Western-influenced dissent, haunted the Soviet Union when I arrived, shortly after Czechoslovakia had embarked on its ill-fated road toward a more liberal, more democratic, more human kind of Communism.

Exactly three weeks after I landed in Moscow, in a speech to the Moscow city party organization, the CPSU's general secretary, Leonid Brezhnev, rushed to meet that threat with a demand for "ideological vigilance" and "iron discipline." He launched a witch hunt against dissidence and non-conformism which has raged virtually unabated to the present day.

Under the pretext of "the acute ideological struggle in the world today," Russians were warned that "imperialism is trying to undermine the ideological and political unity of the working people." They were exhorted to wage an "irreconcilable struggle against hostile ideology, resolutely expose imperialism's plots and cultivate ideological fortitude and skill in resisting all forms of bourgeois influence."

To help drive such warnings home, the theater, literature, art, television, radio, cinema and press were harnessed to polemicize against all foreign influences and churn up a spy scare reminiscent of the darkest Cold War days, and a massive campaign was directed at the slightest displays of liberalism and independent thought within the Soviet Union itself.

Foreigners, both capitalist non-believers and Communist schismatics, are as suspect—and as segregated—in the "right believing" and "right praising" Soviet Union of 1971 as they were in the Russia of centuries ago. They are tolerated, albeit unwillingly, only because in a Russia as contradictory as it was three or four centuries back they are needed.

The foreigner who succeeds in breaking out of the ring of isolation, in penetrating the curtain, finds beyond it a society that thinks in nineteenth-century terms, an economy that has only peripheral relevance to what is happening in the rest of the industrialized world, a standard of living that is lower than Franco Spain's and a collective leadership of *apparatchiki* (party and government officials) who are gray, bland, parochial, unimaginative and utterly ruthless in the preservation of their power.

The Soviet Union, now embarked on the second half century of its existence, can boast of impressive military biceps and an empire that matches in size and influence the realm of the tsars. But behind the Potemkin-village front of its propaganda, the Kremlin has failed to meet the most pressing social and economic problems, has reestablished a class system almost as unbalanced as that of pre-revolutionary days and has nurtured a whole generation of obsequious hypocrites who trade intellectual honesty for mere crumbs of economic payola. The only hope is that the post-Stalin generation, now approaching maturity, will be less pliable and less malleable.

The Soviet Union today enjoys the status of a superpower largely because of its sheer size and mass, because of an effective propaganda effort and because it has elected to put almost all its resources into the building of a military machine and the perfection of a few flashy scientific projects that do not reflect either the real mettle of the society or the potentials of its economy.

Behind the façade of sputniks, luniks, lunokhods and salyuts, atomic bluster and military muscle, the U.S.S.R. is a second-rate economic power which faces a growing technological gap with the West. It can provide the vast majority of its citizens with only a little more than the necessities of life while a tiny minority of the political elite wallows in opulence and enjoys perquisites that no amount of rubles can buy.

It is a society in which corruption pervades industry, trade and politics and alcoholism is a national syndrome.

The U.S.S.R. is ruled, and for the foreseeable future will continue to be ruled, by an oligarchy which relies on a brutal and callous police organization, a mammoth propaganda apparatus and a labyrinthine bureaucracy to stifle initiative, creativity and independent thought.

It is difficult to assess the real quality of life in the U.S.S.R., largely because one never knows which standard to apply: theirs or ours. Naturally there has been progress. What kind of system would it be had there not been? But progress has been by inches while other societies have surged ahead by yards and miles. When Soviet propagandists wax apologetic they are quick to argue that it has been *only* fifty years or so since the Revolution. But one could easily retort that it has *already* been fifty years.

However, regardless of criteria, the fact is that half a century after the Bolsheviks came to power, the U.S.S.R. is barely on the threshold of what West Europeans and most of the East Europeans (with the exception of the Bulgarians) would consider affluence.

Life is cheerless, gray, drab. The supply of consumer goods is sporadic and poor and they are outrageously expensive. It is a society in which shortages, high prices, queues and shoddy workmanship prevail.

Notwithstanding its reputation as an industrial superpower, the U.S.S.R. today is still largely an agricultural country in which almost half the population is rural and one third of the labor force is engaged in feeding the rest. Their efforts, moreover, are woefully inadequate. Soviet agriculture is among the least productive and efficient in the world.

I could devote this entire book to discussing how much of Soviet insufficiency is due to the built-in peccancies of Communism, how much to the traditional lethargy and apathy of the Russian *muzhik* (peasant). Perhaps it is the imposition of Communism on Russia and the Russian way of life that accounts for the continuing shortcomings and malfunctions of the Soviet economy, but it is difficult to tell because the veil of propaganda hides the truth from all but the most perspicacious and disenchanted.

A disillusioned member of the Soviet establishment once told me with considerable rancor: "It is a tribute to the greatness of the Russian people, almost a Russian miracle, that this country exists at all and that its economy functions, no matter how badly, despite fifty years of Communism. Russia was well beyond the takeoff point before the Revolution. Without this system we would be the richest, most affluent country in the world today."

The much hailed economic reforms, conceived by Professor Yevsei Liberman of Kharkov University and enacted—in watered-down form—by Premier Kosygin, have been eroded. Barely introduced when I arrived in Moscow early in 1968, they exist today in name only. Why? Because the Communist Party of the Soviet Union cannot countenance reform no matter how much the economy may demand it. By granting managers more authority and autonomy and allowing scientists more initiative, which after all is what economc reform in Communist countries is all about, the party's monopolistic hold would be threatened. But the party's and the leadership's mood today is to tighten, not to relax that hold.

The de-Stalinization initiated by Khrushchev in 1956 reached its climax with the removal of Stalin's body from the Lenin Mausoleum in 1961. It ended with Khrushchev's own ouster by Stalin's heirs in 1964. Since then de-Stalinization has not only been halted but reversed.

This explains the new freeze that has iced over the literary and artistic thaw of the late 1950s and this is what was behind the gagging of novelist Alexander Solzhenitsyn and his hounding by the Kremlin, for Solzhenitsyn and his novels are the embodiment of de-Stalinization.

The majority of Soviet people have resigned themselves with silence, fear and self-censorship to the end of de-Stalinization, to Stalin's gradual, measured rehabilitation and to the "enlightened" Stalinism practiced in the U.S.S.R. today. A minuscule minority has found the courage to protest. It is a small but brave and tenacious group of non-conformists who wage a lonely and largely hopeless struggle: in the name of freedom, democracy, justice and yes, even the constitution of 1936 which Stalin drafted. But the tide, I fear, is moving against them.

In the more than two and a half years that I spent in Moscow scores of these dissidents—among them some very good friends and close acquaintances—were arrested, tried in kangaroo-like proceedings and sentenced to exile, prisons, labor camps and, worst of all, special prison mental hospitals, a tried and tested Russian means of political suppression since the middle of the nineteenth century.

The prospects for the future look bleak. Change in Russia has always been slow and even in tsarist times it was always imposed from the top by its leaders. It was Peter the Great who made his own revolution, nobody else. And he wasted no time staking out its limits. Lenin merely institutionalized this principle with his theory of democratic centralism and the leading role of the Communist Party.

Thus dramatic changes could come if, for example, there were a Soviet Alexander Dubcek waiting in the Kremlin wings. But if he is there, he has yet to be discovered or noticed. More likely another generation will have to mature and gain power before a different Soviet Union can emerge.

In the meantime there is the clear and imminent danger that the heirs of Stalin now in power will throw the wheel of history into reverse.

Part One

Those who wish to live and to survive in a world different from the one created by Stalin must fight. For Stalin's world has not collapsed. Its essence and its full force have been preserved.

Milovan Djilas, *Conversations with Stalin,* 1961

A Moscow journalist once said to me: "All this liberalism is only for a while. The apparatus created and trained by Stalin has only been temporarily switched off—you know, the way one pulls an electric plug out of its socket. But the machinery itself is intact. Just plug it in and it will work again."

Svetlana Alliluyeva,
Only One Year, 1969

1 Smoke Above the Coffin

Hail, thunderstorms and a cloudburst buffeted Moscow on Sunday, June 21, 1970. Despite the deluge the customary queue of thousands, umbrellas raised, pieces of plastic and newspaper held hurriedly over their heads, continued to shuffle slowly from the Alexandrov Gardens near the Manege through Red Square to visit the mausoleum and view Lenin's waxen mummy. Except for the portentous downpour it was a Sunday like hundreds of others in Moscow.

Some tourists in the queue were the first to notice the difference. Within an hour the news had flashed through Moscow's foreign community: the seven graves of Soviet leaders, including Stalin's, between the mausoleum and the Kremlin wall had been closed to the public and surrounded by a high, roughly hewn wooden fence.

"They are putting up a monument to Stalin," a *militsioner* said laconically to foreign correspondents who rushed to the scene.

For days Western journalists kept a vigil in Red Square and soon they could see above the fence Stalin's granite head. It was merely a question of when and whether the unveiling would be accompanied by a ceremony. Then, at ten-thirty Thursday morning, just minutes after Mitza Ribicic, Yugoslavia's prime minister at the time, in Moscow for an official visit, had laid a wreath at Lenin's tomb and Soviet and Yugoslav dignitaries had departed, the fence was torn down: to reveal gray, granite, ten-foot busts on the graves of Stalin and his erstwhile follower, Marshal Kliment Voroshilov, who had died at eighty-eight in December 1969.

Stalin's bust, sculpted by Nikolai Tomsky, and Voroshilov's are exactly the same height and in the same style as the other five in the row: Yakov Sverdlovsk's, Felix Dzerzhinsky's, Andrei Zhdanov's, Mikhail Kalinin's and Mikhail Frunze's. The late dictator's eyes are downcast and a quiet, almost gentle expression gives his face an avuncular look. A slab atop the grave, which like the others is surrounded by a tiny plot of red and yellow flowers, reads: I. V. Stalin, 21 XII 1879–5 III 1953.

As hundreds upon hundreds of pilgrims shuffled past the grave on that balmy June day there was hardly a flicker of interest on most of the faces. Many, just in from faraway towns, probably never knew that Stalin's grave up until then had been a small, flat stone visible from only a few feet away.

Only a few who knew offered any comment.

"Za chem, za chem (what for, what for)?" asked a visibly shocked forty-year-old housewife.

But the majority, when told that the monument had just been raised, merely shrugged—seemingly unmoved by the fact that a tyrant whose regime of terror afflicted nearly every family in the U.S.S.R., whose cruelty and megalomania took the lives, by conservative estimate, of 20 million victims, had now been honored. They shrugged, perhaps, with an apathy and fatalism nurtured by centuries of despotism.

For almost a decade the body of Stalin had lain in that virtually unmarked grave in the shadow of Lenin's tomb: ever since his remains had been unceremoniously removed from the bier of honor in the mausoleum next to Lenin one dark October night in 1961. That had been the nadir in Stalin's posthumous fortunes. The fresh, austere grave site had signaled a new stage in Nikita Khrushchev's de-Stalinization campaign which exposed the brutality and bloodiness of Stalin's rule.

"Operation Mausoleum," was launched on the morning of October

30, 1961, by Ivan V. Spiridonov, the militantly anti-Stalinist first party secretary of Leningrad region, a close associate of Khrushchev's. At a session of the XXIInd Congress of the CPSU in the Kremlin's sparkling new Palace of Congresses, Spiridonov spelled out many of Stalin's crimes and proposed the removal of the dictator's body from the mausoleum where it had lain mummified and embalmed next to Lenin's since March 1953. Spiridonov's motion was seconded by a small parade of prepared speakers, including an emotional old woman delegate, Dora A. Lazurkina. Lazurkina had joined Lenin's underground party in 1902, served several terms in tsarist prisons, became a party official in Leningrad after the October Revolution, was arrested during the purges in 1937 and spent until 1956 in prisons, concentration camps and exile. Only her faith in Ilyich—Lenin—had kept her alive, she said. Then she told the congress: "Yesterday I asked Ilyich for advice as if he were alive and in front of me. He told me: 'I do not like lying next to Stalin, who brought the party so much harm.'" On that note Spiridonov's motion was carried by a unanimous show of hands and the body was buried the next day.

Not all, however, were certain that this act had killed his spirit. In his remarkable poem *The Heirs of Stalin,* Yevgeny Yevtushenko wrote:

> Thin smoke curled above the coffin.
>> And breath seeped through the chinks
> as they bore him out of the mausoleum doors.
> Slowly the coffin floated,
>> grazing the fixed bayonets.
> He also was mute—
>>> he also!
>>> mute and dread.
> Grimly clenching
>> his embalmed fists,
> He spied from inside
>> only pretending to be dead . . .
> And I, addressing our Government, petition them
>> to double, and triple the soldiers on guard
>> by this slab,
> lest Stalin rise again
>>> and, with Stalin,
>>>> the past . . .

We bore him out of the mausoleum.
But how, out of Stalin, shall we bear
                Stalin's heirs . . .
While the heirs of Stalin walk this earth,
Stalin,
          I fancy, still lurks in the mausoleum.

Yevtushenko had cause to be uncertain as the new monument to Stalin demonstrated. He had even more cause when, fifteen months after that bust was erected, Nikita Khrushchev died in near obscurity. And it was especially fitting that Yevtushenko was among the few who paid their last respects to Khrushchev in the mourning hall of the Kremlin hospital. Standing by the bier and looking at the sunken face of that once impetuous, garrulous and colorful leader of Russia, Yevtushenko clenched his teeth, unashamedly wiped away tears and then left the room in silence.

For nearly forty-eight hours the men in the Kremlin tried to keep from the Soviet people the news that the man who had ruled them for a decade was dead. Then finally *Pravda* published a terse eleven-line announcement on the bottom right-hand corner of page one: "The Central Committee of the Communist Party of the Soviet Union and the Council of Ministers of the U.S.S.R. report with sorrow that on September 11, 1971, after a severe and long illness, the former first secretary of the Central Committee and chairman of the Council of Ministers, special pensioner Nikita Sergeyevich Khrushchev, died in his seventy-eighth year."

It was not the last ignominy to which the man who had unmasked Stalin would be subjected.

Even after removing him from the mausoleum, Khrushchev had allowed Stalin to rest in peace by the Kremlin wall, the Soviet Union's burial place for its most honored dead. Far lesser men than either Stalin or Khrushchev lie there, but for Stalin's successor, so the new tsars in the Kremlin decided, it was too good. Instead they consigned Khrushchev to a remote and unkempt corner of the cemetery at Novodevichy Monastery—next to a bass singer, a diplomat and a former judge of the Soviet supreme court. More famous Russians—Gogol, Chekhov, Prokofiev, generals, marshals, scientists and the wives of Kosygin, Molotov and Stalin—are also buried in Novodevichy, but they lie in other, more attractive and more prominent areas of the cemetery.

Besides foreign newsmen, a few diplomats and scores of police and KGB agents, who sealed the cemetery and kept Russians away and under surveillance, the mourners numbered no more than 150. Most of them were close friends and relatives. Only four wreaths marked the grave site: one from the Khrushchev family, another sent by "a group of comrades," one from former Soviet president Anastas Mikoyan and one sent "jointly" by the Central Committee and the Council of Ministers.

A simple marble slab, whose gold letters read "Khrushchev Nikita Sergeyevich, 17-IV-1894—11-IX-1971," marks the site.

It has now been nineteen years since Stalin died, sixteen since Khrushchev toppled him from his once godly pedestal with his famous "secret speech" to the XXth Party Congress in 1956, a decade since he suffered the ultimate disgrace when his body was torn from its place alongside Lenin's.

Yet his shadow still looms large in every corner of the empire he built with terror and with fear.

"At times it is strange to think of him as dead," a Russan acquaintance once said. "We used to consider him eternal."

Eternal he has remained in many ways. Everything about his memory in the U.S.S.R. is explosive and treated gingerly.

In the spring of 1971 his familiar, pipe-smoking image, played by a Georgian actor, dominated the third installment of a film called *Liberation,* a blood and guts history of what Russians call the Great Patriotic War. Each of his appearances on the screen was still a jolt.

His memory lies in a sort of limbo, not accepted, not banished, but delicately balanced so that each attempt to change his place in history, no matter how slightly, still sends shock waves rolling out through the Soviet Union and the Communist bloc.

True, he accomplished much. He industrialized Russia, educated it and led it triumphantly through the crucible of war—but at a price that was far too high and that is still being paid by the Soviet people.

He left a mute, cowed and exhausted society, a Russia once more isolated from the world, 20 million corpses and an empire held together only by the shackles of his cruelty and ruthlessness. He left a heritage of fear and a mammoth bureaucracy still run to this day by tens of thousands of middle and little Stalins, all moving in grooves carved out decades ago. His legacy is a system that rewards mediocrity and inertia, where the ingrained reflex is to fawn on superiors and grind down those below, where to say *nyet* or to do nothing, where to repeat what has been done in the past, is better and safer than to risk innovation, which might lead to failure.

For a brief period, under Khrushchev, the Soviet Union tried to free itself from the chains of Stalin's bequest. De-Stalinization was Khrushchev's ladder to the pinnacle of power. With his fall in October 1964, the pace of de-Stalinization slowed to a crawl. The exposés on the reign of terror, epitomized by Alexander Solzhenitsyn's *One Day in the Life of Ivan Denisovich,* were no longer published. The pendulum began swinging back. No longer reviled, Stalin soon came to be praised as the wartime hero. Soon Soviet historiography began blaming others for Stalin's crimes. Then the historians stopped mentioning the crimes. Eventually, those who dared to criticize this conspiracy of silence about the past were sent to some of the very same concentration camps where millions suffered under Stalin's terror. They discovered not only tens of thousands of new prisoners but some of the very same guards who did duty there two and three decades ago.

A relativization of crime and guilt began to be applied to the Stalin era. A mask of silence and official censorship covered all the old wounds which had not even begun to heal.

"But we admitted that he committed errors," one Russian once told me. "Isn't that enough? The victims have been formally rehabilitated."

The granite bust erected on his grave persuaded some to explain hurriedly: "It would have been indecent to wait any longer."

"Of course he was a tyrant," a Soviet official said. "And there is hardly a family in the U.S.S.R. that didn't lose at least one relative to him. But the man, after all, forged half our history since the Revolution. To just exclude him from its pages, to make him and the quarter century he dominated into an unperson and an unthing, is ridiculous."

The more sanguine argued optimistically that Stalin had merely been given "equal status" with other great leaders of the Soviet Union. The decision to erect his bust together with Voroshilov's, who had just died, but whose grave in the same row was still unmarked, they contended, represented a compromise between liberals and conservatives, de-Stalinizers and re-Stalinizers in the Kremlin.

If the hard-liners had really predominated in the Kremlin, so the argument went, Stalin would have been honored six months earlier on his ninetieth birthday. On the other hand, to have left his grave bare as one out of a group of seven would have been unseemly discrimination.

Indeed, six months earlier, Moscow had bristled with rumors about Stalin's imminent rehabilitation. A bust, said some reports, would be erected on the grave. More imaginative rumormongers predicted that it would be a 200-foot-high marble or granite column. Some prudent Western correspondent, feeling that anything is possible in the Soviet Union, even kept late-night vigils on the square, but saw and noticed nothing.

Only in Gori, Georgia, where Joseph V. Dugashvili, alias Stalin, was born and is still revered as the local boy who made good, did officials really commemorate the day. They mass-produced and distributed cheap plastic souvenirs which portrayed Stalin and depicted the temple-like pavilion over the log cabin in which he was born.

In Moscow, however, December 21, 1969, came and went with barely a ripple on the surface of Soviet society. A large wreath of fresh asters, roses and carnations and some other bouquets were placed anonymously on Stalin's grave early in the morning. And according to some observers, a larger than usual number of the thousands who line up to see Lenin's remains passed on to visit Stalin's grave as well.

Virtually the only other reminder of Stalin's birthday was a 1300-word editorial article in *Pravda*. Though almost the first formal mention of Stalin in a decade, its tone was surprisingly balanced.

Taken by themselves, out of context from the course of developments, the non-events of December 1969 and the monument in June 1970 seem to represent a sensible compromise. But they cannot be taken out of the context of a systematic rehabilitation of Stalin, Stalinist practices and policies, the reinstatement and promotion of Stalinist officials since 1964 and the methodical suppression of anti-Stalinists. In that context the granite bust by the Kremlin wall is a darkly significant, premonitory landmark. Anyone who doubts it need merely compare it to the perfunctory, fifty-six-word announcement of Khrushchev's death in *Pravda* on September 13, 1971 and the simple burial site to which Stalin's successor has been relegated. The comparison between the two graves is chilling.

The experts may debate how to label what has happened since Khrushchev's ouster and the end to de-Stalinization: neo-Stalinism, re-Stalinization, a rehabilitation of Stalin or perhaps "enlightened" Stalinism. To me the labels, which I may be using interchangeably in the course of this book, seem only vestigial to the ominous portent of the course of events. And if at times I seem to sound alarmist, then let me immediately call as a witness a Communist source whose judgment may bear more weight.

"Stalin's heirs occupy all the positions of power," Frank Hardy, an Australian Communist Party member and writer, said in the fall of 1968 after his last visit to Moscow. "They created the Czechoslovak crisis and used it to intimidate the positive forces which oppose them at home. The old methods of administrative pressure, blanket censorship and even naked terror are on the way back and they trot out old dogmas or invent new ones to justify their actions."

The "heirs" of which Hardy wrote are the successors of Khrushchev, for de-Stalinization was to Khrushchev's rise what "re-Stalinization" was to his fall.

Ostensibly Nikita Sergeyevich Khrushchev was toppled for a combination of factors, among them his China policy, his German policy, the inefficacy of his agricultural schemes, the Cuban missile fiasco, economic bungling and cuts in the military budget and manpower.

These may have been genuine grievances which the Soviet establishment and other leaders held against him. But Khrushchev's successors have not proved much more adept at coming to grips with them. The Sino-Soviet rift actually widened. The rapprochement with West Germany, which Khrushchev merely insinuated, became reality under Brezhnev and Kosygin. Adventurism in foreign affairs, such as the Six-Day War in the Middle East and the invasion of Czechoslovakia, remains as much a policy of the present regime as it was of Khrushchev's. The military-industrial complex, to judge from the frugality of its budget increases, should be as disgruntled today as it was in the early 1960s. The economy and the agricultural sector are still merely stumbling along and growth rates since Khrushchev's ouster are lower than when he was in power.

Not one nor a combination of the issues that constituted the "public" bill of particulars against Khrushchev could have been grave enough to weld the almost unanimous coalition of diverse interests and elements that brought him to fall. On the contrary, they were but necessary pretexts, euphemisms for what the leadership coalition considered his greatest transgression: excessive de-Stalinization as a platform for developing his own personality cult.

The Stalin era had been so atrocious that its repudiation was sure to benefit any succeeding regime. Khrushchev probably knew this better than any of Stalin's other successors. His rise to power was a singularly graphic documentation of his ability to utilize the repudiation of Stalin and Stalinism as a tool in solidifying his own position and purging his rivals. Until he went too far.

But Stalinism is more than just the personal rule of a cruel despot whose tyranny and reign of terror have been matched by, perhaps, only one other Russian ruler: Ivan the Terrible. And it was in this sense that Khrushchev probably miscalculated.

For Stalinism is first of all the extension of one of the three theories about state organization that emerged at the Xth Party Congress in March 1921: rule by the party plus bureaucracy, a system that placed the party and state above the society and above the workers.

By the mid-1930s, when Stalin consolidated his power, the party, in the Leninist sense, no longer existed. Instead it had become a party apparatus wholly subservient to Stalin. The trade unions, which Lenin had envisaged as running the economy within one to two decades after the Revolution, had been reduced to bureaucratized extensions of party power. Dictatorship of the proletariat, which in the Leninist sense had meant dictatorship *by* the proletariat, had developed into dictatorship by the party hierarchy. Soviet power, which had once implied the power of the workers' councils, had become a meaningless phrase, for it was the party hierarchy that ruled, not through the soviets, but through the party organizations and the executive organs of the government. The deputies "elected" to soviets were all handpicked and vetted in advance by the party hierarchy or local party cliques.

Equally significant is the development of the *nomenklatura* system of lists of important positions and lists of certain party and non-party people especially trusted to fill such positions. To be on the *nomenklatura* means to be sufficiently experienced and trusted to fill any post on the list, be it director of a school, farm, factory, movie house, local newspaper or the local soviet. The *nomenklatura* is divided into posts for which the party selects the holder and those for which the relevant administrative organs have responsibility, but with the party's agreement.

Nomenklatura lists exist at all party and administrative echelons. To be promoted from one list to a higher one is not only a great honor but a sure sign of rising in the apparat. *Nomenklatura* jobs are not only well paid but entail a host of privileges and perquisites that no amount of money could buy. To be thrown off the list or demoted to a lower one is usually a financial, social and political disaster.

This Stalinist invention, which had its parallels in the *chinovnich-estvo,* a complicated rank system of tsarist days, served as the basis for the patronage system which Stalin developed and which rules Soviet society today. For there was one criterion for getting on, staying on and rising higher on the list or climbing to one at a higher level: the ability to make things easy for one's party chief at the particular level. The proper mode of *nomenklatura* operation is to get the job done, no matter how much giving and taking of pressure, threats, bullying and ulcers it requires.

What Stalin established was essentially a command society. He created a new class, a new establishment of the privileged, of party *apparatchiki,* government bureaucrats, industrial executives, careerists and opportunists, "farther removed from the people," as one Soviet intellectual put it to me, "than the aristocracy was during the empire."

Of course, the new class also suffered from Stalin's excesses, for no one had been immune. When Khrushchev denounced Stalin's crimes in 1956, the new class approved, as Khrushchev knew they would.

For Khrushchev, a paradigm of nomenklaturism, it was a new role. As late as 1955 he had never said or done anything to suggest that he was anti-Stalinist. His "secret speech" had but one purpose: to undermine the positions of such rivals for power as Georgy Malenkov, Vyacheslav Molotov and Lazar Kaganovich. Eventually he was able to purge all of them by identifying them with Stalin's crimes (of which he was just as guilty as they) and accusing them of forming an "anti-party group."

The 1957 purge laid the basis for a Khrushchev personality cult. To discredit his other rivals, all more or less associated with Stalin, he built a party machine of devoted Khrushchevites. Nothing served his purposes better than to continue to discredit the Stalin regime.

The new class approved of his policies in 1956, but as former accomplices and direct beneficiaries of Stalin's tyranny, they could not really condone the second stage of Khrushchev's de-Stalinization campaign, unveiled at the XXIInd Congress in 1961. Stage two presaged public criticism, spectacular rehabilitations and the raising of a plethora of embarrassing questions about guilt and complicity which threatened the members of the establishment whose careers had begun in the Stalin era.

Difficult as it was to persuade the machine bureaucrats to accept changes that did not curtail their right to rule, Khrushchev signed his own political death warrant when he attempted to circumscribe that prerogative. As he continued to emphasize the crimes and errors of the Stalin era he inevitably discredited the party as a whole and cast doubts on its wisdom, its consistency and its infallibility.

Even under Khrushchev no *real* break with the past was possible nor can it ever be as long as the party is the embodiment of that past. A genuine condemnation of Stalin and Stalinist practices would have required the wholesale dismissal and purge of all the middle and little Stalins who to this day constitute the core of the party apparat. It would have entailed a departure from the system and its ideology which Stalinism had come to represent and embody after thirty years of autocratic rule. A political party whose credo is its own infallibility because it claims to be based on scientific principles cannot really afford to exorcise the policies to which it adhered for three decades. Its leaders cannot afford to acknowledge guilt or responsibility lest they risk throwing their own right to rule and the "leading role of the party" open to serious challenge.

These were the reasons that led to Khrushchev's ouster and the end of de-Stalinization. The final blow probably was his plan to call a meeting of the Central Committee in November 1964 at which he intended to expose a new anti-party group, under the guise of de-Stalinization, which presumably would have included all his remaining rivals: Anastas Mikoyan, Mikhail Suslov, Leonid Brezhnev and Aleksei Kosygin. To free itself from the nightmare of another purge, the party leadership and the bureaucracy pre-empted Khrushchev by deposing him.

Although Khrushchev's motives from 1956 through 1964 were ulterior, his policies, haphazard and periodically frustrated as they were, gave new hope to the Soviet Union and unleashed vital forces of initiative, creativity, pluralism, independent thought and embryonic concepts of freedom, democracy and justice. Ilya Ehrenburg called it *The Thaw* and, notwithstanding new cold fronts which from time to time disrupted it, the Khrushchev era held the promise of a real spring.

Vladimir Vasilyev, a young Russian, reminded the world of this—Khrushchev's greatest contribution—once more as he stood on the pile of dirt by Khrushchev's open grave and told the small gathering who had come to bury him: "It is very difficult for me to talk, but somewhere lost in the forests of the Taiga [in Siberia] is the grave of my father, executed in the tragic year of 1937. It was Nikita Sergeyevich who rehabilitated the honor and dignity of our fallen parents . . ."

To the men who toppled him, however, Khrushchev must have appeared not only as a threat to their establishment but as a traitor to their cause. One of their first logical steps was to halt what he started. They de-emphasized disclosure of Stalin's terror, censored the anti-personality cult literature and gagged its exponents. Slowly they rehabilitated and extolled the favorable aspects of the Stalin era, especially Stalin's role as a military leader. Eventually they re-adopted many Stalinist principles and practices. Today they practice what could be called, for lack of a better term, "enlightened Stalinism."

Their objective was never to rehabilitate Stalin per se, merely to restore confidence in the wisdom of the nation's leaders, specifically in those men who held key posts in the Stalin era, which means anyone over forty-five years of age.

To judge from the new party line that has evolved since 1965, the period of the "personality cult" never even existed. Stalin was not a criminal, merely a Leninist who committed a few transgressions of "socialist legality." His role before and during World War II was beyond reproach. Khrushchev's "subjectivism" contributed to the distorted assessment of Stalinism presented by the XXth and XXIInd Party Congresses.

In the years since Khrushchev the Soviet Union has been inundated with memoirs, novels, party documents, *Pravda* editorials and theoretical ideological essays which, at first, ignored Stalin's crimes, then belittled them, eventually sought to rehabilitate and now actually glorify many of his actions and policies.

Retrospectively, the timetable is clear. It began with the publication in April and May 1965 of the memoirs of three military leaders, none of which contained any of the usual criticism of Stalin. On May 8, 1965, in a speech commemorating the twentieth anniversary of V-E Day, Brezhnev delivered the first positive mention of Stalin as a war hero since 1956.

In September Sergei P. Trapeznikov, a hard-liner who had served as director of the Moldavian Higher Party School under Brezhnev in the early 1950s, was named head of the Central Committee's department for science and education. Trapeznikov has been described by one Kremlinologist as "the closest contemporary equivalent to a little [Andrei] Zhdanov [Stalin's last cultural tsar]." His influence is ubiquitous. Within a month of his appointment, Trapeznikov was in print in *Pravda* with a blistering attack on intellectuals. One week later the writers Yuli Daniel and Andrei Sinyavsky were arrested, Alexander Solzhenitsyn's house was searched by the KGB and several young dissenters were arrested and questioned.

By January 1966 *Pravda* was openly declaring that the campaign against the personality cult had gone too far. The point was not lost on dozens of leading establishment intellectuals. In a letter to Brezhnev, one of the first of the *samizdat* (self-published) protest documents to reach the West, they spoke of their "deep concern and apprehension" over recent tendencies toward "a partial or indirect rehabilitation of Stalin."

The letter, intended to prevent such a rehabilitation, widely rumored to be planned for the forthcoming XXIIIrd Party Congress in March 1966, said in part:

> Until now we have not been aware of a single fact or a single argument which would permit us to think that a condemnation of the personality cult was wrong in any of its respects. On the contrary . . . a large part of the striking, truly horrifying facts about Stalin's crimes has not yet been made public . . . Stalin was responsible not only for the destruction of countless innocent people but for our unpreparedness for the war and for a departure from the Leninist norms of party and state life. His crimes and unjust deeds distorted the idea of Communism . . .

Whether this pre-emptive protest and others like it prevented Stalin's formal rehabilitation at the congress, or whether it was never intended, is something we may never know. The most significant revival of Stalinism at the congress was merely that the name of the party's presidium was changed again to "Politburo" and the first secretary (Brezhnev) was renamed "general secretary." Both titles were holdovers from the Stalin period.

Meanwhile Andrei Sinyavsky and Yuli Daniel had been sentenced to seven and five years respectively, and in mid-February, in connection with his seventieth birthday, newspaper accounts heaped lavish praise on Zhdanov, until his death in 1948 the most hated man in the Soviet Union next to Beria.

Throughout 1966 the ideological line continued to toughen, culminating in arrests of protesters and dissenters and in attacks on writers who portrayed the World War II period "erroneously."

In 1967, the fiftieth anniversary year of the Revolution, the Stalin museum in Gori, closed since 1961, was reopened. And Soviet television began a series of fifty historical documentaries—one for each year since the Revolution—in which Stalin appeared on the screen twelve times, Khrushchev not even once.

One "liberalizing" move during the early post-Khrushchev era to which optimists point was the economic reform sanctioned in October 1965 and introduced in 1966. But it is advisable to remember that the reforms, as introduced, were a devitalized version of what Liberman, with Khrushchev's blessings, had proposed. In practice they have been diluted to the point of ineffectiveness.

A new conspiracy of silence gripped the U.S.S.R. Following the XXth Party Congress in 1956, articles and biographical references about Communist leaders who had been purged and liquidated all ended with the expression "sacrifice of unreasonable repression during the period of the personality cult." Following Khrushchev's fall such biographical references became rarer and it became more difficult for readers to discover the manner in which the person had disappeared, though they continued to indicate for a while that death had been violent during the Great Terror. A remark such as "his life was extinguished in a tragic way" often sufficed to get the message across. In 1968 most references to violent deaths were deleted.

On the other hand, Stalin's "great deeds" have been celebrated in a torrent of memoirs, historical treatises and novels.

Through them the rehabilitation campaign assumes a distinct and unmistakable pattern. Whereas earlier memoirs, following Khrushchev's fall, limited their praise of Stalin to his role *during* the war, later works lauded him for the preparations he made (that is, during the period when he purged the army, concluded the pact with Hitler and apparently did nothing to take advantage of the time he had gained). The most recent books not only throw a soft light on the purges but tend to exonerate Stalin of responsibility by citing examples of men whose lives he allegedly saved from Nikolai Yezhov's and Lavrenti Beria's murder machines.

Censors and editors who "clear" and "correct" such works have no reservations about changing facts and twisting authors' words.

In 1962, for example, shortly before his death, Lieutenant General Boris Vannikov, once People's Commissar for the Armaments Industry, published the *notes* to his memoirs. In them Stalin is portrayed as a brutal dictator who blocked the development of modern arms for the army. In October 1968 the monthly journal *Voprosy Istorii* (Problems of History) published the first part of Vannikov's actual memoirs. In *these* Stalin is characterized as an intelligent politician who looked to the future, who understood well how to get along with his co-workers and whose initiative on the eve of the war was responsible for the entire armaments campaign. In the *notes* Vannikov had described his own arrest and those of many other highly qualified industrial specialists in June 1941, just before the German invasion. The *memoirs* themselves contain no mention of this episode. Instead they praise Stalin as a statesman and specialist, a benign patriarch to whom not only the armed forces but also Vannikov personally were grateful.

An even more glaring example is provided by the memoirs of Ivan Maisky, the wartime Soviet ambassador to Britain whose original three-volume work, *Memoirs of a Soviet Diplomat,* which appeared in 1964–65, was sharply critical of Stalin. In a new edition, published as a one-volume memoir by the eighty-seven-year-old diplomat in 1971, all unfavorable references to Stalin have been expunged. Maisky, it should be added, was one of those who signed the March 1966 letter to the XXIIIrd Party Congress.

One of the more mysterious figures of both the Stalin era and the contemporary U.S.S.R. is General Sergei M. Shtemenko, Chief of Staff of Warsaw Pact Forces since 1968. Shtemenko's meteoric rise under Stalin was matched only by his sudden decline under Khrushchev and his quick re-emergence under Brezhnev.

From 1941 to 1944 he was a colonel serving frequently as chief liaison officer between Stalin and the leading marshals. From 1944 to 1945 he was chief of the Red Army's operations division and deputy chief of the general staff. By 1948 he had been promoted to four-star rank and was a deputy minister of defense, and in 1952 he was named to head Soviet occupation forces in Germany. After Stalin's death Shtemenko was demoted and disappeared from public view. He did not reappear until October 1956—with only two stars on his epaulets—at a Moscow reception for a Yugoslav military delegation. He held a series of subordinate posts until Khrushchev's fall. A year later he was again a deputy chief of the Soviet Army general staff and just before the invasion of Czechoslovakia, by then restored to the rank of full general, he was named to his present post.

In December 1968 Shtemenko's best-selling (200,000 copies of the first edition were printed) book, *The General Staff at War,* was published. It presented an unblemished, highly polished picture of Stalin, whom Shtemenko portrayed not only as a great military leader but as a statesman fully prepared for and expecting the German invasion.

Marshal Georgy Zhukov, for example, depicted Stalin as a "polite person who allowed argument and conversed freely on various topics . . . He does not deserve the reprimand that he had not prepared the country for war . . ." Zhukov called Stalin a "tolerant and wise commander."

Alexander Y. Golovanov, a retired air marshal, illustrated Stalin's benignity and benevolence, not to mention his innocence of crimes, by asserting that it was Stalin who obtained the release from prison of a famous aircraft designer (presumably Andrei Tupolev, arrested in 1938 and freed five years later). Golovanov, who was in command of the long-range bomber force during the war, wrote that he approached Stalin about Tupolev's case and asked whether he really believed the allegations (of espionage) against the designer. "And do you believe them?" Stalin allegedly asked in reply. Golovanov said he did not. "Nor do I," he quoted Stalin as saying. Soon after that conversation, according to the marshal, the designer was out of prison.

Golovanov, whose account of Stalin is the most favorable to date, characterized him as a man who took a friendly interest in the families of his subordinates, had phenomenal capacity for work, never interrupted people when they were speaking and "had an expert knowledge of aviation."

Another aviation expert turned memorialist, aircraft designer Alexander Yakovlev, pictures Stalin as a benevolent father figure who was largely unaware of the purges and mass executions carried out by Yezhov and Beria. In his book *Aim in Life,* Yakovlev quoted Stalin as saying, during one discussion about the lack of qualified staff: "That scoundrel Yezhov finished off some of our finest people. He was utterly rotten."

Soviet Defense Minister Marshal Andrei Grechko has struck the extreme line of actually justifying the Stalinist terror. During a speech commemorating the twenty-fifth anniversary of V-E Day in May 1970, though not mentioning the purges by name, he said that the country had been "steeled ideologically and politically" during the 1930s when "the Party upheld the purity of Marxism-Leninism against distortions by opportunists from the right and by Trotskyites from the left."

The greatest problem facing Soviet historians, so goes a frequently told Moscow joke, is predicting the past. No past seems more difficult to predict than Stalin's. The best evidence of this axiom is a book called *A Short History of the Communist Party of the Soviet Union,* a fat, dry but highly illuminating tome which is a catechism for hundreds of thousands of Soviet students, party workers and functionaries.

Officially, four editions of this book exist. One was published in 1938 under Stalin; the second and the third in 1959 and 1962 under Khrushchev; and the fourth was approved for printing, in a run of 200,000, on November 26, 1969. But a mysterious "fifth" edition was passed for printing in a run of 100,000 on August 28, 1969, three months before the official fourth edition. It was suddenly withdrawn from distribution and Western observers in Moscow caught only a fleeting glimpse of it: enough, however, to demonstrate that despite its favorable view of Stalin, to the neo-Stalinists in the U.S.S.R. it was not favorable enough. They apparently demanded its revocation and revision. A comparison of the two 1969 editions with each other as well as with the earlier Khrushchev versions is highly instructive as to how the wind is blowing in the U.S.S.R. today.

The thrust of both 1969 editions was to shift blame for the purges and terror, for violations of "socialist legality" from Stalin to Beria, who was accused of not permitting "any interference by the Central Committee and the Council of Ministers in the running of the Ministry of Internal Affairs."

The murder of Leningrad party leader Sergei Kirov, in December 1934, has been reinterpreted. The Kirov murder served as the signal that triggered Stalin's mass repressions. The Khrushchev version of the party history not only charged unequivocally that Stalin had seized upon the assassination to deal with all his opponents summarily but also suggested there was something mysterious about Kirov's death. It hinted that Stalin had arranged the assassination as a pretext. The two 1969 versions excluded all this and treated the murder as a closed chapter. More ominously, they seemed to justify the results. The assassination, the books said, "alarmed the party and the Soviet people. It served as another reminder of the need to enhance revolutionary vigilance. The party had to be protected from alien elements so as to forestall actions hostile to socialism and the interests of the Soviet state, no matter how they were camouflaged." This interpretation could have been lifted almost verbatim from Stalin's own 1938 history of the CPSU.

Aside from a lenient evaluation of Stalin's responsibility for the Soviet Union's unpreparedness for the attack by Hitler, the 1969 editions depreciated Khrushchev and elided the host of quotations from and references to him which glorified his role in the 1959 and 1962 editions. Khrushchev's achievements in the fields of socialist legality and justice following Stalin's death and his various reform programs were not mentioned.

The 1962 version condemned Stalin for the purge of the army which deprived the country of outstanding military commanders, who "were subjected to unwarranted repressive measures before the war and lost their lives." The August 1969 edition modulated the paragraph by omitting the phrase "and lost their lives." The definitive November edition omitted the entire paragraph.

In its summary of the 1930s, the 1962 version said: "The Stalin personality cult created an abnormal situation in the party and the country. The development of socialist democracy and the creative activity of the people were handicapped. Many prominent officials, economic executives and military leaders became the victims of unwarranted persecution." Both the August and November 1969 editions omitted the negative phrases and praised the development of Soviet society during that period.

The systematic rehabilitation of Stalin's image entails far more, of course, than merely skillful doctoring of past history.

Numerous Stalin-era institutions, abolished under Khrushchev, such as the Ministry of Internal Affairs (MVD) and the Ministry of Justice, have been restored. Thus far the restoration seems to be merely a semantic one, a terminological reversion. But who is to say, in a society that offers no guarantees against despotism, that in a year or a decade from now these agencies, whose names alone inspire so much fear, will not be exercising their former functions?

During the past five years the Soviet propaganda machinery has deluged the public with books, articles, plays, movies and television programs designed to polish up the image of the dreaded secret police, the KGB, and to portray the KGB agent as Ivan Ivanov's "friend and helper" in the building of Communism. One such screen thriller, *The Dead Season,* opened with a documentary interview of a genuine KGB spy: the late Colonel Rudolf Abel. And in his report to the XXIVth Party Congress Brezhnev went out of his way to praise the KGB for its services to the nation.

The concentration camps are functioning again, as Anatoly Marchenko's grim book *My Testimony* demonstrates. True, as Marchenko himself wrote, nothing on the *scale* of the Stalin camps now exists. Entire categories of the population are no longer imprisoned. And while a hard core of politicals are serving terms, some of them imposed in the Stalin years, there is now at least a semblance of legal procedure under which people are individually convicted on specific criminal or "political" charges, not as members of suspect categories or at the whim of a paranoid dictator. But the scope and size of the camp system is awesome. Western estimates, based on careful analysis of *samizdat* documents, indicate that approximately a thousand camps contain about a million prisoners, of whom tens of thousands are "politicals."

Of course, in Stalin's days the very existence of camps and political prisoners was a closely guarded secret. Today, thanks largely to the underground anti-Stalinist dissent movement, an increasing flow of *samizdat* literature and a colony of foreigners in Moscow— Western and Communist diplomats and correspondents—who are willing to take the risks of moving this information across the borders, we know more.

We know, for example, that the whole southwest corner of Mordvinia, an Autonomous Soviet Socialist Republic in the Russian S.F.S.R. southeast of Moscow, is crisscrossed with the barbed wire, fences, watchtowers and searchlights of the largest concentration camp complex in the Soviet Union. Here, as Marchenko put it, "there are more dogs per head of the population than there are dogs per head of sheep in the Caucasus. Here statistics, in general, have been turned topsy turvy, including the national composition of the population. Russians, Ukrainians, Latvians, Estonians and members of other nationalities have been living here, behind barbed wire, for so many years that they have surpassed all requirements for a permanent residence certificate. The fathers and elder brothers of the prisoners of today have been mixed for ever with the soil of Mordvinia, as bones lost in the sand."

Marchenko served a six-year term in the camps from 1961 to 1966 for attempting to flee the U.S.S.R. In 1968 he was arrested again, ostensibly for living in Moscow illegally, actually because of his political views and his book. Finally released in August 1971 and exiled to Chuna in Siberia, he is one of the activists of the dissent movement. In one of his several open letters he wrote: "The present-day camps for political prisoners are just as terrible as under Stalin. In some ways, true, they are better. But in others they are worse. It is essential that everyone should know this—those who want to know the truth and those who do not wish to know it and prefer instead to close their eyes and ears so that one day they will again be able to absolve themselves by saying, 'Oh, God, we didn't know.'"

It followed naturally that most of the Khrushchevites, including the most ardent anti-Stalinists, would be purged. One of the most recent victims was Ivan Spiridonov, who proposed the removal of Stalin's body from the Lenin Mausoleum. Three weeks after the granite bust was unveiled on Stalin's grave, Spiridonov was deposed as chairman of the Council of the Union of the Supreme Soviet, a post roughly equivalent to Speaker of the House of Representatives of the U. S. Congress.

But a cause for far greater concern is the systematic return and rehabilitation of all the middle and little Stalins: not just the Trapez-nikovs, the Shtemenkos and the *apparatchiki* who run the industrial ministries and undermine the economic reforms, but even the labor camp guards of the 1930s and 1940s.

Though many of the camp personnel were fired after Beria's execution in 1953, a large percentage stayed in the vicinity of the camps, where they obtained lucrative positions in industries based on prison labor. Many bided their time, confident that they would be recalled. And right they were.

"Slowly and on the sly," Marchenko wrote, "they began to return to their posts. They were able to take their uniforms, not yet even faded, out of mothballs, and reappeared as camp commanders, company officers and aides . . ."

Marchenko met many of them. One was Colonel Gromov, the chief of the Dubrovlag complex at Potma in Mordvinia, who has served as an officer in labor camps since the Stalin era. His despotic nature has remained the same. All that has changed is that in the 1940s he was a junior officer, now he heads a whole network of camps. Another is Senior Sergeant Shved, a former major, a sadist who in the 1940s organized "mass escapes" of prisoners, then supervised their mass executions. When Stalin died, Shved was dismissed but later returned to camp guard duties as a non-com.

Of all of Lavrentri Beria's dozens of top aides and henchmen who were tried and imprisoned in 1953–54 following Stalin's death only five are still being held. They are in Dubrovlag Camp No. 3 where they have privileged jobs as librarians, storekeepers, clerks etc. and are members of the prisoners' council. All the others—most of them sentenced to terms of twenty-five years—have been released or pardoned by the courts. The most recent to be freed was S. F. Emelyanov, Beria's plenipotentiary in Azerbaidzhan and that republic's former minister of internal affairs. He was pardoned by the Presidium of the U.S.S.R. Supreme Soviet in June 1970. Yet, many of the prisoners remaining in the camps were incarcerated there originally by the "Beria men." They have not been pardoned or rehabilitated.

Though a new criminal code has been in force since 1961, political prisoners are still called "Fifty-eighters," a reminder of the dread, flexible Article 58 of the Stalin-era code under which millions were convicted, imprisoned, executed, deported and worked and starved to death in the *lagery* (camps).

Even in the Khrushchev period much of the truth about Stalin was embellished and obscured by the stilted, bureaucratic language of the entrenched apparat. Since then the truth has been distorted and censored into the skeleton closets of history.

The parallel between post-Stalin Russia and post-war Germany is striking. In neither country has there really been a *Bewältigung der Vergangenheit*, a coming to grips with the past, though it required my assignment to Moscow, after nearly a decade of covering Germany and German affairs, to convince me that the problem in the Soviet Union was far greater than in either the Federal Republic or the Democratic Republic of Germany. In both West Germany and the U.S.S.R., though much less in the former, where the information media and literature are free, the ugly past has been swept under the carpet by generations of accomplices and beneficiaries who, either for reasons of convenience and power, or out of a sense of profound guilt, wanted to close their eyes to their own history.

The greatest difference of all, perhaps, is that in West Germany the "guilty" generation is leaving the scene of public influence and power, while in the Soviet Union that generation is not only much in control but can be expected to direct the course of events for at least another decade.

Soviet citizens are, naturally enough, incensed at the suggestion of a comparison.

Georgia, Stalin's birthplace, may be atypical. But a lengthy conversation I had with a twenty-three-year-old Intourist guide in Tbilisi has been fixed permanently in my memory. Standing in front of the commemorative plaque on the old Tbilisi Seminary, where Stalin had once studied to be a priest, we got into a heated argument about his role, his crimes and his legacy. The guide, a girl with a college education, defended every one of his actions and policies. "But what about the millions he killed?" I asked her. "Well, he did that to Georgians too," she retorted. "Every family in this city lost at least one member in the 1930s. And how can you compare Hitler with Stalin? Hitler killed millions who were not even Germans."

Andrei Amalrik, author of the book *Will the Soviet Union Survive Until 1984?*, now serving a three-year labor camp term for his writing, told me that when he was exiled to Siberia in 1965 and 1966 he met many student summer volunteers who were extremely tolerant of Stalin.

"They considered him a major historical figure, incomparable to middleweights like Khrushchev or the present leadership," Amalrik said. "What they admired about him is the strong, orderly hand with which he ruled the country."

In Leningrad I once met a Russian student who explained his sympathies for Stalin by saying: "He kept a control on prices. Things were cheaper in his days."

Other Soviet admirers of Stalin and Stalinism justified their views by saying: "What the country needs is a strong leader who knows what he wants and how to achieve it."

A great deal of sympathy for Stalin probably derives from the fact that the Khrushchev era of de-Stalinization forced people to think, to think for themselves and to think unpleasant and dangerous thoughts. Today the backlash represents a natural, predictable escapism for a people conditioned by centuries of having their thinking done for them in the Kremlin or in St. Petersburg.

For many, as memories of the terror fade or lies and propaganda obscure them, Stalin has acquired a romantic, nostalgic glow. They see him as a purposeful, determined man of action who knew where he was going (no matter what the cost), condoned no nonsense and could deal with his country's enemies effectively. They remember him as the charismatic leader, the rallying force and symbol of one of Mother Russia's greatest triumphs and most dramatic historical moments.

Some are simply disgruntled, vengeful victims of de-Stalinization and Khrushchevization who have recognized the opportunity to stage a comeback. Among them are the hard-liners and conservatives of the writers', composers', artists', actors' and journalists' unions who were on the artistic outs during the thaw and are now exacting their pound of flesh from the ostracized liberals. Some of them, as one Moscow intellectual confided, hounded Solzhenitsyn "not because they disagree with what he writes but because he writes so much better than they do."

Not a few are simply opportunists for whom Lenin has never been more than a portrait on the wall, Marx and Engels musty names in a history book. They are the people who, in any society, can recite the credos by rote but snore loudly when the pastor's sermon turns to what it all means.

True, more than nuances distinguish the kangaroo-style trials of present-day dissenters and intellectual mavericks from the Stalin-era deportation and liquidation of millions who not only thought differently but merely thought. A wide chasm of history divides the midnight knock on the door from the KGB agents who arrested Amalrik in May 1970. They produced a warrant and even gave his wife a receipt for the items they confiscated in his apartment and country cabin.

It is one thing when the KGB persecutes a handful of courageous and dedicated dissidents, or writers must smuggle their manuscripts abroad to get them published. It was quite another when millions were liquidated or sent to certain death in the North and Siberia just because a paranoid, tyrannical potentate was consolidating his power.

Perhaps there is solace in the argument that the present leadership is unlikely to turn the wheel of history back to mass terror: because the threat of measured terror suffices to keep the masses obedient and quiescent, because the rulers themselves are afraid of the potential consequences of a new tyranny.

But the mood they have created with "enlightened" Stalinism is grim.

"Yes, I would very much like to have a long discussion with you," the foreign-born representative of a foreign Communist newspaper in Moscow once told me in a place and at a time when we were both sure that we would not be overheard and that our conversation would arouse no undue suspicion. "But you see, I am a Soviet citizen. The days are over when I could meet with foreigners. The pendulum is starting to swing back. I have already been in the camps. I do not wish to go again."

Part Two

Once upon a time there was a cruel and despotic tsar who permitted no other beliefs in Russia but his own. He believed that two plus two equals six and decreed this as the official line with which everyone had to agree, on pain of death. Eventually, to everyone's rejoicing, he died and his son was crowned the new tsar. A liberal man, he immediately recognized the old line as wrong and proclaimed his own: two plus two equals five. This change in policy naturally caused uneasiness and induced intellectuals to think and whisper, always a dangerous thing in Russia. "If the old man said two plus two equals six," they thought, "and the son says they equal five, couldn't two plus two also equal four?" Word of this heresy reached the Kremlin, where, understandably, there was alarm. A public warning was issued: "Be careful, it could be six again."

A widely and frequently whispered parable in Moscow, 1968–71

*That community is already in the
process of dissolution where each man
begins to eye his neighbor as a
possible enemy; where non-conformity
with the accepted creed, political as
well as religious, is a mark of
disaffection; where denunciation,
without specification or backing, takes
the place of evidence; where orthodoxy
chokes freedom of dissent . . .*

Judge Learned Hand
October 24, 1952

2 *Truth in the Powder Keg*

Maly Nikolovorobinsky Lane is an obscure, hard-to-find, elm-tree-lined street near the center of Moscow. Only one block long, it appears on very few maps. Leading off the northern embankment of the Yauza River, it is in one of the oldest sections of the city and in its weatherworn, tumble-down way it is picturesque and reminiscent of better times. A shabby ocher-colored, three-story district courthouse dominates one side of the street.

But for three cold, damp, rainy days in October 1968 the courthouse, chosen deliberately for its obscurity and isolation, was the focus of world attention. On the second floor, in a small, stuffy courtroom, crowded with a largely hand-picked audience of provocateurs who cheered the prosecution and jeered the defense, People's Court Judge Valentina Lubentsova presided over a trial that was making Soviet history.

In the dock sat five defendants: a thirty-one-year-old unemployed college physics instructor named Pavel Litvinov whose grandfather,

Maxim, had been a bank robber, revolutionary, minister of foreign affairs and Soviet ambassador to the United States; Larisa Bogoraz-Daniel, a philologist, housewife and mother, whose husband Yuli had just started the third of a five-year term in a Mordvinian concentration camp; an economist and author of many books and scientific treatises named Konstantin Babitsky; a twenty-year-old college dropout and promising young poet, Vadim Delone previously convicted for "organizing and actively participating in group activities involving a grave breach of public order"; and Vladimir Dremlyuga, a self-educated, twenty-eight-year-old unemployed Leningrad worker, previously convicted of "black marketeering."

At issue was a brief, vaporific "demonstration" which they had staged in Red Square, August 25, 1968, with two others—Viktor Fainberg, an art critic, so badly mauled by the secret police that he could not be produced in court, and Natalya Gorbanevskaya, a poetess, magnanimously released because she had no one to look after her two infants. It was a protest against the Soviet invasion of Czechoslovakia, though by Western standards it would hardly have been a demonstration. The group barely had time to unfurl four homemade posters which read: "Long Live Free and Independent Czechoslovakia," "Shame on the Occupiers," "Hands Off the CSSR" and "For Your and Our Freedom." Then *militsionery,* red-armbanded *druzhiniki* (auxiliary police) and KGB agents, posing as incensed and indignant citizens, swooped in, beat the demonstrators and herded them off in waiting, gray Volga sedans.

Brief as the demonstration was, to the world it gave virtually the only sign that the Soviet Union had a conscience, that not all Soviet citizens approved the Kremlin's ruthless suppression of "Communism with a human face." And certain as the demonstrators were of the consequences of their dramatic act, they felt they had had no choice, they felt somehow absolved.

"For the whole of my conscious life," Dremlyuga later told the court, "I wanted to be a citizen, that is, a man who tranquilly and proudly expresses his views. For ten minutes in Red Square I *was* a citizen."

"I thought that some of our public personages would speak out," Larisa Daniel explained, "but they did not. I was faced with the choice of acting on my own or keeping silent. To have kept silent would have meant joining those who support the action with which I did not agree, and tantamount to lying."

Outside the courthouse, from ten each morning until late at night, friends, sympathizers, relatives of the accused and foreign journalists —those who had been denied admission to what was theoretically a public but in fact a closed trial—mingled and argued heatedly with workers, passers-by, drunks, hired Komsomol provocateurs and KGB agents over the Czechoslovak invasion, freedom in Soviet society and what constitutes due process of law.

Occasionally the arguments turned into personal insults:

"Why don't you dirty parasites shave your beards and cut your hair?" a bulbous-nosed drunken worker from a nearby factory shouted at a group of the defendants' intellectual friends and relatives.

"Why should we?" came the quick retort. "Karl Marx wasn't bald, was he?"

A middle-aged, frowzy-looking bleached blonde from a nearby apartment house repeatedly stirred up the crowd, which varied in size from fifty to three hundred, shouting:

"We oughta kill 'em all, these parasites. Give me a machine gun and I'll mow 'em down right now. What did we win the war for?"

From time to time militiamen escorted the most bellicose provocateurs and dissenters to a safer distance. Periodically rain showers cooled rapidly heating tempers and forced both camps to seek shelter in a ramshackle wooden pavilion across the street from the courthouse. A fading wooden sign identified it as a "Public Reading Room." Pensioners use it in warm weather to read and play checkers, chess or dominoes.

For veteran Moscow correspondents, seasoned by previous trials of Daniel and Andrei Sinyavsky in February 1966; Vladimir Bukovsky and Delone in September 1967; Alexander Ginzburg, Yuri Galanskov, Aleksei Dobrovolsky and Vera Lashkova in January 1968, it was a familiar scene with familiar faces and a familiar cast of characters inside and outside the courtroom.

There was first of all Mrs. Daniel, whose husband had been convicted for sending his satirical short stories abroad to be published under the pseudonym Nikolai Arzhak.

Litvinov, scion of a respectable family of Old Bolsheviks, had already lost his teaching job because of his militant and public defense of Ginzburg, Galanskov and Bukovsky: a defense he undertook, as he explained to friends, "because I want my country to be just."

Delone had been a co-defendant with Bukovsky on charges arising out of their joint demonstration in Pushkin Square on behalf of Ginzburg, Galanskov and Lashkova.

There was Galanskov's wife, Olga, Ginzburg's fiancée and Litvinov's wife.

Periodically Alexander Yesenin-Volpin, a mathematician and son of the famous revolutionary poet Sergei Yesenin, once married to Isadora Duncan, appeared on the street. Volpin, a poet in his own right besides being a scientist, had just recently been released from a special psychiatric prison where Soviet authorities incarcerated him because of his persistent involvement in protest actions against re-Stalinization and injustice.

There was Andrei Amalrik, then still writing his two books, *Will the Soviet Union Survive Until 1984?* and *Involuntary Journey to Siberia.* And, of course, there was Amalrik's beautiful, striking wife, Gyusel, a painter.

Like a figure out of revolutions past, there was stocky, square-jawed Pyotr Yakir, son of one of the nine top Red Army generals and marshals whose execution by the NKVD in the courtyard of the Lubyanka Prison signaled the start of Stalin's 1937 purge of the Soviet military.

And, of course, there was the bald, erect figure of Pyotr Grigorenko, a major general in the Soviet Army and professor of cybernetics at the Frunze Military Academy, the U.S.S.R.'s West Point, until 1964 when Nikita Khrushchev stripped him of his rank and imprisoned him in a mental hospital.

As usual there was the complement of KGB men, Komsomol troublemakers, uniformed police, plainclothes agents who photographed correspondents and dissidents for the secret police archives, and the genuinely curious.

And there was the by then traditional furtive passing of type-written *samizdat* documents—protest letters, petitions and fragments of testimony smuggled out of the courtroom by those few relatives who had been permitted inside.

Equally familiar and predictable was the outcome: long periods of exile to Siberia for Larisa Daniel, Litvinov and Babitsky, labor camp for Delone and Dremlyuga. The trial, part of a pattern of repression of dissidence and non-conformity woven since 1965, was but a charade, a travesty on the often ballyhooed but rarely upheld principles of Soviet justice and socialist legality.

As I observed the events on Maly Nikolovorobinsky Lane, I remembered the words of the Marquis de Custine, written more than 130 years ago. "One word of truth hurled into Russia is like a spark landing in a powder keg."

Today Moscow's rulers again treat their realm like a keg of powder and seem terrified by the threat of truth. And they may have good reason. Behind a wall of complacency and docility erected by the heavy hand of propaganda, indoctrination, police suppression, lack of exposure to democratic traditions and ingrained lethargy grow the seeds of discontent from which revolutions sprout.

It is the discontent of youth with the rigid, no longer viable or pertinent precepts of their fathers; the resentment of a growing intelligentsia toward the ossified, incantational bureaucracy of the ruling elite; the backlash of the U.S.S.R.'s many nationalities and minorities against decades, even centuries of Great Russian chauvinism and colonial oppression; the fear of those who see the apparition of neo-Stalinism.

Because this is happening in the U.S.S.R., a rigid police state whose citizens have been cowed and broken by centuries of tsarist and decades of Stalinist terrorism, where the threat of repression and indiscriminate terror continues to hang heavy, there will not be a revolution tomorrow, next month, next year or even in the next decade.

Nevertheless, for the past five years or so the Soviet Union has produced a phenomenon that no one would have dared to predict: the growth of an articulate and heterogeneous dissent and civil rights movement which has assumed the role of an inchoate political opposition and added an entirely new dimension to Soviet life. Its roots are in the 1965 arrest and subsequent trial of Sinyavsky and Daniel. Between then and the winter of 1970, when Dr. Andrei D. Sakharov, the "father" of the Soviet hydrogen bomb, founded his "illegal" Committee for the Study of Human Rights, intellectual dissenters and non-conformists in the Soviet Union have written, signed and clandestinely distributed hundreds of letters, petitions, appeals, essays, articles and dissertations of protest covering a spectrum of subjects ranging from sociopolitical and philosophical critiques to violations of legal procedure and re-Stalinization.

They range the spectrum from belles-lettres to revolutionary programs, from labor camp diaries to secretly recorded trial records, from vignettes of oppositionist fiction to full-length dramas, from a bimonthly, typewritten journal called the *Chronicle of Current Events,* now in its fourth year of uninterrupted covert publication, to individual letters of protest.

It is all called *samizdat,* literally self, or do-it-yourself publishing, a time-honored and -tested method of outwitting the censors, used by Russian writers since at least the eighteenth century. This outpouring of handwritten, typed, photographed and sometimes barely legible literature not only fills whole shelves of libraries but has given birth to entirely new publishing ventures in the West as well as an embryonic subdivision of Sovietology.

Most *samizdat* materials deal with political protests of one kind or another—petitions, protests, legal appeals and even draft constitutions and political action programs.

But it was also through *samizdat* that Solzhenitsyn's novels *The First Circle of Hell* and *Cancer Ward* became typewritten and many-times-copied best sellers in the U.S.S.R. before the first barely legible copies reached publishers in the West. It is through *samizdat* that his epic *August 1914* is reaching thousands of readers. Amalrik's books; Yevgenya Ginzburg's *Into the Whirlwind,* an epical memoir of the Stalin purges; Lydia Chukovskaya's heart-rending novel about the Great Terror, *The Deserted House;* Anatoly Marchenko's *My Testimony,* the gripping account of Soviet concentration camps today; Sakharov's provocative letters to the Soviet leadership and his essay on *Progress, Coexistence and Intellectual Freedom;* and Grigorenko's *Soviet Military Failure in 1941,* an astute analysis of Stalinist pre-war bungling—all were circulated and eventually smuggled out of the Soviet Union through *samizdat.*

In fact, *samizdat* literature is about the only literature worth reading. A widely told Moscow joke depicts a *babushka* entering a bookshop and asking a clerk for a typewritten copy of Tolstoy's *War and Peace.* "But Comrade," says the clerk, *"War and Peace* is a perfectly legitimate, fully acceptable book. I can sell you several printed editions, it all depends on how much you want to spend." "Oh, I know," says the old woman. "But you see, I want it as a gift for my grandson in the university. He only reads books if they are in typewritten form."

Samizdat's popularity and effectiveness is surpassed only by its electronic alter ego, *magnitizdat,* the expression for protest songs and messages recorded on magnetic tape. As an art and protest form it did not really make an impact until the late 1960s but it now reaches an audience estimated in the millions. Its star performers are more or less clandestine protest singers and poets whose ballads prick the regime and draw on the traditional Russian gift for literary ambivalence and ambiguity, for innuendo and irony. Haunting songs which nettle the new aristocracy and tell of prison camps and psychiatric penitentiaries, they are sung mostly among friends to the accompaniment of vodka and guitar and recorded on the spot. Within a week or two a new tune or a wittier text will have spread across the country through *magnitizdat*.

Some of the performers are nationally and internationally known: Bulat Okudzhava, the forty-five-year-old Georgian-Armenian poet and novelist who has performed publicly and officially in the U.S.S.R., other Communist countries and Western Europe but is engaged in running scuffles with Soviet censorship and authority, and Vladimir Vysotsky, one of the leading actors of Moscow's avant-garde Taganka Theater and husband of the French actress Marina Vlady. Others, such as Yuli Kim, a half-Korean ex-teacher, underground poet and son-in-law of Pyotr Yakir, are less renowned abroad and in official circles, but no less effective. Some are completely anonymous. A few, such as Alexander Galich, an unpublished dramatist who has spent more than fifteen years in prison and camps, are known only to the cognoscenti.

Complementary to both *samizdat* and *magnitizdat* are the low-power, clandestine pirate radio stations which are the bane of censorship and Ministry of Communications authorities all over the Soviet Union. Established by juveniles and radio hams, they operate under such names as "Free Sons of the Ether," "The Smile," "The Black One" or "Sunrise," broadcast pop and rock music and protest songs and are described by officials as "sharply anti-Soviet" and even religious. Most of these stations have a limited range and are soon silenced, but some are known to reach audiences up to two hundred miles away.

The dissent movement has produced not only a vast reservoir of underground songs, literature and documents but has generated the first spontaneous unsanctioned political demonstrations in Moscow since the Bolsheviks consolidated their power.

It has spread the seeds of doubt to enclaves of seemingly orthodox and unshakable Soviet complacency: the military establishment, the scientific institutes and even the countryside. One of its most active members, for example, until he was arrested, tried and sentenced for two years to a special psychiatric prison, was Ivan Yakhimovich, a collective farm chairman in Latvia. Yakhimovich was once considered so paradigmatic of the U.S.S.R.'s new Communist generation that *Komsomolskaya Pravda* lauded him in a feature article as an example for Soviet youth to follow.

Admittedly, despite the attention and interest it has created abroad, however, the dissent movement is not a mass or popular one. A small but defiant group of activists constitute its core and source of momentum. There is really no way to count, or count accurately, those who have been willing to speak out in public, sign, distribute or draft petitions and go on record at party, trade union or other public meetings against government policies or for political freedom.

Amalrik once calculated that "slightly more than a thousand people signed declarations and letters calling for the observance of legality in the four years or so between the Sinyavsky-Daniel case and General Grigorenko's arrest in May 1969."

But signatures on petitions and protest letters are not necessarily indicative of the movement's size. In the current political climate of the U.S.S.R., it requires considerable courage to sign such a document, not to mention drafting or distributing it. The few who are willing to speak out may well be voicing the privately held or discussed views of tens if not hundreds of thousands. One cannot know in a society where ingrained fear has persuaded the masses that silence may not be the road to valor but to survival.

Anatoly Marchenko wrote of thousands of political prisoners in the labor camps and more recent reports and analyses suggest that there may be tens of thousands. But even this is a microscopic nucleus of dissidence when one recalls that the U.S.S.R. is a country of 242 million people. Yet the regime is deeply concerned about the movement's effectiveness and potential impact—far more than the mere number of adherents would indicate.

It is engaged in energetic suppression of the dissenters and has harnessed its puissant forces of surveillance, propaganda and repression to isolate the mavericks, immunize the masses against their message and hound and imprison the non-conformists.

Most of the foreign correspondents who have been expelled from the U.S.S.R. in recent years were ejected because of their contacts with dissenters. It is no secret that the dissidents flood the press corp with *samizdat* materials, not to win headlines abroad but to have a transmission belt for getting their message back to the Soviet people.

Foreign radio stations with programs in the languages of the U.S.S.R. pick up the correspondents' dispatches about protests, petitions and political trials and beam the news back to the Soviet Union—to the audience the dissenters want to but, because of censorship and other restrictions, cannot reach.

There is also a qualitative factor of the movement's strength which far outweighs the quantitative one. The few who are willing to speak out are a select and potentially influential group. According to the breakdown that Amalrik made, some 45 per cent of the signers of petitions were academics (and mostly in the scientific fields), 22 per cent worked in the arts, 13 per cent were engineers and technicians, 9 per cent were professionals such as teachers, lawyers, physicians or journalists, 5 per cent were students and only 6 per cent were workers.

"Also," Amalrik once told me, "you must keep in mind that it is the first opposition of any kind, outside the inner circle of the party, since Stalin triumphed over Trotsky. It may be loosely organized, it may not yet have specific goals, but it is an opposition. And that is significant."

The Kremlin and the dissidents are both aware that similar voices in the nineteenth century helped to weaken the fabric of the tsarist empire. As Grigorenko told me, shortly before his arrest: "Isn't it true that Lenin, together with a small group of intellectuals, helped to make our revolution? That's why it is possible that a small group could make another revolution someday."

Who would have dared to suggest in 1887, when Lenin staged his student demonstration at Kazan University, or during the years of his exile and emigration in Western Europe, that this man and his small band of quarreling followers would someday seize power in Russia and change the course of world history?

Despite the authorities' relentless efforts to crush it, and the arrest of its most articulate spokesmen, the dissent movement continues to grow: because it is spontaneous, emotional, desultory and largely personal. Reasons that may also explain why there are relatively few *stukachi*—stool pigeons and informers—in its ranks. It depends on the closeness and interrelationship of the Soviet intelligentsia, in which almost everyone knows almost everyone else, particularly in Moscow and its environs.

It is linked primarily by ties of blood and friendship which serve not only to protect the movement from subversion but from the authorities' attempts to suppress it. It is a postulate that for each dissident who is jailed the movement will grow by as many as three new adherents: a brother or sister, a mother or father, a son or daughter, a wife or mistress, a husband or fiancé, a cousin or a very close friend.

The cases of Zhores A. Medvedev, the geneticist temporarily incarcerated in a mental hospital in the spring of 1970, Alexander Solzhenitsyn and the cellist Mstislav Rostropovich are perfect examples of this geometric growth of dissident activity.

Until Solzhenitsyn was expelled from the Union of Writers in November 1969, his friend Rostropovich had never exposed himself. But then he rallied to Solzhenitsyn's side and invited him to move to his country dacha and supported him. It was a daring move and Rostropovich realized it soon. Within a month Yekaterina Furtseva, the minister of culture, told him that his partisanship for Solzhenitsyn might cost him his privileges to travel and perform abroad.

Rostropovich, with perhaps excessive confidence and an ingenue's knowledge of the regime's retaliatory power, told Furtseva: "To hell with your travel privileges." There the matter rested for a while.

The regime continued to persecute Solzhenitsyn and one year later Rostropovich was so incensed that he joined the ranks of active dissidents and engaged in *samizdat*. He wrote an impassioned "open letter" (promptly available to Western correspondents, but never published in the U.S.S.R., of course) in which he condemned restrictions on artistic freedom. The letter was made public while he was traveling in Europe. It was to be his last trip abroad for a long time but a good example of how the dissent movement grows.

Another is Solzhenitsyn's involvement in the case of Medvedev.

Solzhenitsyn, though the acknowledged spokesman of de-Stalinization and the embodiment of the struggle against Stalin's rehabilitation, had himself never written or signed a letter or petition protesting anyone's arrest or confinement. That was not his nature: until the Medvedev case broke.

But Solzhenitsyn and Medvedev, who was well-known for his courageous exposure of the Soviet Union's greatest scientific charlatan, Trofim Lysenko, were close acquaintances.

Medvedev, one of the U.S.S.R.'s leading scientists, a biologist, geneticist and gerontologist, was until 1969 a member of the Institute of Medical Radiology and head of the Laboratory of Molecular Radiobiology in Obninsk, a scientific center sixty-five miles southwest of Moscow. In 1965 Solzhenitsyn's wife, Natasha Reshetovskaya, a physical chemist and biochemist, had been selected by competitive examination for the post of senior assistant in the Laboratory of Chemical Dosimetry in Medvedev's institute. But by then Solzhenitsyn was already so unpopular with Soviet officialdom that a protracted behind-the-scenes battle developed to block his wife's appointment to the new post. Medvedev, along with Dr. Nikolai Timofeev-Resovsky, head of the Section of Radiobiology and Genetics in the institute, played—in his own words—"a vigorous part" in the futile effort to bring the Solzhenitsyns to Obninsk.

The effort on behalf of the Solzhenitsyns cost Medvedev a planned trip to the United States in 1966 as an exchange scholar at the Aging Research Laboratory of the Loch Raven Veterans Administration Hospital in Baltimore. Because of his association with the writer and his wife, his "exit dossier" was not approved by the party and the KGB.

Solzhenitsyn's other link to Medvedev was through Timofeev-Resovsky, one of Medvedev's scientific mentors, idols and close friends. Timofeev-Resovsky is also a close friend of Solzhenitsyn. The scientist had been an exchange scholar in Germany in the 1920s and 1930s. When the war started he was formally interned in Berlin though allowed to continue his scientific work at the Kaiser-Wilhelm Institute. Released with the arrival of Red Army troops in the capital, he was subsequently arrested and sentenced, under Stalin, to ten years in prison on trumped-up charges of having been a German spy. In Moscow's Butyrki Prison he shared a cell with a young physicist and army captain: Solzhenitsyn. Later their paths crossed again at one of the special camps for scientists which served as the setting for Solzhenitsyn's novel *The First Circle of Hell*. Timofeev-Resovsky is believed to be one of the characters in the book.

When Medvedev was arrested in May 1970 Solzhenitsyn joined scientists in protesting the incarceration. That was Solzhenitsyn's first active engagement in such overt dissidence and illustrative of how the regime's attempts to suppress dissent recruits new dissenters and galvanizes others into action.

What some call the protest or civil rights movement, others the Democratic Movement, has its roots in the post-Stalin thaw when discontent was voiced largely by the angry young men of literature: poets Yevgeny Yevtushenko, Andrei Voznesensky and Bella Akhmadulina; the novelist and balladeer Bulat Okudzhava; writers such as Vasily Aksyonov, Yuri Kazakov, Vladimir Tendryakov, Yuri Nagibin, Anatoly Kuznetsov; editors such as Alexander Tvardovsky and Boris Polevoi. Their demand in the late 1950s and early 1960s was primarily for a relaxation of censorship and the party's tight control over intellectual and artistic freedom.

Protest and dissent in those days focused largely on either reducing or assuring more intelligent censorship and on opening channels for more and more varied information from abroad. Demonstrations, when they took place at all, consisted of frenetic poetry reading on Mayakovsky Square or the unauthorized, mile-long march in April 1965 from the square to the House of Writers by Moscow's "Smogists."

The Smogists—derived from the Russian initials SMOG for their slogan "*Smelost, Mysl, Obraz, Glubina* (Courage, Ideas, Image, Profundity)" (sarcastically referred to by *Komsomolskaya Pravda* as the "Most Young Society of Geniuses")—were a loosely knit organization of students and non-conformist young intellectuals in their late teens and early twenties. Their primary aim: a return to Russian purity in literature and art.

The turning point was the Sinyavsky-Daniel case, which persuaded the Smogists to put purity in storage and bring out civil rights. On Soviet Constitution Day, December 5, 1965, the Smogists showed up again, this time on Pushkin Square with placards urging "Respect the Constitution" and "A Public Trial for Sinyavsky and Daniel."

The KGB, tipped off in advance, moved in quickly to break up the affair, snatching placards and banners, tearing them up and hauling the ringleaders off to jail. Most were released with warnings. A few were placed in mental asylums.

In a sense it was a logical transition from literary to political protest. What had brought about the September 1965 arrest of Sinyavsky and Daniel in the first place was their frustration with censorship and their publication abroad under the pseudonyms of Abram Tertz and Nikolai Arzhak. The Sinyavsky-Daniel case, a year after Khrushchev's ouster, galvanized the Soviet "liberal" intellectual community, particularly the writers, who sensed their own futures threatened. Sinyavsky and Daniel also provided the spark that welded the hitherto timid and disorganized non-establishment dissidents into a fairly cohesive and vocal force.

In January 1966 the two were tried before a hand-picked audience that excluded foreign correspondents and most friends and relatives of the accused. In Stalin's days they would have been simply shot or sent to Siberia without fanfare. But it was, after all, 1966, not 1937 or 1948. Moreover, the regime hoped to set an example. The outcome of the trial was predictable: seven years for Sinyavsky, five for Daniel.

In March, just before the XXIIIrd Party Congress, sixty-two prominent writers appealed to the party leadership for Sinyavsky's and Daniel's release. At about the same time a small group of Smogists, accompanied by a handful of Old Bolsheviks and party veterans, attempted to demonstrate near Stalin's grave against a return to Stalinist methods.

Fears that the congress would *formally* whitewash Stalin proved unfounded. The establishment intellectuals were placated. The non-establishment dissenters were not. From the streets they turned to their typewriters and *samizdat.*

In November 1966, Ginzburg, the 1954 youth sculls champion of the U.S.S.R., then thirty, a sometime editor, journalist, actor and electrician who had twice been arrested for distributing "anti-Soviet literature," compiled a "White Book" on the Sinyavsky-Daniel case and demanded judicial review. He sent the original of his document to Kosygin, a carbon to the chairman of the KGB. Copies naturally found their way to Westerners.

In December, a close friend of Ginzburg's, Yuri Galanskov, then twenty-seven, entered the picture. A struggling young writer, poet and dedicated pacifist, he had once staged a one-man sit-down demonstration in front of the U. S. embassy in Moscow against the American intervention in the Dominican Republic. Galanskov had had previous scrapes with authority because of his typewritten *samizdat* literary journal *Phoenix.* In *Phoenix-1966* he published a handful of articles highly critical of regime policy, particularly the Sinyavsky-Daniel affair.

In mid-January 1967, about a month after the appearance of *Phoenix-1966*, Galanskov, Aleksei Dobrovolsky, a contributor to the journal, and Vera Lashkova, a student who had typed the manuscript, were arrested.

Several days later some of the Smogists and friends of Ginzburg and Galanskov staged a demonstration in Pushkin Square to secure the release of Galanskov and the others. Among those arrested were Vadim Delone and Vladimir Bukovsky, then twenty-five. Bukovsky had already served a term in a psychiatric prison for his role in the December 1965 Pushkin Square demonstration on behalf of Daniel and Sinyavsky. Ginzburg was also arrested.

Thus the stage was set for the September 1967 Bukovsky-Delone trials and the January 1968 case against Ginzburg and Galanskov.

Enter Pavel Litvinov, whose mother was a friend of Ginzburg's mother, and who knew Bukovsky well. Litvinov's involvement brought him in contact with Larisa Daniel and their joint participation, with Delone, in the August 25, 1968, demonstration in Red Square which led to the subsequent Litvinov-Daniel trial.

Slowly, methodically, through blood relationships, chance friendships or acquaintanceships, pure moral commitment or *samizdat* publication and broadcasts from abroad, the dissident circle grew.

Today the dissent movement and its spirit have proliferated and spread to many other Soviet cities and have become linked with causes and protests that had previously been isolated. To call it a "movement" may be a convenient misnomer: because its active membership is infinitesimal and because it encompasses heterogeneous elements whose own concepts of what they are striving for are not yet clear. But it has become a force with which the Kremlin has had to reckon, a force that baffles the KGB.

Aside from the radicalized youngish littérateurs who served as its nucleus, it includes scholars, scientists, artists and men of letters who have been frustrated by lack of creative freedom, insufficient information, bureaucratization of their work and restrictions on their chances of success. Allied with them are historians, social scientists and writers whose analysis and search for the causes of Stalinism have been frustrated by the regime's neo-Stalinist propensities.

To judge from yet another *samizdat* journal, the *Political Diary,* the existence of which was unknown to foreigners until eleven of its seventy-two typewritten issues were released by underground sources in the summer of 1971, the movement also encompasses party and government officials at the middle and upper level whose dissent is limited to what could be called a "liberal Communist position."

The movement embraces various elements disgruntled by the abandonment of economic reform, especially those who had hopes that the reform would result in the general liberalization of all spheres of life.

Attracted to it are religious believers whose efforts to widen *re-*

ligious freedom persuaded them that this cannot be obtained without greater *civic* freedom.

Individuals and groups who have lost all faith in any democratization of the regime and strive to overthrow it are drawn to the movement just as much as "true" Leninist-Marxists who believe that Lenin and Marx have been betrayed and who oppose the regime from an orthodox Marxist position.

In its ranks are nationalists such as Latvians, Lithuanians, Crimean Tartars and Ukrainians. But most important, the "movement" encompasses "constitutionalists" and "civil rightists," whose strong views about "the rule of law, not men, founded on respect for human rights," is the common denominator of dissent in the U.S.S.R.

"Until now," Viktor Krasin, a dissenter who has been exiled to Siberia for "parasitism," once said, "the Soviet leadership has been above the law. We are agitating to put the law above the leaders."

During a lengthy philosophical discussion Grigorenko expounded on that idea: "We have a constitution which gives us all the basic rights and protections. What we need is to observe it. In the constitution there is no power to censor speech or the press, for example."

The importance of law to the movement is also evident in the program of the Initiative Group for Human Rights, founded in 1968 during United Nations Human Rights Year by fifteen leading dissenters, of whom only eight are free today. A precursor of Sakharov's 1970 Committee for the Study of Human Rights, its program said in part:

> We cannot condone a punitive policy against those who think differently . . . We merely say: "Do not violate your own laws."
> By criticizing the actions of authorities we do not oppose the state. The state must be confined in its actions which encroach on human rights. The characterization of our theories as anti-Soviet would be tantamount to saying that the violation of human rights follows from the very nature of the Soviet system.

A similar devotion to legal principle characterized the Sakharov committee. One of its co-founders, Vladimir Chalidze, a physicist, told my colleague Jay Axelbank, of *Newsweek:*

> "Our committee is legal. Paragraph 126 of the Soviet constitution guarantees citizens the right of association.
> "Our aims are to give consultative aid to the organs of state

power in applying guarantees of the rights of man, to give creative aid to those who study this problem and to provide legal enlightenment. The task of the committee is not to unmask or demand but to study and recommend, taking into account the actual conditions here and the difficulties of the state in this sphere. It demands patience.

"We will not stage a revolution. That is silly. We will merely study human rights as guaranteed in Soviet law. We aim at generalized study without devoting attention to particular cases. We will study the extent to which Soviet guarantees correspond to those recommended by the United Nations, though this will not hinder us in acting in a personal capacity, as we have before, in speaking out in individual cases . . .

"When the public has matured sufficiently to be able to absorb the ideas proclaimed by the French Revolution, then we could say that we have had some influence. And if the government doesn't listen to us, we shall just go on making recommendations and more recommendations."

Two months after its founding the committee was declared "illegal" and ordered to cease functioning, but it still exists.

Legality and the rule of law preoccupy the dissenters and knowledge of the law itself has become a prerequisite to effective dissent. Virtually every non-conformist has a copy of the legal code on his bookshelf. It is this book, not underground *samizdat* or "anti-Soviet" literature from abroad, which a KGB or police agent will look for when he starts to search a dissenter's apartment. A copy of the code on the shelf is a sure sign that the man knows his rights.

One of those who knew them best was Amalrik. He insisted on publishing his books abroad, and demanded the royalties for them, because, as he argued correctly: "Sending and publishing manuscripts outside the Soviet Union is not a violation of Soviet law."

The authorities, of course, will always find a technicality. Amalrik, now serving a three-year term in a "strict regime" camp in the Magadan region of Siberia near the Arctic Circle, was convicted on charges of "systematic dissemination . . . of deliberately false statements derogatory to the Soviet state and social system" under Article 190/1 of the Criminal Code of the Russian Federation. A highly flexible statute, it was enacted in September 1966, apparently for the express purpose of dealing with non-conformists, and has been applied in most cases since then.

Another "legal expert" is Bukovsky, whose final plea in his 1967 trial displayed a masterful knowledge of the constitution and basic democratic principles.

"So, the prosecutor regards our demonstration as impudent, yet here I have the text of our constitution," Bukovsky said, reading verbatim from Article 125, which, in addition to freedom of speech and freedom of the press, also guarantees Soviet citizens the freedom of assembly, including the "holding of mass meetings" and the "freedom of street processions and demonstrations." Why, he asked, was this article put in the constitution? "To legalize the demonstrations of May Day and the anniversary of the Revolution? But that was not necessary. Everybody knows that if the government has organized a demonstration, nobody is going to break it up. What is the use of freedom to demonstrate 'for' if we cannot demonstrate 'against'?"

A sense of justice, alien to Russian tradition, runs like a central theme through the dissent and civil rights movements.

It was devotion to the principles of justice, for example, that motivated Amalrik to polemicize against Soviet novelist Anatoly Kuznetsov, who defected to England in 1969, for having collaborated with the KGB, for writing things he did not believe in and for "thinking one thing, saying another and doing a third."

Amalrik, a loner, who never signed a single protest document or petition, was the dissent movement's most articulate chronicler and a perspicacious analyst of intellectual forces in the Soviet Union.

He was the first to suggest that the dissent movement "is a real embryonic political opposition to the regime. It is a social movement that has given itself the title of 'Democratic Movement.' It has leaders and activists and is based on a large number of sympathizers. It has specific objectives and chooses specific tactics, though both are still rather diffuse."

As such it is a composite of four or five ideologies. While some of its members may espouse, as their personal philosophy, only one of these, others borrow from two or more to construe their ideal world.

Of these ideologies "Marxist-Leninist purity" is the most significant, if only because it echoes the views of influential Communists and Marxists abroad—in Italy, Yugoslavia, France and other countries where Communist parties are at variance with Moscow.

Under the banner of Leninist-Marxist opposition to the present regime, a number of clandestine "True Marxist" groups and parties have been started and quickly broken up again by the KGB. One such group, in the city of Saratov, called itself "The Party of True Communists." In the spring of 1970 six of its student members were sentenced to labor camp terms ranging from three to seven years.

The leading and most outspoken Marxist-Leninists in the dissent movement are Grigorenko, Yakhimovich and Yakir. All were members in good standing of the CPSU until they began criticizing its policies.

Grigorenko always considered himself a staunch Leninist and in his discussions with me used to argue that it was Stalin and the post-Stalin regimes that drifted from the fold. Notwithstanding some modifications from dictatorship to oligarchy which characterized both the Khrushchev and Brezhnev periods, he portrayed them as extensions of Stalinism. For Grigorenko "the Czechoslovak path" was the one "we should be following—in other words: democratization *and* socialism, for there can be no socialism without democracy."

Yakir occasionally receives letters from "ordinary citizens" who equate his criticism of the regime's policies with "defamation of your father's good name."

"My father, like many other honest Soviet citizens, fell victim to Stalinism," Yakir invariably replies. "I am struggling against Stalinism. Do you suppose that thereby I am defaming the name of my father? Unfortunately, there is a tendency today to confuse anti-Stalinism with anti-Sovietism. As a result, Stalinism is identified with Soviet power."

The ethical-Christian-social wing of the movement, most of whose members are in prison or psychiatric hospitals following mass raids and trials in 1967 and 1968, rejects the ethical values of the present Soviet regime. Its more extreme adherents, influenced by neo-Slavophile currents, laid down a specific program with the objective of seizing power in the U.S.S.R. Calling for the "Christianization of politics," they urged, on the one hand, a separation of church and state, but proposed on the other a governmental establishment consisting of a parliament, an executive, and an ecclesiastical-state council, made up largely of metropolitans and bishops of the Church, who would have complete veto power over both the legislature and the executive.

Anatoly Levitin-Krasnov, one of the fifteen founder members of the Initiative Group for Human Rights, is the embodiment of Christian-socialist dissent. A teacher of literature by profession, he spent seven years in Stalin's concentration camps. In the mid-1950s he contributed articles to the official *Journal of the Moscow Patriarchate* but eventually was forced to turn to underground *samizdat* writing. In 1958 he lost his teaching post because of his religious beliefs. Then he held menial jobs to support himself while continuing to write.

In September 1969 Levitin-Krasnov's writings landed him in jail, charged with anti-Soviet slander and fabrications and he is now serving a three-year term in a "general regimen" labor camp.

The most recreant piece of dissent literature to emanate from the "liberal, democratic" faction of the movement is a 14,000-word "Program of the Democratic Movement of the Soviet Union," which calls for "illegal activities" as a means to hasten democratization of the U.S.S.R. It has been tenuously linked to three submarine officers of the Soviet Baltic Fleet who were arrested in May 1969 on charges of establishing a "Union of Fighters for Political Freedom." Thus far, little is known about these officers. Even their full identity has not been established in dissenter circles. Nor is it known whether they authored the "Program," were merely caught with or distributing it, or even whether the program linked to them is the same as one that had been circulating anonymously in *samizdat* form.

Anonymous *samizdat* items, such as "draft constitutions," are usually treated with considerable circumspection by both dissidents and Western observers in Moscow, particularly when they claim to represent "millions of Soviet intellectuals" or "all freedom-loving and democratically minded citizens." Anonymity, in the eyes of most recusants, is not only cowardly but unnecessary. It suggests something illegal or deliberately provocational about the document. The active dissenters always stress that what they are doing is in complete conformity with Soviet law and therefore needs no disguise. They not only sign articles, essays, letters and petitions with their full names but frequently add their addresses and telephone numbers.

Non-conformity in the military, as reflected by Grigorenko and the naval officers, is an important development, though as yet there are only shreds of evidence to indicate its existence. One of the most active military heretics besides Grigorenko is Major G. O. Altunyan, a thirty-eight-year-old Armenian engineer officer who joined the Communist Party in 1957 and for thirteen years, before his dismissal from service, was a lecturer at the Kharkov Higher Military School in the Ukraine. Ostensibly a paragon of Soviet Army virtue,

Altunyan had received fourteen commendations for his excellent service until he was sacked in 1968 for making anti-Stalinist speeches in his party organization. Another of the fifteen co-founders of the Initiative Group for Human Rights, he was arrested in May 1969 and has been sentenced to three years in a labor camp for anti-Soviet slander. The specific charge was that in a conversation he had condemned the invasion of Czechoslovakia and had said that official anti-Semitism exists in the U.S.S.R.

The most mysterious incident suggesting dissent in the military was the "Kremlin shooting" of January 22, 1969. A gunman, later identified as a Lieutenant Ilyin, AWOL from his unit in Leningrad, fired six shots at a limousine in a motorcade bringing the Soyuz 4 and Soyuz 5 cosmonauts into the Kremlin for a reception. The chauffeur reportedly died of his wounds, a motorcycle escort was hurt but recovered. In the car, a huge black ZIL limousine, the second in the cavalcade after the open convertible which carried the returning space heroes, were four other cosmonauts: Major General Georgy Beregovoi, Valentina Nikolayeva-Tereshkova, her husband Colonel Andrian Nikolayev and Colonel Aleksei Leonov, the world's first space walker. They were not injured. But the shots had obviously not been meant for them, anyway.

Ilyin, related to a Moscow militia captain from whom he had borrowed a police uniform to pass through security cordons, was apparently aiming for a more important target: Brezhnev, whom he probably expected to be riding in the second car of the column. When the limousine came into view he saw Beregovoi, who has a slight facial resemblance to the party chief, and fired.

Although most of what is known about Ilyin is rumor or conjecture, there is sufficient indication that he was an impressionable young officer very much disenchanted with his nation's leadership and their policies.

Disagreements between various factions and ideological currents of the Democratic Movement, to judge from the experiences of Russian intellectuals who tried to change things in the nineteenth century, were to be expected. They occur frequently and quite publicly.

Moreover attempts by various recreants to coalesce with dissident Jews proved largely futile because of a basic conflict of purposes. The political dissenters are agitating to improve or change conditions in the U.S.S.R. Most of the disaffected Jews are seeking permission to leave the country for Israel and have little interest in improving anything in the Soviet Union except emigration policy. True, some of the Jewish militants have also been active in the dissent movement. Eduard S. Kuznetsov, one of the chief defendants in the December 1970 Leningrad hijacking trial (he was one of the two originally sentenced to death), had already served a seven-year labor camp term for engaging in "anti-Soviet agitation and propaganda." Leonid Kolchinsky, who was drafted because he applied for emigration papers, then became a *cause célèbre* when he asked to be stationed on the Chinese border where he could fight "one of Israel's implacable enemies," had previously been expelled from high school for speaking in defense of Sinyavsky and Daniel and against the invasion of Czechoslovakia. Some of the Jewish émigrés were active in the dissent movement—the scientist Boris Tsukerman, the mathematician Julius Telesin and Leonid Rigerman, to name a few. The *Chronicle of Current Events* has faithfully recorded all the acts of Jewish dissent and protest. But the conflict of interest remains. As Yakir, himself a Jew, once explained: "The quintessence of *our* struggle is that we must remain and fight here to effect changes." Unlike some of their nineteenth-century antecedents today's Russian dissenters have little desire to leave the country, even if they could, to work for change from a safe haven abroad.

The most prominent dissident today is Sakharov, the nuclear physicist. To categorize him politically or ideologically is difficult because his role has changed from cool, intellectual dispassionate social criticism to active participation in overt courthouse dissent.

Sakharov first gained international attention as a dissenter in June 1968 with his *samizdat* essay on *Progress, Coexistence and Intellectual Freedom,* a document which reflected the views of the non-Marxist "liberal, democratic" school of the dissident movement. A more orthodox work, calling for change within the existing framework of Soviet institutions, is the four-thousand word letter of March 19, 1970, to the Soviet leadership which Sakharov co-authored with another physicist, Valentin Turchin, and Roy A. Medvedev, a historian and the twin brother of the geneticist Zhores Medvedev.

Concerned primarily with the U.S.S.R.'s yawning economic and technological gap vis-à-vis West, the letter said that "the source of our difficulties is not the socialist structure. On the contrary, it lies in those peculiarities and conditions of our life which run contrary to socialism and are hostile to it. Its source is the anti-democratic traditions and norms of public life that appeared during the Stalin period and have not been completely liquidated . . ."

Sakharov believes that democratization and completely free access to and exchange of all information would restore "to our ideological life its dynamics and creative nature and liquidate the bureaucratic, dogmatic, hypocritical style which is so prevalent now."

"What awaits our country if a course of democratization is not taken?" Sakharov asked. "Falling behind the capitalist countries in the process of the second industrial revolution and gradual transformation into a second-rate provincial power."

Sakharov speaks for thousands of Soviet scientists.

True, they are the courted and pampered elite of the Soviet intelligentsia. And well they might be, for it is on the backs of its dedicated scientists that the U.S.S.R. has trudged the tortuous path to superpowerdom.

As a consequence, Soviet scientists have always been more than well treated and rewarded by Soviet standards. For their efforts they receive lavish prizes, comfortable apartments, summer dachas, coveted reservations in the best Black Sea rest homes and automobiles. They have model cities in which to live; greater though not total freedom to travel to non-Communist countries; more right to meet with foreigners; access to special shops where, like party *apparatchiki* and other members of the upper classless, they can buy quality Soviet and foreign goods not available to the U.S.S.R.'s masses. To a degree, they are also entitled to cultural and intellectual amenities denied the mass of Soviet citizens by ideological orthodoxy: movies, plays, books and paintings that would otherwise not pass muster. But only to a degree.

What scientists, like other Soviet citizens, are denied, however, is intellectual freedom and full access to and exchange of information. In short: the right to think for themselves, the right to express their scientific, political, social, cultural and philosophical views.

They argue convincingly, as Sakharov did, that without such freedom there can be no real science and no independent search for the truth which leads to scientific and technological progress.

The gap between the needs of science and the Kremlin's restrictions has fostered widespread disaffection and dissent in the Soviet scientific community.

Scientists were among the most outspoken defenders of Sinyavsky and Daniel. Twenty-five leading scientists, among them many members of the august and influential Academy of Sciences, such as Professor Pyotr Kapitsa, a leading figure of international physics, the late Nobel Prize winner Igor Tamm and Sakharov, publicly warned against the formal rehabilitation of Stalin, rumored for the XXIIIrd Party Congress.

In March 1968, some ninety-five mathematicians, including seven Lenin Prize winners, protested against the detention of Yesenin-Volpin. Among the signers of this petition was the sister of the Academy of Sciences president Mstislav Keldysh, Lyudmilla, and her husband P. S. Novikov, both leading mathematicians and members of the academy.

A party ideologist expressed the dilemma of the discord between scientific requirements and the party's ideology in the theoretical journal *Kommunist* some years ago:

"We cannot but rejoice that Soviet scientists and specialists in many branches of knowledge march in the front rank of world science," he wrote. "But at the same time the party and the people want to see in scientists not only creators and organizers of scientific and technical progress but political workers, active fighters, for the cause of Communism."

Valentin Moroz, a Ukrainian history teacher and dissenter, now serving a nine-year labor camp term, stated the problem from the other side:

"Stalin invented the man projected from above, the man who is a cog in the wheel. The cog is the cherished ideal of any totalitarian system. An obedient herd of cogs can be called a parliament, it can be called a learned council. You will have no trouble or surprises with them. A cog called a professor or academician will never say anything new. The only surprises he will ever spring will be the lightning changes of his convictions within the space of twenty-four hours . . ."

But cogs, obviously, do not produce many scientific innovations.

The case of Dr. Revolt I. Pimenov typifies the quandary. Pimenov, forty-one, is one of the U.S.S.R.'s most brilliant mathematicians. His book *Kinematic Spaces,* also published in the United States, has been hailed as a "most significant work" which attempts to "analyze and extend the general theory of relativity without preconceived physical concepts."

In July 1970 Pimenov was arrested and charged, under Article 190 of the Russian code, with possession and distribution of seven pieces of *samizdat* literature, among them the "Two Thousand Words" of Czechoslovak intellectuals, an open letter by Pavel Litvinov on behalf of Ginzburg and Galanskov and an essay by Milovan Djilas.

For Pimenov it was not the first encounter with authority. In 1949, at age eighteen, he was detained in a psychiatric prison hospital because he had applied to resign from the Komsomol. A psychiatric examination showed him to be completely normal and he was released from the hospital on condition that he withdraw his resignation. In 1951 the Komsomol organization at Leningrad University expelled him from its ranks, then enrolled him again. In 1953 he was expelled a second time and once again taken back. In 1954 he received his bachelor's degree and went to work as a researcher. Three years later he was suddenly arrested and sentenced to six years in a labor camp. The charge: counterrevolutionary activity. The specifications included organizing an anti-Soviet group among students at Leningrad's Institute of Library Sciences and possession of "anti-Soviet" literature. He was freed in 1963.

Within twelve months after his release, Pimenov defended his dissertation for the degree of candidate of science (equivalent to a doctorate). In 1969 he was awarded his doctorate (a rare degree in the U.S.S.R. and comparable to the European life-title of professor).

One year after that award his apartment was searched by the KGB, books, manuscripts and tape recordings were seized and Pimenov was called to Leningrad party headquarters for a Kafkaesque "discussion" with the official in charge of ideology.

"Please understand," said the *apparatchik,* "that we are not speaking about your scientific work. Your scientific successes are very good. But there is something else. You are not living right. A whole collection of anti-Soviet literature was confiscated from you."

"There was not a line that called for the overthrow or weakening of or anything detrimental to Soviet authority," Pimenov replied.

"I am not very good at the legal nuances," the ideologist said. "The investigation will determine whether there was any anti-Soviet literature. But they took from you a whole collection of bad literature . . . Where did you develop the interest in such things?"

"Let me try to explain to you," Pimenov responded. "For some time we scientists have lost our sense of personal security. Roughly since the end of 1966. I'll tell you why.

"To work in science there must be faith in the future. When there is no faith there can only be narrow specialists who are preoccupied with their discipline and have no interest in public issues. The threat to personal security explains my interest in politics. It all began with the trials of the writers. The most important element was how they were conducted: the violations of legal rights which focused attention on the [trials] and aroused public concern."

"If you think we will ever allow somebody to speak and write whatever comes into his head, you are mistaken," the official replied. "This will never happen. We will not permit it. Do you want us to change the ideology? Of course we do not have sufficient power to force everyone to think the same way, but we have enough power to prevent them from doing things that will be harmful to us. There will never be any compromise on ideological questions. Remember this once and for all.

"I can count for you on my fingers the eternal truths that cannot be violated . . . Re-examine your outlook. I understand, of course, that one meeting is insufficient, but I am advising you to think over your behavior thoroughly."

Six months later Pimenov was tried, convicted and sentenced to five years' exile in Siberia. The punishment, by Soviet standards, was mild and the reason may well have been Sakharov's personal interest in the case. He had made formal application to attend the trial and was, surprisingly, admitted.

Disaffection in the scientific community is rooted in the Stalin era when scientists, because of their professional devotion to verifiable facts, were prime victims. Moreover, to a greater extent even than creative artists, they were professionally interested in events outside the U.S.S.R., a particularly hazardous inclination at a time when Stalinist propaganda declared Soviet primacy in every field, including that of technology.

No one has told the plight of scientists under Stalin more trenchantly than Zhores Medvedev in his book *The Rise and Fall of T. D. Lysenko*. It is a scathing condemnation of a system that permitted a ruthless charlatan and quack to dominate Soviet biology and genetics and arrange for the total professional and physical liquidation of his rivals and the cream of this scientific discipline.

In part it was Medvedev's exposure of Lysenko, the circulation of his book in *samizdat* form and its subsequent publication in the United States that led to his two-weeks-long incarceration in a Kaluga psychiatric clinic in May 1970. The other contributing factor was his militant criticism of censorship and restrictions on exchange of scientific information spelled out in two other *samizdat* books (*Fruitful Meetings Between Scientists of the World* and *Secrecy of Correspondence Is Guaranteed by Law*) which have now been published in English as *The Medvedev Papers*.

The Medvedev Papers are a reasoned, logical and highly motivated call for greater access to information. The central thesis is that Soviet science and the Soviet economy suffer immense, irreparable harm from censorship and senseless obstacles raised in the U.S.S.R. against co-operation between Soviet and foreign scientists.

By the time he was spirited away to the asylum Medvedev had already been dismissed from the Institute of Medical Radiology in Obninsk, allegedly on orders of the KBG, high-ranking officials in Moscow and the Obninsk party committee. His incarceration was intended to prevent his attending an international symposium on genetics scheduled in Moscow and to keep him from entering a competition for a new job.

Without so much as a warrant or a scrap of paper a squad of burly *militsionery* and psychiatrists forced their way into Medvedev's apartment, twisted the scientist's arms behind his back and, as his stunned wife, teen-age sons and friends looked on, led him to a waiting car that sped him to the psychiatric hospital.

Only the concerted efforts of the scientific community, led by Sakharov and Medvedev's brother, Roy, and the heavy pressure of world opinion secured Medvedev's release and prevented his permanent commission to an asylum or psychiatric prison.

Justifying the confinement, a psychiatrist (presumably though not necessarily acting on orders from above) told Roy Medvedev: "Generally speaking I found that your brother is suffering from a split personality. He is a biologist, but for some reason he does not concern himself only with biology but with many other things which have nothing to do with his direct duties. Moreover he always seems to be dissatisfied and is fighting something. He was writing other kinds of books besides his learned works."

The Medvedev case was a turning point for the scientific community and a test of courage for Sakharov, who almost single-handedly organized the campaign that led to Medvedev's release.

During the genetics symposium, which Medvedev had been scheduled to attend, Sakharov walked up to the platform and wrote a message on the blackboard informing participants where in the auditorium he was sitting and invited anyone to join him in a protest on Medvedev's behalf. After a while Nikolai Dubinin, the director of the Soviet Institute of Genetics, a man who had been victimized by Lysenko and whose return to the inner circles of Soviet science was due largely to Medvedev's book and articles, went to the board and erased the message. Sakharov wrote it there again. During the afternoon he was unceremoniously ejected from the hall on grounds that he was not a delegate to the symposium.

For Sakharov, the Medvedev case became a watershed that led him from social criticism to active protest. It was the logical first step toward the formation of his human rights study group.

The metamorphosis of "scientific" to "general" dissent required some prodding, however. In fact, the scientists were exhorted and virtually shamed into greater commitment by an "open letter" in the *samizdat Chronicle of Current Events* in the summer of 1970. Directing the attention of the twenty prominent signers of the Medvedev appeal to the plight of less prominent and less influential dissidents, the letter emphasized the common human factor shared by all nonconformists and asked those in an influential position, in Soviet society to be equally concerned about all persons victimized for their beliefs, irrespective of their professional or social standing.

Official reaction to the new militancy among scientists was predictably severe. At the Lebedev Physics Institute, with which Sakharov is closely associated, party organizers have been objurgated for "insufficient ideological and political work" and exhorted to "instill among scientists an irreconcilable attitude to the ideological concepts of anti-Communism and revisionism."

If reprimands and calls for "ideological vigilance" were the regime's chief means of reprisal, there would be little cause for concern. Unfortunately, dissent in most cases is met with the full force a totalitarian regime can muster, short of mass terror.

As we stood outside the courthouse on Maly Nikolovorobinsky Lane in October 1968, stamping our feet to ward off the October Moscow chill and eying each other suspiciously, a KGB agent approached a bearded dissenter and sneered: "In a year we'll have you all in prison."

Though the timetable has not been met the threat may yet be fulfilled.

The methods of repression are becoming more severe: trial and imprisonment, trial and exile to remote areas of the U.S.S.R., exile by administrative fiat, intimidation and the spread of fear, and, perhaps worst of all, incarceration in psychiatric hospital prisons operated or maintained by the KGB.

There may have been a time when some dissenters felt immune from prosecution or persecution because of their positions or family ties or because they had already suffered so much that it would be too embarrassing for the authorities to torment them again. It proved to be a chimerical hope.

Being a famous Old Bolshevik's grandson did not help Litvinov. Nor did being the wife of a man already serving a five-year term protect Larisa Daniel. Even the Daniels' eighteen-year-old son Alexander has been intimidated, denied admission to college or university and prevented from holding a decent job. He was beaten by the KGB for having the temerity to protest his father's treatment in the camps and prison.

Grigorenko believed confidently that he would not be arrested in Tashkent "because I am already too old [he is now sixty-four] and after all that has happened to me it would be too embarrassing to arrest me again." He was wrong.

Even Yakir, who was virtually raised in concentration camps after the NKVD murdered his father, has stopped believing that being one of the chief victims of the Stalin "cult of personality" exempts him from arrest. In the last few months before my expulsion, when I saw him frequently, he would always say, on parting: "Well, I'll see you tomorrow, if I'm still free."

Although the fear of arrest is omnipresent, many of the dissenters have lived with it for so long, or have already served terms in camps, prisons and mental hospitals, that they have sublimated it. They tend to live a game of cat and mouse with the KGB, a sort of Tom and Jerry existence which in the context of this macabre nether world of dissent and opposition to Soviet power is not without its humorous moments.

In May 1970, a few days before he planned to leave for his country cottage in Akulovo to spend the summer, and where shortly afterward he was arrested, Amalrik and his wife came to see us. They ate dinner at our apartment, we drank quite a bit and were in good spirits. Andrei's books had just been published abroad and he felt certain that if he could last through the next few days without being arrested, he would be safe until the fall. The thought that the

KGB might trouble to arrest him in that remote hamlet in Ryazan province seemed absurd.

When they wanted to leave, we had to escort them out of the foreigners' compound and decided to walk our dog at the same time and accompany Andrei and Gyusel for a while. It was a warm, balmy night.

As it was between the May Day and Victory Day (May 9) holidays, the usual portraits of Lenin and the members of the Politburo —in alphabetical order—were still mounted on metal poles on Kutuzovsky Prospect, across from the Ukraina Hotel. Methodically the dog began sniffing at each one of these poles, passing up Pyotr Shelest, Alexander Shelepin, Mikhail Suslov. We were talking loudly and joking about which member of the Politburo he would pee on. Brezhnev? Possibly Lenin?

Suddenly, in the darkness on the all but deserted street, we noticed a *militsioner* sitting on a bench, apparently guarding the portraits and watching us suspiciously. We stopped laughing and pulled the dog away. The prospect of Amalrik going to prison because our dog had desecrated a contemporary icon dampened our spirits.

Amalrik, following his arrest, was taken to Sverdlovsk, a city nearly a thousand miles from Moscow at the foot of the Urals, for investigation and trial. It was not accidental and the choice of venue explained why his arrest had been delayed so long. Sverdlovsk is closed to foreigners. There was no chance that Moscow-based correspondents could go there. And that is what the KGB wanted, for public spectacles such as the Galanskov-Ginzburg or Litvinov-Daniel trial proved too damaging to the Soviet image. The authorities waited long until they found a man with a *samizdat* copy of Amalrik's works in a remote place that would make it possible to try him there.

The techniques of repression and punishment of political miscreants are devious and seem to follow a set pattern of phases. Dismissal from work is usually the first concrete measure, making unemployment a syndrome common to all dissenters. Since they are unemployed, not only is the impression created among casual observers that they are ne'er-do-wells, but they are also made vulnerable to further pressure, for the Soviet system not only guarantees each citizen a job but demands that he must have one. Once they are fired, the KGB usually throws a variety of invisible obstacles in their way to prevent them from obtaining alternate employment.

Amalrik, for example, worked as a part-time mailman until the

KGB pressured his postmistress, who considered him hard-working and reliable, to fire him. Eventually he circumvented the "anti-parasite" laws by becoming a reader for a blind man. Vladimir Bukovsky worked as a secretary for an established and recognized woman writer, until he was arrested again in March 1971. When Yakir was dismissed from his position on the staff of the Institute of Historical Science, he obtained a job as a cataloguer in a library. After getting out of the psychiatric prison the first time, Grigorenko was a warehouse loader until he worked his way up to a position of foreman on a construction crew. Vera Lashkova, the girl student tried and sentenced together with Ginzburg and Galanskov, has been a truck driver since her release from jail.

In Chuna, her place of exile near Bratsk, Larisa Daniel had to haul wet, heavy logs at a sawmill until finally, after many months during which her health deteriorated, she was assigned to a machine in the mill.

Arrest ineluctably means many months—sometimes a year or more —of pre-trial detention in prisons, most of which have not been renovated or modernized since the nineteenth century, and endless interrogation by the inquisitors of the KGB and the *procuratura*.

Trials, notwithstanding the small nucleus of honest, dedicated defense lawyers that has evolved in recent years, are invariably star-chamber proceedings in which, it seems obvious, verdicts and sentences were decided—by KGB fiat—long before the court convened.

The public sections are always filled with hired Komsomol provocateurs and KGB men, to satisfy the formal requirements of a public trial, and to assure that the general public as well as relatives, friends, sympathizers of the accused and foreign journalists are kept out.

One dissenter's wife, Galina Gabai, describing this technique in an open letter of complaint to Nikolai Podgorny, told how a "group of young men, who were not relations, friends or even acquaintances of the accused, were let in immediately," while she and Gabai's mother were refused admission. After a recess, she explained, "the same well-organized group tried to push the rest of us—friends and relations of the accused—away from the courtroom door and did it so roughly that the judge felt obliged to say: 'Let the mother in. It doesn't look well.'"

Once convicted and sentenced to labor camps, a new nightmare begins. Today there are four types of camps, distinguished by the severity of their regimen: general, reinforced, strict and special.

General, the laxest of the four, prescribes normal work in the camp factory or industry at full pay, housing in barracks with free movement within the camp, unlimited though censored correspondence with immediate relatives, ten rubles from earnings which may be spent in the camp shop for tobacco and sundries, receipt of one parcel a month and one "private connubial visit" every six months from the prisoner's husband or wife. This category is rarely used for political prisoners, who are usually sentenced to terms of reinforced or strict regimen.

Reinforced regimen stipulates harder work, a monthly spending limit of seven rubles, receipt of parcels only every three months and one private visit every six months, although the prisoner must continue to work regular hours while the spouse is in the visitors' center.

Strict regimen requires heavy or dangerous work, a spending limit of five rubles monthly, one letter every month, no conjugal visits but one visit from relatives for a period of four hours per year and receipt of one parcel every four months. It is to this type of camp, for example, that Amalrik was sentenced.

Under special regimen prisoners must wear striped uniforms, engage in hard labor such as quarrying, are restricted to two rubles spending money, may write one letter per year and are not permitted any visitors.

Privileges prescribed in the regulations may be, and usually are, suspended at will by warders and camp commandants, and conditions are far more severe than the regulations would indicate. Theoretically, prisoners under strict regimen are limited to 2400 calories of food daily, those in special regimen camps to 1300, though in practice the amount doled out is far less.

"Russia," reads a *samizdat* report, "is entangled in a network of camps where, despite all the international conventions signed by the Soviet government, forced labor and cruel exploitation are the norm, where people are systematically kept hungry and humiliated, where human dignity is debased. Through these camps passes an uninterrupted flow of humanity numbered by the millions, people who are sent back to society in a physically and morally crippled condition."

Early in 1970 Ginzburg, then in Camp 17a in the Mordvinian swamps east of Moscow, about twenty-five miles north of the town of Potma, taped a message on a camp-made recorder which reached Western correspondents in Moscow through dissident sources. It was subsequently broadcast by CBS correspondent Bill Cole in his memorable documentary on the Soviet civil rights movement.

Ginzburg reported that sixteen prisoners had died recently from lack of medical attention and that there was only one doctor, also a prisoner, for every 1000 or 1500.

"Thousands of people are deprived of their freedom and everyone is in danger of his life," he said.

Political prisons, such as the infamous one at Vladimir, a nineteenth-century relic, are infinitely worse than labor camps. Among the better-known dissidents who have served in it are Marchenko and Yuli Daniel, who was sent there because of his publicized protests about the way in which Ginzburg was treated in camp. In his recording Ginzburg described Vladimir as "a living grave." Several months later, as punishment for his clandestine recording, he was transferred there himself.

The normal prison regimen at Vladimir, during Marchenko's detention in 1961, called for a daily diet of 18 ounces of black bread, ½ ounce of sugar, seven or eight stale sprats, a 12-ounce bowl of watery soup, one bowl of cabbage soup which consisted of water with leaves of rotten cabbage in it, 3 to 5 ounces of watery gruel and 3 to 5 ounces of watery mashed potatoes.

Under strict regimen in prison the rations are sharply reduced. Prisoners in punishment cells, in either camps or prisons, receive an even more meager food allotment.

But even in that living grave, dissent continues. From December 5, 1970, Soviet Constitution Day, to December 10, international Human Rights Day, twenty-seven Vladimir inmates, Alexander Ginzburg among them, staged a hunger strike to emphasize their demands for greater rights.

The camps in Mordvinia are only a fraction of the network. In fact, some one thousand camps, each containing approximately a thousand prisoners, bunched in clusters and complexes of from ten to twenty camps, dot the Soviet landscape from the Arctic Circle to the Chita region on the Manchurian border, from Yakutia in northeast Siberia to Odessa on the Black Sea.

"I do not know where there exist anywhere on earth outside our country such conditions for political prisoners: legalized lawlessness plus legalized hunger plus legalized forced labor," Marchenko wrote.

Little about them has changed over the years. Not even the "Stolypin" railway cars used to transport the prisoners to these living hells.

The name "Stolypin" derives from the tsarist Minister of the Interior, P. A. Stolypin, assassinated in 1911, who designed and introduced them. Many of the cars date from his reign of terror.

Even worse than camps or prisons are the special prison mental hospitals where heretics are confined on trumped-up findings of insanity.

As a form of punishment, or substitute for punishment, commitment is not new to Russia. The Marquis de Custine described it vividly in 1839 in the case of the Russian philosopher Pyotr Chaadayev, who "devoured by love of truth—a dangerous passion anywhere but fatal in that country—dared to state that Catholicism is more conducive to the development of minds, to progress of the arts, than Russian Orthodoxy."

He was imprisoned and tortured for months. Then, rather than face the embarrassment of a trial, Tsar Nikolas I ruled him mad and ordered him put into "the care of doctors." This "new form of torture," wrote Custine, "was applied in a fashion so severe that the supposed fool was near justifying the sentence.

"This martyr of the truth was on the verge of losing the sanity denied him by a decision from on high." After three years he was granted a modicum of liberty but by then he doubted his own sanity. "On the faith of the Imperial word, he declared himself insane." This, added Custine, "is a very recent example of the way affairs of conscience are treated in Russia today."

The treatment has proven useful for 130 years.

Hundreds of dissenters have been committed. Most of them are in special "hospitals" maintained by or on behalf of the KGB. Examining hospitals such as Moscow's Serbsky Institute for Forensic Psychiatry and treating asylums have special sections for political prisoners, whose only hope of escaping years in a Bedlam is to "confess" their crimes and accept years of imprisonment in a labor camp instead. General Grigorenko, every bit as sane as Khrushchev was and Brezhnev is, both of whom ordered his commitment, the first in 1964, the latter in 1970, reported in documents smuggled abroad that he frequently saw the Serbsky Institute's infamous Professor D. R. Lunts and other psychiatrists in the special military-style uniform that KGB officers occasionally wear.

"The quintessential horror of this inhuman system," Grigorenko wrote in late 1969, "is that a sane person gradually begins to understand that the longer he stays there the greater is the danger that he will become like those (who are really ill) surrounding him. For a sane man a mental hospital is a horrible experience, if only because he is deprived of all rights, even those due a prisoner . . . His only hope is to find an honest doctor."

Grigorenko obviously didn't find one.

To the average Soviet psychiatrist, not even a KGB man parading in psychiatrist's clothing, a political dissenter of Grigorenko's nature *must* seem unbalanced.

"I remember," Grigorenko recalled, "how I was questioned by a woman doctor in Leningrad [Psychiatric Institute] in 1964. She didn't want to see me ruled insane, but she was a political illiterate and as a result twisted my words during an interrogation so that I must have sounded abnormal.

"'You were earning eight hundred rubles a month,' she said to me. 'Why did you make speeches like that [criticizing Khrushchev and the regime]? What were you lacking in life, what else did you want?' To her anyone as materially well off as I was would have had to be insane to make the kind of statements I made. 'You would not understand,' I told her. 'I had no free air to breathe.' That was obviously the wrong answer! Since then I have learned not to make oral statements to doctors. I insist on writing out everything."

In a sense, Grigorenko's dilemma and that of other dissenters is that anyone who tries to fight *this* city hall must be a bit cracked.

Today Grigorenko is serving his open-ended sentence in Chernyakhovsk near Kaliningrad, the former East Prussian Koenigsberg, where authorities have converted a former Gestapo jail into a special psychiatric prison for political dissidents. Conditions are indistinguishable from those in any other Soviet penitentiary. Grigorenko's wife Zinaida, who is permitted to visit him for a few hours once a month, told me shortly before I left Moscow that, as punishment for the reports on asylum conditions which he wrote, the general is now confined to a stone cell and limited to the use of a pencil for one hour twice weekly. Everything he writes is confiscated.

Before that restriction was imposed on him, he managed to jot down an essay that tells chillingly of conditions in such a hospital.

"My military training and perhaps the iron constitution which my parents passed on to me," he wrote, "enabled me to learn quickly to insulate myself from my surroundings and to survive [his first confinement in 1964] without any particular harm to my psyche. But what I cannot forget, what still sometimes wakes me up at night, is a wild nocturnal cry [of another inmate] mixed with the hollow sound of shattered glass."

Theoretically, anyone who is a political non-conformist faces the threat of open-ended incarceration in a psychiatric prison. Girsh I. Feigin, a former Red Army major and World War II veteran, who succeeded in emigrating to Israel in February 1971, was forcibly placed in the republican psychiatric hospital of Latvia in December 1970 because he had sought to leave the U.S.S.R. and publicly renounced the government decorations he won during the war. The doctor who ordered his hospitalization said that Feigin was abnormal because "normal people do not renounce government decorations."

"All these 'special' psychiatric hospitals," reported the *Chronicle of Current Events,* "have the following features in common: political prisoners, although of sound mind, are kept in the same wards as seriously disturbed psychiatric patients; if they refuse to renounce their convictions they are subjected, on the pretext of treatment, to physical torture . . . The regime is the same as for closed prisons, with one hour's exercise a day. Sometimes, before interrogation, sodium aminate is administered by injection. The staff consists of orderlies recruited from Ministry of Interior forces, their uniforms concealed by white overalls, male nurses chosen from among the criminal prisoner-patients, also in white overalls, and senior and junior medical personnel who are usually police officers. The brick walls surrounding these prison hospitals are even more impressive than those of other kinds of prisons. The most terrifying arbitrary regimes prevail at the Sechyovka and Chernyakhovsk hospitals where the sick patients as well as the politicals are the victims of daily beatings and sadistic humiliations on the part of the supervisory personnel . . ."

One inmate of a psychiatric prison, Vladimir Gershuni, arrested in October 1969 for possessing twenty copies of a leaflet about General Grigorenko, printed in Paris, has smuggled out a graphic description of conditions. He is imprisoned in Oryol, a town 170 miles southwest of Moscow.

"Eight people occupy a cell measuring 16 to 17 square meters," Gershuni reported. "There is no room to move. The toilet is a cesspit: four holes in the ground and two taps for fifty-four people." In December 1970, to commemorate Soviet Constitution Day, Gershuni started a hunger strike. On its forty-third day the warder forbade him to take his daily walk. Gershuni insisted on his rights. "[The warders] grabbed me, twisted my arms behind my back, forced me into the cell and in the doorway the exercise warder dealt me a blow on the jaw. Blood gushed forth. Once I was locked up again, I broke the small pane of glass in the door, shoved my hand through the opening, drew back the bolt and ran out with a piece of glass in my hand so as to settle accounts with Checkist [KGB] pig. But he managed to run away." In the official record the incident was described as "a fit of insanity" during which the patient "smashed the glass with his head, cutting his mouth and breaking his jaw at the same time."

Vladimir Bukovsky, who has already spent six of his twenty-nine years in prisons, labor camps and mental asylums, and now faces another seven-year term, has called his period in Moscow's Serbsky Institute and the Leningrad Psychiatric Hospital "fifteen months of hell."

"There were about a thousand men in the asylum, political prisoners and insane murderers," he has related. "The sick raved, the healthy suffered."

His wardmates during one period were an old Ukrainian nationalist, who had been confined for sixteen years, and a maniac who had killed his children and then cut off his own ears. The Ukrainian spent most of the day raving about Ukrainian independence, the murderer just sat and smiled.

The real authority rests not with doctors but brutal turnkeys and prisoner trustees—criminals from Leningrad Prison—whose reports to the doctors about inmates' behavior frequently resulted in extreme punishment.

On the recommendation of trustees or guards, doctors would inject sulfazine, which caused severe stomach cramps, fever, intense pain and temperatures of up to 104 and left the inmates—already weakened by starvation diets of thin oatmeal, watery cabbage soup, bread and, once a week, fish—close to being physical wrecks.

According to Bukovsky, another drug, aminazine, reserved for serious misbehavior, induced sleep and dulled the senses. Injected daily for ten days, it turned inmates into human vegetables. Some managed to regain their senses after two months, others never did.

Another form of punishment called for swathing prisoners tightly in wet canvas, which shrinks as it dries. This technique, applied with a nurse in attendance, is used until the pulse grows so weak that a doctor orders a halt to the "treatment."

"Only the crafty survived," Bukovsky reported. "You had to be nice to the guards, you had to make friends with them, you had to bribe them. Otherwise they could beat you until you were nearly dead and tell the doctors you had misbehaved, and that would result in special punishments such as drug injections or the 'roll-up.'

"Sometimes they would put inmates into padded isolation cells and beat them almost continuously. I know of several men who died after this.

"And the doctors themselves realized that it was not a hospital but a prison and sometimes admitted it openly," Bukovsky said. "To get out of it you must declare officially that you *are* sick, admit you were wrong, and disavow what you did. People who refused spent many years in such special hospitals."

In Leningrad Bukovsky met a Romanian-born French Communist who had lived for more than a decade in Marseilles before going to the U.S.S.R. to see what Communism was like in practice. He worked in a factory in Moldavia, near the Romanian border, and became disgruntled over the low pay. He encouraged his fellow workers to fight for higher wages and to strike. He was arrested and declared insane, in lieu of trial.

"He just couldn't understand what had happened to him," Bukovsky said, "how Communists could do such things. For him Communism and the struggle for a better life were the same thing. Toward the end of my stay in the hospital he really began to go out of his mind, or so it seemed to me, because he was telling everybody that the Soviet government was under the influence of the Vatican."

The diagnoses given by KGB psychiatrists in some of the political cases would make Sigmund Freud turn in his grave: "psychohetero-mindedness" in the case of Grigorenko; "creeping schizophrenia," in the case of a graphic designer accused of defaming the Soviet state; and "deterioration of the intellect" for an electrician caught with *samizdat* materials.

In January 1971 Bukovsky sent a 150-page documentation on individual cases through *samizdat* channels to the West and appealed to international associations of psychiatrists to concern themselves with the Soviet practice of imprisoning political dissenters in mental asylums. Two months later, on the eve of the XXIVth Party Congress, he was arrested.

Although the use of insane asylums in lieu of prisons to deal with non-conformists was described as long ago as 1839, it was not until the Stalin era that a network of special psychiatric prisons was established. The first was built shortly before World War II in Kazan.

After the war a special asylum colony for political prisoners was built in Sechyovka near Smolensk. In 1951 a special hospital was opened in Leningrad, in 1965 in Chernyakhovsk in East Prussia, in 1966 in Minsk, and in 1968 in Dnepropetrovsk.

According to a 1970 *samizdat* report, by Sergei Pisarev, a veteran Communist Party member, these psychiatric prisons had been investigated by a specially appointed commission of the Central Committee in 1955 and 1956. Although the commission's report was highly critical of the system and its practices, no action was ever taken and the report itself was hidden in the archives of the Central Committee by an official who, according to Soviet underground sources, had been active in the purges of the 1930s.

Pisarev is no ordinary dissenter. He joined the Communist Party in 1918 at age sixteen and fought the Whites in the Civil War. He was an *apparatchik* and later a bibliographical researcher. During World War II he served as an army *politruk* officer (a political commissar), won several medals, was wounded and is now partly disabled.

In 1953, two months before Stalin died, he wrote a letter to Stalin complaining about secret police practices. Pisarev was arrested on the day of the dictator's death, detained for four months in the psychiatric section of the Butirky Prison, then sent to the Serbsky Psychiatric Institute, where, in his words, "they rubber-stamped a diagnosis of 'schizophrenia.'" Sent to the Leningrad psychiatric prison, where he served a term of about eighteen months, he was released and rehabilitated politically in 1955.

Pisarev's four-thousand-word report to the Academy of Medical Sciences includes a brief résumé of his own case as well as a lengthy appeal brief by Olga Kallistratova, Grigorenko's lawyer.

> For decades [he wrote] the Serbsky Institute has made frequent and fatal errors [because] this medical establishment and its special departments have been used primarily for the confinement of political prisoners and have come under the administrative and investigative authorities [KGB] which use them for purposes which contradict the objectivity of medical science.
>
> There is nothing new to this foul practice. Back in 1955 I brought this matter to the attention of the Central Committee of the Communist Party. I gave the names of a number of innocent persons, primarily party officials, scientists and workers in art and litera-

ture . . . some of whom had been compelled to spend eight years among the mentally ill for committing no crime whatsoever.

The Central Committee set up an authoritative commission, headed by A. I. Kuznetsov, a responsible Central Committee official. It included a number of party members and famous psychiatrists. The commission carried out a thorough study, confirmed all the information provided by me and even supplemented that information with facts I had known nothing about.

The commission found hundreds of completely healthy inmates who had been sentenced to unlimited periods of isolation under the guise of mental illness. It pointed out systematic errors in the diagnoses of the Serbsky Institute, in particular by Dr. D. R. Lunts and a number of other psychiatrists. It documented that, because of the failings of this institute, Soviet mental hospitals, in particular the infamous special clinics for political prisoners in Kazan and Leningrad, had been filled regularly with normal people subjected to illegal reprisals . . .

The commission recommended radical changes and that the Serbsky Institute and the Kazan and Leningrad institutions be turned into genuine medical institutions under the full control of the Ministry of Health, not the administrative and investigative agencies.

Despite the persistent efforts of the commission . . . no action was ever taken.

The participants of the study were ultimately dismissed from the Central Committee apparatus under various pretexts.

Psychiatric prisons, labor camps, arrests, intimidation and persecution notwithstanding, the Democratic Movement continues to gain in importance.

To suggest, as some Western observers do, that it is likely to generate a revolutionary situation soon is premature and unsound. Its importance must be measured by more moderate criteria. It demonstrates that a significant body of intellectuals, connected by the most tenuous and amorphous ties, have begun with tenacity and courage to voice their politically dissident opinions, that they refuse to desist or recant, even in the face of certain repression and possible martyrdom. In an unstable sociopolitical and deficient economic setting, this could become a combustible mixture.

For the Kremlin it creates a unique dilemma. As Amalrik said: "If the Soviet Union is to survive, it must undergo a total transformation. But if the present Soviet leadership is to survive, everything must remain exactly as it is."

It is not a new contradiction for Russia, where for centuries the intelligentsia and the ruling elite have been engaged in protracted debate and battle over how the country should be run and which directions it ought to take.

Today that debate seems especially acrimonious because the current ruling elite, the party leadership, propagates the thesis of its own infallibility and identity with the party, with Communism and with the "scientific truths" upon which Communism is allegedly based. Its dispute with the intelligentsia revolves around the naked question of political power. For the past years it has won, and for the foreseeable future it will continue to win, most of the arguments.

But not all of them. The intelligentsia, the dissenters, have over the years achieved some small, tenuous, but nonetheless traceable successes.

There are indications that influential sympathizers with the civil rights movement and its members exist in the party-state apparat. Some, as a consequence of their disillusionment with the swing back to Stalinist practices, have reached a degree of disaffection that surpasses even the mood of militant dissenters. They believe they can effect change from within but the change they are working toward calls for far more than reform.

One member of the party and the establishment told me with the utmost candidness once: "Sakharov and Medvedev are naïve. You cannot moderate this system, you cannot attempt to change it through a policy of gradual liberalization, for gradual liberalization contradicts the monopoly of power which the ruling elite has arrogated for itself. The only answer is the establishment of a completely new system."

How widespread are such views? No one can say. One can merely speculate, conjecture and, perhaps, hope.

One source of hope seems to be the *samizdat* journal *Political Diary,* published monthly since October 1964, whose very existence was not disclosed to Western correspondents in Moscow until the summer of 1971. Soviet sources who made eleven of its seventy-two issues available to New York *Times* correspondent Bernard Gwertzman hinted that its publication had been suspended in late 1970 or early 1971. There is no way to document this, particularly in view of the secrecy that previously surrounded *Politichesky Dnevnik,* as it is called in Russian. It could still be circulating as regularly as it did before some dissenters decided to provide the West with a sample look at the journal.

What is significant about *Political Diary* is that its views and contents hint of a "loyal opposition" among establishment intellectuals, historians, writers, journalists, scientists and government and party officials who are in responsible but not decision-making positions. It appears to be edited by and for people who do not wield great power themselves but are close to those who do.

Although, like the *Chronicle of Current Events,* a typewritten underground organ—with an average of fifty-six single-spaced pages per issue—it differs radically from the *Chronicle.* It is not intimately concerned with practical politics but, rather, with political ideas. A journal for political thinkers rather than for political actors, for people who probably consider themselves above the battle of daily politics and too loyal to engage in overt acts of dissent, *Political Diary* adds another dimension to *samizdat.*

A surprisingly large portion of the content of those issues of *Political Diary* that are available consisted of excerpts from articles printed in official Soviet publications, even *Pravda,* which carried no other introductory comment than the remark that they might be of interest to the reader. About half of the *samizdat* documents contained in the available issues were previously known abroad through other sources. "It would appear," said Dr. Albert Boiter, an American Sovietologist working in Munich, "that a primary function of *Political Diary* may have been to provide a digesting service for the liberal-minded and busy intellectuals who read it." It drew on an amazingly wide variety of materials: from books and articles old and new; from publications in many countries and in various languages; from political gossip or speculation; from *samizdat* petitions and letters espousing liberal causes; from transcripts of closed meetings.

Issue No. 3 dated December 1964, the earliest available, carried excerpts of a speech by Anastas Mikoyan at a Moscow factory in which he explained how and why Khrushchev was forced out of office. Another issue carried illuminating details on the 1957 struggle between Khrushchev and the "anti-party group" in the Politburo led by Georgy Malenkov, Vyacheslav Molotov and Lazar Kaganovich. The June 1965 issue published rumors about an attempt by some Bulgarian Communist leaders to unseat Todor Zhivkov, the Bulgarian party leader. The same issue revealed details on crime in Moscow, given in a lecture by the head of the Moscow Militia, and reported on a conference in the Ministry of Higher Education during which a deputy minister proposed including works of Stalin in the social sciences curriculum. A two-page article in the March 1967 issue reported details on the defection of Stalin's daughter, Svetlana Alliluyeva, to the United States. The June 1967 issue carried a half page of details on how the Politburo dismissed KGB chief Vladimir Semichastny while his mentor, Alexander Shelepin, was ill and in a hospital. Its cultural and literary pages have carried critical and unpublished speeches by Yevgeny Yevtushenko, information on films that have been suppressed, a report that the London *Times* began publishing chapters of Solzhenitsyn's *Cancer Ward,* news of the suppression of an exhibition by young Moscow painters, as well as five pages of details on the results of a readership survey by *Literary Gazette* which so displeased the *Gazette*'s editors that they were not published in that paper. *Political Diary* has introduced its readers to the ideas of Herbert Marcuse and the New Left in the United States, provided them with information on the conflict with China which official Soviet publications would never print and discussed both the computer and the paper shortage in the U.S.S.R.

Over the years *Political Diary* has adopted an editorial policy wholly favorable to the political developments in Czechoslovakia before the invasion and highly critical of the military intervention in Prague. It has been equally critical, to judge from the editors' selection of materials, of Soviet policy in the Middle East, particularly Soviet involvement on the Arab side.

Political Diary's editors, and presumably its readers, are against dogmatism, neo-Stalinism and anti-Semitism. The struggle against Stalin's rehabilitation and the revival of Stalinist practices is an overriding concern and documentary material which serves to undermine the position of neo-Stalinists appears to enjoy priority in the journal. They are thoroughly patriotic, committed to making the Soviet Union a healthy and strong society at home and increasing its influence abroad. They regard themselves as good Communists, though of a critically-minded, tolerant and internationalist hue. Among *Political Diary*'s editors and readers could well be what one Soviet source has described as "the liberal Communist" faction of party intelligentsia, some military personnel, some littérateurs, some party functionaries "and even a not too numerous section of KGB officials" who feel that some reforms are necessary to prevent revolution and whose main criticism of the present regime is that it is insufficiently dynamic, flexible and modern. "This group," said the source, "is continually growing in strength and numbers. It has illegal and semi-legal links with Western Communist parties and enjoys their support."

The allusion to a liberal element in the KGB is of particular interest. No doubt the dread secret police has undergone a certain degree of transformation since the days when Stalin, Yezhov and Beria used it as an instrument of cruel suppression. It has become more professional. It has sought and found intelligent recruits in the universities. Though its quota of professional thugs and goons —whose penchant for brutality is matched only by their proclivity for bureaucratic narrow-mindedness—remains very high, it has attracted others—intelligent and cultivated Russians.

Are they the ones, for example, who make it possible for the *Chronicle of Current Events* and *Political Diary* to continue to appear, are they the ones who have protected certain members of the civil rights movement from arrest? For it would seem, given the power and the resources of the KGB, that the movement would be snuffed out or crippled quickly if someone were willing to pay the price: mass arrests involving several more thousand people. Or would that suffice? Is disaffection and discontent already so far spread that terroristic means to suppress it would merely serve to enlarge the ranks of the disenchanted and the militant dissenters? Are overt dissent and *samizdat* merely the tips of an iceberg?

According to reliable information some twenty senior KGB officers in Moscow and elsewhere were replaced and transferred in late 1969 and early 1970 for giving out information to members of the dissent movement. Retributive action was also taken against some officers who allegedly warned Grigorenko about plans to arrest him in Tashkent. It has also been reported that a number of guards at the Tashkent KGB jail were reprimanded for the fact that some of Grigorenko's notes leaked out as *samizdat* documentation which later reached the West.

Both the KGB and the *procuratura* have tended to become more painstaking and more meticulous in their observance of the law and the legal code. Gross violations of Soviet law, while remaining the rule, not the exception, have tended to diminish, as a result, undoubtedly, of dissenters insisting on their rights and the wide publicity given to violations.

A small but courageous core of defense lawyers has emerged.

Though subjected to considerable pressure from the authorities, their briefs have become consistently more daring and outspoken. The circle of such *advocaty* is small, and deliberate intimidation helps to keep it that way. But their briefs and appeals show that they endeavor to wage a genuine fight for their clients.

This rudimentary legal consciousness has influenced the Soviet legal profession in general. During 1970, for example, a number of articles calling for closer observance of "socialist legality" have appeared in the press. And one series, written by a justice of the Soviet Supreme Court, even demanded an enhanced and strengthened role for defense attorneys in criminal proceedings.

"These developments," Yakir once told me, "encourage us more than anything else, for it is observance of the law which is the soul and essence of our movement."

Yet, on the whole, these are the straws in the wind that one clutches in moments of optimism.

A less propitious straw, in a sense, is the appearance of *Political Diary*. After years of keeping it a secret, why did some Soviet intellectuals finally decide to make copies of the journal available? Only, many observers feel, because the *Diary*'s editors and backers have concluded that their chances of influencing Soviet policy from within have diminished. Their decision to turn to the West could well be a sign of their desperation and a reading of the real climate inside the U.S.S.R.

Pyotr Yakir, in his more pessimistic moods, tells friends of a KGB man who once said to him: "You think you are your father's heir. But you are wrong. We are."

In the macabre context of the system that Yakir's father helped to create, but which snuffed out his life in the Lubyanka Prison, the KGB is proving to be right.

If an individual or a whole country
want to be free, they must achieve
freedom somehow . . . But sometimes,
to obtain this, one must risk even
the little freedom one has.

Andrei Amalrik in
a letter to Anatoly
Kuznetsov, 1969

3 *Profiles in Determination*

The trial of Litvinov, Larisa Daniel, Babitsky, Delone and Dremlyuga was to start at 10 A.M. Precisely on the hour, the crowd of
150 relatives, friends and sympathizers, led by General Grigorenko,
surged toward the courthouse doors to demand admittance. Fended
off by the *militsionery,* they retired to the wooden pavilion on the
other side of the street. There they collected signatures for a petition
demanding an open trial.

The paper was passed around. Suddenly, when fifty-six signatures
were already on it, Oleg I. Alexandrov, a spade-bearded KGB
tough who had been a plainclothes regular at other trials, snatched
the document and tore it to pieces.

Up went the heavy wooden cane of General Grigorenko and
militsionery rushed in just in time to prevent it from crashing down
on the KGB's man skull.

"I want to charge that man with hooliganism," Grigorenko told
an astonished police major. The policeman said he could do nothing

but advised Grigorenko that if he really wanted to file a complaint, the nearest precinct station was across the Yauza River, a few blocks away.

"Come on," Grigorenko told Alexandrov. Then, his battered blue felt fedora plunked squarely on his bald head, his faded blue gabardine coat flapping in the wind, his cane beating a martial rhythm on the pavement, the ex-general marched toward Moscow Militia Station No. 27. In a half run beside him came Alexandrov. A straggling band of the defendants' friends, KGB agents, Komsomol provocateurs and foreign newsmen hurried behind them.

The precinct chief, after listening to Grigorenko's complaint, said he would consider the case. Of course, nothing ever came of it. But Grigorenko had scored another, albeit minor victory for what he considered "genuine socialist legality."

Though he is now locked up in a bleak psychiatric prison cell where he does isometric exercises to keep his mind and body from vegetating into senility, legality—the rule of law not men—remains Pyotr Grigorenko's main aim in life.

He has written and signed countless petitions, appeals, letters and protests. He has peppered the Soviet Union's leaders, the editors of *Pravda* and *Izvestia,* the representatives of foreign Communist parties and the United Nations Human Rights Commission with condemnations of the Soviet invasion of Czechoslovakia.

Grigorenko has written and published abroad the most definitive analysis yet to appear about why the Soviet Union was nearly defeated by Nazi Germany in 1941.

Over the open coffin of a liberal writer-journalist friend he has audaciously promised that "freedom will come, democracy will come." From a podium at a Communist Party meeting he once charged that the Stalin "personality cult was not an accident . . . Now we have the Khruschchev cult . . . We need to change the system to prevent other cults."

He was arrested, incarcerated in an insane asylum in lieu of jail, expelled from the Communist Party, stripped of his general's star, demoted to private, forced to work as a warehouseman and compelled to live with the ominous shadow of the KGB just an arm's length behind him.

In May 1969, though indirectly threatened with arrest if he did so, he flew to Tashkent in Uzbekistan to testify for ten Crimean Tartars awaiting trial on charges of slandering the Soviet Union.

The KGB made good on its promise. Grigorenko was arrested, spent nearly ten months in pre-trial custody and the dread Serbsky Institute, was tried secretly and *in absentia,* and sentenced to an unlimited term in the psychiatric penitentiary in Chernyakhovsk, East Prussia.

But even prison walls, asylum bars, brutal beatings by sadistic guards, forced feedings when he went on a hunger strike, isolation and punishment cells and endless inquisition could not crush this sexagenarian's indomitable spirit or still his pen. From prison he smuggled out a remarkable diary that is both a unique tribute to his courage and a singular indictment of the insidious machinery of persecution, prosecution, pseudo-scientific psychiatry and the network of Bedlams where non-conformists are pressured and tortured to recant.

"All my life I wanted to be true to myself," Grigorenko told me a few days before he left on his fateful journey to Tashkent. "I am not afraid. And I don't care what others say or think about me. Only what I think about myself."

Grigorenko came to this recognition the long, hard way of many an orthodox-Communist-turned-renegade after the death of Stalin.

A big, bony man whose erect 6-foot-4 frame and strident gait reveal his military background, Grigorenko is as bald as and bears a striking facial resemblance to Nikita Khrushchev. Born of Ukrainian peasant parents in 1907, he joined the Communist youth league as a teen-ager in 1922, became a full-fledged party member in 1927, studied engineering, won a candidate of science degree and entered the Soviet Army as a career officer.

A lieutenant colonel when the Germans invaded, Grigorenko saw front-line infantry duty, was decorated for heroism and wounded twice. For most of the post-war period, until he was cashiered from the service, Grigorenko was professor of cybernetics at Frunze Military Academy with a general's star on his shoulder boards.

Married to a statuesque strawberry blonde, once as orthodox a Communist as he but now one of the most outspoken dissenters, and the father of five sons (the oldest forty-two, the youngest twenty-five), Grigorenko seemed well on the way to a successful career in the Soviet party and military hierarchy.

"I protected the Stalin regime in an honorable way," he once confided. "I believed."

But then came Nikita Khrushchev's "secret speech." For Grigorenko it was a personal catharsis that "turned all my feelings around." When he realized that Stalin had not acted alone but that the whole system was at fault, he decided to do something about it.

The occasion was a borough party meeting in Moscow in September 1961. His "first performance," as he put it with a smile. From the podium Grigorenko charged that Stalin's personality cult was not an accident, that every Communist country had such a cult and that the only way to prevent them was to change the system.

Of course, it was phrased more tactfully than that. But the audience applauded enthusiastically. His superiors at the military academy called him in the next morning, ordered him not to deliver his scheduled lectures and dismissed him from the faculty. While his local party organization deliberated on the reprimand which he received a few months later, Grigorenko circulated an open letter to Moscow voters in which he lamented "restrictions on freedom" in the U.S.S.R. and criticized the "unreasonable and often harmful activities of Khrushchev and his team."

Grigorenko soon found himself in the boondocks of the Far East —in Vladivostok. Stripped of his degrees and professorship, he continued, however, to make speeches and write protest letters. In February 1964 he was arrested and arraigned before a court-martial of generals who decided, instead of a potentially embarrassing trial, to pack him away in the Leningrad psychiatric prison, where he spent fourteen months—*after* Khrushchev's fall. Meanwhile he had been expelled from the Communist Party, removed from the officers' lists, demoted and discharged and deprived of his pension rights.

Grigorenko was no sooner out of the hospital and working for a Moscow construction trust when he began petitioning on behalf of his own rehabilitation and pension as well as against the rehabilitation of Stalin. Soon he was out on the streets demonstrating on behalf of Sinyavsky and Daniel and other dissenters.

By mid-1966 he was a central figure of the civil rights movement. His crowded apartment on Moscow's Komsomolsky Boulevard, which he and his wife shared with some of their sons and their families, became a mecca for intellectual rebels not only from the Moscow area but from other cities as well. It was raided and searched eight times in three years by the KGB. The battered old typewriter, taken during the final search following Grigorenko's arrest in Tashkent, was the third that had been confiscated from him in twelve months. It was on them that he pecked out his essays, letters and petitions inveighing against Soviet injustice and demanding observance of constitutional guarantees.

Grigorenko is fearless. On the streets in front of courthouses he argued his points for legality with all comers and in complete disregard of the secret police agents and *Komsomoly* who were around.

When his friend Aleksei Kostyerin, an outcast expelled from the Communist Party and the Soviet Writers' Union, died in November 1968, Grigorenko organized the funeral and cremation ceremony in the face of vile KGB harassment and machinations. In his oration at Kostyerin's bier in Moscow's main crematorium, he told mourners and the listening KGB agents of his vow to fight "the damned machine" against which Kostyerin had battled.

Later, the morgue director approached him to apologize for all the difficulties that had been placed before the ceremony and pleaded, "It wasn't my fault."

"I could express no sympathy for him," Grigorenko said afterward. "I considered and still consider that only a man can make himself a man . . . In our country there are many people—unfortunately very many—who only have to hear the magic word KGB and at the order of a man representing that organization will commit the most shameful acts. At some point one must break the habit and must remember those fine words—'human dignity.'"

He exhorted the Crimean Tartars to "Stop begging. Take back that which was taken from you unlawfully." He encouraged them to present their case outside the country to the UN and bluntly charged that what was done to that minority group was "genocide —pure and simple."

Of the self-immolation of Jan Palach in Prague, Grigorenko said:

"We, all of us, bear the burden of guilt for his fate . . . By our support, approval or simple silence toward the military intervention in Czechoslovakia, we are making it possible for living torches to burn on the streets of Prague . . . The greatness of a country lies not in the might of its armies, unleashed against a numerically small, freedom-loving people, but in moral strength."

And of himself and his role, he once said:

"Obviously, if you believe that the only normal Soviet man is one who bows his head meekly in face of each arbitrary act by a bureaucrat, I am certainly 'abnormal.' I am not capable of that kind of humility no matter how long I must continue to fight."

A staunch Leninist who argues that it is Stalinism and the heirs of Stalin who drifted from the true fold, he once told me:

"Lenin wrote of a difference between bourgeois and proletarian democracy. In bourgeois democracy there is freedom only for the rich, in proletarian democracy freedom for everybody. But here, in our society, there is freedom for nobody. What I want is democratization and socialism, for there can be no socialism without democracy."

Grigorenko is fully aware of the long road ahead.

"I began alone but I am no longer alone," he said to me. "There is always hope when you have an idea. But it would be much better if we had a way to speak to the people directly. We could change many things if we had the means of mass communication."

But now, limited by his warders' censorship and the virtual absence of pencil and paper, Grigorenko's platform is even smaller.

"Only now do I truly understand the terrible desperation of those who died by the millions in Stalin's jails," he wrote in his prison diary. "The physical suffering can be endured. But people were deprived of the smallest hope and were convinced of the omnipotence of the dictatorship. This is unbearable . . .

"The whole conduct of my case shows they were looking not for proof of my guilt but for means to twist the law so that I could be thrown into prison without trial and without a defense. In short: punishment for one's convictions by means of false and untrue accusations, isolation and the psychiatric prison—confinement for life."

*　　*　　*

Vladimir Bukovsky writes and speaks like a bookish young man. Soft-spoken, contemplative and reflective, blessed with a keen mind and a sharp intellect, he is a thinker. And why not? The son of a privileged Communist Party member who was a respected Moscow journalist associated with the more orthodox and conservative literary journals, young Bukovsky grew up, by Soviet standards, with a silver spoon in his mouth.

You would expect him to be as mild and gentle as he speaks. But Bukovsky is hard and tough. He has the physique of a stocky middleweight boxer, muscles that bulge underneath his ill-fitting shirts and jackets, scars on his face that tell of many bloody scraps and the gait of a man always wary of trouble lurking beyond the next corner. In January 1971 when he and an American corre- spondent were mugged by five KGB hirelings, as part of a campaign to intimidate dissenters and foreign journalists, Bukovsky, fists flying, acquitted himself masterfully. Despite a heart murmur and a rheu- matic ailment, the result of six years in Soviet labor camps, prisons and psychiatric penitentiaries, Bukovsky is tough. The system has made him that way.

For the sake of the cause he believes in Bukovsky was prepared at any time to go back to the hell that forged his adult life.

"Don't threaten me," he once told a Moscow prosecutor who was questioning him about the interview he had given Holger Jensen, an Associated Press correspondent, in which he spelled out the details of life in Soviet prisons and psychiatric hospitals. "I am not afraid. If one trial is not sufficient, if my last speech was not enough, there will be a second one—and after my release, more material for another interview."

"I absolutely do not repent of having organized the demonstra- tion," he told a Moscow City Court judge in September 1967. "I believe it has done its job and when I am free again I shall organize other demonstrations."

And to his dissenter friends, just before he was shipped to a labor camp in the Voronezh region three hundred miles south of Moscow in 1967, he said: "Sooner or later we will all go to prisons and insane asylums. But we will come out and fight even harder."

In January 1970, after serving a three-year term, he was released and, true to his word, fought harder than ever—in the sure knowledge that it would just be a matter of time before he was imprisoned again. In March 1971, the KGB obliged him.

"I can be arrested at any moment," he once told me. "Because I am meeting with you or giving you *samizdat* materials, because of what I say or what I write. They'll find some excuse. In the camps we used to say: 'When they've got the man they'll always find the law to nail him.'"

Bukovsky is young enough to be Grigorenko's grandson. Nearly forty years—an epoch of Soviet history that includes the October Revolution, the Civil War, Stalin's reign of terror, World War II, Beria's execution and the rise of Khrushchev—divide them. If Grigorenko embodies the dissenter who turned 180 degrees from loyal service to Stalin to open opposition, Bukovsky typifies the generation that is too young to remember the dictator's rule. He was ten when Stalin died.

And yet they are linked by the common experience of psychiatric prisons, publication and protests through *samizdat,* street demonstrations and a passionate addiction to the principles of democracy and the rule of law.

And like Grigorenko, everything in Bukovsky's background suggest that he should be an orthodox, conformist, prosperous supporter of the regime, not the renegade rebel he has turned out to be. Instead he turned to protest early.

Born in Belebey in the Bashkir Republic where his mother had been evacuated during the war, he was raised mostly in Moscow. As a teen-ager, he was a bright and promising student at Middle School No. 59. But as a senior he started to discover the inequities and repressive aspects of Communist society. He helped publish an underground satirical humor magazine, called *Martyr.* It not only caused his expulsion but the dismissal of the school principal and several teachers for lack of vigilance, and a reprimand from their party organization for Bukovsky's parents for having failed to raise him "in the proper spirit."

Bukovsky was thus barred from a higher education. Somehow, he registered at Moscow University anyway and studied biophysics for a year before authorities discovered who he was. Expelled, he worked as a museum handyman and spent his nights on Mayakovsky Square with the young poets and littérateurs who later formed the nucleus of the SMOG movement.

Bukovsky was very much a part of that movement. He was a contributor to the 1961 edition of Galanskov's *samizdat* journal *Phoenix.* He took part in unauthorized poetry readings, helped organize an illegal exhibition of abstract art by Moscow painters, and in 1963 was caught by the KGB for possessing and circulating "anti-Soviet documents": photostats of parts of Milovan Djilas' book *The New Class.* Arrested and under investigation, he was sent to the Serbsky Institute, which, predictably, declared him insane and committed him to the prison asylum in Leningrad, where he spent fifteen months.

Released in December 1964, shortly before his twenty-second birthday, he plunged back into the non-conformist movement.

His freedom was short-lived. A year, to be exact. He helped organize the 1965 Constitution Day demonstration in Pushkin Square calling for an open trial for Sinyavsky and Daniel and was soon arrested, again put through the mill at the Serbsky Institute and committed to an asylum. He attributes his own unexpected release a half year later to the fact that Amnesty International took an unusual interest in his case and demanded his freedom.

In January 1967, following the Pushkin Square demonstration for Galanskov and Dobrovolsky, which he organized, Bukovsky was arrested a third time. His trial, together with Delone and Yevgeny Kushev, in September resulted in the three-year camp sentence that he completed in January 1970.

Until he was again arrested, in 1971, Bukovsky shared a two-room apartment in a dilapidated old building on Furmanov Street in Moscow's Arbat section with his mother, sister, her husband and their baby. From time to time he did free-lance technical translations. He had taught himself English in prison and the asylum. And then there was the fifty-rubles-a-month job as secretary to a sympathetic writer.

"Of course I know I am being followed," he said once, "and it is obvious that my telephone is tapped. I am under constant surveillance."

And yet, he went on with his struggle. In the spring of 1970, to draw attention to the plight of political persecutees in the U.S.S.R., he sent an open letter to Greek composer Mikis Theodorakis, just released from a Greek political prison, inviting him to the Soviet Union to inspect prison and camp conditions:

> I imagine you as a man of courage, honesty and principles who would not depart from his views either for money or under pressure.
>
> You can understand better than anyone else what a police state is, what prosecution of those who think differently means and what struggle against illegal actions under these conditions implies. As a creative man you cannot remain impartial to the fate of those who are deprived of their freedom to create. As a former political prisoner you cannot remain impartial to the conditions under which political prisoners in other countries are kept. And as a fighter for democracy you cannot remain impartial to the fate of those who openly defend their civil rights . . .
>
> Some years ago the leaders of our country used to state that

we did not have political prisoners. They cannot state this now
as the world knows their names. There is no secret about the
addresses of the camps, prisons and psychiatric prisons where they
are kept . . . And there is no reason for refusing you permission
to visit Soviet camps, prisons and asylums provided there is no
wish to hide the facts of illegal actions and arbitrariness.

You could, for example, compare the conditions of political
prisoners in Greece and the U.S.S.R. . . . I am appealing to you
as one former political prisoner to another former political prisoner
with a request to help our friends, the political prisoners in the
U.S.S.R.

The letter was never published in the Soviet Union, nor did
Theodorakis acknowledge it. On the contrary, when he did come
to the U.S.S.R. several months later, it was as a propaganda object
of the regime, which had invited him to recuperate from the physical
and spiritual strain of imprisonment in Greece.

"Typical," Bukovsky told me when he heard about that. "But
I think I scored a point."

Bukovsky's views and aims are best summed up in his 1967
courtroom testimony.

"As an opponent to all forms of totalitarianism," he said, "I have
made it my aim in life to denounce the anti-democratic laws which
lead to political inequality in our country . . . Demonstrations such
as the one I organized are, in my view, a legitimate form of protest
and of struggle for the abolition of anti-democratic laws. Article
125 of the constitution grants us this right; the only breach of
public order in the square was committed by the *druzhiniki* ['voluntary' auxiliary police] and I cannot understand how we can be tried
for it . . .

"Protest demonstrations are a powerful weapon in the hands
of the workers and the right to hold them exists in every democracy. And where is this right denied?" Bukovsky asked, calling
the court's attention to a *Pravda* item reporting that May Day demonstrators had been convicted in Madrid, Spain. He said: "Note the
touching unanimity of fascist and Soviet law."

"The essence of our struggle," Bukovsky believes, "is against
fear, the fear which has gripped the people since the time of Stalin
and thanks to which this system continues to exist, the system of
dictatorship, of pressure, of oppression. In that struggle the personal
example, the example which we give people, is very important.

I spoke out on the occasions when I wanted to and I am alive. Not only is it necessary, but it is possible to fight."

* * *

That he is even alive today is a small miracle. That he is not only healthy of mind and reasonably healthy of body is even more remarkable. That he is the acknowledged leader of the civil rights movement with a fearless devotion to principle, prepared momentarily to face again imprisonment and a living hell is astounding. But then, Pyotr Ionovich Yakir, forty-eight, is an astounding man in many ways.

Bukovsky is typical of the political dissident who was too young to remember Stalin. Grigorenko is typical of the onetime establishment Communist who made Stalin possible but abjures today everything Stalin stood for. Yakir is the living symbol of the injustices, the murders, the crimes and the suffering for which Stalin was responsible. Understandably, the focus of his dissent activity is to prevent a rehabilitation of Stalin and a recurrence, no matter in how diluted a form, of the system Stalin created.

He sees a clear and present danger of both.

"Eventually," he once said to me, "all of us who take part in the Democratic Movement may be arrested. But that is not so important, for if we are not here others will be. The young generation will not permit the regime to go back to what used to be. Their struggle will be a hard one, but they will struggle. They may beat us, kill us, imprison us, but people will go on thinking differently."

Yakir began thinking differently at an early age. He was fourteen years old on May 31, 1937, when NKVD men boarded the Kiev-Moscow express at Bryansk and arrested his father, Army Commander Iona Yakir, hero of the Revolution and the Civil War, bundled him into a Black Maria and drove him at top speed to Moscow and the Lubyanka Prison. He was locked in a solitary cell, his medals and rank insignia were ripped off. For nine days he was subjected to torture and interrogation, but Yakir refused to buckle and did not confess as so many of Stalin's other victims had. The trial was perfunctory, probably lasting no more than a few minutes. The sentence was a foregone conclusion—death. On June 11 or 12, the exact date is not known, General Yakir, Marshal Tukashevsky and seven other top commanders of the Soviet Army were led into the courtyard of the NKVD building on

Dzerzhinsky Square. While truck engines were revved up to drown out the noise, they were shot.

Mrs. Yakir and young Pyotr were immediately exiled to Astrakhan, where they met the families of the other executed officers. At the beginning of September she was arrested. Pyotr was sent to a children's home. Two weeks later, at night, the NKVD came for him and put him first in prison, then a concentration camp.

For the next seventeen years—until 1954—Yakir was in the camps. There he grew up, met his wife, also a prisoner, and married. It was in the camps that his daughter was born.

Yakir had Nikita Khrushchev to thank for his release and rehabilitation and as a consequence a close personal association developed between them. Periodically, until Khrushchev's death they telephoned each other and discussed events or Yakir visited the deposed leader in his country dacha. In September 1971 when he wanted to attend Khrushchev's funeral, Yakir and his wife were arrested outside their apartment house entrance, taken to a police station and detained for intending to "commit an anti-social act" until the *militsionery* were informed that the funeral had ended.

He and his wife live in a cramped, book-filled, two-room flat on Moscow's Avtozavodskaya Street which they shared, until recently, with their daughter, now married to the poet and underground protest singer Yuli Kim, and until her death in July 1971 with Yakir's aged, nearly blind mother, Sarah. (The elder Mrs. Yakir was given an official funeral arranged by the Soviet Defense Ministry.)

Though a Jew, Yakir is a collector of icons, crucifixes and other Orthodox artifacts, which cover those walls of his apartment not hidden by bookshelves. To Yakir they are symbols of Russia and Russian suffering.

He still considers himself a Marxist-Leninist but many long conversations over far too many glasses of whisky and vodka finally persuaded me that his faith in the Communist ideal is wavering. He has seen and suffered too much.

Once, during an evening spent with a couple of active dissenters who are unusually religious and have complete trust that God will deliver them and the Soviet Union from evil and suffering, Yakir turned to me and said softly:

"Their naïveté sometimes drives me crazy. But I admire them, more than that, I envy them. They have faith, they believe in something. They can fall back on something. I have nothing."

He is the driving spirit and force of the civil rights movement. And notwithstanding his academic approach to many problems, he is an effective agitator and propagandist.

Following the invasion of Czechoslovakia, for example, Yakir encouraged scores of Moscow dissidents to walk around the city for months with little metal Czechoslovak flags pinned to their outer clothing.

Several years ago, in response to a number of articles extolling Stalin's role in World War II, Yakir sent a letter (never published in the U.S.S.R.) to the editors of *Kommunist,* the party's theoretical journal, suggesting a posthumous trial of Stalin on the basis of a seventeen-point indictment which he compiled.

The charges, all covered by specific articles of the penal code, included "abuse of power," "illegal imprisonment," "physical pressures in legal investigations," "instigation to suicide," "premeditated murder," "acts of terrorism involving murders of private citizens, members of the government or other public officials with the aim of undermining or weakening Soviet power," "violations of equality of nationalities and races," "sabotage and other actions or inactions designed to undermine industry, transportation and agriculture," "desecration of tombs and graves," "desertion in wartime," "criminal negligence of the nation's defense bordering on treason."

"It is not my purpose to confront Stalin with all the accusations he deserves," Yakir wrote. "But although our list is far from complete his acts, as set forth in this statement, constitute a substantial body of crimes as defined by Articles 64, 68-17, 69, 74, 88-1, 88-2, 10-17, 10-70, 113-17, 126-17, 130, 131, 170, 171, 229, 230 and 247 of the penal code of the RSFSR [the Russian Republic]. In studying Article 38 of the penal code, dealing with extenuating circumstances, one can find nothing that justifies mitigating the sentences in Stalin's case."

"Well, why not?" countered Yakir with professed innocence. As he paused to think he ruffled his massive crop of curly hair and stroked his bushy pepper-and-salt beard. Then he added: "Look, if you can have posthumous rehabilitations such as my father's, I don't see why a posthumous conviction wouldn't be possible."

Though Yakir's background as one of Stalin's chief victims probably gives him immunity—the uproar among Communist leaders in other countries would be a higher price than the Kremlin is willing to pay to silence him—he is forced to play a continuing game of cat and mouse with the KGB. They do not frighten him, however.

The night before my departure from Moscow, Yakir and his wife came to our apartment to say good-bye. On the street was a heavy KGB stakeout and when the Yakirs entered the compound they were photographed, accosted and molested by the agents, who grabbed Yakir's wife roughly by the arms. The next day she had bruises. Yakir angrily telephoned a high-ranking KGB officer and complained.

"Those weren't our people," the official lied. "They must have been street hooligans."

"I know the difference," Yakir retorted. "I've been dealing with your people for thirty-three years and I know who works for you and who doesn't."

* * *

So does Andrei Amalrik, although he was born only one year after Yakir's father was arrested and executed, eight months after Yakir himself was sent to a concentration camp.

Andrei was not yet fifteen when Stalin died and like Bukovsky he is relatively free of the fears which are second nature to the older generation.

Shortly before his arrest in May 1970, Amalrik explained that freedom from fear in a letter to the editors of the German news magazine *Der Spiegel*.

"Until now I have enjoyed more freedom than most Soviet citizens," he said, "but I have only myself to thank, because I wanted to be free. Thus, I acted as any free person can and must. I sent my books abroad under my own name and have insisted on all author's rights.

"Even if and when they put me in jail I hope to stay freer than millions of my and your countrymen who 'in freedom' screamed 'hurray' for Stalin and Hitler and believed in the omnipotence of the organizations created by these dictators."

Arrest really came as no surprise for Amalrik. On his thirty-second birthday, a few days before he and his beautiful sloe-eyed wife Gyusel left for their cottage in Akulovo, 170 miles southeast of Moscow, he told me:

"The KGB will arrest me when the fuss abroad has died down and interest in me has waned. They won't get me for my books but will trump up some minor pretext. But now that my books are out and

I have said what I wanted to say, I don't really care whether I go to prison or not. It's been worthwhile."

For Amalrik, a slight, frail, nearsighted man with a congenital heart ailment, arrest was no new experience. But he is going to need every ounce of his strength, all of his inner freedom and all of his wryness and dispassionate sense of humor to come out of the strict regimen labor camp on the Kolyma River as spiritually and physically unscathed as he returned from exile to Siberia in 1966.

My last memory of Moscow, which I left two weeks before the start of his trial in Sverdlovsk, was the final meeting with Gyusel. She had come to our apartment for lunch and accompanied my wife and me partway to the airport. We let her off somewhere on the Sadovo Ring before turning out on Leningradsky Prospect to Sheremetyevo. With tears in her eyes she said, *"Ya boyus, ya boyus* (I am afraid)." I could barely look at her as I replied, more to persuade myself than Gyusel: "He'll make it, he'll come through."

In March 1971 he almost didn't make it. Meningitis contracted in prison put him in a coma for ten days and nearly killed him.

To me Amalrik was more than one of the dissenters. He was my friend. His 12-by-15-foot room in a five-room pre-revolutionary flat shared by five families on Vakhtangov Street in the Arbat section was an oasis of relaxation, intellectual exchanges and plain good fun. It was crowded with a double bed, a grand piano which Andrei had inherited from his aunt but could not play, a desk that doubled as dining table, a wardrobe, two old chairs, a wall of books and bookcases, Gyusel's makeshift easel on which she shoebrushed portraits of her friends and occasionally the wives and children of Western diplomats, and paintings by unofficial avant-garde artists.

Life in such *kooperativniye* flats, where five (and sometimes more) families share one kitchen, one toilet and one bathroom, is difficult for any Russian. For Andrei, visited periodically by artists, nonconformist intellectuals, foreign correspondents and diplomats, it was often compromising because neighborliness in such communes is predicated on the principle of one neighbor spying on the others.

To the chagrin of the KGB, at the Amalriks it didn't *always* work that way. One day several years ago, when the secret police raided and searched the room, a cantankerous old woman who lived in the flat barged in. Thinking the agents were more of the Amalriks' friends, she berated them for making so much noise, disturbing peaceful Soviet citizens, and threatened to call the police on them.

Probably, the friends usually *were* noisy. That is endemic to discussions about art, politics, philosophy and religion that last late into the night. Such discussions, underscored by the sound of baroque music from the record player and the clinking of glasses, were a frequent occurrence there.

In the Democratic Movement Amalrik was an outsider, a chronicler so to speak, whose observations about his fellow dissenters were sometimes as caustic and wry as his commentaries about the foreign correspondents and diplomats he knew.

His most salient characteristics are his individuality, his consistent refusal to compromise his beliefs, his determination to act in strict accord with his own principles and his dry humor and admirable ability to laugh, not only at others, especially the pompous representatives of Soviet officialdom, but at himself.

These are character traits that got him into trouble at an early age. While a student in the history department of Moscow State University Amalrik wrote a term paper entitled "The Normans and the Kiev Principality," in which he suggested that the ninth-century Russian state in Kiev owed much of its civilization to the Normans. It is a view shared by most objective historians, including many eminent pre-revolutionary Russian ones. But it contradicted the official Communist view that the proper conclusions should stress the Slavs as the true founders of the first Russian state. Amalrik's professor recommended that he submit merely the dry facts and delete his conclusions. Amalrik refused. The professor refused to approve the dissertation. Amalrik protested. He was expelled from the university.

His intellectual interests and curiosity focused on underground writers, poets and artists and led him to such people as Alexander Ginzburg, the painters Anatoly Zveryev and Dmitry Plavinsky, as well as members of the foreign diplomatic and press community.

In their attempt to maintain surveillance over such persons, the KGB approached Amalrik in 1961 and, in his own words, "politely suggested that I write general reports on the mood of the intelligentsia. I, with equal politeness, refused. And there the matter rested."

For two years. In 1963, according to Amalrik, "I was driven to the Lubyanka at night and told to write a denunciation against an American diplomat, to the effect that he was subjecting me and other Soviet citizens to harmful ideological influence. I again refused, although this time they threatened me with criminal proceedings."

Though none of Amalrik's activities were in fact illegal, they did fall into what he has termed "a broad, gray belt"—activities that the law neither formally forbids nor condones but which are proscribed in practice. After Khrushchev, official tolerance straitened and the "gray area" once again fell into the category of "anti-Soviet" activity. Amalrik was one of the first victims of the new stringency. Arrested in May 1965, he was first charged with writing, producing and disseminating "pornographic" plays. When the prosecutor realized he could prove neither their "pornographic" nor their anti-Soviet content, Amalrik was charged with "avoiding socially useful work" and leading an "anti-social, parasitic life." In a one-day sham trial Andrei was sentenced to exile in Siberia for two and a half years with obligatory physical labor.

Thanks to the diligent efforts of a principled Moscow lawyer, an acquaintance of Ginzburg, the verdict and sentence were repealed by the Russian Supreme Court and Amalrik was "pardoned" fifteen months after his conviction. He had spent his exile working on a kolkhoz in the Tomsk region, where Gyusel had joined and married him. His experiences in exile are the basis of his book *Involuntary Journey to Siberia.*

Amalrik has no illusions about the Soviet Union or its political system. He sees no hope for liberalization and views the progressively draconian measures of repression as an expression of the regime's growing loss of control. He predicts, and probably hopes for, catastrophe.

Though he is incensed by the regime's injustices, he cannot really commiserate with its victims, for he believes that "no rule by force can exist without people who are ready to submit to that rule. If we want to change it we must fight it. It is a bad system. It makes me physically ill to the stomach. But no one living under it is absolved of blame for its being bad."

For all his opposition to the system, however, Amalrik says categorically that he would never want to leave Russia. "This is the country in which I was born. Perhaps, if I had had a choice beforehand, I might have preferred to be born elsewhere. But all that remains to me now is to hope and strive for changes that will make this country a better one."

Literature is a fearful mass weapon.
You cannot play around with it. It
prepares revolutions but, as we know,
it can also prepare counter*revolutions.*

Vsevolod Kochetov, editor-in-chief of
Oktyabr, conservative Soviet literary monthly

I divide all works of literature into
those that were authorized and those
that were written without authorization.
The first are obnoxious filth, the latter
are a stolen breath of fresh air.

Ossip Mandel'shtam,
Soviet poet and victim of the Stalin purges

 Russian Winters

"A great writer," Alexander Isayevich Solzhenitsyn wrote in *The First
Circle of Hell,* "is, so to speak, something like a second government.
That is why no regime, anywhere, has ever loved its great writers,
only its minor ones."

During the past two centuries Russia has probably produced more
good writers than any other country. And nowhere have writers been
as persecuted, berated, muffled, censored, imprisoned, banished, exiled and, under Stalin, systematically liquidated, as in Russia.

Nor have writers anywhere been as politicized, as involved and
engaged, albeit with less demonstrable success, as in Russia. And
in no other country have the writing intellectuals served so obviously
as the nation's genuine progressive force and conscience as in pre-
revolutionary Russia and in the post-Leninist Soviet Union.

Because authentic and effective political opposition was weak or
absent, the littérateurs assumed the role of a vicarious opposition

and became the only group from whom political and social criticism emanated. Great writing and political opposition became symbiotic.

The list of Russia's literary martyrs is a long one, beginning with Alexander Radishev, initially sentenced to death, then banished to Siberia in 1790 because of his polemical essay on serfdom, *A Journey from Saint Petersburg to Moscow.*

Alexander Griboyedov spent five months in jail in 1823 for his play *Woe from Wit.* A satire on high Russian society, it was banned by the censors, though copies of the manuscript circulated illegally—an adumbration of *samizdat.* The play was not published, and then only in a sharply censored version, until 1833, five years after the author's death.

Alexander Pushkin, Russia's greatest poet, was once sent into exile because of an anti-monarchist ode. Mikhail Lermontov was banished because of a poem in which he blamed the tsar for Pushkin's death.

Fyodor Dostoyevsky was almost executed in 1849 because of his association with a revolutionary socialist society. He was already on the scaffold with the noose around his neck when the sentence was commuted to four years' imprisonment in Siberia.

Ivan Turgenev was banished because of his attacks on serfdom. Alexander Herzen was exiled twice before he emigrated to England where he continued his opposition to the tsarist monarchy with Russia's most famous émigré journal *The Bell.*

Nikolai Chernishevsky, who perfected the Russian tradition of using fiction for the discussion and dissemination of social ideas, was arrested in 1862, spent two years in the grim Peter and Paul Fortress of St. Petersburg, then was sent to Siberia, where he lived for seventeen years.

Leo Tolstoy was excommunicated from the Church because of his views and could publish many of his books only abroad.

Maxim Gorky was an émigré twice—from 1906 to 1913 and again from 1921 to 1928. The only time that Russians could see an uncensored, unexpurgated version of his great play *The Lower Depths* was during a brief period of thaw following the October Revolution. Today, the same lines are censored from it, and probably for the same reasons, as were cut out in tsarist days. Gorky was typical of the dozens of great writers who first welcomed, then became disillusioned with Soviet power.

Ivan Bunin, the first Russian to win the Nobel Prize, immigrated to France in 1920. Alexander Blok, the leading Russian symbolist poet, originally welcomed the Bolshevik Revolution but by 1921 had become one of its chief critics. Sergei Yesenin, who had dreamed of a peasants' paradise and became the Bolshevik bard, committed suicide in 1925, a disillusioned man. Vladimir Mayakovsky, the futurist, killed himself five years later, thoroughly disenchanted with the Communist Party.

The purges of the 1930s murdered Boris Pilnyak, Isaac Babel, Mikhail Kholtsov and Ossip Mandel'shtam, to mention only a few who went to the camps and never returned. Then the *Zhdanovshchina* of the post-war years silenced Anna Akhmatova, Mikhail Zoshchenko, Lev Kasil and countless others.

The Khruschchev era produced Dudintsev, Yevgeny Yevtushenko, Andrei Voznesensky and Solzhenitsyn but gagged and killed Boris Pasternak.

Today it is Solzhenitsyn who plays a special role and is a unique symbol. He and his novels personify the vicissitudes of political-literary thaw and refreeze, the incarnation of de- and re-Stalinization.

Following publication of *One Day in the Life of Ivan Denisovich*, the names Stalin and Solzhenitsyn were juxtaposed as counterbalances. Today, as one Soviet dissenter lamented, "the balance has shifted. We are exhuming the corpse of Stalin and burying Solzhenitsyn alive."

Solzhenitsyn has become a symbol. His photograph—frequently yellowed and dog-eared—can be found on nearly every Soviet intellectual's wall or bookshelf. In the crowded, dingy rooms and apartments where dissidents and members of the intelligentsia light their candles of passive or active resistance, it is never Lenin or Marx but Solzhenitsyn who hangs icon-like in a place of honor.

Like Gleb Nerzhin, the autobiographical protagonist in *The First Circle of Hell,* Solzhenitsyn has been "robbed of everything. He is no longer in *their* power. He is free again." And because he has gained his freedom, Solzhenitsyn is able to formulate and analyze, more eloquently and more trenchantly, what the Soviet misery is all about.

When six of the seven members of the Ryazan branch of the Union of Writers met on November 4, 1969, to expel him, Solzhenitsyn told them:

> Stalin's crimes cannot be forgotten indefinitely. One cannot always run against the truth. These crimes concern millions and they must

be revealed . . . As long as they are kept secret nothing prevents their repetition.

Free speech, honest and complete free speech—that is the first condition of health for every society, including ours. Anyone who abjures free speech for our country is indifferent to the needs of our fatherland and thinks only of his own, narrow self-interests. He who does not want free speech for the fatherland also does not want to cure it of its illness but to drive the disease inward so that the rot begins from there.

Solzhenitsyn's ordeal as a writer began when he first exposed the Soviet sickness to public scrutiny, when he initially burst into print. He is a literary iconoclast whose first published work was a catharsis of apodictic revelations that challenged the establishment of Stalin's heirs.

Alexander Tvardovsky, then the editor of the U.S.S.R.'s most liberal literary monthly, *Novy Mir,* planned to publish *One Day in the Life of Ivan Denisovich* as soon as he read the manuscript. But he knew that without official support at the very highest level he would never clear it through censorship. Tvardovsky sent a copy of the manuscript to Khrushchev, who personally authorized its publication in the November 1962 issue of *Novy Mir.* The story of Ivan Denisovich fitted perfectly into Khrushchev's endeavor to unmask and exprobrate Stalin.

For a few months Solzhenitsyn was panegyrized by the paladins of the Soviet literary establishment. An unknown high school physics teacher until his sudden success, he was invited to join the Writers' Union, whose board even waived the normal entrance requirements.

The following January Tvardovsky published "Matryona's Home," a long story which, in my opinion, more than anything else he has written, establishes Solzhenitsyn as one of the greatest Russian writers. But criticism of Solzhenitsyn and Khrushchev's policies was already mounting and the story sparked a vicious campaign by the literary hard-liners, who fulminated against the author's "narrow-mindedness" and "shortsightedness."

Seven months later, when Tvardovsky published "For the Sake of the Cause," a story that described a technical school principal's unsuccessful struggle against the arbitrariness of a party bureaucrat, the conservative literary and party establishment excoriated both the author and the editor.

Tvardovsky answered the criticism by filling the next few issues of

Novy Mir's correspondence column with letters of praise and adulation from Solzhenitsyn's devoted readers. But Solzhenitsyn's voice was too dissonant, his pen too truthful for the Soviet Union of the mid-1960s. Nearly three years passed before he was again in print, in the January 1966 issue of *Novy Mir,* with a fictionalized essay, "Zakhar Kalita," in which the action centers around the custodian of the visitors' book at Kulikovo, the historic site of the 1380 battle between Russians and Tartars. A short work characterized by clarity, lyricism, unobtrusive patriotism and profound love of humanity, it portrays Kalita as a living link between Russia's past and future.

"Zakhar Kalita" was the last of Solzhenitsyn's work to be published in the Soviet Union. That it got into print at all is probably due to Tvardovsky's pertinacious support of his protégé and the stupidity and inefficiency of the censors, who failed to catch the essay's hidden meanings and critical innuendoes.

The years between the publication of "For the Sake of the Cause" and "Zakhar Kalita" were crucial ones in the history of the Soviet Union, punctuated by Khrushchev's fall, the end of de-Stalinization and the beginning of Stalin's rehabilitation.

By mid-1966, *One Day in the Life of Ivan Denisovich* was being discreetly withdrawn from library shelves around the country. Solzhenitsyn himself reported on this angrily during a confrontation with the secretariat of the Writers' Union in September 1967.

"The technique," he said, "is to tell readers that the book is in the bindery, that it has been lent out, that there is momentarily no access to the shelves on which it is kept. Librarians are under instructions to refuse to circulate it. Here, for example, is a letter I received from a reader in the Crimea: 'I am an activist of our local library and was told confidentially of an order that your book be removed from circulation. One of the women working in the library wanted to present me with a souvenir copy of *Novy Mir* containing *One Day in the Life of Ivan Denisovich,* because the library no longer needed it. Another librarian stopped her and told her that once a book had been assigned to the "special section" it was dangerous to make a present of it.'"

For Solzhenitsyn it must have been clear at an early stage of his literary career that his novel *The First Circle of Hell,* which he began writing in 1955, two years after his release from the concentration camp, and completed in 1964, would never be published in post-

Khrushchev Russia. But he was justified in thinking that his other major novel, *Cancer Ward,* stood a better chance, despite the fact that one critic, an old Stalinist writer, told Solzhenitsyn that the novel "makes me vomit when I read it," and the conservative literary *apparatchiki* opposed it because it did "not tell of happy things."

Tvardovsky wanted to publish it and fought tenaciously for it. But by 1967 Solzhenitsyn's fortunes had ebbed sharply. For one thing, he had just recently amassed a host of new enemies because of his blunt criticism of the Union of Writers and literary policies in the U.S.S.R. Having been deliberately passed over as a delegate to the Third Congress of Writers in the spring of 1967, Solzhenitsyn sent the congress and the union an acrimonious but scathingly truthful letter in which he decried censorship, bureaucracy and the poltroonery and obsequiousness of the union and the Soviet literary establishment. To the delight of his malefactors, *samizdat* copies of the letter reached the West, throwing Solzhenitsyn open to charges of serving the "bourgeois enemy."

Solzhenitsyn and Tvardovsky had miscalculated the mood of the Kremlin and underestimated the power and influence which Solzhenitsyn's enemies had on the party leadership. The first installment of *Cancer Ward* was set in type and a protracted battle to publish it began. Finally, Tvardovsky, believing he had won, scheduled publication for the December 1967 issue of *Novy Mir.* Just before deadline, the secretariat of the Writers' Union, which owns *Novy Mir,* on direct instructions from Leonid Brezhnev, overruled Tvardovsky.

A systematic campaign to ruin and defame Solzhenitsyn followed. He proved easy prey. *Samizdat* circulation of *Cancer Ward* and *The First Circle of Hell* assured copies of both manuscripts reaching the West, where, understandably, they were immediately rushed into print. The effect was to intensify the campaign of vilification at home, where Solzhenitsyn could be accused of giving aid and comfort to the enemy.

The KGB did its part to assist.

In the 1950s, shortly after being released from camp, Solzhenitsyn had written an angry and bitter play, strongly critical of all aspects of Soviet society. Entitled *The Feast of the Victors,* he later repudiated and disavowed it, saying that the play had been written by an embittered prisoner of Stalin who, emotionally, philosophically and professionally, was no longer identical with the post-Stalin author of *One Day in the Life of Ivan Denisovich*. Solzhenitsyn never attempted to publish the piece and, according to him, only one copy of the manuscript existed. In 1967, while on a trip to Moscow, he left a suitcase containing that manuscript with a friend. A short time later the friend's apartment was burglarized, apparently by the secret police. Soon the play was being offered by KGB emissaries to publishers, particularly Russian émigré groups, in the West in an obvious attempt to discredit Solzhenitsyn in the U.S.S.R.

Less than two years passed between the final decision not to publish *Cancer Ward* and Solzhenitsyn's expulsion from the Union of Writers. The illogic that dictated the ouster was expressed by Vasily Matushkin, one of the little-known Ryazan writers who led the discussion at the decisive meeting. "It is true that we do not know his latest works," Matushkin said. "We have not read them. But they go against all that we are writing ourselves, and the West uses his name to sling mud at our motherland, which is sacred to us."

For Solzhenitsyn expulsion meant little more than formal ratification of his status as an outcast. Although he never availed himself of them, he was formally deprived of the perquisites and emoluments that accrue to members of the Writers' Union. Otherwise there was little change.

His chances for publishing his latest novel, *August 1914,* first of a trilogy dealing with Russia in World War I, the Revolution and the Civil War, were neither improved nor reduced by expulsion. Its rejection by Soviet publishers was predictable. And while there were justified fears that the authorities might take punitive action against Solzhenitsyn as "an unemployed parasite" or on grounds of publication of his work abroad, to date the worst thing that has happened has been ceaseless harassment by the authorities and a vituperative, calumnious campaign in the press. Of course his works, long criticized and condemned by hack literary circles, became dangerous to discuss, possess and distribute.

Eleven months after his formal relegation to the status of an unperson, this "man of steel," as his friends call him, enjoyed the ultimate triumph of any writer and the greatest vindication he could expect in his lifetime: the 1970 Nobel Prize for literature.

The award placed the Soviet regime in a quandary. In 1958, when the prize went to another literary outcast, Boris Pasternak, Khrushchev forced the author to decline. The prize itself, in Soviet propaganda terms, became synonymous with "capitalist, bourgeois plots" to embarrass the Soviet Union. Seven years later, in 1965, the Nobel committee awarded the prize to another Soviet writer, Mikhail Sholokhov, a paragon of virtuous Communist orthodoxy who in 1969 was to stoop so low as to call Solzhenitsyn a vermin. Sholokhov and the Kremlin accepted with alacrity. Thus in 1970 the sorry performance of 1958 could not be repeated.

Solzhenitsyn was not forced to decline. He was merely prevented from going to Stockholm to accept the prize. Offered an exit visa with no assurance of being permitted to return, Solzhenitsyn, a Russian patriot to the marrow, a man with close emotional ties to the Russian language and Russian soil, decided to stay home. Because news of the award could not possibly be censored even in the Soviet isolation ward, the propaganda machinery vented its anger on the Nobel committee, which it called a tool of the "imperialist conspiracy" playing an "unseemly game." The award was termed a "deliberate provocation" by "reactionary circles" against Soviet literature. And, predictably, the defamation campaign against Solzhenitsyn reached new heights.

He has been vilified in the press and attacked from the lecture platform. He has been barred from receiving most of the Nobel Prize money which he needs desperately. And he has been subjected to continuing abuse and constant surveillance by the KGB. That police persecution reached a macabre climax in August 1971 when Alexander Gorlov, a friend of Solzhenitsyn's, discovered a squad of KGB men rummaging through and confiscating papers from the writer's dacha in the village of Rozhdestvo, forty miles southwest of Moscow, while Solzhenitsyn was in the city.

The writer, who had fallen ill in Moscow, had asked Gorlov, a construction engineer, to go to the cottage and pick up a spare part for his car. When Gorlov approached the dacha he noticed the lock missing from the door and could hear voices inside. He entered and found about ten men in civilian clothes. One of them, apparently the senior officer, shouted: "To the woods with him and silence him." Gorlov was knocked down, bound, dragged into the forest and beaten viciously while the other agents carried packages of papers and various objects, including, as Solzhenitsyn surmised, listening devices, to their cars. Gorlov fought back, alerting neighbors, to whom the agents identified themselves. Gorlov was detained and taken to the local police station, where the senior KGB officer demanded that he sign an oath of secrecy. He was threatened with imprisonment and the ruin of his career and family if he told Solzhenitsyn what had happened.

Gorlov did tell Solzhenitsyn, who immediately wrote a scathing letter to Yuri V. Andropov, the head of the KGB, which was made available through *samizdat* channels to Western correspondents within two days of the incident.

"For many years," Solzhenitsyn wrote Andropov, "I have borne in silence the lawlessness of your employees: the inspection of all my correspondence, the confiscation of half of it, the search of my correspondents' homes and their official and administrative persecution, the spying around my house, the shadowing of visitors, the tapping of telephone conversations, the drilling of holes in the ceilings, the placing of recording apparatuses in my city apartment and at my garden cottage and a persistent slander campaign against me from speakers' platforms by employees of your ministry . . . But after the raid yesterday, I will no longer be silent. I demand from you, Citizen Minister, the public identification of all the robbers, their punishment as criminals and an explanation of this incident . . ."

Solzhenitsyn himself never got an explanation, although his friend Gorlov did receive an apology of sorts. Police explained to him that they had gone to the dacha in an effort to trap a burglar. They had mistaken Gorlov for the criminal when he entered the cottage.

The dilemma that Solzhenitsyn and his work, the embodiment of political and cultural de-Stalinization, pose to Stalin's heirs was succinctly presented by Anatoly Marchenko in his *samizdat* report on contemporary concentration camp conditions. "Get lost with your Solzhenitsyn," he quoted a KGB major at one of the camps as saying. "What makes you think he's a writer? He's nothing but a disgrace to the profession of writing. What he writes is an insult to the Russian language. Your Solzhenitsyn distorts life. My two daughters—at school both of them—went and read *Ivan Denisovich* and then imagined that they could start criticizing me, their father. Questions, reproaches, tears almost every evening. In the beginning I explained it all to them nicely. But eventually I had to throw the magazine [*Novy Mir*] in the fire and that was the end of it."

Just as Solzhenitsyn and *Ivan Denisovich* personified de-Stalinization, so the muzzling and defamation of Solzhenitsyn personify the backward swing of the pendulum under Khrushchev's successors.

Criticism of Stalin and disclosure of his crimes, particularly in the form of "camp literature," have become taboo. Conversely, works unquestionably apologetic, even laudatory, of Stalin and Stalinist practices have been published. The most glaring examples are Vsevolod Kochetov's novel *What Do You Want?*, a humdrum dissertation of neo-Stalinist precepts against any manifestation of liberalism in the arts, and Ivan Shevtsov's blatantly anti-Semitic and neo-Stalinist diatribes *In the Name of the Father and the Son* and *Love and Hatred,* both best sellers with initial print-runs of 100,000 and 200,000 respectively.

Experimentation in artistic forms, never really free even during Khrushchev's most liberal cultural period, has been sharply curtailed. Writers and artists are continually exhorted to pay more attention to the principles of "socialist realism" and urged to fall back on "production" or "factory" and kolkhoz themes and heroes. "Positive" characters who personify the stilted, cardboard Communist ideal of the worker or farmer in love with their lathe or tractor instead of a girl are again in demand, on orders of the party.

Ideological deviations, especially those suggesting "ideological co-existence with the enemies of the working class," have again become the bane of the literary establishment. Vigilance campaigns to censor them out of literature and art have increased in frequency and intensity.

Responsibility for enforcing the new line has slowly been transferred from the party's traditional watchdog organs such as the KGB, Glavlit and the ideological departments of the Central Committee to the trusted orthodox *apparatchiki* of the creative unions themselves. These conservatives and hard-liners, who are now unmistakably in majority control of all the unions with the exception, perhaps, of the Union of Soviet Composers, have been more than happy to oblige. Ostracized, ignored and ridiculed during the thaw, they now vilify and persecute their liberal colleagues with a vengeance.

Not just Solzhenitsyn but most of the other men of the thaw—novelists, poets, playwrights, critics and editors—have been systematically bridled, silenced, intimidated or persuaded to change their line. Scores of films and plays have been withheld from public screens and stages because their themes ran counter to party dogmas.

Konstantin Simonov's 1941 war diary was banned because in the footnotes he referred to "political and military errors" made (implicitly by Stalin) at the time.

Yevgenya Ginzburg's son, Vasily Aksyonov, the favored writer of Soviet youth in the early 1960s because of stories and novellas such as *Halfway to the Moon* and *Ticket to the Stars,* has been gagged. During the past three years Aksyonov wrote four plays, all of which were bought by Moscow theaters but never staged. The censors ruled against them.

Yuri Bondaryev, whose novel *Silence* was hailed in the early sixties as "one of the first Russian novels to tell us what life was *really* like in Moscow immediately after the war," has turned to writing apologias for the Stalin era. Today he openly questions the desirability of telling the truth about the Stalinist past, and has shifted his allegiances from the liberal monthly *Novy Mir* to Kochetov's arch-conservative *Oktyabr.*

Even that paradigm of ideological orthodoxy, Sholokhov, had difficulty getting clearance from the censors for his new novel *They Fought for the Fatherland* in 1970 because it contained passages too critical of Stalin. Sholokhov, a full member of the CPSU Central Committee, is in a class by himself. According to reports circulating in Moscow at the time, he took his case to Brezhnev directly and insisted on unexpurgated publication. Brezhnev compromised and relented, on condition that the author modify some of his criticism. Sholokhov doctored the manuscript accordingly.

Andrei Voznesensky, at thirty-seven no longer a youthful *Wunderkind,* is still the Soviet Union's most unorthodox and uncompromised, as well as probably its best living poet. His latest collection of poems, *The Shadow of Sound,* was published in a print-run of 100,000 copies in April 1970 and sold out on the first day. But he has had more than his share of troubles.

Khrushchev criticized him. Orthodox critics called him a formalist. In 1967 his planned trip to the United States was canceled and because he had the temerity to protest in public, it took four years before he had another opportunity to go abroad. Voznesensky spoke for many writers when, protesting the cancellation of his U.S. trip, he said: "I am a Soviet writer, a human being made of flesh and blood, not a puppet to be pulled on a string. Clearly the leadership of the Union of Writers does not regard writers as human beings . . . We are surrounded by lies, lies, lies, bad manners and lies."

What Solzhenitsyn was to prose, Yeygeny Yevtushenko was to poetry. Time, success and pressure have mellowed him. He will still say categorically that "the young generation in the United States is pregnant, Russia's new generation is asleep." But the bust on Stalin's grave didn't seem to disturb him. "I am not concerned," he told me a few weeks after it happened. "You know how much I hate him, but this is just a rectification of history."

Yevtushenko was one of the few writers to speak out forcefully and publicly against the invasion of Czechoslovakia. In a telegram to Kosygin and Brezhnev on August 21, 1968, he said:

"I don't know how to sleep. I don't know how to keep on living. All I know is that I have a moral duty to express to you the feelings that overpower me. I am deeply concerned that our action in Czechoslovakia is a tragic mistake . . . It lowers our prestige in the world and in our own eyes. It is a setback for all progressive forces, for peace in the world, and for humanity's dreams of future brotherhood."

The authorities' punishment was the sudden cancellation of Yevtushenko's play *Bratsk Hydroelectric Station* from the repertoire of a Moscow theater.

In March 1970 a new edition of his selected poems, running to 60,000 copies, was published. Conspicuously missing from the collection were three of his most outspoken ones. His long epic poem *Kazan University,* written and published to commemorate the hundredth anniversary of Lenin's birth, was severely criticized for its "ideological errors" because it suggested that Lenin became a revolutionary only to revenge his executed elder brother, Alexander. This postulate has been repeatedly rejected by the Leninist hagiographers, who contend that Lenin turned to revolution through his spontaneous, independent discovery of "scientific Marxism."

In 1968 Yevtushenko was proposed for the Oxford Poetry Chair. He became the focus of massive criticism from Western writers who felt he had sold out and had capitulated before the administrative pressure that the Writers' Union and the Communist Party brought to bear on him.

"What do they want from me?" he told Frank Hardy, the Australian Communist writer. "I can say nothing now. I must try to remain calm in these times."

Although Yevtushenko subsequently dissociated himself from his telegram to Kosygin and Brezhnev, calling it a "mistake," he was the only speaker at the Fifth Soviet Writers' Congress in July 1971 to display even a modicum of rebellion or independent thought.

The speech, while no manifesto, was nevertheless a breath of fresh air in what otherwise were humdrum, bureaucratic proceedings which had nothing to do with literature but served merely as a platform for the party to reiterate its ideological views. Yevtushenko attacked the pusillanimity of his colleagues, raised the generation conflict and denounced the gerontocracy of the Soviet literary world today.

Touching on politics he said "there should be no forbidden themes . . . Nothing is so dangerous as a question that one has been forced to suppress . . . The silence observed concerning one or another episode of our history, or the treatment of the facts from a particular standpoint dictated by considerations of the current situation [is a policy] fraught with consequences, for literature is emotional information and the reader who is misinformed or ill-informed is an invalid member of our society."

Those were strong words that referred back to the era of de-Stalinization. Yevtushenko made it plain when he said: "We are the children of the XXth Congress that denounced the cult of personality and the practice of regarding man as a small screw in a big machine."

In the summer of 1969 Yevtushenko, Voznesensky and the playwright Viktor Rozov were fired from the editorial board of *Yunost* magazine, the largest and most popular of the literary monthlies.

"I was dismissed," Yevtushenko told me, "because Anatoly Kuznetsov concocted a report for the KGB saying that I and some other writers were hatching an anti-Soviet plot and were preparing to publish an underground magazine." Kuznetsov, who admitted feeding the KGB this fabrication, was appointed as the only known "liberal" writer to replace Yevtushenko, Voznesensky and Rozov on the *Yunost* board. Two weeks after his appointment, Kuznetsov, the author of the novel *Babi Yar,* defected to England.

This was but the first of a long series of crises for *Yunost* and its relatively liberal editor, the novelist Boris Polevoi. It has been repeatedly criticized for not publishing enough articles and fiction dealing with "the life of young working people" or "the problems that are being solved on collective farms and in factories" and for its "ironic attitude toward the positive and constructive type of hero."

When he surfaced in London, Kuznetsov said he once told Polevoi, whose years of literary infighting in the U.S.S.R. have made him his own best censor: "You are a frightful cynic." Polevoi replied: "Yes. And so what? You think you're going to write and I'm going to carry the can? The writing is yours, the backsides are ours."

Probably the broadest and most scarred backside in Soviet literature belongs to Tvardovsky, forced out of the editorship of *Novy Mir* in February 1970. For months the party's ideologists and the union's philistines, the hard-liners and the hacks had tried to get rid of him.

"You just don't know what Alexander Trifonovich had to go through," a Moscow writer whispered when the deed was done. "It was exactly like Dubcek before he was dismissed."

Questioned about Tvardovsky's dismissal, a Moscow translator and poet said: "Not in many years has there been such an air of pessimism and hopelessness among intellectuals here. Tvardovsky gave us a little sense of comfort. He fought back a little for all of us. He made us feel that not all was lost when we picked up a copy of *Novy Mir.*"

For sixteen years while Tvardovsky edited the "journal with the light blue cover," it was a court of last resort for voices in the wilderness, a refuge where banned writing might see the light of day.

Despite its obvious appeal to a small intellectual elite, high literary criteria and high price by Soviet standards (the magazine costs eighty kopeks, compared to three kopeks for *Pravda*), *Novy Mir* is vastly popular and in great demand. In more remote and provincial areas of the country, far from the centers of culture and intellect such as Moscow and Leningrad, its circulation is limited and copies frequently sell secondhand and on the black market for five to ten times their official price. "We think nothing of laying out a ten-ruble bill for one," a young music student once told me in Alma-Ata.

Tvardovsky, himself an able but by no means great poet, whose wartime verses of heroism made him immediately popular, had long known what it meant to be on the firing line. He became editor of *Novy Mir* in 1950 and after Stalin's death he laid the groundwork for its reputation for liberalism. His "thaw" articles advocating "sincerity" in literature as well as *partiinost* (party-mindedness) incurred the wrath of Stalinist diehards and paved the way for his removal as editor in 1954. He was replaced by Konstantin Simonov, who fell into disfavor in 1956 for publishing Vladimir Dudintsev's controversial novel *Not by Bread Alone*. By 1958 Tvardovsky, then forty-seven, was back as chief editor of the journal.

Tvardovsky was an improbable candidate for the role of St. George in Soviet literature. The son of a prosperous kulak farmer, he had become a popular but never great poet. He was not a de-

tached intellectual critic. He was not a pure aesthete. Moreover he
had the sort of credentials that would tend to make him a com-
promiser rather than a fighter. At fourteen he became a Komsomol
correspondent for a local newspaper in Smolensk and a few years
later he was breaking into print with poetry that contained peasant
themes of love of the soil. In the early 1930s he became imbued
with the idea that collectivization was necessary, despite the fearsome
human toll. His writing easily passed muster in that day.

During World War II Tvardovsky went to the front lines as a war
correspondent and wrote a series of patriotic adventure stories laced
with humor and his usual down-to-earth language. Their hero, Vasily
Terkin, became a household character in Soviet literature. Tvardovsky
won a Stalin Prize.

Undoubtedly his ties to the Soviet people, his popular, easy-to-read
prose and poetry and his Communist Party orthodoxy formed the
basis of his strength and the loyalties of fellow writers and kept on
winning him hearings for the maverick views he expressed as editor
of *Novy Mir*.

One long-time Moscow resident once compared Tvardovsky to
Earl Warren, "a middle-of-the-roader, almost a plodder, who came
to the Supreme Court and developed a conscience and intellectual
conviction that made him one of the most outstanding and controversial chief justices. Tvardovsky's life has been something like that."

Tvardovsky not only tried to keep banality out of Soviet literature
but attempted to maintain a recognizable frontier between art and
propaganda which official literary policy had blurred out of sight.

During his tenure as editor-in-chief there was hardly an issue
that he didn't have to defend against attacks and criticism from the
party's ideologists and the hard-line *apparatchiki* of the literary establishment.

But Tvardovsky's finest hour was undoubtedly his defense of
Solzhenitsyn and his months-long struggle to publish *Cancer Ward*
against the objections of the Writers' Union secretariat and the party
leadership.

Much of that struggle is revealed in a lengthy letter that Tvardovsky
wrote to Konstantin A. Fedin, the aging, embittered and miserly
chief of the U.S.S.R. Union of Writers.

There is no need to enumerate all the more or less well-known
writers here and abroad who warmly or enthusiastically greeted

[Solzhenitsyn's first story, *One Day in the Life of Ivan Denisovich*]. I shall name only two: you K.A., and Mikhail A. Sholokhov . . .

Solzhenitsyn concerns us now . . . because through numerous circumstances he stands at the crossroads of two opposed tendencies in the social consciousness of our literature: one which strives to go back, the other which strives to progress in accordance with the irreversibility of the historical process . . .

What is extremely sad is the position which you have adopted recently concerning the so-called Solzhenitsyn "affair." You say that Solzhenitsyn must first give a rebuff to the West, which has raised an unbridled anti-Soviet campaign in the press and on the radio in connection with his "letter" [protesting censorship in Soviet literature to the 1967 Writers' Congress]. Otherwise you will not publish his [new] book. You will not protect Solzhenitsyn, a member of the Union of Writers, from the widespread fabrications concerning his past . . .

To hear from you, K.A., a great Russian writer, a friend of Gorky and a follower of his tradition in the leadership of literature, the terms of your proposal are strange and incomprehensible . . .

Your insistent demand that Solzhenitsyn should state "his attitudes," that he should "give a rebuff to the West," as a pre-condition for his further literary and civic career sounds strange coming from you, because it obviously tends in the direction of long-condemned and -rejected practices. Such "confessions" do us immense harm because they create an impression of writers who are morally and ethically indiscriminating, who are deprived of a sense of their own dignity or who are wholly dependent on "instructions" or "demands." Do you really think that such confessions are to the advantage of the Union of Writers or strengthen its authority?

Tvardovsky's dogged support of Solzhenitsyn was unsuccessful. *Cancer Ward* was not published. Instead, *Novy Mir* and its courageous editor came under sharp political fire from the party and the conservatives in the Writers' Union.

The campaign to dislodge Tvardovsky began in earnest in the summer of 1969. It was spearheaded by Mikhail Zakharov, who called himself "a lathe operator, an ordinary worker," but was also a candidate member of the Central Committee. Zakharov's platform was the newspaper *Socialist Industry,* a "factory worker's *Literary Gazette,"* which was revived in 1969, after twenty-eight years of suspended publication, in an attempt to press home the ideological campaign at the workbench level.

"I have been reading the magazine regularly," Zakharov said in a letter addressed to Tvardovsky, "but somehow I have not found it publishing the kind of things that make one rejoice . . . Why is the working class not evident in the pages of *Novy Mir?* During the past two years there haven't been more than two or three stories about the working class. And in those stories it was portrayed so primitively: wallowing in the ways of the past, without ideals, never without a glass of vodka in their hands . . ."

Tvardovsky began swimming energetically upstream with a Custer's last stand for intellectual and artistic integrity that ruined his health and sometimes led him to the bottle.

Tvardovsky, along with many other establishment intellectuals, feared that Stalinism was ineluctably creeping back into Soviet life. He wrote a long poem which admonished that Stalin's crimes "still threaten our sleep." In it he warned of the "silence which is pressing down on the past," and the need to "explain . . . the whys." It is not known whether he ever submitted the poem or could not get it past the censors. But "On the Ashes of Stalin" circulated in *samizdat* form and soon made its way to the West, where it was published in Italy, France and Germany, including the Russian émigré journal *Grani.*

This, according to a reliable Soviet source, prompted the final move against Tvardovsky. The decision was probably reached at a high-level ideological meeting involving leading artists, writers, composers and editors in December 1969. In February the secretariat of the Writers' Union, meeting without some of its more liberal members such as Simonov and Polevoi, dismissed four of Tvardovsky's most trusted assistants on the editorial board of *Novy Mir* and replaced them with ultraconservatives. Tvardovsky protested and offered his resignation, which the rump secretariat accepted with alacrity.

Several months later, Tvardovsky, already suffering from lung cancer, had a nearly fatal stroke.

Tvardovsky's replacement was not an unknown quantity. V. A. Kosolapov is a former editor-in-chief of the Writers' Union's weekly *Literary Gazette* who had been dismissed from that post in 1962 after publishing Yevtushenko's poem "Babi Yar" and refusing to print an attack on abstract art.

Nor has the magazine degenerated into quite the banal propaganda journal which everyone expected it to become. Its print-run was increased from 110,000 to 160,000 and it now usually comes out on time—a sign that its new editor is having less difficulty with the censors and the union's secretariat. But Kosolapov still had a lot of scripts in the drawer which Tvardovsky had bought and he has not shied away from publishing them. On the contrary, to judge from the criticism of *Novy Mir* by the union's secretariat and *Literary Gazette* in January 1971, its troubles with the establishment are far from over.

"It is still rare for *Novy Mir* to publish significant works of fiction about the present day and major works about the working class," the secretariat complained. The editors were accused of laxity in their "demands on ideological and artistic content." The editors were told to abide by "the precise criteria of the party spirit and popular nature of the literature of socialist realism."

This most recent criticism of *Novy Mir* points to the basic dilemma of Soviet literature.

As Solzhenitsyn said in his controversial letter to the delegates of the 1967 Writers' Congress:

"Literature cannot develop between categories of 'permitted' and 'not permitted.' Literature that does not breathe the same air as contemporary society, that cannot communicate to it its pains and its fears, that cannot warn in time against moral and social dangers, does not deserve the name literature."

But for decades Soviet literature has been constricted to these very categories of "permitted" and "not permitted," for it is based on the idea of an organized, censored literature serving a political purpose.

Through the Union of Writers and the mysterious censorship bureau named Glavlit, the Communist Party exercises control over the life of literature and the lives of writers. Ultimately it is the party that not only decides who can publish what but who should have access to a typewriter, an apartment, a dacha, foreign currency with which to buy prized goods in special shops, who can give a public lecture, who may travel abroad.

Presided over by Fedin, the chairman of the board, and run by Georgy Markov, the first secretary, a secretariat of 44 other members and a board of 235, only a few of whom are liberals, the union has 7290 members. It and its republican and local subsidiaries are the law, the final arbiter of literature in the U.S.S.R. It owns, runs or controls a couple dozen publishing houses, publications and magazines, among them the weekly *Literaturnaya Gazeta* (*Literary Gazette*), *Oktyabr, Novy Mir, Yunost, Teatr, Znamiya, Neva* and *Moskva.*

Headquartered in a yellow, neoclassical *palais* built in 1802 for Prince Dolgoruki on Moscow's quiet, tree-shaded Vorovsky Street, the union is many things: a private club, a professional association, as well as editor and publisher, critic and censor of all writing in the U.S.S.R.

The union building and two adjacent structures which form the complex of Moscow's House of Writers, the *Dom Literatov* (one of these a Stalin-era pretension facing Herzen Street, the other a turn-of-the-century mansion built by a merchant prince) are in their way symbolic of literature in the Soviet Union today. It is official.

By late afternoon or early evening it is usually difficult to find a parking place in front of the complex—the spaces having been taken up by the private cars, some of them foreign models, of the union's most prosperous members. Most of these automobiles have license plates from the Moscow suburbs, where their owners live in the secluded, privileged compounds of the upper classless of the Communist elite.

Inside, the air is a dignified mélange of hotel lobby, university musty meeting hall: thick carpets, huge portraits of Lenin and past luminaries of Russian literature, wood-paneled walls, bulletin boards library and private London club with here and there the touch of a with announcements for lectures, exhibitions, concerts and recitals— open to members only—a quiet, posh restaurant with waiters in tails, starched clean tablecloths and some of the best food in town. There is also a snack bar, in bistro style, whose walls are covered with caricatures of famous members and the scratched and daubed signatures of important visitors.

The union is committed by statute to the promulgation of only one kind of literature. As its 1934 bylaws say, its purpose is "The creation of works of high artistic significance, saturated with the heroic struggles of the world proletariat, the grandeur of the victory of socialism, which reflect the great wisdom and heroism of the Communist Party; the creation of works of art worthy of the great age of socialism."

Those were not always the ground rules for Soviet literature. In the first decade after the Revolution there was room for a wide spectrum of literary moods and forms which could be expressed with more or less freedom. True, a fairly tight censorship was exercised by Glavlit, but its function was largely to prevent publication of openly "counterrevolutionary" works. Soviet prose during this brief "golden age" of artistic freedom was relatively objective in portraying the realities of the Revolution, the Civil War and the tumultuous period of the New Economic Policy.

Most of the best writers during these years were in a category which Trotsky dubbed the "fellow travelers." Intellectuals by origin, their degree of loyalty to the new regime varied considerably, but like certain other bourgeois specialists they had skills that made them indispensable to it.

In the early post-revolutionary years this afforded them protection from excessive interference by the so-called "proletarian" writers, who were as loud as they were untalented. Not necessarily workers or peasants by origin, they were grouped in the Association of Russian Proletarian Writers (RAPP), which attempted to establish hegemony over the fellow travelers, who belonged to an organization called the All-Russian Union of Writers.

Until 1929, the year in which Stalin consolidated power and Anatoly Lunacharsky was removed as Commissar (Minister) of People's Education and Enlightenment, the proletarians received relatively little encouragement. In fact, Lunacharsky's stewardship of literature, education and the arts produced a brief but nonetheless unprecedented period of cultural flowering.

These were the great years of Mayakovsky and Yesenin, Babel and Pilnyak, of Yevgeny Zamyatin and Mikhail Bulgakov, of Konstantin Paustovsky and Valentin Katayev, of Venyamin Kavyerin and Leonid Leonov, yes, even of Mikhail Sholokhov and Konstantin Fedin, who are now fuglemen of the literary unions and writing *apparatchiki*.

Today, Sholokhov, one of the richest men in the U.S.S.R., arouses nothing but contempt among Soviet intellectuals. Fedin, whose miserliness is legendary in Moscow, is despised, if not feared. In the wake of the dispute over Solzhenitsyn's *Cancer Ward* many angry Russian intellectuals mailed back to Fedin autographed copies of his works. The post office in Peredelkino was ordered not to forward them to the old man. His more determined and ingenious critics traveled to the village, went to Fedin's dacha and tossed the books over the high green fence into the garden, where a big shepherd dog promptly chewed them to shreds.

The 1930s were, Stalin's purges notwithstanding, not the worst years for Soviet literature. They began after 1946. But the thirties saw the establishment of those features which make it unique: the imposition of "socialist realism" as the doctrine and common denominator of all creative activity; the disbandment of RAPP and the All-Russian Union of Writers and their amalgamation into the present Union of Soviet Writers, in 1934; the subordination of literary activity to the political demands of the Communist Party; the ascendancy of police terror as a means to keep writers on the ideological straight and narrow; mass repression and liquidation of non-conformist writers, and centralized control of all means of publication and expression. To be a writer one not only had to be a member of the new union but also to subscribe to the "method" of socialist realism, promulgated officially by Andrei A. Zhdanov, Stalin's cultural tsar, at the First Congress of Soviet Writers in 1934.

Writers were to model their works on the nineteenth-century classics and adopt a kind of composite style of the language of Turgenev, Tolstoy and Chekhov, eschewing all the modernist movements of the beginning of the century and the early Soviet period, which were rejected as aberrations and "formalism."

The purges, the *Yezhovshchina,* that soon followed confronted most writers with an agonizing choice: either collaborate or cease writing, possibly living. In his letter to the Fourth Soviet Writers' Congress in 1967, Solzhenitsyn spoke of more than six hundred writers who had died in the camps and he spoke bitterly of the Writers' Union, which had "obediently handed them over to their fate in prisons and camps."

The outbreak of war in 1941, as Pasternak described it in a passage toward the end of *Dr. Zhivago,* "broke the spell of the dead letter." All writers rallied to the cause of the nation's defense and both police and ideological pressure relaxed. In the spirit of wartime camaraderie people began to trust each other again. Writers served at the front, either in action or as correspondents. Freed of doctrine and the hypocrisies of peacetime, they wrote with relative truth and sincerity about real people again.

But it was a thaw of brief duration. It ended abruptly in 1946 when Zhdanov launched the so-called "anti-cosmopolitan" campaign, whose first chosen scapegoats were Pasternak, Anna Akhmatova and Mikhail Zoshchenko. It culminated in the deepest freeze ever.

What the Writers' Union did not enforce on its own, Glavlit enforced for it. Glavlit and the Union of Writers, as one Soviet intellectual has described them, are "Siamese twins."

Glavlit, the official euphemism for Chief Administration for the

Preservation of State Secrets in the Press, is supposed to "exercise all aspects of politico-ideological, military and economic control over productions of the press, manuscripts, photographs, pictures, etc. intended for publication or distribution and over radio braodcasts, lectures and exhibitions." According to its 1931 statutes, it may prohibit publication and distribution of works that contain "agitation and propaganda against the Soviet regime and the dictatorship of the proletariat . . . and . . . arouse nationalistic and religious fanaticism." It determines not only what may be published in the U.S.S.R. but what books, films, photos and recordings may be brought into the U.S.S.R. from abroad.

Because the Soviet constitution and Soviet laws do not provide for censorship, the words "censor" and "censorship" are themselves banned by Glavlit's censors and immediately struck from any manuscript that might contain them.

Its main offices in Moscow, on the sixth floor of the Ministry of Electric Power building, are guarded by uniformed and armed police. Visitors are admitted only if they have an appointment and their passes are valid only for entry into a specific censor's office. In addition there are hundreds of Glavlit offices and plenipotentiaries around the country. In the larger publishing houses, editorial offices, printing plants, broadcasting and television studios, customs and post offices they occupy rooms or whole suites marked with large "No Entry" signs. The entire apparatus consists of approximately 70,000 people, who, by Soviet standards, are quite well paid.

Although Glavlit is also responsible for determining which books shall be "removed from circulation" in libraries and what kind of ideological and literary or artistic material crosses the Soviet frontiers, its main purpose is to check printed works for deviations from the approved political line and for the presence of any information considered inimical to state security.

Prohibited items are listed in a thick book, accessible only to the censor, which is known colloquially as the "Talmud" and which is amended annually. The censors themselves are strictly supervised. They attend frequent seminars and other courses of instruction, but their most important asset is their "political nose," which tends to be overly sensitive.

Until the late 1930s Glavlit's omnipresence was displayed openly on all printed matter with the licensing visa of Glavlit or its local organs. This imprint used to take the form of the words "Plenipotentiary of Glavlit," followed by his serial number. For example, on Volume 32 of the last page of the first edition of the Large Soviet Encylopedia, there is the notation: "Plenipotentiary of Glavlit B-24884." Since then, probably to obfuscate the fact of censorship, only the serial number itself has appeared.

Every piece of printing, from a book to the label on a beer bottle, must be read by an official censor—twice: before it is sent to the printers and again before it is actually put on the press. Printing anything without censorship approval is punishable with a prison sentence of up to eight years.

The identities of censors are closely guarded secrets, never known to the writers, only to editors and responsible officials in the Central Committee's departments of ideology and culture. And even important editors often know the identities of only one or two censors —the ones they regularly deal with. The only exceptions to the rule of secrecy are the head censor himself, Pavel Konstantinovich Romanov, a professional *apparatchik,* who is chairman of Glavlit, and Aaron Vergelis, editor-in-chief of the Yiddish journal *Sovietish Geimland.* Vergelis was formally appointed his own censor, and even given a stamp with a serial number, because no one in the Glavlit operation could be found who reads Yiddish.

Besides being anonymous, the censors, to quote Anatoly Kuznetsov, "understand as much about art as a pig does about oranges." He once described them as "people who in place of brains have a collection of quotations and fears."

The censors work in tandem with the conservative, cautious functionaries who comprise the leadership of the Union of Writers and the editorial boards of most Soviet periodicals. They make a formidable combination.

The first hurdle, according to Kuznetsov, is an editor who frequently turns out to be a considerate, understanding person who proposes a few deletions from the manuscript. The editor-in-chief then makes more drastic corrections which the author tolerates because everyone tells him that "they" (the censors) will object.

"Ivan fears Pyotr, Pyotr fears Semyon, Semyon fears Yemelyan and so on up the ladder," Kuznetsov explained. "It is a pyramid with its apex somewhere in the party Politburo. But nobody knows anything definite. By the time this filtering process is over and the manuscript passes to the official censor, the author is already pinned down."

When Kuznetsov showed his first novel, *The Continuation of a Legend,* to the editors of *Yunost* in 1958, they said they liked it very much but could not publish it because it was too realistic. It showed life in Siberia as it really was, not as the party propaganda machine wanted it to appear. This, in short, is the difference between "realism" and "socialist realism."

Of course, Kuznetsov was told, there was a way to publish the book: remove the more gloomy passages, add some cheerful ones and infuse a few slogans to give it the proper spirit of Communist optimism.

"More experienced writers," Kuznetsov explained, "advised me that everybody did this."

At first Kuznetsov refused to play. Finally he capitulated and made some changes that still did not satisfy the *Yunost* editorial board. Months later, however, without notifying him and without asking his agreement, the magazine's editors doctored the novel on their own and published it. Kuznetsov said he was furious at the time. But he also became famous. *Continuation of a Legend* was praised in the Soviet press, placed on the reading lists for Soviet school children and translated into thirty languages.

When a French translation, deleting most of the balderdash that *Yunost* had inserted, appeared in France, Kuznetsov was accused by Soviet authorities of writing an anti-Soviet book. As an alternative, he was told, he could sue the publisher. Although he knew that the abridged French version came closer to what he had really wanted to say than the Soviet edition, he sued. He won the case, though he never received a sou or a kopek of the money awarded him by the French court. One of the first things he did after defecting to England in 1969 was to apologize to the French publisher.

All writers, according to Kuznetsov, indulge in self-censorship because there is no alternative under Soviet conditions. Nobody can openly announce that "the emperor has no clothes." It is a form of inner censorship psychologically conditioned from the time the writer, or any other citizen, starts kindergarten and learns to express only ideas that are politically suitable and safe.

Kuznetsov tried several magazines with his second novel *In Your Own Home* but could find no editor willing to print it. Finally someone from *Novy Mir* phoned him and said the magazine would publish the novel if he would agree to a few cuts. Kuznetsov acquiesced because, as he said, "It is better to have something published than nothing at all. Moreover I had always respected *Novy Mir* and I decided to leave the cutting to them. Then the phone calls to my home in Tula began: every other day or so, with the news that they would have to cut this chapter or that passage."

The final version, he said, was one-third shorter than the original manuscript and politically twisted by 180 degrees. He dissociated himself from the novel though it sold hundreds of thousands of copies, was declared one of the ten best books about life in the Soviet Union and awarded a diploma by the Komsomol which Kuznetsov "did not bother to go and receive."

Then he wrote *Babi Yar,* which, drastic cuts and revision notwithstanding, became a Soviet and international best seller. When he fled to England, Kuznetsov disowned the book and sat down to rewrite it, using a 35-millimeter film of the original, unexpurgated manuscript to piece it together again. The new edition, in which the censored passages, sentences, phrases, sections and chapters are printed in bold-faced type, was published in 1970. It is a singular demonstration of both the insidiousness and inanity of censorship in the U.S.S.R.

From the Soviet point of view, much of what was cut from *Babi Yar* deserved to be sliced out, for Kuznetsov had told not only of German atrocities but of Soviet crimes as well. He wrote about the strong Ukrainian opposition to Soviet rule in the 1930s and early 1940s, that Hitler's armies were met with considerable welcome and good will, that Soviet atrocities matched some of those of the Germans and that the massacre of Jews at Babi Yar would not have been possible without the complicity of virulently anti-Semitic Ukrainians.

The excised passages did indeed contain, as Kuznetsov later said, "the main sense of the book and the reasons why it was written." But they also reflect a deliberate attempt to elide everything that struck the censor as mildly critical of Soviet policies past and present.

The fact that the Germans were well equipped—censored.

That one German soldier was a "good-looking" boy—censored.

That the Red Army retreated in a hurry, some "without even their weapons"—censored.

Adjectives, nouns, verbs, phrases showing that Kievites welcomed the Germans—censored.

That Soviet soldiers were "poor devils, hungry and barefoot"—censored.

That Ukrainian girls talked to the German soldiers "with a laugh"—censored.

All that is understandable. But how does one explain that the censor *permitted* a passage in which Kuznetsov described how his grandfather took the Soviet flag, ripped it off its pole and told his wife to stuff it in the fire, but *deleted* his remark that the pole was all right and would do for a broom handle?

That references to the widespread drunkenness of Russians would have been censored seems logical in view of official embarrassment over this widespread and traditional Russian malady. But why did the censors cut out all references to Russian and Ukrainian girls who were raped by the Germans? Because the Russians did that when they got to Germany?

References to the NKVD were all excised. So were remarks about panic among the population. And Glavlit was sure to expunge the line about a Communist who "joined the party like everybody else, so as to survive." But why did the censors insist that Kuznetsov describe the stench in the Babi Yar ravine as "heavy" instead of, as in the original, a "heavy stench of flesh from the mass of fresh corpses?"

Frequently censors prove to be either stupid or inefficient. Things slip by them. Often this happens in allegorical writing and Soviet science fiction is notorious in this respect.

From time to time, science fiction writers such as Arkadi and Boris Strugatsky are also "unmasked" by the party's ideological watchdogs.

In one of their recent books, *The Inhabited Island,* the Strugatsky brothers placed the action in a country ruled by a seemingly benevolent group of "Unknown Fathers" who resemble the Soviet Politburo and Central Committee. They came to power after overthrowing an oligarchy remarkably similar to tsarism. Most of the population lives in dire poverty but the Unknown Fathers make it appear that the society is just and progressing. Their propaganda system depends on a network of towers that emit a type of radiation that makes all citizens, except the "Freaks," accept unquestioningly the false picture of the world promulgated by the Unknown Fathers. The Freaks, immune to the radiation, are the only people who can see through the pervasive official propaganda "shouted by the newspapers, pamphlets, television, radio, by teachers in schools and by the officers in the barracks." The Freaks, an underground resistance movement, are hounded by the secret police, arrested, tortured to confess, tried in kangaroo courts, imprisoned in concentration camps and banished to remote parts of the land. But as a tiny minority, they do not really count. The populace at large, deprived of the faculty to question because of the radiation, accepts the propaganda "as the only truth" and the Unknown Fathers as the repository of political wisdom, though all the Fathers are interested in is perpetuation of their own power.

This novel was actually published in the U.S.S.R. Moreover, stories by the Strugatsky brothers continue to appear in such journals as *Baikal, Molodaya Gvardiya* and *Angara,* though not without severe criticism and occasional reprimands for the editors who publish them.

"This allegedly imaginary story is nothing more than a libel of our reality," one critic of the Strugatskys wrote in 1968. "The authors do not say in which country the action unfolds . . . but the whole tenor of the narrative and the events and arguments contained in it make their implications quite clear."

The editor-in-chief of the *East Siberian Almanac* was fired in 1969 for publishing another Strugatsky story. But the books continue to circulate, secondhand copies bring high prices on the gray market and political science fiction, which can legitimately hide behind the skirts of fantasy, is a growing medium for critical literature.

But censorship continues and rare is the member of the Union of Writers who at one time or another has not bowed to the pressure of Glavlit.

"The uncontrolled manipulation of texts and elimination of whole chapters have become the rule," Grigory Svirsky, a novelist, short-story writer and essayist complained at a meeting of the Communist Party group of the Moscow municipal writers' union in 1968.

> We are told [said Svirsky] that "this is not the time," that "circumstances do not permit it," that we "must wait." We wait a year, two, ten . . . Lenin said that one must not lie, even to one's enemies. Here people lie to friends. And how they have lied. They lied about Pasternak, about Solzhenitsyn, Voznesensky, Yev-

tushenko, Yevgenya Ginzburg, Bulat Okudzhava. What haven't they lied about?

Yes, we demand freedom. Not freedom outside the party, the party of which we are flesh and blood. We demand to be freed from the perversions of the party line brought about with impunity by the militant cliquists . . .

How many years have we talked about cliquishness in the Writers' Union? We inveigh against it, we demand reconciliation between groups. Some say that writers are divided by genres, others that they are divided by age, and still others allude to literary prejudices and publishing connections. That is all empty twaddle. Yes, there are two groups of writers in the union. The dividing line between them is not age, genre or literary prejudices but the XXth Party Congress [when Khrushchev denounced Stalin].

For his outburst Svirsky was expelled from the party, though not yet from the Writers' Union.

The "clique" Svirsky talked about: who are they? The conservatives, the dogmatists, the hacks and the opportunists who make up the majority and the most influential group on the board and secretariat of the union. Their attitudes emerged during the 1967 exchange with Solzhenitsyn and Tvardovsky over *Cancer Ward*.

Here are some excerpts:

Fedin: "This bartering as to how many months we are entitled to examine your manuscript, Alexander Isayevich. Three months? Four months? Is that really so terrible? It is far more terrible that your works are used there, in the West, for the basest of purposes."

Aleksei Surkov, poet, former first secretary of the Union of Writers, former editor-in-chief of *Literaturnaya Gazeta,* former editor-in-chief of *Ogonyok:* "If *Cancer Ward* were to be published it would be used against us and would be more dangerous than Svetlana Alliluyeva's memoirs . . . The works of Solzhenitsyn are more harmful than those of Pasternak."

S. A. Baruzdin, a member of the board of the Union of Writers: "*Cancer Ward* is an anti-humanitarian book. The end of the story suggests that a 'different road should have been taken.'"

Petr Brovka, a Byelorussian poet, writer and editor and a secretary and board member of the Union of Writers: "Before us stands a genuinely acknowledged talent, and therein lies the danger of publication. Yes, he can make you feel the pains of your country, to an extraordinary degree in fact. But you do not feel its joys. *Cancer Ward* is too gloomy and shouldn't be published."

Berdy Kerbabaev, a Turkmenian writer, playright and translator, head of the Turkmenian Union of Writers: "Why does he see things only in black? I always try to write about joyful things."

Leonid Novichenko, a Ukrainian writer, critic and literary historian, a secretary of the Ukrainian and U.S.S.R. writers' unions: "Even if this novel were put into some kind of shape it would not be a novel of socialist realism but merely an ordinary, competent piece of work."

Surkov: "Alexander Isayevich, you should state whether or not you are renouncing your role of leader of the political opposition in our country, the role they ascribe to you in the West."

Solzhenitsyn: "Aleksei Alexandrovich, it really sickens me to hear something like that, and from you of all people. An artist with words is supposed to be the leader of the political opposition? How does that figure? . . . My every line is suppressed while the entire press is in the hands of the union . . . In the West they say that the [Russian] novel is dead. And all we do is gesticulate and deliver speeches saying that it is not dead."

That dramatic encounter in the plush rooms of the old Dolgoruki Palais, to which Tvardovsky's letter to Fedin was a sequel, was the beginning of Solzhenitsyn's end as a writer in the U.S.S.R., for two years later he was expelled from the union.

The cultural *apparatchiki* were quick to deny it, of course. Solzhenitsyn, they said in a chorus, can continue to write and if he writes something suitable it will be published. "He has merely been excluded from a voluntary organization of writers because his behavior was incompatible with continued membership."

The truth is not that simple. Individual writers must be members of the union before they can participate in official literary activities. And "unofficial" activities are forbidden. It was a point on which the courts left no doubts in the trials of dissenters beginning with Yosif Brodsky in 1964.

Brodsky, a brilliant, promising poet in Leningrad, was asked by his judge:

"Who gave you the right to call yourself a poet?"

He was then asked to produce "documentary evidence" attesting to his right to write poetry.

Similarly, in 1966, when the poet Vladimir Batshev was sentenced to exile in Siberia, the court accused him of "engaging in so-called literary activities without being a member of the Writers' Union."

Not that membership is a guarantee of bliss.

"For a third of a century," Solzhenitsyn remarked acidly to the Fourth Writers' Congress, "the union has not defended either the 'other' rights or even the copyrights of persecuted writers. Many of them have been subjected during their lifetime to abuse and slander, violence and personal persecution. Not only did the union not make its own publications available to these writers for the purpose of reply, not only did it fail to defend them, but . . . it was always among the first of the persecutors. Names that adorned our twentieth-century poetry were on the list of those expelled from the union or not even admitted to it in the first place. The union's leadership simply abandoned those for whom persecution ended in exile, labor camps or death."

A thinly veiled enforcer of CPSU policy, though only a minority of its members belong to the party, the union works hand in glove with the party apparat, Glavlit and the KGB—an unholy trinity of cultural diktat in the U.S.S.R. of today.

According to Kuznetsov, "the KGB's tentacles reach like a cancerous growth into the world of Soviet literature." The KGB even has its own top confidant in the leadership of the union—Konstantin Voronkov, a secretary and member of the board.

Voronkov, said Kuznetsov, "isn't even a writer. He is responsible for ideological questions and administers all the personnel dossiers of the union. And the dossier determines what kind of a person you are."

Kuznetsov's dossier was so-so. At first he co-operated with the KGB, then ignored and finally co-operated with them again.

"If you co-operate," he explained, "you prosper. If you acknowledge your duty but refuse to collaborate directly, you are deprived of a great deal, particularly the prospect of traveling abroad. If you brush them aside you are not published and may find yourself in a concentration camp." Those who do not co-operate are kept under constant surveillance. They are provoked by KGB informers, who, to judge from Kuznetsov's story, are all around.

"I have lived in Russia all my life," Kuznetsov said in self-justification after obtaining asylum in England, "and I know no other way of life. Life there is such that only he survives who is constantly looking out for himself."

Andrei Amalrik disagreed. In his open letter to Kuznetsov he wrote:

> You seem to be saying, "I was given no choice" . . . It sometimes seems to me that the Soviet creative intelligentsia is, as a whole, an even more unpleasant phenomenon than the regime which has formed it. Hypocrisy has become so much a part of it that it considers any attempt to act honorably as either a crafty provocation or madness. It is always better to be silent than to utter falsehoods, better to refuse to publish any of your books than to put out something which contradicts what you wrote in the beginning, better to refuse a trip abroad than, for the sake of one, become an informer.

The few established writers who follow those precepts write for the drawer or simply keep out of sight and wait for better days. In Moscow that is known euphemistically and literally as "taking to the dachas." The vicissitudes of Soviet cultural policy have caused many exoduses to the dachas.

By the spring and summer of 1969 the party's message was more explicit. A *Pravda* editorial warned delegates to a conference of "young Soviet writers":

> The significance of work with young writers is particularly great now when the world is engaged in a tense ideological struggle, when the writer's public role has increased in importance and when hostile propaganda exerts every effort to lead our young people away from correct ideological positions. We cannot overlook the fact that some young writers view "fashionable ideas" from the West uncritically. As a result their works occasionally show tendencies toward "de-heroization," indifference to politics and sometimes even a serious distortion of our reality and of Soviet spiritual values.
>
> It behooves every professional organization to heighten responsibility for the work of every writer, to create an atmosphere of fidelity to principles and intolerance of ideological wavering. An artist must have a clear party attitude toward the most important problems of our time.

Vasily Aksyonov, dropped from the editorial board of *Yunost,* was singled out for sharp criticism. "His characters," said *Literaturnaya Gazeta,* "speak a jargon instead of the idiom of the people.

They are filled with bravado and nihilist skepticism rather than profound emotions connected with the moral principles of the people. Heroes of this kind can be found in all countries but they are no more than scum on the surface of a nation's life. Scum, as everybody knows, disappears quickly."

In December 1969 a semi-secret meeting of the leaders of all the creative unions—writers, artists, composers, dramatists and cinematographers—was held in Moscow to set down the ideological guidelines for the forthcoming Lenin centennial celebration. The participants were, largely, the most doctrinaire and dogmatic leaders of the unions and the chieftains of ideology from the party and government.

Few of the speeches were ever published in full and only hints of the tough new line became public. But *Pravda* undoubtedly reflected the general tone when it trumpeted that "there is no higher calling and duty for the Soviet artist and writer than service to the people . . . and devotion of their talent and their craftsmanship to the process of building a Communist society." The creative intelligentsia was called upon to "fight actively against alien, bourgeois ideology."

When Demichev spoke, the opening remarks to the conference in the Hall of Columns of the Trade Union House in downtown Moscow were televised. These were meaningless platitudes. As soon as Demichev launched into the essence of his text, the sound went— and stayed—off. From what one could see, however, it was a tough talk to a somber and subdued audience.

Most likely it paralleled his essay in the January 1970 issue of *Kommunist,* the Central Committee's theoretical monthly. In it he wrote:

> Sometimes we are reproached for "inconsistency." It is said that we sometimes support this or that writer actively, then start criticizing him. Yes, this happens, but not due to our inconsistency. It is rather because of the vacillations of that artist who succumbs to the influence of petit bourgeois ideology, to false imperialist propaganda . . .
>
> For more than half a century now our country's enemies, who sometimes pretend to be our friends, have "worried" about the freedom of creativity in the U.S.S.R. But we know very well what is concealed behind all this! We know what "freedom" they want!
>
> An artist's quest for the new is something perfectly legitimate.

But genuine quest for the new is incompatible with experiments of the modernistic type . . . Modernism fosters indifference to politics in the perception of reality, inculcates elitist views and concepts. This is why Soviet men of art . . . refuse to accept modernism, no matter under what slogans it may appear.

In March 1970 the Third Congress of the Russian Republic's Union of Writers was held in Moscow. Sergei Mikhailkov, a mediocre poet and political dogmatist who for many years had headed the Moscow writers' organization, was elected first secretary of the Russian Republic's group. That in itself was a tocsin. Mikhailkov's credo is that "tolerance of the intolerable is harmful to our cause . . . There is no place for any all-forgiving liberalism and bleeding hearts."

The congress ended on a note of heightened militancy which was expressed by *Trud,* the Soviet labor union daily:

"Literature," said the paper, "plays an immense role in the bitter ideological struggle of the two worlds . . . [an] honest writer today cannot keep aloof from the most acute problem of our time. To expose warmongers and their servitors, to struggle for peace and progress—those are the paramount tasks of Soviet masters of the pen. The best of them and their books fight like soldiers on this front which covers our entire planet."

The demands for militancy in the arts, for vigilance against ideological subversion, for positive heroes, the calls for literature, drama and films that eulogize the military, factory workers and collective farmers are trumpeted louder and more frequently month by month.

Leonid Finkelstein-Vladimirov, a Soviet journalist and popular science writer who defected to the United Kingdom in 1966, has summed up the results of Soviet cultural policy with acrimonious accuracy. "During the half century of its existence," he said, "Soviet dictatorship has been strikingly successful in its main crime: that of deforming the reader."

It is a crime that the Brezhnev leadership has abetted more than any other Soviet oligarchy with the exception of Stalin.

*The pitiful and wretched thing that
pretends to the title of the theater of
socialist realism has nothing in
common with art . . . Where once
there were the best theaters in the
world, now everything is gloomily
well regulated, averagely arithmetical,
stupefying and murderous in its lack
of talent. Is that your aim? If it is—
oh—you have done something
monstrous. In hunting down formalism,
you have eliminated art.*

Vsevolod Meyerhold on
June 14, 1939, one day
before his arrest

The Devils in the Prompter's Box

"World primacy in the field of the theater belongs without doubt to Russia," Sergei Mikhailkov, the first secretary of the Russian Federation's Union of Writers, once boasted. "Europe has admitted that we alone have preserved the art of the stage."

Preserved—that may be one word for it. Embalmed and desiccated would be more accurate.

Viewed from other European drama centers such as East and West Berlin, London, Paris, Prague, Warsaw, Wroclaw and Zurich (New York, for better or worse, is in a category by itself which has no relevance to the repertoire and ensemble theaters of Europe), Moscow, the traditional capital of Russian drama, is stale, jaded, outdated and incredibly dull.

The city's most renowned playhouse is the Moscow Art Theater (MAT). Founded in 1898 by Konstantin Stanislavsky and V. I. Nemirovich-Danchenko, it was there that the Stanislavsky Method of acting was born and there that Anton Chekhov and Maxim Gorky introduced their dramas to the world. Today it is little more than a monument to itself. There is not an ounce of Method to its methods. Some of its acting, with a catalogue of gestures for a corresponding list of emotions, smacks of the eighteenth century. The rest is nineteenth-century melodramatic. Many of the productions have not been updated since Stanislavsky died in 1938. The same applies to some of the actors.

The reason for the decline of one of the world's most famous theaters is not hard to find. In the 1930s, when Zhdanov proclaimed "socialist realism," the Stanislavsky system was elevated to a dogma of its expression in drama. Whereas Stanislavsky's ideas greatly influenced modern acting abroad, the use made of his system during the Stalin era not only killed theater in the Soviet Union but ruined the MAT.

The MAT's only hope may be that in 1970 Oleg Yefremov, founder, director and leading actor of the Sovremennik (Contemporary) Theater on Mayakovsky Square, became the Moscow Art Theater's chief producer. For fourteen years Yefremov was to drama what Yevtushenko was to poetry: a breath of new life. Whether Yefremov's transfer from the audacious Sovremennik Theater was a punitive action or not, for the MAT it can only mean cultural salvation.

At the other end of the spectrum, Moscow's most vibrant and avant-garde theater is Yuri Lyubimov's Comedy and Drama Theater on Taganka Square. Lyubimov, born in October 1917, the month and year of the Revolution, is a former director and actor of the Vakhtangov Theater in Moscow and the Vakhtangov Theater Studio, where he was a teacher. His Taganka ensemble, founded in 1964, is a collective of his best former students, most of them in their late twenties and early thirties. A director's theater, it brought Brecht to Moscow in the form of unusual and heterodox productions of *Galileo Galilei* and *The Good Woman of Setzuan;* Yesenin's *Pugachev,* which tends to be declaimed to the audience; Peter Weiss' *How Mr. Mockinpott Absolved Himself of His Troubles;* Gorky's *Mother;* Voznesensky's *Anti-Worlds;* and a dramatization of John Reed's account of the Russian Revolution, *Ten Days That Shook the World.*

Lyubimov, whose office walls bear the admiring graffiti of Sir Laurence Olivier, Kenneth Tynan, Lillian Hellman, Jean Vilar, Anna Magnani and Arthur Miller, believes in a theater that moves away from closed, conventional plays toward theatrical events, happenings, so to speak, directed at and involving the audience. He has come closest to achieving that in *Ten Days*. The spectator is drawn into an authentic revolutionary atmosphere before the curtain even goes up. Actors wearing greatcoats and peaked caps of the Red Army serve as ushers and spear tickets on the long bayonets of their World War I rifles as the audience files into the lobby.

Notwithstanding the sensation it has caused—no Moscow theater's tickets are as scarce and premiers as discussed—the Taganka is little more than a revival of the earliest, liveliest period of Soviet theater. Its style is not an innovation but a return to the experimental audacities of men like Vsevolod Meyerhold, Yevgeny Vakhtangov and Alexander Tairov. As such, to foreigners, it is nothing new. But for an entire generation of young Muscovites it means the reincarnation of theatrical techniques and concepts that were stifled by official fiat under Stalin and Zhdanov.

Founded in the last year of Khrushchev's relatively liberal stewardship, the Taganka Theater today is the nemesis of dogmatic guardians of artistic freedom. Timid as its departures from the established norms may seem to Western observers, even these hesitant experiments with the theatrical forms and techniques of the 1920s and early 1930s went beyond official strictures.

Lyubimov's theater was controversial from the outset but its real difficulties began in 1968 when Lyubimov wanted to stage a highly unorthodox version of *Tartuffe* which the censors read as an indictment of Communist bureaucracy and Marxist liturgy. Glavlit's plenipotentiary probably realized that Lyubimov would bring the house down in a scene where Tartuffe takes out a notebook and jots down an overheard conversation in the best tradition of the KGB informer. The premiere was held up for months and the compromises Lyubimov made to obtain final clearance remain a well-guarded secret of the tightly knit Taganka ensemble.

His next major engagement with the party, Glavlit and the Ministry of Culture was fought over Voznesensky's *Watch Your Faces,* a theatrical compendium of poetry, imaginative pantomime, topical humor and relatively mild social message.

A series of sketches, the production included Voznesensky songs sung by Vladimir Vysotsky, the Taganka actor and *magnitizdat* balladeer. One of these songs likened modern society to a band of merciless hunters who shoot defenseless animals. The production included mild digs at hippies, Moscow's obsession with the Asian flu and the continuing struggle between liberals and conservatives in the arts.

Political comment was set in a soccer context with the lines: "The left doesn't know what the right is doing and no one knows who is on the right or who is on the left." At the end of that sketch the soccer player scored a goal against himself and complimented himself on his scoring style.

In accordance with the censorship rules, a Glavlit and Ministry of Culture commission watched three rehearsals of the play and, after some revisions, gave it a stamp of approval on February 6, 1970. It opened before an enthusiastic audience of invited guests on February 9. There were performances on the tenth and eleventh and then posters went up around Moscow announcing further performances for February 17, 20, and 24.

Then the censorship commission reversed itself, ruled that the play had serious "ideological defects," was partly anti-Soviet and ordered it withdrawn from the repertoire. The posters around Moscow were covered up and a signboard in front of the theater was painted over in black. Lyubimov protested and even offered to make changes in the script, but *Watch Your Faces* never reopened.

The following season Lyubimov faced potentially similar difficulties with a dramatization of Chernishevsky's nineteenth-century novel *What Is to Be Done?* The public premiere was held up several weeks as Lyubimov battled with the censors and showed the play privately. What compromises he finally made may never be known because he threatened to fire any Taganka employee who allowed a copy of the script to leave the building or be seen by anyone else. The scripts were numbered and Lyubimov locked them in a safe each night until final approval was given and the play opened.

Expurgations, even of standard play texts, are frequently demanded of Lyubimov. His scintillating production of Brecht's *Galileo,* for example, conveniently skips over the scene in which Andrea Sarti smuggled manuscripts across the border to Holland.

But struggles with the censors are the least of Lyubimov's worries. In May 1970, during the Twelfth Congress of the All-Russian Theatrical Society, a "creative union" of 25,000 playwrights, directors, producers, actors, dancers and singers, the group's president, Mikhail Tsarev, a Moscow actor, warned Lyubimov and his ensemble to pay more attention to the "contents" of the Taganka's art and to "defining its place in the ideological battle now going on in the world." Tsarev referred to "faults in the theater's repertoire and its use of ideologically dubious plays" which have failed "to show the way of Communism."

Six months later Viktor Grishin, the Communist Party chief of Moscow and a member of the ruling Politburo, accused the Taganka of "substantial shortcomings" and the theater's party cell of "improper and insufficient influence on the choice of repertoire and the creative life of the company."

Between the extremes of the MAT's stodginess and the Taganka's "heresies," theater in Moscow is, for the most part, a gray void of thirty professional playhouses in which political conformity and artistic mediocrity set the strictures for dramas, stagings and acting which are uninspiringly archaic.

Periodically there are striking exceptions that support the axiom that theater in the Soviet Union is the hardiest and most resilient of the arts. Were it not, theater would have died decades ago under the stifling, restrictive hand of the Communist Party's control. What is so amazing about the Soviet theater is that time and time again it gets away with as much as it does—to the utter delight of its audiences.

The official pressures and constraints are enormous, and well they might be, considering the history and tradition of theater in Russia.

Since the time of its first great—and, naturally, censored—comedy, Griboyedov's *Woe from Wit,* Russian drama has taken political, social and moral corruption as its theme and the struggle on stage has been basically a conflict between the upright hero and depraved society. Usually the hero is destroyed but remains the moral victor. Sometimes there is no hero at all, only a villain: humanity or society. It is easy to see the problems raised by this kind of theater for Communist doctrine which holds that extant Soviet society is free of corruption and turpitude.

Essentially it was always a serious and, on the whole, somber theater, which was bound to lead to conflict with a cultural dogma calling for optimism and joy in the service of propaganda.

Theater was among the first arts to be brought forcefully into the new line laid down by Stalin. The Method was systematically reduced to a cliché and Stanislavsky, as officially revered as Gorky, died a largely disillusioned man in 1938. The plays of Mayakovsky were proscribed and the expressionist directors were censured, hounded and, in the case of Meyerhold, physically liquidated. Brilliant playwrights such as Yevgeny Shvarts, Bulgakov and Nikolai Erdman, whom Gorky had once called "our new Gogol," were forced into silence. It was not until after the dictator's death and the first thaw that Mayakovsky was rehabilitated, Shvarts' fantasies were first performed and Meyerhold's stagings shown to a new generation. The rehabilitation is far from complete. Even today Erdman is virtually an unperson, only two Mayakovsky plays are in the current repertoire of Moscow theaters, and until late 1969, when a second-rate playhouse staged his satire *Ivan Vasilyevich,* Bulgakov's sole representation was *The Turbin Family,* a play that Stalin had approved and admired.

Since March 1968 Soviet theater has again been going through a tense period from which no relief appears in sight.

Viktor Rozov, whose three-act drama *Alive Forever* was turned into the prize-winning Soviet film *The Cranes Are Flying,* has been repeatedly censured for ideological deviation and was, as I pointed out earlier, removed from the editorial board of *Yunost.*

Edward Radzinsky, not yet thirty, has been attacked for two of his plays: *We Are Making a Movie* and *104 Pages About Love,* both of which deal with unhappy people caught in ill-starred love affairs. The criticism: his characters' emotions bring them into "blind alleys, to loneliness and finally to death. Are blind alley situations typical of Soviet youth? Of course not."

Aleksei Arbusov, whose 1959 two-acter *It Happened in Ikrutsk* won him acclaim at home and abroad, is in trouble because two of his recent plays, *The Promise* and *Happy Days of an Unhappy Person,* make heroes of "warped personalities" and "failures in life."

Even Valentin Yezhov, author of *Ballad of a Soldier,* is in difficulties because of his latest play, *The Night of the Nightingales,* which centers around an unhappy love affair between an AWOL Soviet Army sergeant and a German girl.

The new freeze has taken its toll of foreign plays and playwrights too. Jean-Paul Sartre has been declared persona non grata because of his protests of the Czechoslovak invasion. In early 1969 a student production of his *No Exit* was banned at the Moscow State Theatrical Institute. Arthur Miller's works have been struck from the repertoires of all Moscow theaters because of the sharp criticism of Soviet cultural policy in his and Inge Morath's book, *In Russia.*

Periodically Soviet "theater workers" are reminded that "Soviet drama must participate actively in the Communist education of the working people and in shaping the lofty artistic tastes of Soviet citizens." It should offer a "life-asserting message," instill optimism and reflect "the nature of the Soviet citizen's world outlook . . . Its supreme criteria are the Leninist principles of the Communist Party."

"The summit of party-mindedness, the climax of artistic skill," a theater critic suggested in 1968, "is the theme of Lenin on the stage. Of course, that does not necessarily mean to show Lenin on stage in person. Previously, artists strove to produce a concrete visual image of Lenin on stage. More recently, producers have started looking for other ways. To speak of Lenin is to write and show our contemporaries the character of a man inspired by Leninist thoughts."

"Party-mindedness" is required not only of dramatists, producers, directors and actors but of critics and journalists concerned with drama as well.

One who failed to live up to these demands was Yuri Rybakov, editor-in-chief of *Teatr* magazine, dismissed in December 1969 for "ideological shortcomings." Rybakov's firing climaxed an eighteen-months-long struggle between the liberal editor and the conservative leadership of the Writers' Union which owns the magazine. Rybakov's crimes included publishing "dramatic works of a decadent, pessimistic nature, and plays filled with mockery of Soviet reality," failing to "fight for the creation of works that would foster in every Soviet person ideological conviction, a sense of Soviet patriotism and proletarian internationalism and irreconcilability toward all manifestations of bourgeois ideology," "ideological inexactness" and heaping lavish praise on the Taganka Theater's production of Gorky's *Mother.*

Yet Moscow's theaters are capable of the most fantastic Hydra-like, protean feats which infuriate and confuse the censors and ideological watchdogs. A troublesome play is lopped off the repertoire of one theater, but another is added elsewhere. A devastating line is scratched from the text but an even more devastating nuance or visual effect is added. In Moscow an actor's eyes or gestures often say more than a soliloquy of censored words.

One way to avoid the censors, at least for a while, was through the classics. Not the classics staged by the MAT, of course, but carefully tailored productions at the Taganka, Sovremennik, Malaya Bronnaya and Vakhtangov theaters. It did not take *Literaturnaya Rossiya,* a weekly cultural paper, long to discover they were "public meetings on the stage directed against contemporary society."

Because discussions of contemporary bureaucratic infighting are taboo on the stage, Moscow's Mayakovsky Theater produced an updated version of Sukhovo-Kobylin's 1869 masterpiece *The Death of*

Tarelkin, which, in the words of one sympathetic critic, "represents a kind of social order in which there is no freedom of expression, open courts or official responsibility to the public."

To dwell on the anti-intellectualism that lurks in Soviet society would be unthinkable, if presented in a contemporary context. But a modernized version of Ostrovsky's *A Lucrative Post,* written in 1857, drew capacity audiences at the Satire Theater and caused ripples of identification when Yusov, the anti-intellectual chief clerk in a tsarist office, talked about his pleasure in suppressing "those modern educated ones" and his preference for promoting nonentities because they tended to remain indebted to him.

Stalin's crimes are also proscribed on the stage. But the relatively conservative Central Theater of the Red Army managed to allude to them by dusting off and reviving Aleksei Tolstoy's century-old classic *The Death of Ivan the Terrible.*

One way to emphasize certain themes of contemporary significance in classical drama was to repeat or stress the lines that the director considered significant. Anatoly Efros thus succeeded in giving a decidedly Freudian interpretation to the frustrations of Chekhov's *Three Sisters.* As he directed it, the girls' yearning "to Moscow, to Moscow" had as much to do with sex as a desire to be closer to the intellectual life in the city.

Efros, who had been fired in 1967 as producer of the Lenin Komsomol Theater (a dozen actors demonstrated their solidarity by walking out with him) because his direction "failed to reflect the most important problems of our life, the tasks of youth in the building of Communism," paid for his audacity. After a short run his version of *Three Sisters* was banned at the Malaya Bronnaya Theater, where he had become director.

"Some phenomena in the theater," Sergei Mikhailkov warned, "are alarming. It is not a secret that in their productions some directors arbitrarily interpret the texts of classic works—through coloration of lines—to give them a contemporary ring. Even if this is done merely for the sake of effect and without malicious intent, it is still an act of political and civic irresponsibility."

Nothing is quite as classical as the Bolshoi Ballet.

Its 1968 production of Aram Khachaturian's *Spartacus* was the first breath of artistic fresh air to sweep through that venerable old house in three decades. Ideologically speaking it was a painful birth —delayed and postponed time after time for reasons of doctrine. But when it was finally premiered, the production proved that political and social strictures notwithstanding, the Bolshoi had the dancers, choreographers and designers to bring this once great company into the competitive world of contemporary ballet. Thus far, unfortunately, *Spartacus* with its expressionism and body-stockinged performers has remained an adumbration of what the Bolshoi's chief choreographer, Yuri Grigorovich, can achieve when given the chance.

At a press conference several months after the premiere, Minister of Culture Yekaterina Furtseva, obviously talking about *Spartacus* and looking straight at Grigorovich, who was on the platform with her, said: "But I do think that of late there has been a little too much sex in our ballet." From the other end of the table, Igor Moiseyev, director of one of the U.S.S.R.'s best-known dance companies, speaking barely loud enough for the audience and Furtseva to hear, said: "But *Tovarishch* Minister, sex is life." Furtseva shot him a quick glance and said acidly: "I don't think that is at all funny." Moiseyev had to atone for his sin, like a naughty schoolboy, by writing a lengthy dissertation in *Literary Gazette* condemning modern dances such as the twist, frug, slop and monkey.

As a national art since tsarist days, ballet is lavishly subsidized and popularized. Literally tens of thousands of youngsters who elsewhere would be playing in sandboxes are already donning ballet slippers and dreaming of a glamorous career someday with the Bolshoi.

Yet for all its popularity and its unmatched machine-like precision, the Bolshoi lives in the past, bogged down by staid, tradition-bound thinking, staging and choreography. Sets are ornate but, with few exceptions, oppressively realistic. Stage effects are so circus-like— with burning cities, raging floodwaters and gliding swans—that the dancers sometimes seem like forgotten adjuncts.

Stravinsky's *Rite of Spring* was not added to the Bolshoi's repertoire —and then hesitantly—until 1964. And even Khachaturian's *Spartacus* was fourteen years old when premiered by Grigorovich in 1968.

The illustrious Bolshoi is sometimes even used for the crudest type of propaganda. White colonial hunters in sun helmets oppress poor Africans who finally break their chains. Wall Street tycoons exploit the downtrodden on its stage. And coveralled Soviet workers still find terpsichorean happiness in a new model tractor or machine lathe.

The Bolshoi usually seems like ice when it should be like fire, and here as in most Soviet theaters, it is yesterday's vignette, not tomorrow's promise, which meets the party's approval.

*Art is always and everywhere the
secret confession and, at the same
time, the immortal movement of its
time.*

Karl Marx, 1854

Pictures Without Exhibitions

Nowhere is the iron hand of the conservative Soviet cultural establishment felt more strongly, nowhere are the strictures of Socialist
realism more apparent, than in the fine and visual arts.

Officially, fine art in the U.S.S.R. consists of the work produced
by the 12,000 members of the Union of Artists. For the most part,
their creations—more propaganda than art—are banal, mediocre and
nauseatingly conformist. Then there is a vast "gray area" of applied
art and illustration in which, from time to time, the discerning con-
noisseur will find hints of stifled originality and talent.

But far more important, politically and artistically, are the U.S.S.R.'s
several hundred "underground" or unofficial artists: painters, sculp-
tors, illustrators whose work is non-representational and avant-garde,
ranging the spectrum of styles from post-impressionist to construc-
tivist, from purely abstract to symbolist, from suprematist to Pop.

Their exact number may never be ascertained: among the artists
themselves I have heard estimates that ranged from "a few hundred
in the whole country" to "about one thousand." The majority are untalented mediocrities who paint for themselves or their friends the
same way unofficial writers, good or bad, compose for their desk
drawers. Lacking talent, they will go on deluding themselves for
years that, because they are clandestine, they must be good. A few
score are good. Of these some have sold their works to foreigners
through whom they reached museums, galleries and private collections
abroad.

Middling, good or inferior, the "underground" artists all have several things in common. They are outcasts of the system, pariahs in

the eyes of Soviet officialdom. Most of them tread a narrow line between grudging toleration and public condemnation. At home, they are outsiders, condemned to a life of impoverishment on the fringes of society. Social acceptance will be denied them until they are prepared to compromise their political and artistic principles.

A few are lucky. Their work is purchased not only by diplomats, correspondents and foreign art lovers, but by a handful of Soviet cognoscenti—scientists, writers, musicians, actors and, yes, even politicians such as Khrushchev's son-in-law Aleksei Adzhubei, or, more surprising, Leonid Ilyichev, Khrushchev's chief of propaganda and ideology who is now a deputy foreign minister. He railed and ranted against non-conformists publicly but is reputed to have, privately, one of Moscow's largest collections of underground art. Some owe their unofficial prominence and their modicum of success directly to collectors such as Ilya Ehrenburg and Yevgeny Yevtushenko; some to experts such as Alexander Glezer and George Kostaki, the latter a Greek citizen, working for the Canadian embassy, resident in Moscow almost five decades since he was eight years old, and the owner of probably the largest private collection of Chagalls, Kandinskys, Tatlins and Maleviches anywhere.

Occasionally a few unofficial artists cause excitement with unsanctioned exhibitions. Usually these "shows" are so brief that only a handful of supporters, collectors, foreign correspondents and diplomats have a chance to see them before they are closed again. The most recent of these, in May 1970, lasted all of thirty-five minutes. It was a one-man show by Oleg Tselkov, thirty-seven, a gifted and enigmatic neo-Dadaist, whose works were hung in the White Room of Moscow's House of Architects. When it happened at eleven o'clock one weekday morning, about forty people, invited by word of mouth, were present. At eleven thirty-five an official of the Union of Architects came in and told everyone to leave. He promised that the show would reopen at 5 P.M. Visitors who returned then were told flatly: "There is no exhibition."

Otherwise the standards of art in the U.S.S.R. are set by the party's ideologists and the heads of the Union and Academy of Arts, painters who won their laurels with photo-like Lenin portraits, revolutionary scenes or idyllic canvases of happy collective farmers, enthusiastic workers, dams and hydroelectric stations. They are not about to cede the terrain or open even the anteroom doors to those who preach or paint according to another gospel.

These are the people who argue that abstractionism and such "pseudo-objective avant-garde" trends as Pop art or kineticism express "bourgeois society's confusion in the face of the contradictions of the present-day world."

They fulminate against "people who call themselves artists, fawn upon the intellectual philistinism of the West, ape elements of modernism in their works, then smuggle them abroad to be exhibited."

They bask in the reassurance of a static world when the Communist Party's Central Committee proclaims that: "Only realistic works of art, profound in content and perfect in mastery, can satisfy the Soviet people today . . . The Soviet artist must always display ideological staunchness and irreconcilability toward all forms of alien influences."

Few men represented this kind of entrenched "establishment painter" of "socialist realism" better than the late Vladimir Alexandrovich Serov, president of the Soviet Academy of Arts, who in his lifetime painted more portraits of, and scenes including, Lenin than any other man.

Dapper, voluble, polished and blatantly hypocritical, Serov was the living champion of socialist realism, the implacable foe of what he considered "abstract nonsense."

"In the West," Serov told my predecessor, Robert Korengold, "they are always claiming that we have no 'artistic freedom' because the government is the purchaser. They say that they are free because they can compete with each other. That's just the point. They cannot seek their own path. They must do what pleases the buyer. To me that is not freedom, that's slavery.

"We view art as a way of communicating the ideas for which we live and fight. Art was always for the masses. History demonstrates that. The Greeks used art for propaganda. Those beautiful statues were put up to propagandize. Christian art was propaganda—great propaganda, but propaganda nevertheless. History was always a battle for high ideas in art. Why should we renounce that now?

"I don't understand abstract art. It is monstrous. Why should any artist want to ignore the beautiful things in life for these sick concoctions? Nor would the masses understand abstractions. They wouldn't understand it and no one would go to an abstract exhibit. But they understand our art. Thousands of people line up to see our exhibitions."

Serov was the "king of the conservatives" whose tirades against contemporary Soviet abstractionists were the law of the academy he ruled. But he vented his spleen not only on the "unofficial" artists eking out a clandestine living in Moscow garrets and basements but on his nation's own famed artists of the 1920s and 1930s—Marc Chagall, Vasily Kandinsky, Vladimir Tatlin, Kasimir Malevich, Lazar Lissitsky, Robert Falk, Pavel Filonov, Naum Gabo, Natalya Goncharova and Lyubov Popova—artists whose work has not been shown in the U.S.S.R. for forty and more years.

"Theirs wasn't revolutionary art," Serov argued shortly before his death. "It was a deformation of our idea of art. Real revolutionary art was always that which helped the Revolution and the work of the people."

Serov is dead. So is Alexander Gerasimov, Stalin's "court" painter whose assembly-line portraits of the leader in an endless flow of new poses hung in every office, classroom, factory, living room and nursery in the U.S.S.R. But their spirit remains alive and the artist *apparatchiki* who have replaced them in the hierarchy of the union and academy are cut from the same mold and think alike.

Thanks to them Moscow's Tretyakov and Leningrad's Hermitage museums keep their treasures of Chagalls, Kandinskys, Maleviches and Tatlins under lock and key, out of sight from an entire new generation of Russians who have been systematically deprived of a major link from their heritage. Because of them an exhibition of Picasso's work remains a once-in-a-decade sensation in the Soviet Union.

Once, in 1967, Moscow's Institute of Advanced Physics held a private show devoted to Russian art in the 1920s and 1930s which included works by Falk, Lissitsky and Filonov. But in the summer of 1968, when a scientists' club at Akademgorodok near Novosibirsk arranged to hold a representative exhibit of Chagall's work, the Ministry of Culture interfered and canceled it.

"Some of them are great masterpieces," Furtseva admitted. "But we have so many great masters. Unfortunately our facilities are not such that all of them can be shown."

The arbiters of Soviet art even endeavor to wield their influence abroad. In February 1971 a major exhibition of post-revolutionary Russian art in London's Hayward Gallery had to open with one room sealed at the insistence of Soviet officials. The room contained structured wall reliefs by Lissitsky. Also removed from the show on Soviet request were works by Tatlin, Popova and Malevich. Soviet Ministry of Culture representatives threatened to withdraw everything they had lent to the show unless the sponsors, the London Arts Council, complied.

Regimentation of art is nothing new in Russia. On the contrary, for most of its history, art in Russia has been in bondage—first to the Church, then to the aristocracy, and now to the Communist Party apparat. For centuries the iconographer's lot was not to question but to reproduce faithfully the models created in Byzantium. Originality or departure from established norms of portrayal were tantamount to heresy.

Today the same principle prevails in the name of socialist realism. It is an art of the ideal—the Marxist ideal. Theoretically, its form is limited to the photographic or naturalistic portrayal of man and his environment. In practice, however, it is a photographic or naturalistic portrayal of how the party *wants* man and his environment to appear. Gerasimov, greatest of the socialist realist artists, was a master at that. Though Stalin was a short man, shorter than most of his compatriots, Gerasimov always painted him as the tallest figure in the group.

The range of subject matter, not to mention style, available to the artist under the precepts of socialist realism is extremely narrow. In addition to the official homage paid to Lenin and the party leadership, the artists' choice of subject is almost entirely confined to the general theme of the "new Soviet man" and the "new Soviet society." This does not mean that socialist realist art consists only of scenes of industry, construction sites, dams, collective farms and hydroelectric stations, but it does require art to be representational and above all optimistic.

Only once can I recall seeing a negative canvas in an official Soviet exhibition. It was a painting, in dark blue, gray, black and umber, that depicted a group of obviously lonely, frustrated teen-agers, one with a guitar, standing idly and aimlessly on a street corner at night. The painting, an untalented but remarkably accurate portrayal of the condition of Soviet youth, was the focus of many heated discussions between older and younger visitors to the show. Once a young artist got into an argument with a minor party bureaucrat about the canvas. The youth defended the picture for its "realistic" portrayal of life while the *apparatchik* considered it "decadent." How the painting got into the exhibit, sponsored by the Union of Artists in its gallery on Moscow's Kuznetsky Most, remains a mystery to me.

A young Soviet painter of even minimum talent, coming up today, can count without fear on a relatively well-paid, secure life—provided he eschews "pessimistic" themes like the one described and conforms to the official vision of what Soviet art should be. Plenty are willing. To turn out the socialist realists and Lenin portraitists of the future, the U.S.S.R. has sixty secondary art schools and seventeen that rank at university level. The most prestigious are the Repin Institute in Leningrad and the Surikov Institute in Moscow.

Once he has finished the institute, a young artist fixes his sight first and foremost on getting into the Union of Artists. He must submit a representative sampling of his work and have the recommendations of three other members in good standing to apply.

It is the union that will get him an apartment, a studio, provide him with quality paints, brushes and canvas and underwrite his "get acquainted with life" trips around the country. It will arrange for the sale of his painting—to adorn the limitless wall space of the Soviet Union's factories, houses of culture, administrative offices and hotel rooms. Some painters, of course, sell to friends, acquaintances or anyone interested enough to look them up. But there are few galleries where Soviet citizens can drop in and pick up an oil or a piece of graphic art. Moscow has two, Leningrad one. All of them, with the exception of the sales salons in the Baltic capitals of Riga and Tallin, confine themselves to mediocre outpourings of socialist realism.

In Tallin, however, where life and the arts are infinitely freer than in Moscow or other Central Russian cities, I once bought a completely abstract lithograph for forty rubles in the state-run gallery. The same work in Moscow would have been considered strictly unofficial and available only from an underground artist. In fact, one of them said: "If you hadn't shown me the receipt I would not have believed that you bought this in a salon. With my conservative abstractions I would become a millionaire in Estonia."

Most official art is sold via the union and usually to the state. The union thus is an artist's guarantee of an income. It sends out salesmen—*zakazchiki*—throughout the country—usually for another Lenin, revolutionary scene or Russian landscape.

The orders are then spread among the members with an eye more to internecine connections, political pull and financial subsidy than talent. If one painter has already had three orders the next ones will be funneled to those who have had less, unless, of course, the more active artist happens to be a friend of the union official who distributes the work and the money.

Even the most average union painter can expect to earn a minimum of two hundred rubles a month for normal work turnout. The bigger names and better-connected artists can reach monthly averages of several thousand rubles—thanks not only to orders, private sales and official commissions but royalties on the reprinting and exhibition of their works. Some are millionaires.

But even membership in the union is no guarantee of admission to a land of security and benefits if the artist, like Ilya Glazunov, is a maverick. Glazunov, a portraitist, expressionist and neo-iconographer whose main work dwells on old Russian traditions and Russian history, pressured his way into the union from above with the help of his main clients—foreign diplomats, visitors, heads of state and the international jet set. Ever since he became a member in 1967 he has been paid back in kind for his unorthodox tactics and art. "They gave me a union card because they were forced to," said Glazunov, a nephew of the famous composer and a nephew by marriage of the actor Peter Ustinov. "But they don't buy anything from me." Glazunov is fortunate enough not to need the union's patronage.

His main sources of income are not his Dostoyevsky-inspired scenes of Leningrad, subtle aquarelles of abandoned Orthodox churches and the barren Russian countryside, and much less his huge, garish Pop-icon renditions of *Boris Godunov,* the *Murder of Tsarevich Dmitry* and other quasi-religious, quasi-historical motives. The latter, in fact, typify Glazunov and his art. But the canvases, running to 6 by 9 feet, are eminently unsuited for contemporary housing conditions and may be even too large for certain museums.

Glazunov is a sort of court portraitist for the diplomatic corps and top-level foreign visitors to Moscow—from Gina Lollobrigida to Averell Harriman. In addition to teaching art to the wives of American diplomats, he hobnobs with the cream of the foreign colony. Everyone from actors and artists to prime ministers may seek him out when they come to the U.S.S.R. Among his satisfied clients he numbers premiers and the entire royal family of Laos.

Born in Leningrad in 1930, Glazunov entered the Repin Institute in 1951 and for a number of years worked hard at his studies—he is an excellent technician—and turned out a number of pictures in the approved manner. But he became dissatisfied with the limitations of socialist realism and soon turned to the theme of love. One of his first unorthodox paintings depicted a man and a woman embracing against the dark, somber background of a Leningrad apartment house. The painting was exhibited at an international competition in Prague, where, even during the darkest years of the Gottwald and Novotny era, artistic orthodoxy was never drunk straight. He won first prize.

Sudden fame in a "fraternal socialist country" secured Glazunov's painting a showing in Moscow but also the heightened opprobrium from the socialist realists of the Union of Artists.

Fortunately for Glazunov, he had other things going for him as well. Blessed with charisma, a tremendous drive and self-confidence, he also has a Madison Avenue sense for personal publicity in addition to a genuine talent for portraiture. In 1961 he met Gina Lollobrigida at the Moscow Film Festival, pleased her with a quick sketch and wound up not only with her invitation to come to Rome to paint her portrait in oil, but also permission from the Ministry of Culture to stage a showing of his works there. It wouldn't have happened to a man of comparable charm and talent ten years later.

On his triumphant return to the U.S.S.R., though still not a member of the Union of Artists, he insisted on a studio and an exhibition in Moscow itself.

His studio—in the turret of a post-revolutionary apartment house that was sealed tight in Stalin's days because of its rifle's-sight view of the dictator's regular route along Arbat Street from the Kremlin to his suburban dacha—would be the envy of any artist in New York or Paris. Hung with one of Moscow's finest private icon collections, it is today one of the chief intellectual salons of the Soviet capital. So many foreigners, young artists and writers (Glazunov has even published his autobiography in *Molodaya Gvardiya,* a monthly magazine for young readers) use it as base that it is a wonder he gets any work done. The studio is a mecca for struggling hopefuls and nonconformists. He and his dark-haired wife Nina, herself a graphic artist, virtually hold court all day amid old cups, half-empty wine or cognac bottles and the tens of thousands of dollars' worth of icons.

Glazunov also got the exhibition—a five-day show of his paintings in the Manege Hall next to the Kremlin. Had his old enemies in the union kept quiet, the exhibit might have passed with modest success and been forgotten. But union officials tried to postpone the show indefinitely when they saw block-long lines of eager young Muscovites queuing to get in. Postponement notices were put up and the crowd staged a sit-in. The doors were not opened until Glazunov agreed to remove two paintings: a neo-icon of Ivan the Terrible and another of a woman watching her husband being taken to exile.

Glazunov got his studio and his show. But it took him another five years to become a member of the union. And then it was a moral, not a financial victory. Today, though an official artist, he continues to paint and behave in an unofficial manner.

The world of unofficial Soviet art is a large one, but nobody, not even the artists, knows for sure how large. Moreover it raises a problem of identification. Who is an unofficial artist? Does this term include the dozens, possibly hundreds who do conventional work all week but paint abstract canvases on Sunday? It could if, for example, the artist engages in the other work to avoid prosecution or deportation as a parasite, or simply to support himself.

And what about the unofficial painters who work most of the time as commercial artists or book illustrators? Are they really members of the underground? Especially those among them who are members of the graphics section of the Union of Artists?

One such graphic artist is Ilya Kabakov. As an illustrator, largely of children's books, he not only earned enough to build a genuine studio but he is even a member of the board of the graphics section of the Moscow artists' organization. Yet Kabakov is one of the most unorthodox of the maverick painters, as well as one of the most talented. His work uses elements of surrealism, Dadaism and Pop art to create a special prism through which one sees uniquely Soviet images. One of his recently completed works is a medium-sized canvas covered entirely with blue paint. Near the center of it he painted a life-sized, ordinary housefly. That is all, except for two inscriptions at the upper left- and right-hand corners of the picture which read: "Is this the fly of Kabakov?" "Yes, this is the fly of Kabakov." In a similar vein he has a large canvas of solid light blue in the corners of which are the small, carefully lettered words: "It is a lake," "It is the sea," "It is fresh air," "It is the sky."

Kabakov himself says he is not sure what it is or that it matters. Some people are amused by his works and admire his scurrility and whimsicality. Others say his paintings make them melancholy. But one thing is certain, of the underground artists Kabakov is among the most exhibited and most frequently shown abroad.

Kabakov sells to foreigners when they come to him and show an interest in his work. But unlike some unofficial artists, who hope and hint for invitations to diplomatic receptions where they distribute calling cards and buttonhole prospects, Kabakov never seeks out foreign buyers.

Some artists, on the other hand, are reluctant to sell to foreigners and a few sometimes refuse to sell at all, even to Russian collectors.

One of these is Boris Sveshnikov, a shy, soft-spoken expressionist who spent eight years in a Stalinist labor camp. Sveshnikov, now forty-four, is a perfectionist who leaves nothing to chance in his softly illuminated, lightly colored canvases, in which he attempts to express the frustrations, the poverty and the oppressiveness of Soviet life. One entitled *Soviet Citizen,* shows little more than a tiny, walking figure, throwing a long shadow on a high, towering wall—the embodiment of the individual's loneliness and helplessness in the face of overpowering state authority. Sveshnikov is reluctant to sell because, as he once told me, these pictures are his life, a part of him and his experience. Nor does he really have to sell. He is one of Moscow's most sought-after book illustrators.

Although some of the best non-representational artists, such as Falk, Filonov (who died in the famine during the wartime siege of Leningrad) and Alexander Tyshler survived the purges and the *Zhdanovchina,* it was not until after Khrushchev's 1956 secret speech that the present underground movement developed. The temperate cultural climate of the thaw drove young art students to the homes of unofficial artists who previously had moved only among friends. Their kitchens and bedrooms were turned into studios and quietly the teaching of modern art was resumed.

No specific school or style has evolved from it. And as East-West cultural exchanges began, tourists flowed into the Soviet Union and greater contact with the modern art movement in the West was established, a variety of influences, often strongly marked by Russia's own heritage of the Great Experiment, streamed in. Some are cubists, some do complete abstracts, some are symbolists, Dadaists, futurists, constructivists, suprematists, surrealists and a few dabble with a primitive Pop art.

As Ilya Ehrenburg, one of the main collectors of modern art, complained in his memoirs:

"Our museums possess superb collections of the 'left art' of the early post-revolutionary years. It is a pity that these collections are not open to the public. You cannot throw out a link from the chain. Yet, I know young Soviet artists who were 'discovering

America' in 1960. What they were doing (or to be more precise, trying to do) was what Malevich, Tatlin, Popova and Rozanova had already done in their time."

One of the most difficult to categorize is Vasily Sitnikov, a fifty-five-year-old autodidact whose work ranges from portraits to pure abstractions, from erotica to intricate scenes of imaginary monasteries and kremlins in which scores, sometimes hundreds of figures are engaged in pursuits ranging from simple conversations to drunken orgies.

A wiry, slim, engaging man with a Mephistophelean beard, he is an extrovert and an individualist in a society where neither of those qualities seems desirable. A victim of the Stalin purges, he was arrested shortly before World War II and spent the war years in a psychiatric prison. The experience not only left an indelible impression on him but made him, like many other unofficial artists, a legal invalid. He receives a pension of thirty rubles a month, which frees him from having to take on work as a commercial artist, illustrator or museum restorer as a cover for his other activities. Having once been ruled, officially, a lunatic, he can now act like one whenever it pleases him. And it pleases him when it displeases the authorities.

At one time during his incarceration in Moscow he was held by the NKVD in the Lubyanka Prison, where he was interrogated and severely beaten. During the thaw and after many years as an outcast, Sitnikov was provided with a room in a communal flat—across the street from the Lubyanka. There Sitnikov lived until 1968, when he obtained two rooms in a new apartment house on the edge of Moscow near the Ismailova Park of Culture and Rest. When we first met him, several months after he had moved in there, he was not working, because, as he explained, "I am too busy moving." A year later Sitnikov—frequently he refers to himself in the third person—was "still busy moving."

He has probably the largest collection of unfinished work in Moscow and for the past year or so has not sold more than a painting or two. The lucky buyers are those who come in and succeed in convincing the master that whatever is on the easel is "finished enough."

Once when I visited him with another artist, Sitnikov displayed one of his "fantastic monasteries." As on most of them, the scene was covered with a profusion of intricately painted snowflakes. The detail, according to Sitnikov, is an expression of what he considers the most important thing in art: *kachestvo*—quality.

"You're cheating," said my friend, who, like many of Moscow's younger unofficial painters, had once studied under Sitnikov. "The snowflakes in the upper left-hand corners are not yours. They lack quality. One of your students painted them."

"You're close," said Sitnikov, donning a wide-brimmed black cowboy hat and preparing to plunk himself in the middle of the floor where he intended to expound, more fully, his views on quality in art. "Not a student but my wife."

At the door of his apartment is a large sign which reads "Here lives the artist Vasily Yakovlevich Sitnikov." The apartment itself is a congeries of books, shelves filled with indeterminate objects: icons, shoebrushes (which he often uses in place of paintbrushes), odd bits of wood, a high-powered shortwave radio which he accepted in lieu of payment for one of his pictures from a Western diplomat. There is no furniture to speak of. Meals—it is customary to bring a bottle along and the master will come up with salted fish, sausage, cheese and black bread—are served on planks of wood propped up at each end by rickety chairs. The guests use an ancient, lumpy sofa covered with a moth-eaten bearskin. Sitnikov himself prefers the floor, where he either hunches or sits yoga-like.

Two of his paintings are in New York's Museum of Modern Art. Many others are in private collections. But during the last few years Sitnikov has sold little, preferring to push the very inferior work of his students, of whom there appears to be an endless flow in his cramped apartment.

A feeling of strong sensuality predominates in his early work of the 1950s. These include many sketches executed in pencil or in his inventive adaptation of shoebrush and shoe polish, a technique which is used by many of his students, including Andrei Amalrik's wife, Gyusel. Necessity—the lack of art supplies and equipment which all the unofficial painters face—was the mother of this invention. These earlier works occasionally picture sexual acts, though never in a vulgar or pornographic form but with exceptional tenderness.

A recurring theme in many of his works is the plowed field, in which he uses both regular and shoebrush technique to achieve a subtle integration of form and color. In the early 1960s he turned, occasionally, to abstraction.

Sitnikov himself considers his portraits as his most serious works. More than any of his pictures, they demonstrate his exceptional talent. But the fantastic scenes of Russian monasteries and citadels are obviously the form from which he and his admirers derive the greatest fun. Their intricate details require long study. Usually they will include at least one drunk being led off by a *militsioner,* a one-legged beggar, a mother scolding her child and a bearded, mischievous, gnomelike man sitting far off in a corner of the canvas.

"That's Sitnikov," said Sitnikov, pointing at the gnome.

Even by the criteria of Moscow's underground art world, Dmitry Plavinsky's work is avant-garde. Yet Dima Plavinsky, a stubby, bearded, hard-drinking and very congenial thirty-three-year-old, now has a good chance of becoming a member of the Union of Artists, more specifically its graphics section. His candidature was accepted in the fall of 1970.

It was Dima's second application. The first time, he got so drunk beforehand that he appeared in the august offices of the union with a portfolio of empty sheets of art paper and smelling as if he had just crawled out of a vodka bottle. A third marriage to a tough little woman, herself an artist, has apparently contributed to his increasing sobriety and growing maturity.

Plavinsky had professional training at the Art Academy of the 1905 Revolution, one of Moscow's best schools. And the training shows in both his paintings and his graphic works. He is a meticulous draftsman with a lively imagination and a careful eye for detail, structure, surface, color, form and composition.

In his paintings, many of which are in private collections in the Soviet Union and abroad, Plavinsky frequently uses a three-dimensional collage technique, employing plastics and plaster of Paris. Bits of cloth, coins and, frequently, Cyrillic letters or ancient Slavic runes, cut from cardboard, are glued onto the canvas and then covered with paint or acrylics. Between these, with brush and paint he weaves magnifications of nature and organic matter—leaves, feathers, fish skeletons or the filigreed pattern of a moth or butterfly wing. Plavinsky has a special relationship to nature and organic matter which manifests itself in his steel and copper engravings. On the bookshelf in his cramped studio-living room is the cross section of a log he found in a forest near Moscow. It is, to the non-artist's eye, an ordinary piece of wood. For Dima it became the background and framework for an intricate engraving of flowers, butterflies, moths, other insects, leaves, Slavic letters and runic symbols which, when viewed from a distance of a few feet, seems to be an entire world of nature in its own.

Fascinated by ancient Russian architecture and sculpture, he has made abstract engravings based on the photos he has taken of monastery and church ruins in Central Russia.

Plavinsky has recognizable periods, but they are often dictated by the availability of materials. He concentrated on engraving and graphics for a while when he had no money for canvas but did have a good supply of gray market zinc and copper.

Just before I left Moscow Dima had run out of paper for his engravings, was unable to procure additional metal but had sold enough graphic work to buy canvas for a dozen paintings and was busily preparing them with base white.

As unofficial artists go, Plavinsky lives relatively well. He and his wife share a small, two-room apartment in a new housing area near the city limits not far from Patrice Lumumba University. It consists of a 7-by-10-foot bedroom, bare except for a rickety bed and a crib for their newborn baby, and a 7-by-10-foot living room crammed with bookshelves, easel, drafting table, couch and a huge engraving press.

The objects that are Plavinsky's art are all around him: dried fish, a dog's skull, pressed leaves and flowers, a tortoise shell, an icon or two and the only painting Dima has been unable to sell—a canvas filled with cutout Slavic letters which, arranged in a cross, represent the opening words of the Bible. It is 6 feet wide and 7 feet tall.

"Don't you want to buy that?" he once asked me.

"I would if I had a place to put it," I replied.

"That's the trouble with it," Plavinsky sighed. "Nobody has room. Neither do I."

Soviet policies toward the unofficial artists have changed with the times. For years the artists themselves were hounded and persecuted by the KGB. A foreign collector's visit to an artist's studio could often end by watching as the police raided the place and confiscated the completed and partially finished works. Yet the artists were often free to visit the foreigners' compounds.

This was followed by an era in which no unofficial artist dared to visit a diplomat's or correspondent's apartment. The "national day" receptions of embassies were devoid of the avant-garde artists who used to rush there in the hope of meeting prospective customers. The customers themselves, however, felt no inhibitions about visiting the studios, which became private enclaves of "internal emigration."

Today artists have as few qualms about visiting foreigners in their "golden ghettos" as the foreigners have about going to the studios. The atmosphere surrounding underground art appears to be, on the surface, free of restrictions. One artist, Boris Baruch-Stenberg, a three-dimensional collagist who works mainly with scrap metal, says frankly that he expects no trouble. "I sell a thousand to fifteen hundred rubles' worth of pictures a month," he explains. "All to foreigners. These are people who have exchanged their foreign currency for Soviet money. Ergo, I am bringing the Soviet state a thousand to fifteen hundred rubles' worth of foreign exchange every month. Nobody will bother me."

He's right. No one will bother him. But what about the customer? It has become next to impossible to export unofficial art from the Soviet Union legally, or at least without paying a heavy duty of, usually, 100 per cent of the purchase price. The alternative is to smuggle. Baruch's works don't lend themselves to that. Heavy, bulky, based on wooden backs with layers of tin on them, they cannot be taken out in suitcases.

Huge and rigid canvases are something Alexander Kharitonov does not worry about. A pointillist who does fantasies, beautiful dreams of fairy tales with castles and enchanting princesses chasing rainbows, Kharitonov's often measure no more than 9 by 12 inches.

Their small size is by no means their only attraction. Kharitonov, forty-five, is a remarkable artist. His paintings reflect his enigmatic personality. They tell of an escape into a fairy-tale world of Russian folklore, mystery and legend. Meticulous in his technique, he will work several months on some of his larger canvases (and charge accordingly). He uses minute, short strokes almost in the manner of Seurat. He is concerned with chromatic vibration and the rhythm produced by merging color and form. Pearly grays, pinks, light blues and greens are his world.

Deeply religious, his subject matter occasionally turns from the fanciful fairy tale to the ecclesiastical—crucifixes, priests, bishops and churches—but the style remains unchanged. From a distance it is two-dimensional, almost primitive in form. Viewed from close up it takes on a sharply three-dimensional aspect dependent entirely on the play of light on the many layers of paint that have been applied with small brushes.

Unlike other unofficial painters, Kharitonov, a stocky, balding, blond man who is unmarried and shares a minuscule one-room apartment with his aging mother, makes no compromises with his art. He does not work as a commercial artist or illustrator but frequently supports himself and his mother driving a taxi.

And he is not a Bohemian. The tiny flat, in a nondescript pre-fab building of one of Moscow's anonymous residential areas, is meticulous in its appearance, almost Spartan and bordering on the petit bourgeois. The view from the window in the half of the room that he occupies—a thin plywood partition divides it from his mother's half—is depressing: factories, smokestacks, garbage containers, high-tension wires and telephone poles. It is ugly as only Moscow can be ugly, an ugliness that Kharitonov's meticulously executed fantasies with their effusion of flowers, trees and soft, luminescent colors seem deliberately to ignore, to sublimate into the subconscious.

As an unofficial artist Alexander Kharitonov is atypical. He is never seen at foreign receptions. His room is not a vibrant center of discussion or debate. He is rarely seen in the studios, apartments, basements and cubicles of other artists. He doesn't look like a painter and the half room on his side of the plywood wall could be occupied just as well by a bookkeeper as an artist. There is no easel, there are no visible paints, no brushes, none of the pandemonium which one tends to associate with art. Yet in his aloofness and isolation he is typical, for he paints his dreams largely for himself.

In September 1970 the Museum of Fine Arts in Lugano, Switzerland, showed 380 pictures by 58 Moscow underground artists. I know that it was not Kharitonov, but it could easily have been this soft-spoken man who wrote anonymously to the organizers of that exhibit:

"All that you are doing for us is splendid. Only there is no need for politics. Please change the title of the show from 'Forbidden Artists' to something else. Leave politics out of it. Let our pictures speak. Consider our position as that of dogs without rights . . ."

Part Three

The policy of Russia is changeless . . . Its methods, its tactics, its maneuvers may change, but the polar star of its policy—world domination—is a fixed star.

Karl Marx, 1867

This great Eastern Slav empire . . . has entered the last decades of its existence. Just as the adoption of Christianity postponed the fall of the Roman Empire but did not prevent its inevitable end, so Marxist doctrine has delayed the breakup of the Russian Empire—the Third Rome—but it does not possess the power to prevent it.

Andrei Amalrik, 1969

*The unity of the multi-national Soviet
people is as solid as a diamond. As a
diamond sparkles with multi-colored
facets, so does the unity of our people
scintillate with diversity of nations,
each of which lives a rich, full-blooded,
free and happy life.*

Leonid Brezhnev, 1967

*It is not inconceivable that in the next
several decades the nationality problem
will become politically more important
in the Soviet Union than the racial
issue has become in the United States.*

Professor Zbigniew Brzesinski, 1968

5 *The Simmering Melting Pot*

To the men in the Kremlin, the wave of nationalism that has gripped the rest of the world was a predictable, ineluctable phenomenon. According to Soviet ideologists, the emergence of black militants in the United States, Catholic rioters in Ulster, separatists in Quebec, Basque guerrillas in Spain, as well as battles between Flemings and Walloons on the streets of Brussels and civil war in Pakistan, had all more or less been foreseen by Marx and Lenin, who said that the nation and nationalism are the unavoidable products of capitalism.

But the U.S.S.R. is supposed to be different, for under socialism the division of mankind into small states will be abolished and the races and nationalities will be merged. As long ago as 1921 Stalin said "the only regime capable of solving the nationalities question [in Russia], of ensuring the peaceful co-existence and fraternal co-operation of different nations and races is the Soviet regime."

In the U.S.S.R., to judge from the glossy propaganda brochures, cheerful co-existence and co-operation are already a way of life. They depict the world's largest and most heterogeneous state, in which even the money is printed in the fifteen most common languages, as a harmonious melting pot. They portray more than a hundred racial, ethnic and national groups—ranging in population from 120 million Russians to a few hundred Aleuts and Yugakirs—as one big, harmonious family happily and confidently moving toward a bright Communist future. Colorful political pageants feature almond-eyed Tartars and fair-haired Estonians, ruddy-faced Russians and olive-skinned Azerbaidzhanians in a polychromatic palette of national costumes striding enthusiastically toward a better future.

"All our people live in full harmony and confidence," Justas Paleckis, former president of the Supreme Soviet's Chamber of Nationalities, has said. "They help each other like brothers. They are all equal, not only before the law but in fact . . . The implementation of Lenin's nationalities policy has resulted in the establishment of a socialist brotherhood. The U.S.S.R. offers a model for the solution of complex problems of national relationships."

On paper, perhaps. But behind the screen of glowing propaganda the Soviet Union is a simmering melting pot in which nationalism, particularism and racial animosities smolder menacingly. Some observers forecast a "nationalist explosion in the U.S.S.R." by the 1980s.

In the Ukraine scores of intellectuals who pleaded publicly and privately for more cultural and economic autonomy have already been herded off to prisons and labor camps on charges of "anti-Soviet agitation." Dozens of Crimean Tartars who have petitioned, demonstrated and rioted for full rehabilitation and the right to return to the Crimea, from which they were deported during World War II, have been incarcerated. Militant Jews, agitating for more cultural freedom, greater rights and the opportunity to emigrate to Israel, have staged sit-in demonstrations and peppered the authorities with appeals, petitions and protests. Within recent years there have been violent and bloody nationalist demonstrations in Uzbekistan, Kazakhstan, Azerbaidzhan, Armenia and Georgia. Half the political prisoners in Soviet concentration camps are so-called "bourgeois nationalists"—mostly Latvians, Lithuanians, Estonians and Ukrainians.

Undeniably, the problems that confronted Soviet leaders, from Lenin to Brezhnev, have been staggering. Some were a legacy of the tsars, many more have been of their own making. But the

Kremlin has not solved them. It has failed to find the proper synthesis between the Communist theses of internationalism and anti-colonialism and the antitheses of pragmatism and reliable old Russian imperialism.

With the Revolution the Great Russians—now a bare majority of only a little more than 50 per cent of the Soviet Union's total population, and on the verge of becoming a minority themselves—inherited the world's largest multi-national and multi-lingual empire.

An underdeveloped people, the Russians were masters of a huge realm of races, ethnic groups and nationalities some of which were remarkably more advanced, others considerably more backward than their rulers. Forged by tsarist conquest, rampant with the traditional animosities that had turned Georgian against Armenian, Uzbek against Tadzhik, Ukrainian against Russian, Russian against Tartar and all against Jew, it was a domain raging with irredentism in the Ukraine and the Baltics, mired in nomadism and feudalism in Central Asia.

Fifty years have sufficed to eradicate the feudalism and nomadism but not the irredentism and certainly not the animosities. A blond, garrulous Moscow secretary who spent her first vacation in Sukhumi on Georgia's Black Sea coast in the summer of 1968 told me she would never go there again "because all the people are so dark down there."

Once I nearly had an altercation with a drunken Russian who tried to prevent me from taking photographs in the Tashkent bazaar. "When you are in the bazaar," said a friendly, skull-cap-wearing Uzbek farmer who had rushed to my defense, "you are *our* guest. Please feel at home." He then spoke contemptuously of the *Roosky gooligan* (Russian hooligan) who had caused the disturbance, stressing the word *Roosky,* not *gooligan.*

In Samarkand a Tadzhik cab driver, hurtling me through the labyrinthine streets of the old quarter in his mud-splattered taxi, sputtered out an anti-Semitic tirade that ended with the laconic remark: "Hitler's greatest mistake was that he didn't get rid of *all* the Jews."

"Of course no *Georgian* woman would become a maid or a waitress," a Tbilisi girl, otherwise well indoctrinated in such Communist virtues as labor, proletarianism and racial and sexual equality, once told me. "That kind of work is left to Russians, Poles and Muslims.

If they work at all, Georgian women become teachers, scientists and doctors."

Soviet propaganda about tolerance and amity between the races and nationalities is but a thin veneer masking intolerance, mutual contempt, hostility, arrogance, distrust and chauvinism.

Russians disdain the U.S.S.R.'s more backward, and envy its more advanced peoples, and they have an amplitude of pejorative names for the other nationalities: *khokhol* for a Ukrainian, *katso* for the Georgians, *chernozady* for an Azerbaidzhanian, *chuchmek* for an Uzbek, Turkman or Tadzhik. Most Russians are convinced that the other peoples of the Soviet Union live better and work less than they do: the Georgian farmers who fly their tomatoes and peaches to Russian markets where they sell at outrageously inflated prices; the Estonians who enjoy a standard of living that can be measured by Western criteria; the Armenians who are, by reputation, the U.S.S.R.'s wiliest *bizinesmenki;* the Ukrainians who are accused of grabbing too much political power in Moscow; or the Central Asians who are reputed to be getting the largest share of investment funds.

"We all hate the Kazakhs and they all hate us," a young Russian engineer in Alma-Ata said curtly. "Listen, these *zholtashi* [literally, yellow men] never had it so good."

"Intermarriage?" countered a Russian worker after many glassfuls of vodka in an Alma-Ata restaurant. "With one of them? Don't be ridiculous."

"Look at these Uzbek *militsionery,*" said a Russian in Samarkand, watching a native policeman ticket a Russian woman for jaywalking. "They're greasy, dirty like swine. But stick a pencil and a ticket book in their hands and they think they're really somebody."

"When you go to the Baltic republics," a middle-aged Muscovite advised candidly, "don't speak Russian in public. I know of people who were beaten up in Tallin because they spoke Russian. They hate us there."

Once in a while a Soviet publication will admit that "the national problem is among the most complicated and politically touchy of Soviet life." But the general practice and official policy is to ignore it, to accuse those who raise it as "anti-Soviet agitators" or agents of foreign propaganda.

"It is the biggest problem we face," a Moscow journalist and close acquaintance once confided to me. "No one likes the Russians and the Russians don't like any of the other people. And they all hate each other. But the government and party do nothing but paint a portrait of perfect harmony. How are you going to solve a problem if you don't even admit that it exists?"

Escapism, ambiguity and political ambivalence have characterized Soviet nationalities policy from its post-revolutionary beginnings. And to this day Soviet scholars cannot even agree on a common definition for the concepts "nation" and "nationality."

Ever since Bolshevik moral preachings about the evils of tsarist imperialism collided with the need to consolidate the empire the tsars had amassed, Moscow has been treading the high wire between theory and practice, as a consequence of which history has been rewritten and policy altered countless times.

Caught between recurrent and sometimes concurrent assimilation and diversification drives, the entire nationalities policy seems predicated on antithetic premises. On the one hand, nationalism is condemned as a bourgeois cancer, internationalism lauded as a Communist blessing. On the other hand, the entire state structure of fifteen nominally independent republics, twenty autonomous republics and eighteen autonomous regions, each with its own language, is based on the idea of multi-nationalism.

The pattern of contradictions was set decades ago by Stalin when he was Lenin's chief expert on the nationalities question. "Of course," he said, "the border regions of Russia, the nations and tribes which inhabit these regions, possess the inalienable right to secede from Russia. But the demand for secession at the present stage of the Revolution is a profoundly counterrevolutionary one."

The same view is promulgated today, only less menacingly.

"Byelorussia cannot do without the U.S.S.R.," Sergei Pritytsky, chairman of the Byelorussian Supreme Soviet's presidium, said on the fiftieth anniversary of that republic's revolution in 1969. "The Byelorussians were able to preserve themselves as a nation and nationality only through their alliance with the Great Russian people and other peoples of the U.S.S.R. Of course, each republic has the right to leave the union, but no republic has ever exercised that right. I do not believe that any of them ever will, for that would be contrary to its national interests. The very idea of such a step seems strange to us."

Lenin considered the "national problem" a transitory one. But the transition period is turning into a permanent state of affairs. In fact, national feeling is not only the most entrenched of pre-Communist loyalties to uproot, it is becoming stronger.

Ironically, it was the Bolshevik Revolution itself that unleashed national feelings that previously had been largely latent or suppressed under imperial rule. For when Lenin seized power, the Bolsheviks magnanimously declared the rights of all minorities to self-determination and overtly displayed great tolerance. To the Ukrainians they gave back the national banners and relics which had been held in St. Petersburg. To the Muslims they returned the sacred Koran of Osman which the tsars had locked up in the Imperial State Library. In Kazan the Tartars were encouraged to restore the symbol of the crescent atop the Sumbeki Tower in the city's ancient kremlin.

It was a policy of many promises, made largely to solicit the support of the other nationalities in the Civil War. Although the Communists came to power on a platform of renouncing tsarist claims to the Empire, by the end of World War II Moscow had re-established its suzerainty over nearly all the territory controlled by the tsars. The only notable exceptions: Finland and those parts of Poland that had not been ceded to Stalin in the Molotov-Ribbentrop pact of 1939.

Today, following two recent mysterious fires in the Ukrainian National Library in Kiev, possibly set by the KGB, countless Ukrainian cultural relics and documents are lost forever. The Muslims still have their Koran but their religion is suppressed. And the crescent has long since disappeared again from the Sumbeki Tower in Kazan.

It was also a policy of experimentation in autonomy, semi-autonomy, federation, confederation and centralization which in fifty years has resulted in the renaming of regions, areas and republics, the redrawing of borders and the reconstitution of statutes with dizzying frequency and arbitrariness. There is no guarantee that the present structure of the U.S.S.R. is permanent.

During five decades of Soviet rule Kremlin nationalities policy has oscillated wildly with changing foreign and domestic requirements from what Stalin once called indigenization to intense Russification. Stalin could be heard one day warning that the Great Russians were in danger of "inequality vis-à-vis the other nationalities," on another day warning against Great Russian chauvinism.

Partly to facilitate indigenization, a policy designed to build up local cadres, the Russians began to reconstruct the native Central

Asian languages by introducing the Latin alphabet for all those which had previously used Arabic script. The purpose was twofold: to aid the drive against illiteracy and to combat the influence of Islam. Latin was also prescribed for some of the primitive peoples of northern Russia and Siberia. In fact, Latin was hailed as the alphabet of the world Communist society and attempts to propagate Cyrillic were branded as counterrevolutionary. One scholar who fought to preserve the Cyrillic alphabet in Ossetia, where it had long been in use, was accused of "great power chauvinism" and of being a class enemy.

Suddenly, in 1938, the policy was reversed, along with a decree making Russian a compulsory language in all non-Russian schools. The Cyrillic alphabet was introduced as mandatory for all the nationalities previously affected by Latinization. Even Moldavian, a Romance language, was adapted to the Cyrillic alphabet when Bessarabia was absorbed into the Soviet Union in 1940.

The regime's propagandists were quick to praise the sudden change as a "boon to the development of the languages." Some years ago the monthly journal *Voprosy Istorii* (Problems of History) said: "To have adopted the Russian script in the first years of the Soviet regime might have been interpreted as a relapse into the old Russifying policy of the tsars. When the change to Cyrillic was finally made it did not signify any kind of subordination to Russian culture but . . . represented an act of friendship toward the Russian people and a manifestation of the international unity of the Soviet peoples."

Other rapid shifts have resulted from the fifty-year-old debate over whether the national cultures should be allowed to "flower" or undergo *"rapprochement."* This has led alternately to the propagation of two different lines. One is the "Russian elder brother" concept, which portrays the Great Russians as helping their Ukrainian, Uzbek, Kazakh "little brothers" achieve their "social and national liberation." The other focuses on the "rediscovery" of Central Asian culture.

The histories of the non-Russian peoples have been interpreted and reinterpreted to suit whatever happened to be the party line in Moscow or the changing needs of Soviet policy. Predicting the past, so to speak, of the non-Russian peoples could drive an honest historian insane.

The question most frequently subjected to review concerned the significance of tsarist annexation of non-Russian territory and the character of pre-revolutionary national movements against Russian rule. During the initial period of Soviet power, annexation was considered to have been an "absolute evil" and the risings of subjugated people were interpreted as progressive national liberation movements, even revolutionary in character. In the 1930s the "lesser evil" formula was discovered. It held that while annexation had undoubtedly been evil, considering that it had taken place under the tsars, it was a lesser evil than absorption by some other imperialist power would have been. Ultimately, in the 1940s, during the era of glorification of everything Russian, the "lesser evil" theory succumbed to the doctrine of "absolute good." The facts of tsarist colonial oppression were effaced and only the beneficial aspects of annexation, such as exposure to the "advanced culture of the Russian people," were emphasized.

This interpretation was once more reversed at the XXth Party Congress in 1956. Since Khrushchev's fall, the movement has been back to the concept of "absolute good."

The dilemma these interpretative vicissitudes posed for historians was graphically presented in Edward Radzinsky's popular and controversial play *We Are Making a Move* which had its premiere at the Komsomol Theater in Moscow in 1966.

"I began as a historian," says one of the characters, "and my first work was about Shamil [a nineteenth-century religious and political leader of the North Caucasus Muslim people]. Shamil as the leader of a national liberation movement. But opinions changed and at the end of the 1930s Shamil began to be considered an agent of imperialism. I confessed my mistake. Then, during the war, he again became the leader of a national liberation movement. I then confessed that I had made a mistake in confessing my mistake. Later, in 1949, Shamil was again considered an agent of imperialism, and I confessed that I had made a mistake. I had been mistaken so often that it seemed to me, at one point, that I was a mistake myself."

Moscow has encouraged large-scale immigration of Russians into the Ukraine and of Russians and Ukrainians into the other republics so that the indigenous population's share of the total has dwindled steadily. Uzbeks, Latvians, Georgians, Moldavians account for only two thirds of the population of Uzbekistan, Latvia, Georgia and Moldavia; the Tadzhiks account for only 55 per cent of Tadzhikistan, the Kazakhs a mere 32.4 per cent of Kazakhstan. Even the Ukrainians make up only three fourths of the Ukraine's population.

One Lithuanian commented plaintively that the only town in his republic worth living in these days is Kaunas. "It has no Russians, no Poles, no Jews. Just us." Until the 1970 census Lithuanians were a minority of 40 per cent even in their own capital—Vilnius.

In Latvia I heard the apocryphal story of two Russians sipping tea in Riga's Luna Cafe. One said to the other: "It's time to pay and leave." His friend, perplexed because they had just arrived, asked why. "Too many Latvians around."

The Russians are ubiquitous. They outnumber the Kazakhs in Kazakhstan's universities and colleges. In Uzbekistan there are almost as many Russian specialists with a higher education as there are Uzbeks, in Moldavia of 113,000 specialists and technicians working in the economy, only 35,000 are Moldavians.

Nominally indigenes are responsible for their own destinies and their republics are sovereign. In practice it looks quite different. Although Communist Party chiefs and government premiers in the fifteen republics are usually indigenous they are often merely figureheads. Real power is vested in Slav politicians who, as second secretaries or vice-premiers, control the *nomenklatura,* the cadres and the entire party and government apparat. They are *apparatchiki* who are at the Kremlin's beck and call. In Kazakhstan in February 1971, the second secretary of the Kazakh Communist Party Central Committee was unceremoniously removed and replaced by another man who at the time of his appointment was not even a member of the Central Committee of which he is now second secretary.

Georgians delight in telling the story of one of their most popular and respected writers, Konstantin Simonovich Gamsakhurdiya, who some years ago, wearing national costume, rode a white horse up to the steps of Tbilisi's Central Committee building, knocked on one of the windows with his riding whip and asked to see the second secretary of the Georgian CC, a Russian. The Russian appeared, and Gamsakhurdiya greeted him politely—in Georgian. The Russian smiled, waved his hand and said that, unfortunately, he did not understand Georgian. At this Gamsakhurdiya shouted—again in Georgian: "How can you rule Georgia if you cannot even say 'good morning' in our language? We don't need people like you. Get out of our country at once." Then he galloped away.

Nominally the fifteen union republics are autonomous and have the right to secede. But the original law, that any modification, restriction or abrogation of this right requires the consent of all the republics, has quietly disappeared from the books. Each of the republics has a foreign minister. Stalin tried to procure all of them, plus the U.S.S.R. itself, a seat in the United Nations and finally compromised on membership for only two: the Ukraine and Byelorussia. But their memberships in the UN are as insignificant as their foreign ministries are ceremonial sinecures for loyal party workers. Balzhan Bultrikova, Kazakhstan's foreign minister, was genuinely baffled and embarrassed when a group of Western newsmen once asked her what her duties were.

Some industrial responsibilities have been transferred to republican supervision but heavy industry remains the purview of Moscow. On the whole, republican officials and institutions remain largely conveyor belts for economic directives from the center.

The absence of economic—not political—autonomy is the major source of discontent, particularly in those republics, such as the Ukraine and the Baltics, where the feeling is widespread, as one young Kiev engineer told me, that "we are the draft horse pulling the whole cumbersome Soviet cart." An Estonian put it even more pithily. "The reason we live so much better than the people in the other republics is because we do more with what we have. But we'd be nowhere if we really followed the instructions from Moscow. We circumvent them."

*   *   *

With a population of 47 million and a territory of 223,000 square miles, the Ukrainian Soviet Socialist Republic ranks as the sixth largest country of Europe.

By any yardstick it is one of the world's industrial powers, producing ocean-going vessels, transport planes, automobiles, synthetic diamonds and machine tools, and from 7 to 10 per cent of the whole world's steel, cast iron, coal and tractors. Its reputation as one of the great granaries of Europe and Asia is unsurpassed. It is rich to the point of abundance in iron, coal, manganese and titanium. In 1969 geologists discovered gold deposits in the Ukraine's Ivano-Frankovsk areas, and there is oil.

Stretching from the forest-grown banks of the turbulent river Tissa in the west to the industrialized basin of the Donets in the east, from the Pripet Marshes in the north to the sun-flooded shores of the Black Sea in the south, the Ukraine is as beautiful and variegated in landscape and climate as France.

Moreover, so says an official Intourist brochure: "The Ukraine is completely sovereign and independent."

"Yes," said a disenchanted Ukrainian intellectual, "we now live in a proclaimed sovereign republic, just as we have proclaimed freedom and proclaimed socialist justice."

In fact, the Ukraine, its membership in the United Nations, its diplomatic mission in New York and its foreign minister notwithstanding, is about as sovereign as a *département* of France. And while the Soviet constitution gives the Ukraine the right to secede, Ukrainian nationalist intellectuals who dared to propose such a step have been herded off to prison camps in droves.

Between the propagandistic promise of Ukrainian sovereignty and the fact of Russian suzerainty there is a credibility gap wider than the expanses of Siberia. In it has grown the fruit of a dissident nationalism unmatched by any in the U.S.S.R. In fact, on the day when Moscow must face the demand for independence from the people it rules, the first confrontation is most likely to take place in the Ukraine.

That would be one of the great ironies of history, for the Ukraine is the real cradle of Russian civilization. Even the name—*ukraina,* which means literally "at the border" or border region—is a relatively recent concept, first adopted by the romantic intellectual movement of the early nineteenth century. Until then it was known simply as "Little Russia" and its inhabitants as Little Russians in contrast to the White Russians of the north and the Great Russians who inhabited the vast expanses to the east.

And paradoxically, Kiev, with the golden onion domes of its monasteries and churches, was not only the font of Russian civilization but over the centuries has been a historical mirror of the Ukraine's fortunes and misfortunes.

The city can trace its existence from the eighth century. And it was there in 988 that St. Vladimir, the princely ruler of the East Slavs and the Kiev Rus, laid the foundations of the Russian Empire.

Vladimir and his son Yaroslav made Kiev into one of the great states and powers of the Middle Ages. But its glory was short-lived. Sacked by the Tartars in 1240, occupied by the Lithuanians in 1362, taken by the Poles in 1569, it returned to the fold of the Russian Empire in the seventeenth and by the end of the eighteenth century was little more than a provincial administrative center. From 1917 to 1919 it changed hands several times, was occupied part of the time by the Germans and served as the capital of various transitory Ukrainian nationalist governments. In 1920 it was taken briefly by the Poles. From 1941 to 1943 it was occupied once more by the Germans.

With a checkerboard history like that, it is no wonder that Ukrainian intellectuals face a crisis of identity.

The Ukrainians are an East Slav people, descended from the tribes which inhabited the southern part of Kievan Russia. After the Mongol conquest they moved west into Galicia and Volhynia. When the Tartar danger receded they spread eastward again, gradually colonizing the whole of the present Ukraine.

Distinctive features of the Ukrainian language can be identified in written sources dating to the Kievan period, but it was not really until the fourteenth and fifteenth centuries, under Lithuanian and Polish domination, that the Ukrainians began to develop a separate identity and a degree of national consciousness. That was under the aegis of the Zaporozhe Cossacks, whose free spirit, innate sense of independence, rudimentary form of direct democracy and strong sense of religious and ethnic unity influence Ukrainian thought and attitudes to this day.

The Zaporozhians' military headquarters, the Sich, was the provenance of Ukrainian nationhood. Made famous in song and legend, especially in Nikolai Gogol's sword-and-blood epic *Taras Bulba,* it was located on Khoritsa Island in the big Dnieper bend in what is now the Ukraine's Zaporozhe *oblast* (province), one of the republic's most important industrial regions. Fierce warriors and renowned as the fastest swords in Eastern Europe, welded by a strong sense of comradeship, they were equals and freemen, not serfs. Linked by a legendary capacity for *khorilka,* a fiery, still-popular Ukrainian vodka, and an almost messianic faith in Orthodox Christianity, the Zaporozhe Cossacks were the rallying force of Ukrainian struggle against national, social and religious oppression. Their history is that of one long battle against one form of domination or another, including Russian.

Although they formally recognized the suzerainty of the Polish kings, the Cossacks, for all practical purposes, had complete political independence until the sixteenth century, when the Polish government attempted to reinforce its control over the Ukraine and the Zaporozhian Sich. Coupled in 1596 with Polish persecution of the Ukrainian Orthodox Church and the rise in the Western Ukraine of the Uniate Church, this policy touched off repeated rebellions by the staunchly orthodox Zaporozhians. Finally, in 1648, led by their hetman, Bogdan Chmielnicki, they began a series of campaigns that eventually freed the Ukraine from Polish rule and brought a brief four-year period of national independence.

Polish military pressure on the Cossacks became so great, however, that Chmielnicki entered a protective agreement with Moscow which, while recognizing Muscovite suzerainty, was to leave the Ukraine largely autonomous and independent. But the Russians soon began encroaching on Ukrainian rights and four years later the Ukraine attempted to throw off Russian protection to become an equal partner with Poland and Lithuania in the Polish kingdoms. The result was a war between Poland and Russia which left the Ukraine partitioned in 1667.

Thirty-eight years later the Zaporozhian hetman Ivan Stepanovich Mazepa tried to free the Ukraine once more from Russian domination by collaborating with both Poland and Sweden. In 1708 during the so-called Northern War, Mazepa joined Charles XII of Sweden in an effort to invade Russia from the south through the Ukraine. Both were completely defeated by Peter the Great in the Battle of Poltava in 1709.

To Ukrainian nationalists Mazepa is still a hero. The Russians, understandably, consider him a blackguard. "Mazepa, the Ukrainian traitor," is how a Russian guide, showing me around the museum and the battlefield at Poltava, referred to him. "The Ukrainians," she insisted when I questioned her pejoration, "always wanted to be part of Russia."

On the contrary. From Peter's time to the present, Ukrainian history has been one of steadily diminishing political autonomy punctuated by brief but persistent agitation for Ukrainian independence and the union of all Ukrainian lands. The Ukraine came closest to realizing that hope after the Russian February Revolution in 1917 when the provisional government granted the Ukraine autonomy and recognized the authority of the Ukrainian central *rada* (council). The *rada,* headed by Mikhail Hrushevsky as its president, proclaimed a sovereign Ukrainian Republic after the Bolsheviks seized power in October. As an experiment in independent nationhood it was short-lived. The Ukraine became a pawn in the multi-cornered battles between Germans, tsarist Whites, Bolshevik Reds and the newly independent Poles. In 1920 Soviet power was finally established in the Ukraine.

The initial Soviet policy called for "Ukrainization." A campaign that lasted through the 1920s, it roused the ire of Russians and Jews living in the Ukraine.

In the 1930s Stalin tergiversated and introduced the policy of Russification, which is at the root of the malcontent and the currents of nationalism sweeping the Ukraine today.

Khrushchev began his term as first secretary of the Ukrainian CP in 1938 by decreeing that Russian be taught throughout the Ukrainian school system. All citizens, including those in rural areas, were to be able to converse fluently in simple Russian and read and write the language. Increasingly Russian was depicted as superior to Ukrainian, not only as "the language which Lenin used," and the language common to the whole Soviet Union, but as the bearer of an advanced, revolutionary, proletarian culture.

The problems were aggravated by the advent of World War II, not only because Stalin felt that only the Russian people were wholly committed to the defense of the U.S.S.R., but by the incorporation into the Ukraine of Ukrainian territories that had previously belonged to Poland, Czechoslovakia and Romania. The peoples in these territories were militantly nationalist and unwilling to accept Soviet rule.

Ironically this amalgamation of "lost" Ukrainian territories—southern Bessarabia and northern Bukovina, eastern Galicia and the Carpatho-Ukraine—made the Ukraine the one non-Russian Soviet republic which is clearly the most viable and most capable of standing on its own feet. And the Ukrainians know it.

Some, especially in the Western Ukraine, were determined to force independence at any cost, including collaboration with the Germans. In fact, nationalist guerrilla bands were operating in the Ukraine, primarily in the west, as recently as 1952. Eventually they melted into the woods or were destroyed or resettled by Russian forces. But their legacy continues.

I was reminded of them, not in the Ukraine but on a park bench in Tashkent, Uzbekistan.

"Do you know who Stepan Bandera was?" asked the intense and excited young Ukrainian who had struck up a conversation. The mention of this extremist Ukrainian national leader who was assassinated by Soviet KGB agent Bogdan Stashinsky in Munich in

October 1959 is enough to demand the utmost caution anywhere in the U.S.S.R.

"Yes, I've heard of him," I replied.

"Well," he announced in a defiant, clearly audible whisper, "I'm a Banderist. In the Ukraine we are all Banderists. We refuse to be a province of Russia."

It was an extremist view, as I discovered later on visits to the Ukraine itself, though it demonstrated that Soviet officials are far from finding a solution to the Ukrainian problem.

The post-Stalin formula has been a partial retreat from Russification to an emphasis of the role the Ukrainians might play as the Russian people's "chief partners." It is an unacceptable formula to Ukrainians because the partnership is not wholly equal. The Russians are still considered the *"principal* bearers of the great revolutionary ideas of freedom and progress."

Even Soviet officials admit that "separatism remains a factor" in the Ukraine. "But it is not the Bandera organization people look to," I was told in Lvov. "Those types discredited themselves under the Nazis. You know, 150,000 people in this city were killed, 200,000 deported. That is hard to forget."

What is it then that Ukrainians are looking for?

"More sovereignty, more autonomy within the union," a young Kievite confided. "In 1939 the people in the Western Ukraine were all for union with the U.S.S.R. and the rest of the Ukraine. Now they feel it was a mistake. But all Ukrainians know that we have played history's whipping horse too often, that as an independent state we would probably end up playing it again."

"We Ukrainians are like the Poles: very nationalistic, very proud," a student in Kharkov explained. "But we are not militantly nationalistic or anti-Soviet. What we really want is more economic sovereignty, more independence to make local decisions. We're tired of having Moscow decide every little question for us and tired of economic subordination."

Though it could turn into something far more combustible tomorrow, particularly if Moscow does not show more circumspection, the nationalism rampant in the Ukraine today is largely of an economic and cultural orientation. The objection is to the de-Ukrainization of the urban population through the steady infusion of Russians; the systematic reduction of the teaching of Ukrainian in urban schools; the dearth of Ukrainian schoolbooks and university texts and Ukrainian publications; the conduct of almost all official matter in Russian; the seemingly deliberate neglect or distortion of Ukrainian history and culture; and the emasculation of the Ukrainian party and government.

Ostensibly, Moscow supports, even encourages the expression of national identity through the cultivation of customs and mores. Folk song and dance groups are lauded in the Soviet press. Intourist brochures and propaganda magazines effuse slick color photographs and saccharine prose about the Ukraine's customs.

But when Ukrainians express their culture spontaneously without the advance approval of Intourist, the Komsomol or the Ministry of Culture, it is with a conspiratorial air. On Kiev's wide, tree-lined Khreshchatchik Boulevard, not far from the music conservatory, one summer evening, a circle suddenly formed and twenty young people began singing Ukrainian folk songs. Some Russians approached, listened a moment, then said with audible contempt:

"Oh, Ukrainian. Well, I don't understand it anyway."

After a half hour the impromptu session broke up.

"What were they singing?" I asked a bystander.

"Oh, just some Ukrainian songs," he said, "just Ukrainian songs."

"Do they do that often?" I asked.

"No, not often," he replied sadly and, looking furtively at a man watching us, walked away.

In the economic sphere the Ukrainians object to the imbalanced structure of their republic, to the fact that they were forced to Russify, to build up heavy industry at the expense of more profitable and more important light and medium branches. "The underdevelopment of certain branches of industry," according to *Ekonomika Radyanskoi Ukrainy,* the republic's chief economic journal, forces the Ukraine to import a "vast array of goods" which it could be producing "better and cheaper" on its own.

"What infuriates us," confided my Kiev acquaintance, "is economic and cultural Russification, having to come down, so to speak, to the Russians' levels."

A remark as innocent as that could be interpreted today as an expression of "bourgeois nationalism" and "anti-Soviet," to judge from the flimsy evidence that has been raised against Ukrainians whose trials are reported in the famous *Chornovil Papers.*

Vyacheslav Chornovil, thirty-three, is a graduate of the University of Kiev's journalism department. He worked as an editor and reporter for the Lvov television studios and on the editorial staff of several publications. In the fall of 1965 he was assigned to cover the trials of a number of Ukrainian dissident intellectuals. For nearly two years these trials and others—in Kiev, Kharkov, Lvov, Ivano-Frankovsk—involving scores of Ukrainian nationalist dissenters, were kept a secret: until 1967, when a few pages at a time, Chornovil's *samizdat* report on them reached the West. Chornovil himself was arrested in November 1967 and sentenced to eighteen months in a labor camp for anti-Soviet slander and refusing to appear as a witness in what he considered an illegally conducted trial of a Ukrainian dissenter.

Said Chornovil:

"According to the constitution of the U.S.S.R., anyone who criticizes the current nationalities policy or its departure from Leninist norms has every right to do so. But according to the criminal code of the Ukraine, the same individual can be deported to a labor colony because his criticism is considered 'anti-Soviet propaganda.'"

Chornovil's documents are more than a scathing condemnation of totalitarianism and the arbitrary suppression of even the slightest signs of national awakening. They testify to the intellectual affinity between the Democratic Movement of Russia and the nationalist movement in other republics. Moreover they are a posthumous indictment of Stalinist cultural policies. For nowhere else in the Soviet Union did Stalinism wreak as much devastation in the arts and sciences as in the Ukraine.

In Russia the intelligentsia emerged after the death of Stalin, if not intact, then at least viable and strong enough to express a measure of indignation and dissent. In the Ukraine, however, the intellectuals, haunted by the stigma of nationalism, were in a state of spiritual paralysis. Not until the 1960s was there an intellectual rebirth through the so-called *shestydesyatniki* group, "the men of the sixties." Among them were writers and poets such as Ivan Drach, Mykola Vinhranovskyy, Vitaly Korotych, Robert Tretyakov, Lina Kostenko and the two literary critics Ivan Dzyuba and Ivan Svitlychnyy.

These writers, poets and critics have been involved, directly or indirectly, with the underground pleas for greater Ukrainian autonomy which resulted in three main waves of arrests and trials—in 1961, again in 1965–66 and, possibly, though little is known about it, in 1968.

In 1961 the KGB uncovered allegedly secret organizations dedicated to the overthrow of Soviet power. A typical example was the Ukrainian Union of Workers and Peasants, seven members of which were tried and sentenced in Lvov in May 1961. They were charged, among other things, with advocating secession from the Soviet Union. The group appears to have been neither anti-Marxist nor anti-Leninist, but merely defended the right of self-determination.

One of the accused, Stepan Virun, had equated the regime's refusal to grant this right with "racism." Another member, Lev Lukyanenko, criticized past and present Soviet policies in the Ukraine as a complete departure from Lenin's views on the nationalities question. A third member, Ivan Kandyba, charged that "the Ukraine has become an appendix of Russia with two thirds of her natural resources being transported beyond her boundaries."

In 1965 and 1966 about a hundred persons, mainly young intellectuals, were arrested. Among them was Valentin Moroz, a Ukrainian historian, who was sentenced to a five-year labor camp term from which he was released in January 1970. Eleven months later, in November, he was tried and convicted again, receiving a sentence of nine years. Besides Moroz, some twenty or thirty were eventually tried in 1966 and 1967 on charges of "disseminating anti-Soviet propaganda" and "anti-Soviet agitation." Their terms ranged from six months to six years. Most of them were deported to labor camps near Potma in the Mordvinian autonomous republic.

This prompted Moroz to comment acidly:

"The Ukraine, according to its constitution, is a sovereign state and a member of the UN. Yet her courts sentence thousands of Ukrainian citizens and . . . send them abroad [to other Soviet republics]. It is an unusual precedent—a state sending its prisoners abroad. Is it possible that the Ukraine, like Monaco, lacks space for prison camps? Room has been found for 7 million Russian settlers, yet there is not enough room for Ukrainian political prisoners in their native land."

This was the group about which Chornovil reported. It did not seem to be particularly organized or even self-conscious as an intellectual movement. Their crimes included possession of pre-revolutionary Ukrainian history books or copies of speeches by Pope Paul VI and President Eisenhower. Few had written anything to attract more than routine attention. Their protests and the reasons for their arrest and trial run the spectrum of dissent.

Mykhaylo Horyn, a research worker in the Lvov Institute of Labor Psychology, was sentenced to six years because he had deplored the absence of educational and cultural facilities for millions of Ukrainians living in the Russian Federation.

Opanas Zalyvakha, a painter from Ivano-Frankovsk, received a five-year term for advocating a "national basis" for art. He had once said publicly: "We believe that love of one's country is not a crime but a citizen's sacred duty."

Ivan Dzyuba, the critic, also arrested in 1966 but released again presumably because of his serious tuberculosis, had argued in one treatise that the Soviet regime's Russification policy was responsible for discontent in the Ukraine. He likened the present oppressive policies to a direct continuation of tsarist traditions.

Another defendant, a teacher, got five years for possessing "anti-Soviet documents" which turned out to be a pre-revolutionary history of the Ukraine and a hundred-year-old poem by Taras Shevchenko.

The Ukrainian dissent movement, with its strong nationalist overtones, is growing. Periodically *samizdat* publication turns up petitions from Ukrainian mothers who object to the neglect of the Ukrainian language in kindergartens and by workers who say they are afraid to speak Ukrainian in their factories. One petition, signed by 139 Kievites, among them 14 prominent writers, a leading film director and 20 physicists and mathematicians, warned that "in the Ukraine, where violations of democracy have been compounded by malpractices in the national question, the symptoms of Stalinism reveal themselves even more clearly and brutally [than in Moscow]."

From Dnepropetrovsk, where Brezhnev made his start—but as a Russian, not a Ukrainian—have come reports of attempts by KGB agents and local officials to level the hill-like graves of Cossacks, to plunder old castles and tear down churches, all under the guise of combating "religious superstition and bourgeois nationalism."

But as Chornovil said shortly before he himself was imprisoned:

"The people who are being tried as bourgeois nationalists do not even remember the bourgeoisie. They belong to a generation which grew up under Soviet government and which was educated in Soviet schools and in the Komsomol . . . No one has thought of looking for a deeper cause [of their unrest] than the irksome nonsense about the effect of bourgeois ideology and bourgeois nationalism."

Svyatoslav Karavansky, a fifty-year-old Ukrainian translator of Byron, Shakespeare and Kipling, now serving a term in one of the Mordvinian camps, seems to have discovered the cause. He was imprisoned primarily for writing a letter to Poland's former Communist Party chief Wladyslaw Gomulka. In it he called for a world Communist conference dealing with the nationalities question and said: "The causes for so-called Ukrainian nationalism are to be found in the uninterrupted application of an anti-Leninist nationalities policy over the past thirty years: Russification of the population, the mass deportation of Ukrainians to Siberia, Kazakhstan and other far-removed regions, and the settlement of Ukrainian cities with non-Ukrainian, usually Russian, people."

* * *

Why is the Kura River, which runs through Tbilisi, capital of the Georgian Soviet Socialist Republic, so dirty?

"Because," explained our guide, "it comes from Turkey."

Why are so few icons of value left in Tbilisi's many churches?

"Because," said the guide, "they were stolen by the Persians and the Turks."

A huge statue of Mother Georgia now stands on Mount Mtatsminda, looming over Tbilisi. In one hand she holds a bowl, in the other a sword.

"Wine is in the bowl for friends," explained the guide. "The sword is for foes."

In the two thousand years of its existence, fifteen hundred of them as a Christian kingdom, Georgia seems to have had more foes than friends. Tbilisi, now a sprawling metropolis of 900,000, has been invaded and destroyed forty times—an average of once every half century. But the Georgians always prevailed. Thus it is not surprising that they greet each other not by saying "hello" or "good day," but with a lusty *gamarjveba,* which means "victory."

With a population of only 4.7 million and a territory of about 57,000 square miles, Georgia is one of the smaller Soviet republics. But to hear Georgians talk, it is the most important.

The Georgians have been called the Texans of the Soviet Union. They talk a bit bigger, act a bit bolder and seem a bit wealthier than their Russian comrades. They are also noted as one of the most enterprising of the peoples under Communism's theoretically equalizing way. Reportedly they have the highest per capita ownership of automobiles, television sets, refrigerators, and other prime consumer goods in the U.S.S.R. But the statistics are Georgian.

Like Texans about other Texans, Georgians will not knock a Georgian. Stalin, his crimes notwithstanding, remains a hero to this rugged, wine-drinking and independent-minded mountain people.

Shoeshine parlors, fruit and vegetable stands and, no doubt, hundreds of private homes still display his portrait.

Like most of the Soviet republics, Georgia has been under Russian protection or rule since the eighteenth century. It was not until the Bolshevik Revolution that it enjoyed a brief period of independence. Its government was Menshevik. At first fully autonomous, then suddenly under British occupation and mostly at war with Armenia and Azerbaidzhan, Georgia fell to the Ninth Red Army in 1921 and was transformed into a Soviet republic. The invasion took the lives of four thousand young Georgian soldiers.

On the whole Georgians seem to have contented themselves with that arrangement. Under it they certainly flourished. The fact that it was a local boy giving the orders in the Moscow Kremlin may have been a contributing factor. The question of what might have been had things turned out differently in 1921 is rarely raised, at least in public.

Their nationalism manifests itself largely in braggadocio, unbridled condemnation of de-Stalinization and incredible vehemence toward the neighboring Armenians.

The Georgians' contempt for the Armenians is legendary and few Georgians take pains to disguise it. Especially not the guide who showed me through the Stalin museum in Gori, the dictator's birthplace. Stopping in front of a photograph that showed Stalin together with Anastas Mikoyan, I remarked that Mikoyan had been lucky to survive the purges which took the lives of Stalin's closest associates. "Well, what do you expect?" the guide snapped back. "He's an Armenian. They always manage to wiggle their way through to success."

*   *   *

The Armenians are in many ways the most nationalistic of the large Soviet minorities. Oddly, they are also the happiest under Soviet rule because it has, for the first time, created *an* Armenia.

Of course, this Armenia ought to be larger, to listen to the people in Yerevan, its capital, a city which boasts that it is as old as Babylon. Parts of Armenia, they claim, are in the neighboring Soviet republics of Azerbaidzhan and Georgia, some of it in Iran. Another part, the most important, is in Turkey. There is Mount Ararat, the symbol of Armenian nationalism. Visible on a clear day from Yerevan, Armenians refer to the mountain as "Our Father who art in prison."

Compared to many other minorities in the U.S.S.R., the Armenians, who constitute 86 per cent of the republic's population, have fared surprisingly well. They have resisted assimilation successfully and managed to keep their identity as well as indigenous control over the republic.

Before the rise of nineteenth-century nationalism, Armenians tended to regard themselves as belonging more to a particular locality than to a "nation." Their most important bond after 2500 years of subjugation: they were Christians in a sea of Moslems and almost all belonged to the Armenian Church, founded in the fourth century. In 1828 Russian armies defeated the Persians and annexed eastern Armenia. Many Armenians regarded the Christian Russians as deliverers. In a way they were. When Russia adopted Christianity from Byzantium in 988, the emperor on the throne in Constantinople was an Armenian: Basil I.

For a brief, unhappy period after the Bolshevik Revolution, a coalition of Armenian nationalist parties declared the independence of eastern Armenia and proclaimed a republic. By November 1920 Kemal Ataturk had defeated and conquered it. The Turkish occupation, however, was shorter-lived than the independent republic. The Red Army swooped in and forced the Turks back almost to the 1914 Russo-Turkish frontier, leaving the new Armenian Soviet Socialist Republic in its wake.

As an independent state, Armenian Deputy Premier Larisa Stepanyan told a Western correspondent, "we would fall under Turkish rule again. We cannot live without the Soviet Union. What Armenia has today is due to the help of the Russian people. We were the victims of [Turkish] genocide and the Russians came and stood us on our feet."

Such arguments can frequently be heard from republican party and government officials but in the case of an Armenian it sounds credible. The memory of Turkish massacres in 1915, which took the lives of 1.5 million Armenians, is vivid.

Though not an independent state, Soviet Armenia today can well be described as another Israel. Moscow has built up the image of the tiny republic as the homeland of all Armenians and since 1920 has lured some 300,000 of them from France, Spain, Lebanon, Egypt, Syria, Latin America and even the United States. An estimated 1.5 million Armenians are dispersed around the globe.

Today the Armenian S.S.R. is a distinctly Armenian political unit located on at least a major portion of ancestral Armenian territory. It is the portion they do not have that is the focus of Armenian nationalism today and the source of conflict between Yerevan and Moscow.

More than 30 per cent of all the world's Armenians live in neighboring Georgia and Azerbaidzhan. According to Yerevan, they not only desire to be a part of the Armenian S.S.R. but live on territory that is rightfully Armenian and should be ceded by the other republics. The far more serious territorial claim is on western Armenia, which is located in Turkey, a country with which the U.S.S.R. has been trying to improve relations.

In 1965 and again in 1966 thousands of young Armenians demonstrated on the streets of Yerevan to commemorate the anniversaries of the Turkish massacre in 1915. Dozens of youths were arrested following the second demonstration, which had been prohibited by local authorities.

To Moscow it presented an alarming picture of the kind of nationalist fervor that could easily have developed an anti-Soviet thrust as well. The violence of the demonstrations refuted Soviet claims that all the republics and minorities of the U.S.S.R. were developing a new "socialist consciousness" which transcends old nationalist sentiments.

The Armenians' irredentist claims on Turkey serve as a constant reminder to Moscow that not only Armenian nationalism but nationalism as such has not disappeared in a sea of socialist brotherhood. Today's Yerevan can be tomorrow's Kiev or Tallin, perhaps next year's Baku or Tashkent.

* * *

"With the aid of the proletariat of the advanced countries," Lenin once said, "backward countries can go over to the Soviet system and, through certain stages of development, move to Communism without having to pass through the capitalist stage."

The Soviet Union has tried to prove that tenet in Muslim Central Asia and Kazakhstan by creating a model of how Communism succeeds. Undoubtedly it is a good show. The development is impressive whether you come from Baghdad or Denver. But it is a lot more impressive if you come from Baghdad. And equally impressive if you come from Peking.

The dazzling success of the Ferghana Valley, where the republics of Uzbekistan, Tadzhikistan and Kirghizia meet, impresses China's agronomists and industrial experts as much as it does the non-Chinese minorities in neighboring Sinkiang. And Peking's propaganda runs into trouble when its audience in that region has Kirghiz, Tartar, Uigur, Kazakh and Tadzhik cousins just across the border in the Soviet Union.

To take advantage of this, the Russians have established propaganda committees for an "Independent East Turkestan" in Alma-Ata and Tashkent which broadcast regularly to China to foment risings in Chinese Sinkiang.

Someday this ploy could ricochet with grave repercussions for Russia and one wonders whether Moscow has already forgotten the anti-Communist, anti-Russian Basmachi resistance movement that virtually controlled all of Central Asia from 1918 to 1924. The Basmachi, originally brigands, were employed as military forces by the anti-Bolshevik autonomous Turkestan government in Kokand. After the Turkestan government's suppression, many of its adherents, including the prime minister, fled to the Basmachi and organized them as guerrillas. The movement spread throughout Turkestan and at times reduced Soviet authority to the main cities and the railway lines. In 1924 the Basmachi were finally crushed, except in the mountains, where they were intermittently active as late as 1933, organizing resistance to forced collectivization of agriculture.

Nowhere did it take as long to establish Soviet power as in Central Asia and who is to guarantee that if "eastern" Turkestan rises against Peking with Moscow's backing, "western" Turkestan might not rise against Moscow to form a genuinely independent federation of all the Turkic-speaking peoples in Central Asia.

Of the five Soviet republics that comprise the region, Uzbekistan and Kazakhstan are the largest and most important. Uzbekistan with nearly 12 million inhabitants and an area of 173,000 square miles straddles the ancient Silk Route and was for years a land of thirst. Some 60 per cent of its territory was once nothing but desert, another 20 per cent is covered by the Tien Shan and Pamir mountains. Kazakhstan has almost 13 million inhabitants and more than 1 million square miles of territory, making it the second largest Soviet republic in area—next to Russia—and the third largest in population. Most of the territory, however, is still steppe, desert and mountain.

Lands of nomads, they have now entered the twentieth century with cotton and grain, coal and oil, textile mills and the rudiments of industry.

Soviet achievements there are impressive by any criterion, but one could well ask: at what price? Soviet rule, once resistance was crushed, has undoubtedly been enlightened colonialism. But it was colonialism nevertheless. The resentments it generated, far from subsiding, are being fanned back to life.

In April 1969 a soccer match between a Tashkent and a Moscow team touched off violent anti-Russian demonstrations in the Uzbek capital. The following month, according to reports that reached Moscow later, Uzbek nationalists organized a number of mass meetings at which young militants shouted, "Russians get out of Uzbekistan." Tashkent was surrounded by troops and about 150 people detained or arrested. Among them, according to one unconfirmed but reliable report, was the daughter of Sharaf Rashidov, Uzbek Communist Party chief and a candidate member of the Soviet Politburo.

Kazakhs, numbering about 4 million, are a minority in their own republic, though in Alma-Ata, its capital, they are still very much in evidence. Some continue to wear their traditional fur-trimmed caps, beards and mustaches, but the majority look completely Europeanized.

Officials assert that Kazakh culture is stronger than ever. Maybe it is true that 98.5 per cent of the Kazakhs continue to speak their native tongue, as Soviet officials contend, but if so they speak it at home, not at work. All official business is conducted in Russian.

Visitors are told, in fact, that the native language is compulsory in all schools throughout the republic, even in predominantly Russian areas. But this, apparently, did not become a rule until September 1968 and was then implemented by giving first-grade pupils one hour of instruction a week.

Culture in general is undergoing changes that make it all but unrecognizable to the older generation. Russian officials point proudly to the Kazakh operas, sung in the native language and based on old folk legends, which are in the repertoire of the Alma-Ata opera house. But the opera form itself is foreign to Kazakhstan, having been introduced by the Russians. The music is based on European models and is played on European instruments by predominantly non-Kazakh musicians.

In Alma-Ata I heard and saw one such opera, *Birzhan and Sara,* described as a classic work of Kazakh culture. Written during World War II, European in style, except for the costumes, the libretto propagandizes against arranged marriages, still a widespread custom in Central Asia, and shows Muslim mullahs as the bulwark of conservatism. The opera house was virtually empty, as it usually is, so an Alma-Ata music student told me, when "native" works are performed.

Alma-Ata, a city of 730,000, now boasts a music conservatory which claims to have the only organ in Asia—made in East Germany. Besides the standard instruments, however, students perfect their command of native ones. A graduate student, performing for a group of foreign correspondents, demonstrated her skill at playing Mozart on a dombra, an ancient two-string instrument. She seemed to be prouder of that achievement than the intricate fingerwork and musicianship she displayed when performing lively Kazakh folk melodies.

Alma-Ata, situated beautifully in the foothills of the Tien Shan Mountains, 160 miles from the Chinese border, is a modern city with faint traces of its nineteenth-century re-creation following two centuries of non-existence. By sharp contrast, Tashkent, Samarkand and Bukhara in Uzbekistan border on the exotic. They are the Orient, good and bad. Picturesque, yes. But in Bukhara more than half, in Samarkand and Tashkent more than one third of the population still live in warrens of crooked alleys and mud houses that form the old native quarters—without sanitation or running water. True, on their peripheries the new cities are growing. But these are the same acres and acres of drab, unimaginative, shoddily built box-like apartment houses that one finds in Omsk, Tomsk, Minsk, Pinsk and, of course, Moscow.

Progress? Yes. But at the price of Russification of native culture. And worst of all, perhaps, the new apartment boxes are instant slums, shoddily built, cracking up and falling apart into the moon-scapes of rubble that surround them before they are ready for occupancy. "I think I'd prefer to stay in the native quarter," said one young Uzbek in Bukhara. "We may not have running water, but it's our culture and it is not dehumanized."

The tergiversations of Moscow's policy toward Islam mirror its foreign affairs. The present alliance with Arab countries, for example, is a boon to the U.S.S.R.'s own Muslims. Attacks on Islamic "obscurantism" have stopped. A new edition of the Koran has been published. Bukhara boasts a madrassa attended by sixty students (there used to be dozens of them in the city and many are now being restored as cultural-architectural monuments and museums). Even the *hajj* to Mecca is allowed to faithful and "trusted" individuals.

But decades of Soviet rule have broken Islam's traditional hold. Few religions are as intertwined with a way of life, ranging from attitudes toward women to the style of architecture, and when the Communists arrived to change the way of life, they inevitably struck at the roots of Islam. Nevertheless, the imprint left by a thousand years of Muslim culture remains visible—in dress, in behavior, in attitudes. The vast majority of the Central Asian people still readily admit to being Muslims, even if they do not go to the mosque to pray, and several years ago *Voprosy Filosofii* admitted candidly that the proportion of religious believers in the Central Asian republics is higher than in any of the others.

Soviet power has failed completely to fuse Muslim and non-Muslim peoples or to eradicate traditional animosities. Socially Europeans and Muslims remain apart, though they rub shoulders in the factories, collective farms, the army, the universities. But their family and sex relationships, their behavioral and moral standards and their leisure habits remain markedly different. Uzbeks still hate Tadzhiks and vice versa, both hate the Jews and all are resentful of the Russians, while the Russians are contemptuous of all.

*   *   *

"What happened to your nation," General Grigorenko told a group of Crimean Tartars in the fall of 1968, "was not the work of Stalin alone. He had many accomplices. Not only are they still alive but they hold responsible positions. They fear that if you are given back what was taken from you unlawfully they may eventually be called upon to answer for their part in his arbitrary rule."

For Grigorenko and other political dissenters, the case of the Crimean Tartars is as important as the fight for legality and justice and they see in the plight of these deported people a symbolic cause. For Grigorenko it was so important that he braved arrest and renewed confinement.

The Crimean Tartar case underlines that some of the Soviet Union's minorities are less equal than others. The Tartars appear to be the least equal of all.

A Turkic-Mongol people of Islamic faith, they were deported

more than a quarter century ago from their native Crimean Autonomous Soviet Socialist Republic to scattered areas of Russia's frozen
north, Siberia, Kazakhstan and Uzbekistan: allegedly for collaborating with the Nazis. Like the six other national groups deported by
Stalin between 1941 and 1944—the Volga Germans, the Chechen,
Ingush, Kalmyk, Karachay and Balkar peoples—the Crimean Tartars have been formally "rehabilitated." But it took them longer
than any of the others—until 1967—to achieve that rehabilitation.
And despite it, the Tartars claim, they are still victims of discrimination. Moreover, they have been denied the right to return to their
homeland on the Crimean peninsula—territory that has been incorporated into the Ukraine—and to re-establish the Crimean
A.S.S.R., one of the first such autonomous republics created by Lenin
after the Revolution.

The peninsula, jutting into the Black Sea, was occupied by the
Tartars of the Golden Horde in 1239 and in 1475 by the Turks.
In 1783 it was annexed to Russia and the majority of Tartars left.
Those who remained were designated a nationality group after the
Revolution. In 1936 the Crimean A.S.S.R. had an estimated Tartar
population of 200,000.

Their loyalty to Moscow was never certain and during World
War II when the Germans occupied the Crimea, the peninsula was
the scene of fierce fighting and some of the Tartars collaborated
with the Wehrmacht.

In 1944, when the Soviet Army drove the Germans from the
Crimea, Stalin, as he had done with the other suspect nationalities,
ordered the deportation of all Tartars to outlying areas of the Soviet
Union and the dissolution of the Crimean A.S.S.R.

The collaboration of some Crimean Tartars with the Germans
seems, however, to have served Stalin merely as a pretext for their
deportation. There were contributing factors. As Moslems and moun-
taineers they possessed a strong sense of historical and cultural unity
which neither the tsars nor the Soviets had been able to shatter.
They had resisted Communist penetration for two decades. Khrushchev, on the other hand, suggested that the choice of the Crimean
Tartars had been largely arbitrary. "The Ukrainians," he said in his
"secret speech," "were spared [the same] fate largely because there
were too many of them and [Stalin had] no place to deport them."

It all happened within one month—May 1944—and at a cost of
incalculable hardship and suffering. Thousands of Tartars died:

victims of deliberate liquidation in camps and prisons, or of the subhuman conditions during the journey and in their places of banishment.

Two years later *Izvestia* announced the retroactive law that the Crimean Autonomous Republic had been turned into the Crimean *oblast*. The official explanation: "Many . . . Crimean Tartars, at the instigation of German agents, joined volunteer units organized by the Germans and, together with German troops, engaged in armed struggle against units of the Red Army . . . The mass of the population of the Crimean A.S.S.R. took no counteraction against these betrayers of the fatherland."

"It is inconceivable," Nikita Khrushchev said ten years later, "that whole nations could be held responsible—women, children, old people, Communists and Komsomol members. It is inconceivable that repression could be used against them all for the hostile acts of individual persons or groups of persons."

Khrushchev's speech signaled the rehabilitation of deported peoples. A year later the Kabardar-Balkar and Chechen-Ingush autonomous soviet socialist republics were reconstituted and the Kalmyk and Karachay-Cherkess autonomous *oblasts* were formed.

Although their autonomous republic was never re-created, the Volga Germans, who had been relocated prophylactically, like Japanese-Americans from the West Coast, were rehabilitated in 1964. They were allowed German-language schools, radio programs and even a daily newspaper, *Freundschaft,* which is published in Zelinograd in Kazakhstan, the new German-speaking center.

But it took the Supreme Soviet until 1967 to exonerate the Crimean Tartars and it was only a qualified exoneration. Announced only in the Central Asian republics, never published in any of the national papers, it described the original accusation against all Crimean Tartars as unjust, but alluded to "certain segments" who were guilty of collaboration. Worst of all, according to Crimean Tartars, it specifically barred the re-establishment of the Crimean A.S.S.R. and referred to the Crimean Tartars not as a distinct national group (there is a large Tartar A.S.S.R. with Kazan as its capital, five hundred miles east of Moscow) but as "citizens of Tartar nationality who used to live in the Crimea."

For the Crimean Tartars this discrimination became the focus of discontent and protest. For political dissenters the Crimean Tartar cause became part of the struggle against neo-Stalinism and violations of socialist legality. For Soviet authorities both the Tartars and the intellectuals became the objects of witch hunts.

Trials, protests and repression have followed each other in a vicious circle. Some have been violent and bloody.

Delegations of hundreds of Crimean Tartars have converged on Moscow in recent years, to protest and deliver petitions to the authorities, only to be herded out of town, beaten by police and arrested.

By far the most spectacular confrontation took place in April 1968 in Chirchik, a town near Tashkent, where many of the Crimean Tartars live. The local Tartar community wanted to celebrate Lenin's birthday because, as they explained, "Lenin, as the sponsor of the Crimean A.S.S.R., is especially dear to our people." Local officials refused to sanction the celebration.

On the morning of the planned demonstration police stopped all cars and trucks going to Chirchik, forced passengers out of them and summarily lifted all driver's licenses. Police and army troops were posted around the town. Nevertheless thousands of Crimean Tartars headed toward a public park where they sang folk songs, danced and played traditional games. Suddenly troops and *militsionery* surrounded the park, turned on pressure hoses and moved in, truncheons swinging. Hundreds of people were arrested. For the remainder of the day Chirchik was a town gone mad as police battled Crimean Tartars trying to celebrate Lenin's birthday.

In July 1969 ten prominent Crimean Tartar protesters, among them a few World War II veterans and Rollan Kadiyev, a brilliant thirty-year-old physicist whose discoveries in the field of the relativity theory had only recently been praised in Soviet publications, went on trial in Tashkent accused of anti-Soviet slander. This is the case in which Grigorenko wanted to testify as a "public defender," a frequently used technique in Soviet law. The slander accusation against the ten stipulated that in their various appeals and petitions they had repeatedly alleged that 46 per cent of the Crimean Tartars had perished during the forced deportation of 1944. The government contended, however, that this was an erroneous figure because official statistics listed the number dead as 22 per cent. The Tartars' counterargument was that 22 per cent represented those killed in prisons and camps, the other 24 per cent had died as a consequence of the cruel and inhuman conditions of the deportation itself. Grigorenko, of course, never got to testify. He was arrested before the trial started. The defendants were sentenced to terms of up to three years, the maximum.

The Crimean Tartars appear determined to pursue their quest for justice.

"In the course of our struggle," reads one of their recent appeals, "we have collected more than 3 million signatures on all the various petitions we have addressed to the authorities. This means that every adult Crimean Tartar has signed at least ten petitions. But this ten-times-repeated appeal of 300,000 people has been in vain. Not a single party or state agency has ever replied to us and not a single Soviet publication has ever mentioned our struggles."

* * *

By comparison, Russia's Jews have fared much better. Perhaps this is because there are ten times as many of them as there are Crimean Tartars. More likely it is because they have millions of influential brethren abroad and the force of world public opinion behind them.

It is largely world public opinion, however, formed by propaganda in and outside the Soviet Union, that has contributed to a distorted picture of the plight of the Jews in the U.S.S.R.

As long as Jewish militants in the United States and elsewhere scream hysterically "Let my people go," threaten Soviet diplomats, disrupt performances by Soviet artists (most of them Jews themselves) and vandalize Soviet diplomatic, journalistic and commercial offices, as long as the Soviet authorities trumpet the lie that there is no anti-Semitism in the U.S.S.R. and that Jews in the Soviet Union have never been as well off, that picture is not going to be in focus.

In one sense the plight of the Jew in the Soviet Union is that of the Jew anywhere, except in Israel.

If his situation in Russia, the Ukraine, Byelorussia, Moldavia and Uzbekistan, where anti-Semitism has a long and violent tradition, is worse than his position in France, Britain or the United States, it is largely because as a Jew he is a member of a minority in a country in which all minorities are more or less oppressed. His nationality is stamped into his passport. Often his physical appearance identifies him. He is subjected to a delicate system of quotas designed to maintain a balance of proportional representation of nationalities in the economy and in high government and party organs such as the Council of Ministers, the Politburo and the Central Committee. He is scorned and discriminated against in a society of more than a hundred nationalities, nearly all of whom scorn and discriminate against each other.

In some ways his situation is worse than that of the other nationalities: a consequence of the confusion, first of all, whether his is a nationality, an ethnic group or a religion. Undeniably, it is the only nationality group that is also a religion, an inherently difficult situation in a state that professes atheism. Moreover it is a religion that has been the traditional object of intense discrimination in Russia, where chauvinism and Orthodoxy went hand in hand. Furthermore it is a religion that tends to be tribal rather than ecumenical. Jewish culture as a whole presents difficulties for Soviet ideology.

Finally, he is the only member of a minority group that is genuinely extraterritorial. Not only do most of his brethren live outside the Soviet Union, but 2.5 million of them live in a state that calls itself *his* homeland and competes for his loyalties. Worst of all, that state is at war with a group of countries whose principal ally and supporter is the Soviet Union. Because of the Soviet Union's propaganda against that state, anti-Semitism has again become acceptable, if not actually fashionable, in the U.S.S.R.

The plight of no other Soviet minority group has received as much attention outside the U.S.S.R. as that of the Jews. Some of it has been justified. Some of the attention has been blatant propaganda and the product of confused emotions growing out of the belligerent relationship between two sovereign states: Israel and the U.S.S.R.

Overstating the problem has merely worsened the predicament of the Jews in the U.S.S.R. And to assess their real situation, fact must be separated from fiction.

It is a fact that for many years very few Jews were able to leave the U.S.S.R. But some *did* leave: at an average rate of 150 monthly, even after the Six-Day War in 1967. At times the number rose to 300 a month, at times it was as low as 80. Most of those who emigrated for Israel processed through the consular section of the Dutch embassy in Moscow, caretakers for Israeli interests since diplomatic relations between Moscow and Jerusalem were broken off. This figure, small as it may sound in the light of Israeli and Zionist claims of tens of thousands who want to leave, is the highest emigration rate of any nationality group of the U.S.S.R. Israel has been receiving the highest number of Soviet emigrations since 1967. The

United States is a poor second, Canada, sought out mostly by Ukrainians, is an even poorer third.

It is also a fact that in early 1971 the number of Jews permitted to leave increased sharply, as a consequence, apparently, of intensified propaganda abroad and more militant agitation in the U.S.S.R. itself. Most of the émigrés, however, were those Jews who had aggressively pressed their demands. Between January 1 and May 31, an estimated 3500 had emigrated. The Kremlin apparently decided to get rid of "troublemakers," particularly those Jewish militants who had formed links with the dissident movement.

But it is a fiction that Jews are being *discriminated* against in their desire to leave and a deliberate distortion of the facts to imply that vast waves of Jews are just waiting for exit visas.

"This country," Vladimir Bukovsky once said, "is like a mousetrap. You can enter but you can't exit." It is a description applicable to many Communist countries, which view emigrants as people who vote with their feet. Anatoly Marchenko, it should be remembered, was convicted of treason and spent six years in prison because he attempted to flee the Soviet Union. The writer Anatoly Kuznetsov collaborated with the KGB for years just to obtain the visa to England that enabled him to defect. In London he said that he had already trained himself in frogman techniques and would have swum the Black Sea underwater to escape, if the journey to the United Kingdom had not materialized. The Kremlin views the desire to leave as an expression of disloyalty and makes little distinction between Jews who want to go to Israel, Ukrainians who want to emigrate to Canada and Russians who want to leave for anywhere because they are weary of an economically deprived life in one of the world's most regimented dictatorships. In the case of Jews the Soviets are likely to be doubly restrictive because of the potential economic and military complications that a large exodus would have on the Middle East situation.

Who wants to leave and why?

Israeli and Zionist sources have spoken of "tens of thousands." It is an accurate figure, but cloaked in a semantic play to the grandstands. Joseph Kazakov, the fifty-year-old Moscow engineer who organized and led the letter-writing and petition-signing campaign of Jewish dissenters until he was finally permitted to leave for Israel in February 1971, told me that Jews who want to leave represent about 5 per cent of Soviet Jewry. That would mean approximately

103,000 people based on a 1970 Soviet census figure of 2,151,000 Jews.

"Perhaps," he once said, "if all of them were suddenly allowed to emigrate without difficulty, others would be encouraged to apply for visas and the number might double. But 10 per cent is the maximum."

How many of these 5 or 10 per cent, I once asked him, want to leave because they are Zionists, religious or consider themselves, as Jews, victims of special discrimination? How many simply want to leave the U.S.S.R. because it is an unpleasant place to live in, but have no special affinity for Israel?

"I don't know," Kazakov said. "Maybe half and half."

A joke making the rounds in Moscow before I left posed the question of how many Jews would emigrate if all restrictions were suddenly lifted. The answer: 200 per cent. "All the Jews, and as many non-Jews who would pose as Jews just to get out of here."

Actually, hundreds of thousands of Jews would elect to remain in the U.S.S.R. Assimilated, prosperous and Sovietized, they consider themselves Soviet citizens first, Jews second: like most Jews in the United States, France or Britain.

The Kremlin made this argument effectively in March 1970 when it staged a press conference by a group of prominent Jews who professed their loyalty for the U.S.S.R. and their condemnation of Israeli foreign and military policy.

On the platform in Moscow's House of Friendship for the two-hour news conference were thirty-one Jews from the Soviet establishment, led by Venyamin Dymshits, one of the U.S.S.R.'s nine deputy prime ministers and the highest-ranking Jew in the governmental hierarchy. Beside him were three uniformed and bemedaled Soviet army generals; a kolkhoz chairman from the Ukraine; Alexander Chakovsky, the conservative editor-in-chief of *Literaturnaya Gazeta;* Aaron Vergelis, the editor of *Sovietish Geimland;* government officials; scientists; the Stalinist philosopher and party ideologist Mark Mitin; and the popular Soviet comedian Arkady Raikin, who had just recently stalked off the stage of a theater in the Ukraine because someone from the audience had called him a Yid.

They delivered themselves of anti-Zionist and anti-Israeli diatribes which were repeated in a long statement, signed by those on stage and twenty-two others. Among the signers were the Bolshoi's prima ballerina Maya Plisetskaya, movie director Mark Donskoi, the leading theater actress Yelena Bystritskaya, Leonid Kogan the violinist, the physicist Gersh Budker, and three major generals, three lieutenant generals and one colonel general of the Soviet Army—all Jewish.

In the West this curious display of loyalty by prominent Jews was immediately written off as a "put-on" job by "tame house Jews." Indeed, no American Jew would be likely to go before a press conference to beat his chest and proclaim his loyalty to the United States. On the other hand, why shouldn't these Jews have said what they did? They are among those who made it to the top and have a vested interest in the Soviet Union.

One of the signatories did tell a Western journalist that he had signed the statement under threat of being denied a trip abroad. But on the whole, these fifty-three Jews represented hundreds of thousands of less prominent Soviet Jews who do not care whether or not Jewish culture is suppressed or Yiddish theaters and magazines exist, whether or not there is a Yeshiva and whether or not prayer shawls and prayer books are available for the believers in the synagogues. They do not care because they are assimilated in the Soviet culture around them.

Dissenting Jews complain that "young Jews cannot read Jewish books because the Jewish language is not taught in a single school in the Soviet Union." That is true and that is part of the discriminatory picture, but it means little to the majority of Jews, who would not read a book in Yiddish if the Kremlin gave them out free.

When assessing the status of Soviet Jews Western observers find it difficult, if not impossible, to make objective judgments, to separate fact from emotion.

To draw an accurate picture certain facts should be borne in mind. The Jews are virtually the only minority—the Volga Germans are also an important exception—who did not become part of the old Russian Empire through conquest and colonialism. Anti-Semitism is deeply rooted, and reached exceptionally violent proportions, among many of the U.S.S.R.'s nationalities, especially the Russians and Ukrainians. The present Soviet regime is not anti-Semitic, but it is anti-Zionist and through its propagation of anti-Zionism it ineluctably kindles anti-Semitism because its propaganda is crude and the masses at whom it is directed cannot differentiate between the two.

On the other hand, professionally, Jews are very well off in many fields, including art, music, science, literature, engineering and law. Although they represent less than 1 per cent of the total Soviet population, they account for 14.7 per cent of all physicians, 8.5 per cent of writers and journalists, 10.4 per cent of all judges and lawyers, 7.7 per cent of actors, musicians and artists.

Of some 650,000 scientific workers in the U.S.S.R., 55,000 are Jews. Fourteen per cent of the Jewish population has a higher or specialized secondary education, a rate almost triple that of Russians. In the U.S.S.R. as a whole there are 166 students per 10,000 population in institutes of higher education. For Jews the figure is almost double—315. Of 844 Lenin Prize holders, 564 are Russian, 184 represent all the other nationalities and 96 are Jews. And where else but in Israel itself would one find that many Jewish generals?

Yet Jews seem to be deliberately barred from the government and Communist Party hierarchy and their role in both has decreased steadily since the days when most of the Bolsheviks were also Jews. In 1939 Jews accounted for more than 10 per cent of the Central Committee membership; today they represent less than 1 per cent. They are proportionally underrepresented in the Supreme Soviet and the republican soviets. They have almost no role in the foreign service and in journalism many Jews feel they must adopt Russian-sounding pseudonyms to get ahead.

The Jew's success in certain fields is also his cross. His success is begrudged him. And even in a Communist society Jewishness is associated with business shrewdness.

In 1969 consumer goods-hungry Russians had staged a run on state jewelry shops, buying up virtually all available gold items. The regime, in an effort to soak up excess purchasing power, raised the price of gold and jewelry. A few months later, in Samarkand, a Russian told me angrily: "You know why the price of gold and jewelry went up? All those Jews in Bukhara were hoarding it."

I met some of those Bukhara Jews. A tolerant young Uzbek took me to the city's remaining synagogue, a freshly painted but otherwise ramshackle eighteenth-century building where a handful of gnarled old men, wearing the same quilted coats as local Muslims, were engaged in prayer. They are in one of the few Jewish enclaves in the U.S.S.R.—Georgia is another—where Yiddish was never spoken. Theirs is a Persian dialect brought into Central Asia centuries ago. Although the city has a population of about 20,000 Jews, the synagogue attracts an average of only 200 worshipers on a Sabbath. Most of them are old men.

"I don't understand why they're not liked," said my Uzbek friend.

"My people are all down on them. They say Jews don't farm but only work as tailors, shoemakers and craftsmen. But that's only because they were never allowed to farm. And why do we always say Karl Marx was a German when he was really a Jew?"

He was one of the most unprejudiced men I ever met in the U.S.S.R.

Most of the nationalities have their own territories, where the language is their own and where most officials—if not necessarily the key ones—are of their nationality. Theoretically the Jews have Biro-Bidzhan, the Jewish Autonomous Region on the Chinese border, established in 1934. It is about as Jewish as a ham sandwich. Of a total population of 180,000 only 20,000 are Jews and of these only 30 per cent give Yiddish as their mother tongue.

Until 1970 the first secretaries of the regional Communist Party committees have been Russians and Ukrainians. Now, at last, the party chief is a Jew.

Culturally and politically the dominant role in Biro-Bidzhan has been played by Russians, not Jews, and only in 1970 was an attempt made to redress the balance. In the libraries and bookshops there are few shelves of Yiddish books. There are no shops catering to kosher requirements and there is in the city of Biro-Bidzhan itself only one synagogue, called "the prayer house for Judaists," which serves the whole region. Yiddish is not taught in any of the schools, no special courses in the history of the Jewish people are given, there are hardly enough settlers left who write Yiddish well enough to contribute to the region's small daily newspaper, *Shtern,* and of the five deputies which the region sends to the Soviet of Nationalities, only two are actually Jewish.

The Jew thus is the eternal stranger. Since Jews tend to assimilate into the Russian culture rather than the indigenous culture of the non-Russian areas in which they live, they are further suspected as agents of Russification.

Thus, in areas of traditional anti-Semitism such as Moldavia and the Ukraine, the Jew is doubly damned: for being ethnically Jewish and culturally Russian. In Russia, they are suspected of harboring dual political and psychological loyalties to a homeland other than the U.S.S.R., a suspicion that Israeli and Zionist propaganda has not allayed but merely fostered.

Unquestionably the Jews today are infinitely better off than they were under the tsars. What is dismaying is that despite their undeniable attainments since the Revolution, there have been many changes for the worse again in the last twenty to twenty-five years.

Jews flocked in great numbers to the revolutionary banner in the early 1900s. The overthrow of the tsar gave them a chance to leave the Pale of Settlements and to escape, hopefully forever, from the threat of pogroms. Jews like Trotsky, Zinoviev, Kamenev, Sverdlov and Litvinov were indispensable to Lenin in making the Revolution. And as long as Lenin lived anti-Semitism was held at bay.

In the early, heady years of Soviet power, after centuries of oppression, Jews flooded into institutions of higher learning, into important posts in the government and party. Their generally higher literacy and educational background, in fact, made them indispensable to the revolutionary regime.

Of course, anti-Semitism did not die. But the state and party fought against it with egalitarian fervor, occasionally trying factory workers who had insulted Jews.

By 1939 anti-Semitism in all its varied manifestations had receded into the background. True, Stalin had purged the party leadership of most of its Jewish members, but the motivations were political and his own surge for ultimate power.

An ominous reversal followed the Hitler-Stalin pact. Foreign Jewish Communists who had found refuge in Moscow and survived the purges of the Comintern membership suddenly found themselves being shipped to Germany and Hitler's concentration camps. Soviet propaganda swung onto the Nazi line.

After the war, Stalin cracked down in earnest. His campaign against "rootless cosmopolitans" resulted in the shutting down of virtually all Yiddish cultural institutions, from theaters to newspapers. In 1952 approximately thirty leading Jewish writers and intellectuals were liquidated as Stalin set the stage for the "anti-Zionist" purges that gripped his satellites Hungary, Czechoslovakia and East Germany. Finally the "Doctors' Plot" was in motion. If Stalin had lived it would surely have led to pogroms.

Khrushchev once denied publicly that anti-Semitism exists in the U.S.S.R. But it was under Khrushchev that dozens of Jews were shot as economic speculators and their Jewish names prominently published in the press. It was under Khrushchev also that the furor started over Yevtushenko's poem "Babi Yar."

What Stalin started and Khrushchev finished, in his own way, was the destruction of Jewish cultural life. Under Brezhnev, as a consequence of the Six-Day War and Soviet commitments to the Arab countries, anti-Zionism and an official anti-Israel policy have been unleashed.

Until 1967 the dilemma of the Jews in the Soviet Union had been that the majority were ceasing to be Jews.

"In America," said one Jewish teacher in Moscow, "a Jew can assimilate or not as he wishes. But here a Jew is practically forced to become Russian in outlook. If you want to raise a child as a Jew it is impossible. Hebrew does not exist and Yiddish is being wiped out. This is tragic."

Now, as a consequence of Moscow's campaigns against Israel and Zionism even some assimilated Jews have been reimbued with a sense of their own Jewishness.

Each year more young Jews turn out to sing and dance in front of Moscow's Central Synagogue, one of the sixty still functioning in the U.S.S.R., at Simchat Torah. They now number thousands. It could be simply a recrudescence of religious fervor, for the number of young people who attend Orthodox Easter services also increases each year. But among the Jews there are more portentous signs. Some Jewish youths, for example, have taken to wearing Stars of David and to learning Hebrew from short-wave Israeli radio broadcasts.

Most significant of all, however, are the spirit of militancy which has gripped the Jewish communities in the U.S.S.R. and the draconian measures which Soviet authorities have employed to suppress it.

Scores of Jews have sent and signed petitions to the Kremlin demanding exit visas. Dozens have staged hunger strikes in Riga, Vilnius and Moscow and dozens more have engaged in sit-in strikes in both the reception offices of the Supreme Soviet and the Central Telegraph building in Moscow. In August 1971 an estimated three thousand Lithuanian Jews staged a march to commemorate the deaths of Soviet Jews killed in World War II. The demonstration began on the outskirts of Vilnius, capital of Lithuania, and after marching about six miles the demonstrators were met by police roadblocks. Police ordered the marchers to disperse. They refused, sat down by the roadside and began a thirty-minute period of silence. When police again demanded that the demonstrators turn back, the Jews threw bunches of flowers into the road and pinned Stars of David, made of yellow paper, on their clothing. Nine marchers were arrested at random and sentenced to brief jail terms of eight to fifteen days.

Dozens of others all around the U.S.S.R. have been arrested, questioned, intimidated, convicted and jailed for demonstrating or demanding their rights and emigration visas.

In the autumn of 1970 the *Chronicle of Current Events* started publishing a regular section entitled "The Jewish Movement for Emigration to Israel." Culled largely from the usual underground channels of the Democratic Movement and a Jewish *samizdat* journal called *Exodus,* it tells a gripping but familiar story of KGB persecution, deliberate provocation and intimidation by the authorities. Despite the obvious conflicts of interest between militant Jews and non-Jewish dissidents, the Jewish movement has helped to galvanize dissent in general. In fact, it was at the Soviet Supreme Court appeal hearing in the case of the Leningrad hijackers in December 1970 that Western correspondents first saw physicist Andrei A. Sakharov, the most prominent dissenter, in person. Dr. Sakharov attended the hearing and reported on the results to friends and relatives of the accused outside the courtroom. It was the *Chronicle* that published the most complete transcript of the original trial.

Inadvertently, the Kremlin has fostered Jewish awareness, and thereby added yet another ingredient to the simmering melting pot of national and racial unrest.

6 *Russian Is Beautiful*

From Moscow's huge new steel-and-glass Rossiya Hotel, Europe's largest, the tourist's view is spectacular.

To the west lie the crenelated walls, star-studded towers and gilded cupolas of the Kremlin and the gaudy aberration of St. Basil's Cathedral, a sixteenth-century Russian adumbration of Disneyland, with a chaotic array of multi-colored spires and onion-shaped domes.

To the north, on a street that curves gently around the long, functional façade of the hotel, Russian masons, bricklayers, plasterers, craftsmen and artisans have carefully restored five churches, the ancestral palace of the Romanov family and Ivan the Terrible's old "English Court." As recently as the fall of 1969 they were all dilapidated workshops and storerooms.

Cathedrals, palaces and battlements—a kaleidoscopic panorama that is stunning but anomalous in a Communist state which professes atheism and five decades ago sent its tsar and aristocracy packing in a revolutionary cataclysm of massacre, murder and exile.

The first inclination is to call it a stupendous façade, a tribute to Communist shrewdness in making a successful bid for the hard currency of Western tourists. That, indeed, may have been the original motivation: to inveigle foreigners with their cash to the Soviet Union. But today, Moscow's is only one of dozens of kremlins that have been restored across the breadth of Russia—many of them in cities that tourists do not normally, or are not even permitted to, visit. They attest a national revival of Slavophilism, patriotic fervor, a search for links with the past and religion.

Ancient towns with such historic names as Pskov, Novgorod, Vladimir, Suzdal, Yaroslavl, Rostov-the-Great, Borisosglebsk, Kizhi, Kargopol and Pereslavl, turned drab by twentieth-century Communist austerity, are regaining the patina of their sixteenth- and seventeenth-century splendor. As Russians have rediscovered Russia, churches, kremlins, palaces and other historic and architectural monuments neglected after the Revolution or destroyed during World War II are being renovated, restored and preserved.

The amount of money required taxes the imagination. In Leningrad alone the state has spent 200 million rubles to restore such eighteenth-century masterpieces as Peterhof, Pavlovsk, the Catherine Palace and dozens of churches. Throughout the country fifty special workshops employing more than 10,000 artists and artisans are engaged in restoration and renovation work.

Novgorod, one of Russia's oldest cities, is being turned into a tourist mecca replete with more than seventy historical and architectural monuments, among them a seventy-five-acre park called "Eleven Centuries of Novgorod" where eventually there will be thirty ancient wooden houses and churches, many of them to be brought log, shingle and carvings from northern villages. Not far from the ancient city center municipal officials are planning a large tourist complex—for Russians, not foreigners—complete with hotels, motels, camping sites, restaurants and cafes.

The historical center of Suzdal, an eleventh-century Russian town, is being reconstructed to approximate, as closely as possible, its appearance of centuries ago. That will require removing all overhead wiring and the replacement of asphalt with cobblestones. Step by step Suzdal's eight cathedrals and thirty-eight churches—only one of which is active—are being restored. The Monastery of the Savior and St. Euphemiyus is being turned into a lovely park that will ultimately include a hotel. Shops featuring medieval handicrafts such as candlestick and brooch making, basket weaving and ceramics are being opened.

Equally ambitious projects are planned for some of the remotest areas of Russia. On the shore of Lake Sever in the north, the Kirillo-Belozer Monastery, a fourteenth-century complex, has already been restored.

On the isle of Kizhi in Lake Onega, 250 miles northeast of Leningrad, a dozen spectacular wooden structures, to be joined eventually by sixty others, have been rebuilt or transported there to faithfully recreate a seventeenth-century Russian community. Dominating it is the remarkable twenty-two-domed wooden Church of the Transfiguration, built, according to local legend, in 1714 by a craftsman named Nestor who used not a single nail but so precisely slotted the beams and joists that the structure has stood without reinforcement for 250 years.

Nowadays Russians who shuffle and rubberneck through these museums, palaces and churches outnumber foreigners a hundred to one. In fact, harried Intourist guides sometimes have difficulty herding their foreign charges through the hordes of school children and collective farmers who gawk their way through the *pamyatniki* (monuments). The daily queue outside Moscow's Panorama Museum, a structure on Kutuzovsky Prospect that houses a huge circular painting that depicts the Battle of Borodino in 1812, between the forces of Napoleon and Marshal Mikhail Kutuzov, is almost as long as the line at the Lenin Mausoleum.

The Russians are rediscovering Russia and their past.

The coats of arms of hundreds of old Russian towns have been revived. Cast aside in 1917 as trappings of the tsarist system, they are now manufactured as wall plaques, lapel pins and pennants, which are sold in state shops. Many cities use them for civic decorations. Yaroslavl's bear with an ax on its shoulder is the emblem of a truck produced in the city. The Volga passenger car has a silhouetted running deer as its emblem—the coat of arms of Nizhny-Novgorod, or Gorky as it is now called, the city in which the automobile is made. Many of the symbols have a religious significance. The emblem of Perm, an ancient city at the foot of the Urals, depicts a bear carrying a gospel on its back. In pre-Christian times there was a bear cult in the area. The bear continued to appear on seals used by officials and local princes even after the advent of Christianity. But in 1672 when a church commission began registering coats of arms, the clergy added a gospel to the bear to symbolize the victory of Christianity over paganism.

Groups, study circles and associations, such as Moscow's *Rodina* (motherland) Club, devoted to the study of history, architecture and art have been established. The largest and most influential of these are the republican and All-Russian societies for the Preservation of Ancient Monuments, among whose founders were the novelist Leonid Leonov and pianist Svyatoslav Richter. They now have a total membership of 10 million. In addition to trying to fill the cultural vacuum of fifty years of deliberate dissociation from the legacy of the past, these societies militate for the preservation of important historic and cultural sites. And they are surprisingly effective at it.

The original intention, when construction of Moscow's colossal Rossiya Hotel started, was to demolish virtually all the churches and ancient buildings in the area—one of the oldest of the city. "We fought to preserve the district," Professor Pyotr A. Volodin, a Ministry of Culture official and active leader of the Moscow Society for the Preservation of Ancient Monuments, told me. "As you can see, we won." The result was an ensemble of striking harmony between the old and the new.

Some years ago plans were made to build a new highway between Moscow and Domodedovo airport. It was to pass right through Kolomenskoye, a thirteenth-century village that for centuries served as the summer residence of the tsars. Among its treasures are the Church of the Ascension, built in 1532 by Vasily, father of Ivan the Terrible. Vibrations from the heavy stream of traffic on the highway, the preservation society argued, would seriously damage the unique building in the village. Bypassing the hamlet, representatives of the Ministry of Transportation Construction argued, would cost hundreds of thousands of additional rubles.

It was not the first time that Kolomenskoye had been the focus of a dispute between artistic interests and governmental penuriousness. In the seventeenth century Tsar Alexis built a palace entirely of wood there. More than 20,000 sheets of gold leaf were needed to decorate its interior chambers and Simeon Polotsky, a seventeenth-century writer, called it the eighth wonder of the world. When the capital of Russia was moved to St. Petersburg, the palace fell into disuse. Finally Catherine the Great ordered it completely demolished because she refused to spend the 56,934.27 rubles required to restore it. All that remains is a twentieth-century wood carver's model of what it may have looked like.

The Soviet government apparently is less powerful than Catherine's. After a protracted battle the ministry lost and the new highway now circumvents Kolomenskoye at a sufficient distance to assure its preservation.

Reweaving the threads to Russia's past involved not only architects, artisans and history buffs but has pervaded such mundane fields as the state-run restaurant industry. Soviet restaurants are infamous not only for their atrocious service and mediocre cuisine but for their garish, pseudo-modern neon and chrome decor. Since 1967, however, there has been a drive to make restaurants not only more cozy but to give them a historical atmosphere and traditional flavor. In Novgorod, for example, a restaurant has been installed in one of the towers of the city's restored kremlin. It features bare stone walls, wrought-iron fixtures, wooden soup bowls and typical Russian dishes.

There is more, however, to the panoply of golden cupolas and onion domes, the brilliant arrays of wooden churches and reconstructed provincial kremlins with their drama theaters, art galleries and tower restaurants than merely a tourist attraction or a desire to forge links with a neglected past. The façade of renovated beauty is the lid of a Pandora's box which contains a potent, potentially heady mixture of Russian patriotism and chauvinism, rustic ruralism, mysticism, spiritualism, remnants of Stalinism, and religious revival—all spiked with a large dose of neo-Slavophilism. Like a genie from the lamp, these currents were rubbed into life by the Kremlin's leaders but must now give them sleepless nights.

Russia's Revolution was staged by a handful of Western-oriented, cosmopolitan intellectuals supported by a small army of proletarians barely graduated from feudalism. Like other revolutions, Russia's strove to sever the fetters of the past by destroying not only the hated instruments of suppression—the tsarist tyranny and the Orthodox Church—but their symbols as well. In the process the Bolsheviks turned their backs on Russia's history.

To instill revolutionary fervor and pave the way toward what they hoped would be a better future, they emphasized and praised the new, eschewed and rejected the old. Like nouveaux riches, the uneducated Russian mass spurned its handicrafts, ancient architecture and traditions. It turned instead to the garish modern, the bizarre and the often shoddy imitation of what it believed life in the advanced and technological superior societies was like.

As the churches were secularized they became factories, warehouses, barns, apartment houses, movie theaters, dance halls and cafes. Magnificent palaces were turned into rest homes, hospitals, army barracks and offices. Preoccupied with the task of building a new society, nobody had the time or desire to think about or pine for the glories of the old.

It was not until World War II, when Stalin deliberately reopened the floodgates to Russian patriotism, and with it, ineluctably, the influence of the Orthodox Church, that the Bolsheviks began to look backward as well. Because of the exigencies of the war and his own Russophile predilections, nurtured in the very un-Russian environment of Georgia, Stalin rewove the broken threads between the Soviet Union and the Great Russian past.

The fabric is by no means completed, and during the rule of Nikita Khrushchev the work was deliberately interrupted. But today Russia is not only restoring the physical symbols and architectural relics of its pre-revolutionary millennium but reverting to a Slavophile view of the world. It is an intensely patriotic view in which, as a consequence of the symbiotic relationship between Russian state and church, religion and the messianic concept of Russia as the Third Rome play a distinctive role.

The symptoms are ubiquitous: in the thousands who queue daily to view the circular painting of the Battle of Borodino; in the meticulous reconstruction of a nineteenth-century triumphal arch to commemorate that battle on the avenue which bears Marshal Kutuzov's name; in the staging of festivals to celebrate famous events such as Alexander Nevsky's victory over the Teutonic Knights in the Great Ice Battle on Lake Chudskoye in 1242; in the erection and restoration of countless monuments to the tsars, princes, boyars, monks and patriarchs who fought Teutons, Tartars and Turks, not to mention their own fratricidal frays, for the greater glory of Russia.

The neo-Slavophile movement, half political and half philosophical in its orientation, undeniably anti-urban and preoccupied with the conservation of the Russian and Slav past—in word, picture and architectural symbol—arose in the mid-1960s with the apparent support of the authorities in an effort to offset the expanding influences of the Western-oriented intelligentsia. But the party soon lost control over it.

Outraged by Soviet policy between the Revolution and World War II when the state struggled against all manifestations of Russian nationalism and patriotism, the neo-Slavophiles denounce the era "when a Russian was forced to forget that he was a Russian" and compelled to see himself as a "cosmopolitan without kinship." They are proud that they are "children of glorious Russia."

Russia, to the neo-Slavophiles, means not only Great Russia, but the country's entire territory. To them the name Russian implies all the people living within the territorial limits of the Soviet Union.

Its more religious and philosophically inclined adherents are "god-seekers," that is, they search for answers to social questions in religion. Their inspirations come from Dostoyevsky and the nineteenth-century philosophy of Vladimir Solovyov and the neo-Christians such as Nicholas Berdayev, Dmitry Merozhkovsky and Sergei Bulgakov.

"By the unparalleled profundity of his creative work, Dostoyevsky anticipated the revolution in scientific thinking and the universal problems of the twentieth century," one of the movement's essayists says. "The whole spiritual and moral life of mankind, as it revolves around the axis of eternal problems, was presented by Dostoyevsky."

The neo-Slavophiles feel that literature must serve high purposes: one's country and truth. Like the young Smogists of the mid-1960s they fight for the preservation of the beauty of the Russian language, whose character, they contend, lies in its semantic content, its moral virtue and its austerity of aesthetic taste. They fight for the preservation of old Russian words and names and for the removal of foreign and technical phrases from Russian. And it is not accidental that many of the Smogists are neo-Slavophiles today.

The movement's adherents come from the young to the early middle-aged. The officers' corps and quite a few younger party members secretly encourage it. Even some officials of the KGB are reported to sympathize with it, though neo-Slavophilism is by far the strongest non-Communist movement in the Soviet Union today.

Among its leading spokesmen are the literary critic and cultural historian Viktor Chalmayev, according to whom Peter the Great's merit was not that he opened a window to Europe but gave Europe a window to Russia; Vladimir Soloukhin, a frequently published poet; and Konstantin Yakovlev, a linguist. But it also includes dissident writer Andrei Sinyavsky and Soviet literature's most gigantic figure, Alexander Solzhenitsyn, of whom it has been said that he has essentially two ideas: faith in God and faith in the greatness and mission of the Russian people. One reason why he did not push for publication of *August 1914* in the U.S.S.R. and authorized a Russian-language edition abroad was because Soviet censorship rules proscribe printing the word God with a capital "G." Solzhenitsyn, incidentally, has stipulated that the royalties from that edition be contributed to the construction of a Russion Orthodox church somewhere in the West.

For Solzhenitsyn those two faiths—God and Russia—are an inseparable concept. So they are for the neo-Slavophiles and most of Solzhenitsyn's friends. One of them, who predicted, erroneously, that the writer would go to Stockholm to receive the Nobel Prize, suggested that divine forces would bring Solzhenitsyn back to Russia even if Soviet authorities were to deny him a re-entry visa. Looking at me meaningfully he said in all seriousness: *"Bog znayet, on budit vozvrashatsya* (God knows, he will return)."

During the 1966 trial, when the prosecutor called him a "cosmopolitan," Sinyavsky emphatically described himself as a "pan-Slav." He had an inordinate interest in Russian antiquities and religious ideas. Svetlana Alliluyeva, who was associated with Sinyavsky at the Institute of World Literature, described in her book *Only One Year* how Sinyavsky and his wife, Masha, traveled for long weeks through northern Russia collecting icons, old books in Church Slavonic, peasant costumes, embroideries, utensils of bone and birch, and taking photographs of village architecture.

Many of the unofficial artists not only surround themselves with icons, but some have turned to painting largely religious and pseudo-religious themes. One, who used to do only abstract canvases until a few years ago, now paints only religious motifs: faces and figures of an emaciated, icon-like Christ engulfed by the hell-fire of a Communist inferno. Another, who paints still lifes, Russian peasant scenes and religious themes, once told me emphatically that "Russia's only salvation lies in a return to God." Ilya Glazunov, the neo-iconographer, has turned one whole corner of his studio into a replica of a Russian peasant *izba*—complete with split logs, samovar, embroidered towels and low-hanging ceiling.

Chalmayev, the most articulate neo-Slavophile publicist, idolizes not only Peter the Great and Ivan the Terrible, but also, by implication, Stalin. Chalmayev contends that the unification of Russian lands reached its "rightful conclusion only through the genial statesmanship of the twentieth century." In other words: Stalin's conquest of the "lost territories" and Eastern Europe. He equates Stalingrad with the Battle of Poltava in 1709 and says that the Russian people "go into such a battle once in a hundred years but prepare for it for centuries." To support his theories he even falsifies and distorts Marx, to whom he attributes an admiration for "the genius of Russian statecraft." He eulogizes the nineteenth-century mystical philosopher Konstantin Leontyev, whose creed was to halt the spread of disruptive and decadent European ideas of freedom and democracy.

The Slavophiles of the nineteenth century thought of the tsar as the successor to the Byzantine emperors and provided the ideological underpinnings for Russia's expansionist policies. One nineteenth-century extremist envisaged the double-headed eagle of the Romanovs flying over Constantinople and expected the tsars to assume the Byzantine emperor's title of cosmocrator, ruler of the world. Today's Slavophiles shun historical claims and imperial visions. But they are the spiritual descendants of the early Slavophiles and pan-Slavists because they are imbued with the same sense of mission and spiritual superiority of the Russian people, especially of the Russian peasant.

The poet Soloukhin idealizes the countryside and peasant labor and believes that the idea of collectivization is natural to Russians who grew up in the traditions of the peasant commune, the *obshchina* or the *mir*. Like other neo-Slavophiles he echoes the views of the *Narodniki* or peasant socialist ideologists of the nineteenth century. Some neo-Slavophiles write a great deal about the positive influence of nature on the spiritual nature of man and all of them inveighed against pollution of the environment long before the ecology question became an issue in the West, not to mention in the U.S.S.R. They oppose industrialization of the country.

Anti-Americanism and anti-Western precepts run like a thread through their implicitly anti-Semitic works and they claim a spiritual superiority for Russia. "Thanks to the national genius, health and breadth of the Russian soul," one of them said recently, the Russian people have resisted the ideas of consumerism and cosmopolitanism and the "pernicious influence of soulless American civilization."

Although a *samizdat* neo-Slavophile journal, called *Veche* (the name of the town assembly in medieval Russia), made its debut in February 1971 (edited, reportedly, by Vladimir Osipov, one of the original Smogists), the chief platforms are two very official and influential magazines: *Nash Sovremennik* (Our Contemporary), a youth magazine of the Russian Federation's Union of Writers with a monthly circulation of 150,000; and *Molodaya Gvardiya* (Young Guard), the monthly literary journal of the Central Committee of the Komsomol. It has a circulation of 220,000 and has been described by one Western Sovietologist as "the house organ of the Russophiles."

Whereas the movement originally had the party's blessings, today it meets considerable opposition from an official and unofficial coalition of ideological and political factions as heterogeneous as the movement itself. Those opposing it are the orthodox Communists grouped around the CPSU's chief ideologist, Mikhail Suslov, who see neo-Slavophilism as incompatible with the party's creed of internationalism; the modernizers and big industrial interests; the Western-oriented liberals in the scientific and cultural intelligentsia; and the militant atheists whose house organ *Nauka i Religiya* (Science and Religion) has sighted its ideological guns on *Molodaya Gvardiya* and *Nash Sovremennik* because of the neo-Slavophile tendency to exalt the great ethical and historical heritage of the Orthodox Church under the guise of Russian patriotism.

References to white stone churches and golden domes, Russian saints portrayed as national heroes, religious imagery, bells and ardent passions adorn the articles of some *Molodaya Gvardiya* authors, *Nauka i Religiya* complains:

> These are not just literary mannerisms or individual peculiarities of artistic style . . . These authors continually turn to religious subjects, the history of the Church and the activity of certain Russian preachers whom they regard as an important part of Russian national culture, as one of its universally important achievements . . . We, too, are proud of our creative, brave, freedom-loving and life-affirming traditions. But these have nothing in common with religion, even if often they appeared in history under a religious cloak. We agree that the Russian people have a great spiritual heritage, but it is not to be found among the Orthodox saints.

The sort of separation of history and religion, church and state which the atheists and party ideologists desire is impossible in Russia, where the spiritual and imperial mission were embodied in a single concept.

Saveli Yamshchikov, a young icon restorer and author of a popular book, *Ancient Russian Painting—New Discoveries,* once said: "I cannot look unmoved at the saints on the icons of Rublyov and Theophanes, although I believe in neither God nor the devil. To me these saints are living beings—earthly and comprehensible, but with tremendous will and spirit and power of love and hate. Their eyes and hands, their whole appearance, reveal more to me about my people's past than history's volumes."

Conversely, believers such as the imprisoned members of the All-Russian Christian Social Union for the Liberation of the People are passionately Russophile. One of them recently smuggled a poem out of a labor camp, which reads:

> Yesterday's students and soldiers,
> We wanted to think and to dare,
> For this, Rus, our own mother,
> Clothed us in prison garb.

The Pandora's box seems to contain a confusing tangle of mysticism, patriotism, religious ardor, icon worship and fuzzy philosophical concepts from which intellectuals have drawn an eclectic mélange of diverse theories. These range from the "godseeking" to the doctrine of *sobornost*—an organic concept of ecclesiastical consciousness which, externally, placed the Russian synodal system above papal absolutism and the Protestant individualism of the West and which, internally, defined the Church not as a center of teaching or authority but as "a congregation of lovers in Christ."

The spectrum of religious thought to be found among Soviet intellectuals today ranges from active participation in the rites of the Orthodox Church through the search for "eternal truths" to the neo-mysticism of those who are rediscovering Russia and assimilating the ideas of the nineteenth-century Slavophiles.

Where it will lead one cannot say now. But obviously the Communists are concerned.

"Patriotism and national pride," said *Nauka i Religiya* in one essay, "are great sentiments that enrich the spiritual life of every honest, thinking person. But we must never forget that by poisoning and distorting them, our enemies have always tried to turn them into weapons against Communism. We must treat these questions only from clear Marxist positions with the utmost sense of responsibility."

But how? That is the question.

How, for example, does one explain the icons and the frescoes in restored and renovated churches to people in an avowedly atheistic society based on "clear Marxist positions"?

"It's difficult," Romuald Shafranovsky, an architect and director of the restoration efforts in Novgorod, told me. "The children are not really taught the meaning of what they see in churches, though history courses now include material on the art of the period. Occasionally museum guides visit schools to show slides and films and explain, so that the children will have some concept of what it is all about."

There has definitely been a change since the 1930s, when André Gide noticed a fresco of Christ in a church in Sebastopol with the inscription: "Legendary character who never existed."

"My generation was told that everything the Church did was bad," said a Rostov housewife and mother in her mid-thirties. "We were taught that religion was *nekulturna.* We found out nothing, unless we had religious parents or grandparents. But things are changing. People are beginning to realize how much Russian history was influenced by the Church and that the Church had positive aspects. Obviously something has to be done. What's the point in teaching young people about art or architecture, in showing them icons and wall paintings, if they don't even know the Bible stories or who the saints were who are depicted?"

In 1967 Moscow's Political Literature publishing house issued a Russian translation of a book by a Polish author, Zenon Kosidowski, entitled *Tales from the Bible.* A reviewer in *Novy Mir* described it as "the first break in the exorcism by silence" that surrounds the Bible in Communist countries. The book sold out almost immediately and was reissued in several additional editions—all beautifully bound, illustrated and rather expensive by Soviet standards.

Notwithstanding more than fifty years of official atheism, religion and the Orthodox Church are enjoying a remarkable recrudescence today.

There are approximately 50 million Orthodox believers, of whom 22 million, according to the Moscow patriarchate, are regular churchgoers. This would represent about half the "nominal members" which the Russian Orthodox Church claimed in 1914, the last available pre-revolutionary figure.

(Soviet official propaganda speaks of 30 million Muslims, though this appears to be primarily an ethnic designation for Central Asians, not a religious one. How many of the 30 million are believers is not known. There are also from 2.9 million to 4 million practicing Catholics, depending on whether one accepts the Vatican's figure, the lower one, or Radio Moscow's. The number of practicing Lutherans is estimated at 1 million and Baptist communities also have an estimated 900,000 to 1 million full members.)

Obtaining accurate information about the Church in Russia is not easy. Soviet official sources disclose no information that can be relied upon and the Moscow patriarchate is not exactly forthcoming either. I once spent almost an entire day of telephoning to squeeze the fact out of the patriarchate's press office that there are three functioning Orthodox seminaries. Thus other figures are estimates culled from a variety of sources. The number of active Orthodox churches is now around 10,000, one fifth of the pre-revolutionary figure, one half of what it was nine years ago before Khrushchev launched a massive anti-religious drive, but twenty-five times more than what it was on the eve of World War II when all but 400 churches in the Soviet Union had been closed.

Although there are only three seminaries there are an estimated 40,000 clergy, who, incidentally, earn more and live better than many high priests of Communism. Church salaries for priests and bishops range from five hundred to a thousand rubles a month—four to eight times that of an average skilled industrial worker's pay.

Church attendance is obviously rising. So are the number of baptisms and conversions. Sects opposed to party and state are spreading, as are *samizdat* religious literature and internal opposition within the Orthodox Church to the state-controlled hierarchy by younger priests who desire to free Russian Orthodoxy of its conservatism and superstitiousness.

Polls and sociological surveys indicate that the majority of newborn children in Russia are baptized. More than 60 per cent, for example, in the industrial city of Gorky, and up to 80 per cent in some rural areas of the country.

Church weddings have become so popular that the Komsomol press found it necessary in the fall of 1970 to wage a propaganda campaign against them.

Work stoppages on religious holidays, unmarked in Russia, are frequent and on the increase, particularly in collective farms and villages.

Government surveys indicate that, otherwise, most believers are model Soviet citizens. A 1968 study, for example, revealed that 60 to 80 per cent of believers either hold the title "Shock Worker of Communist Labor" or are candidates for this honor. Moreover re-

1. *Yuli Daniel and Andrei Sinyavsky in prisoners' dock at opening of their trial on February 10, 1966.*

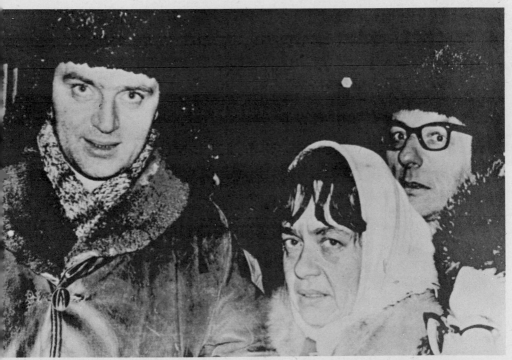

2. *Pavel Litvinov and Larisa Daniel outside Moscow courthouse following trial of Alexander Ginzburg, Yuri Galanskov, Vera Lashkova and Aleksei Dobrovolsky, January 12, 1968.*

3. *Crowd waits with flowers for the defense lawyers at the Litvinov-Daniel trial, October 1968. The tall young man with hat, muffler and glasses near the fence is one of General Pyotr Grigorenko's sons. Some of the hand-picked members of the audience—largely KGB men and Komsomoly—are engaged, on their way out of the courthouse, in arguments with the defendants' supporters, who had not gained admission.*

4. *General Pyotr Grigorenko and wife. This picture was taken when Grigorenko was still in the army.*

5. *Anatoly Levitin-Krasnov, now serving three-year prison camp term.*

6. *Vladimir Bukovsky.*

7. *Pyotr Yakir.*

8. *Andrei Amalrik, Pavel Litvinov and Amalrik's wife, Gyusel (from right to left), in summer of 1968 before Litvinov's trial and exile to Siberia.*

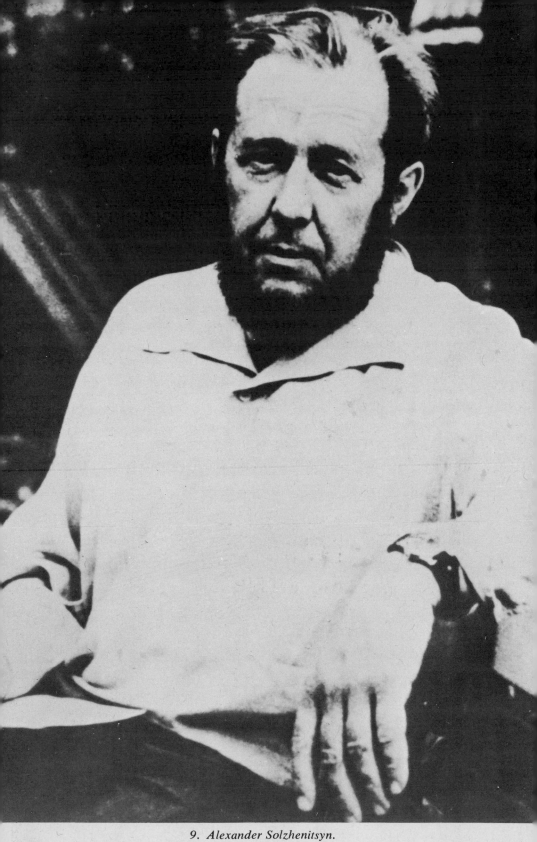

9. *Alexander Solzhenitsyn.*

10. *Visitors to Lenin Mausoleum pass by newly unveiled, 10-foot-high granite bust of Stalin along Kremlin wall. This picture was taken several hours after fence surrounding Stalin monument was removed on Thursday, June 25, 1970.*

11. *Scene in Moscow's permanent Exhibition of Economic Achievements, where Stalinist architecture abounds. At left is the pavilion for the coal industry. At right foreground a section of a gilded fountain eulogizing the multi-national character of the U.S.S.R.*

12. *Restrictions on artistic freedom are much more lax in the Baltic Republic than elsewhere. This sculptural work, at an exhibition in Riga, would be considered underground work in Moscow.*

13. *View of the modern Rossiya Hotel in Moscow with reconstructed churches and historic monuments around it.*

14. *Interior view of the Palace of Congresses, a six-thousand-seat theater in the Kremlin, showing the usual backdrop of Lenin and stylized red banner. Presidium on stage includes the highest-ranking party and government officials. The man in the tenth seat from left is Podgorny, eleventh is Brezhnev, thirteenth is Kosygin. The speaker is Politburo member Kirill Mazurov. The occasion: fifty-first anniversary session on November 6, 1968.*

15 and 16. *Brezhnev enjoying the privilege of position: hunting and examining a gift race horse.*

17. *Pilgrims and religious believers on the grounds of the Zagorsk Monastery near Moscow.*

18. *May Day parade, Red Square, 1968. Defense Minister Grechko's convertible approaches the troops for review.*

19. *The front of the Lenin house in Ulyanovsk.*

20. *An old woman on park bench in Lvov, Ukraine, underneath a glass-encased photo of Lenin sitting on a similar bench.*

21. Street scene in Bukhara, Uzbekistan. This is the view from the front entrance of the main Intourist Hotel. Most Bukhara housing has no running water and it must be obtained from public hydrants.

22. Public transportation for kolkhozniky. Although taken on Kiev's Khreshchatchik Boulevard, this open truck with benches is typical of farm transport.

23. *A herb and spice seller in Tashkent's peasant and kolkhoz market. The headgear is not oriental, but is the beret of the author's wife. Our Uzbek friend insisted on wearing it for the picture.*

24. *View of the main beach in Odessa on the Black Sea. Dredger and oil pipelines run right through the area.*

25. *Street scene in Samarkand, Uzbekistan. The woman at right is selling eggs.*

26. *View of part of the main square of Kazan. Horse carts are ubiquitous in this city of 869,000. The posters are advertisements for movies playing in the city.*

27. *A student at the all-girl pedagogical college in Alma-Ata, Kazakhstan, performing on the traditional native string instrument—the dombra—for visiting correspondents.*

28. *Women can be seen doing the heavy work in most places. Because they treat employment as a means of supplemental income, they tend not to obtain qualification for some of the better jobs. This woman gardener was observed on the grounds of Pavlovsk Palace at Pushkin outside Leningrad.*

29. *Street scene in Kiev, Ukraine. This is not private enterprise. The scales are state property and the man who operates them—ten kopeks for an accurate weighing, no fortunes told—is employed.*

30. *View of Khreshchatchik, Kiev's main boulevard, during rush hour.*

31. *New apartment-style housing on a sovkhoz near Alma-Ata. Apartments were on an average of two to three rooms with a total floor area of less than 30 square yards. The bus was one which brought correspondents to this "model" settlement.*

32. *The queue: this one, in Kazan, shows men and women lining up to buy kerosene for stoves or lamps from a tank truck.*

ligious belief and practice is three times higher among people with a partial or completed secondary education than it is among those who did not go to high school.

As a consequence of the spreading fervor, the regime has displayed considerable concern over the influence of religion. But to distinguish it from previous campaigns, the current anti-religious propaganda effort is more selective, more subtle and directed at the believers themselves, not the Russian Orthodox or established minority churches.

A few years ago it was a traditional practice of the Komsomol to organize gangs of youngsters who deliberately hampered and disrupted Easter services. Armed with guitars, vodka and beer bottles, they would surround the churches around midnight and jeer and heckle the priests and believers as they made their traditional processional circles around the church. Today the youths still come, but so do the police: to protect the church and priests.

Easter 1970 we went to Moscow's four-hundred-year-old Novodevichy Monastery in the hope of watching the service in Trapeznaya Church, the only one still in use on the monastery grounds. The churchyard was filled to riot proportions with teen-agers and youths, some carrying guitars, some nursing vodka bottles, but a surprisingly large number also holding devotional tapers. Precisely at midnight the great bells in the monastery's eighteenth-century belfry donged out the monotonous, off-key litany that calls the faithful to Easter matins, the most important celebration of the Russian Orthodox Church. Then the doors opened to let out the procession of priests and altar boys for their traditional walk around the building. As the crowd outside surged toward them, a cordon of mounted police materialized to hold them back. One man in the crowd, obviously a militant atheist, sneered loudly: "Since when does the state protect the Church from the people?" It is indeed a strange twist to Soviet policy.

The growing threat of Christian revival caused the Soviet government two years ago to send an "atheist missionary ship" to cruise the inland waterways of Vologda province, where the Old Believers, a sect that broke with established Russian Orthodoxy in the seventeenth century, are most strongly ensconced.

To combat the spread of religion among youth, *Komsomolskaya Pravda* has begun reporting about young people who have been expelled from the Komsomol and their colleges or fired from their jobs for getting married in churches, converting or becoming godparents of their friends' children.

None of these youths were really believers, the paper hastened to emphasize, just misguided "atheists who took part in religious ceremonies as 'a prank' out of respect for the past and because they considered them romantic." But, it inveighed, "our cultural heritage and church rituals are two different things."

It expressed alarm over those youths who are "discovering religion not as obscurantism but as a beautiful archaism with attractive rituals. An iconostasis appears above a modern sideboard, someone starts wearing a cross (of course, as an *objet d'art* and to be in style) and before you know it people are holding church weddings out of 'respect' for tradition."

Particularly alarming, in its opinion, are younger, more intelligent priests who attract youth with interesting sermons and discussions and good choral music. (In addition to pop, rock and jazz, Western recordings of Russian church music, by émigré choirs in Paris, for example, bring high prices on the Soviet black market.)

"The clergy," warned *Komsomolskaya Pravda,* "are adapting to changing times. One priest from the Baltic region bought a television set to attract his parishioners, another wanted to put together a volleyball team from among his believers. What is all this for? To ensnare a few young people . . ."

The Komsomol organ insists it is not concerned about serious students of iconography who differentiate clearly between religion and art. But it cautions that icons are becoming a hobby for many people and the hobby has gone so far that even salesclerks in a Moscow department store have started wearing crucifixes.

"One can accept or reject various 'fads' such as miniskirts and long beards," the paper said, "but when fashion leads people to church do we have the right to remain indifferent?"

"Indifference" also seems to be a problem in the armed forces, to judge from exhortation in *Krasnaya Zvezda,* the Defense Ministry daily, to increase atheist propaganda in the services. Calling attention to the number of young recruits and even career soldiers and Communist Party members who are religious, *Red Star* said: "It is too early to believe that the opium of the Church has lost its influence on our people."

A visit to a Russian Orthodox church anywhere for a regular service suffices to demonstrate why the authorities are so concerned.

It is even more apparent on major holidays such as Easter or Christmas, when the churches are crowded to bursting. Thousands will fill them in a swaying, singing, candle-burning and praying mass of humanity for hours while thousands more mill in the churchyards outside.

How much of this fervor is genuine belief, how much is tradition? That is hard to say.

But around Easter, for example, there is hardly a Russian housewife who is not busy coloring eggs, baking or buying *kulich* (Easter cakes and pies) and preparing for *paskha,* as Easter is called. Perhaps not all of them take their paschal cakes to be blessed in the churches on Holy Saturday, but on Easter Sunday nearly every grave in Russian cemeteries has scatterings of pieces of cake, egg, a handful of rice or wheat germ on it to symbolize the resurrection and to pay homage to the spirit of life in a better world.

Moreover, in cemeteries that are less official than the one at Novodevichy (even there the graves of some Communist luminaries bear the traces of scattered food), most graves have crosses. At the villege cemetery behind St. John's Church in Kolomenskoye, for example, 95 per cent of the graves, including the most recent, are Christian. The crosses may be only pieces of pipe or iron tubing. Some are fashioned from steel rods or bent wire, probably filched from construction sites. But they are crosses.

Anatoly Levitin-Krasnov, the religious dissenter, has defined the attitude toward the Orthodox Church as a generational one. The most progressive and energetic members of the revolutionary generation, according to Levitin-Krasnov, despised the Church as the mainstay of the tsars. With them hatred of the Church frequently turned into anti-religious fanaticism. The second, post-revolutionary generation, that is, the parents of today's young, grew up at a time when organized religion was driven underground and was ignored by the majority of Russians. The third generation, today's youth, has been stirred up and the breakthrough to religion, when it occurs, is intense and powerful. Such breakthroughs are far from isolated events.

"Yes, we are believers," said a young student and his wife, both holding candles as they stood on the grounds of Novodevichy Monastery during Easter services in 1970. "The Komsomol? Oh yes, we belong to that too." It was an answer typical of the hundreds one could have gotten in the yards of Moscow's forty churches that night.

The young are inquisitive and curiosity often leads them to church. I saw many of them there, probably on their first visit and brought by a friend. They were baffled by the ritual and mystified by the liturgy in Church Slavonic, but attracted by the beauty and the music.

"It is like the opera," said one young Russian. "I enjoy it."

A recent survey of high school students by *Voprosy Nauchnovo Ateisma* (Problems of Scientific Atheism) suggests, however, that many see more than a performance in religious ritual.

"Religion gives people hope for something in life," wrote a Leningrad senior. "What a man believes may be mythical, but without faith one cannot live."

"Why does religion exist?" wrote another student. "Obviously because man yearns for something pure and exalted. Religion satisfies this yearning."

The idea that religion is the "only mainstay of morality" appears to be widespread among the younger generation, according to this atheist journal, and this may explain why the evangelical churches, originally alien and historically new to the Russian scene, seem to benefit even more from the new upsurge of religion than Orthodoxy.

The prayer houses of the Baptists, a product of the nineteenth-century religious reformation in Russia, are never big enough to hold the faithful, perhaps because the liturgy can be understood and they are not tainted by the Orthodox Church's history of corruption and subservience which repels some intelligent youths who have turned to religion.

Forces of renewal and revival are at work in the established church too, behind whose institutional ceremonies there is a latent church of independent searchers and younger priests who are as oppressed by the hierarchy and Church institution as they are by Communist officialdom.

The most celebrated case of rebellion involved two Moscow priests, Nikolai Eshliman and Gleb Yakunin, who in 1966 in letters to President Podgorny and the late Patriarch Aleksei accused the regime of suppressing religion and the Church hierarchy of complicity in that suppression. They wrote about antagonism between "Holy Russia, which continues to live in the believers," and the "other" Russia. Aleksei ordered the suspension of Eshliman and Yakunin, both thirty-five years old at the time.

Similar views have been expressed by Levitin-Krasnov, who in defense of Eshliman and Yakunin wrote Patriarch Aleksei an open letter, subsequently published in the West, in which he accused the Church leader of failing in his duty. "I am writing," he said, "because you are silent. You should be ashamed. The Russian Church is ill, seriously ill and its most serious ailment is the age-old one of Caesaro-Papism, subjugation of the Church to the narrow nationalistic interests of the secular state."

But these are largely ripples on otherwise untroubled waters, for the Church is flourishing and flourishing largely because it pursues traditional policies.

Russian Orthodoxy's conviction that God meant it to help extend Russia's spiritual empire over heretics and heathens coincided neatly with the imperialistic ambitions of the tsars. To millions of Russians the fate of the Church and the destiny of the *Rodina* became virtually interchangeable. Tsars might come and go, but the Church, as a guardian of the true faith, was—and to the devout still is—the glory of Russia's manifest destiny.

A middle-aged Russian woman, who is not a believer, once told me that when she dies she would like her body to lie in state in an open coffin in a church and the mourners to file by. "I want to be buried the Russian way," she said. In a society where church and state have for so long been intertwined, even a church funeral is, in a sense, the Russian way of death.

*The shield of Communism is marked
by many battle scars. Some of them
were inflicted by the class enemy.*

An Austrian Communist, 1968

7 The Disintegrating Commonwealth

Looking at a sketchy, uninformative TASS communiqué about a
meeting of Soviet, East German, Polish, Bulgarian and Hungarian
Communist leaders in Moscow one spring day in 1968, a Yugoslav
journalist frowned and said: "Once it was a community of fourteen
nations. Now it seems to be only five. By the time the Russians have
whittled it down to one country, their own, they will still be 'strengthening Communist unity.'"

That, succinctly, is the dilemma of the U.S.S.R.'s disintegrating
Communist commonwealth and Moscow's inept way of meeting the
problem.

When Yugoslavia's Tito embarked on his own road toward socialism almost a quarter of a century ago, Stalin branded him a traitor,
read him out of the Cominform and proclaimed to the world that the
Communist movement had never been more united.

When Mao Tse-tung leaped forward on his inscrutable footpath
of Communism, taking Albania with him, Khrushchev responded

with colorful, gutter-like invectives and *de facto,* if not *de jure,* excommunicated the Chinese. Although the Sino-Soviet rift split the Communist world, Khrushchev proclaimed it more unified than ever.

If Mikhail Suslov and Leonid Brezhnev were determined to accomplish anything when they ousted Khrushchev in 1964, it was to restore the unity of and Soviet hegemony over the Communist movement. History, aided by their clumsiness, was against them. They restored a measure of hegemony, it is true—through the brute force of arms and continued saber rattling. In the confrontation with China they succeeded in escalating an ideological dispute into bloody military conflict on the Sino-Soviet frontier. But even more than Khrushchev, his successors, in their own way, have presided over the dissolution of the Communist movement. Vicissitudes of policy notwithstanding, they have widened the rupture with Peking.

There were 240,000 Bolsheviks when Lenin seized power in Russia in 1917. Today there are 111 parties and 50 million or more Communist Party members in the world. But only half of them follow Moscow's banner and many dispute the Kremlin leadership's right to wave it.

When Khrushchev left the scene the movement was undeniably polycentric, with Peking, Moscow and Belgrade each vying in their own way for influence. Today it is acentric beneath a veneer of unity glued on with Soviet tanks and guns.

My assignment in Moscow spanned what may well have been that movement's most turbulent years.

A few days before arriving in the U.S.S.R. I was in Budapest, where I covered the dramatic March 1968 walkout of the Romanians from a preparatory meeting for the world Communist summit conference.

Six months later I sat in the eye of the storm as the Soviet Union and four other Communist countries invaded Czechoslovakia. In September 1968 I watched the slow formation of Brezhnev's doctrine of the limited sovereignty of the Communist countries, which gives Moscow and the other Communist states the right to interfere and invade any Communist country in which the Soviet Union considers "socialism threatened."

In March 1969 fighting erupted between Chinese and Soviet border troops on the Ussuri River, leaving scores dead and wounded on both sides.

Three months after that the long-delayed world conference of

Communist parties was finally held in Moscow. But only nine of the fourteen "ruling" parties and sixty-six of the ninety-seven "non-ruling" ones attended. Of those who did come fourteen either refused to sign, or signed with certain reservations, the basic policy statement of the conference.

Finally, just six weeks after I left the U.S.S.R., riots and strikes in Poland brought down the regime of Wladyslaw Gomulka and put, as is now known, Soviet forces on the alert again, ready to interfere in the affairs of yet another Communist country.

The crux of the problem is the basic disagreement over what unity of the movement really means, what Communism is all about and what the role of the Soviet Union, the world's first Communist country, should be. It is a debate that has been going on for more than five decades ever since the founding of the Third International, or Comintern, in 1919, which Grigory Zinoviev, its first secretary-general, blatantly described as "a single Communist Party having branches in different countries."

Almost from the start the Soviet Union's domestic and foreign goals and requirements determined the policies of the Comintern. One of its members, Mexico's Manuel Gomez, once said: "The first and strongest impression that was made upon me as a delegate to the Third International was the Russian-ness of it, the way the Russians were organized to take everything over. That was something for which no foreign delegate was prepared."

Never much more than an ex officio instrument of Soviet power, the Comintern was soon castrated by Stalin and its apparatus turned into a tool of his secret police. And by the time the Comintern held its Sixth Congress, in 1928, as Gomez recalled, the Soviet party completely dominated all others. "No matter how strong their position might be at home, no matter how popular the individual local leaders might be," Gomez said, "they knew they had no chance if the Russian party was against them."

Though the Comintern and its successor, the Cominform, have long been dissolved, this inherent conflict between Moscow and the other Communist parties of the world remains unresolved to this day.

"The Soviet leadership insists that solidarity with and approval of the U.S.S.R. is the criterion of whether another party is Marxist or not," a Yugoslav acquaintance in Moscow once said. "In fact there is no right of Communist primogeniture."

At the 1969 Moscow conference the remarks of three key leaders of the Communist movement—Bulgaria's Todor Zhivkov, Romania's Nicolae Ceausescu and the Kremlin's own Suslov—brought the dispute into focus.

"We are long accustomed to hearing," said Zhivkov, "that our parties are allegedly dependent on the Communist Party of the Soviet Union, that we are 'agents of Moscow.' Recently such fabrications could even be heard from some members of the fraternal parties . . . For a half century, Communism and the U.S.S.R., Communism and the CPSU have been indivisible. We cannot imagine any socialist commonwealth without the Soviet Union, nor a world Communist movement without, let alone against, the Communist Party of the U.S.S.R. That is a basic truth."

Replied Ceausescu:

"Toward the end of the nineteenth century Lenin said something that is still topical: the Russian socialists must affect an independent study of Marx's theory because it offers only general, guiding principles which under the specific conditions of Great Britain are applied differently than in France, in France differently than in Germany, in Germany differently than in Russia.

"Nobody can pretend to hold the magic key to all problems. What was right yesterday could become obsolete today . . . The forms of revolutionary struggle that proved valid in certain circumstances cannot mechanically be applied to other situations or stages of development."

In a theoretical article, published just before the start of the conference, Suslov argued:

"Adversaries of Leninism try to portray it as a purely 'Russian' phenomenon with no international relevance. Some say that the path of the October Revolution is suitable only to economically backward countries . . . Others maintain that the Soviet Union's path has only 'European' validity and is not, therefore, applicable to Afro-Asian and Latin American countries. There is not a grain of validity in either of these concepts."

The argument is really whether the Communist world should be an empire or a commonwealth, and the more the Kremlin tries to make it an empire, the more centrifugal it becomes.

Commonwealth or empire, it exists only since World War II when Stalin turned the Soviet Army's conquered and liberated East European territories into the alliance of satellites and buffer states for which Russian rulers had always yearned. The instrument of his expansion was Communist ideology—just as the tsars attempted to use Christian Orthodox ideology to create a *cordon sanitaire* around Russia.

Russian ideological leadership and Soviet hegemony over the newly created Communist world were largely uncontested during Stalin's lifetime. They were challenged only once: by Yugoslavia's Tito, whose punishment was formal excommunication from the Cominform in June 1948.

Tito's exclusion, however, failed to solve the Russians' problems, for the forces of self-determination and the desires for independence that Tito's heresy unleashed were already well at work before Stalin died. After his death the Soviet leadership attempted to adapt to them.

But nationalist currents were soon followed by the ideological doubts which Khrushchev evoked with his speech exposing Stalin. By questioning Stalin's infallibility Khrushchev ineluctably challenged Russia's role as the model for socialism and revolution and the very assumption that a model is needed at all.

The seeds of doubt he sowed led to the uprisings in Poland and the Hungarian Revolution of 1956. When developments in Hungary threatened to break Soviet hegemony over Eastern Europe, Khrushchev responded with tanks.

In November 1957, after celebrating the fortieth anniversary of the Bolshevik Revolution, delegations from sixty-four parties, including all the ruling ones, met in Moscow to work out a new general line. Ironically, it was largely because of Chinese pressure that the declaration issued at that meeting emphasized unity, the importance of "proletarian internationalism" and the leading world role of the CPSU: principles that have come back to haunt Peking. Because the declaration sanctioned the invasion of Hungary retroactively, Tito refused to sign it. The Belgrade-Moscow split was rekindled.

It was not long, however, before differences between Peking and Moscow mounted, leading not only to the Sino-Soviet rift but to the formation of two opposing wings within the movement, one led by Moscow, the other looking to Peking for support, as well as the emergence of so-called "neutrals" and "independents."

As the debates became more acrimonious, the Soviet leaders made several efforts to hold another international conference to resolve the dispute and reunite the parties. That conference was finally convened in early November 1960 in Moscow with eighty-one parties attending. It lasted into early December, although it was not until it was almost over that the Russians even admitted a meeting had taken place.

While the Soviet-Chinese rift was the basic line of division at that meeting, it was not the only one. Some of the Latin American and Asian parties objected to the policy on the anti-colonial struggle. Some of the hard-line East Europeans wanted a tougher condemnation of Yugoslav revisionism. And the Albanians, who supported the Chinese on most issues and whose Enver Hoxha vilified Khrushchev personally, even urged the establishment of a Yugoslav Communist Party "in exile." After more than a month of squabbling, the conference produced a declaration of common principles designed to resolve the disputes. All it did, however, was paper over the cracks.

During the remainder of Khrushchev's rule numerous efforts were made to reconvene yet another conference. The ostensible objective was to deal with the Sino-Soviet rift, though by then the Kremlin was faced with the growing autonomy of many parties. The Romanians, notably, displayed extreme reluctance to be drawn into public criticism of any other party on the premise that any attacks in which they might engage could, in time, be turned against them. When, shortly after Khrushchev's fall, the CPSU scheduled a "consultative meeting" in preparation for a full-dress conference, it had to assure those invited that they would not be called upon to excommunicate or condemn anybody.

In March 1965 Brezhnev and Suslov convened that meeting with only nineteen of twenty-six invited parties attending. Differences of opinion among the nineteen were so great, however, that the conference served more to focus on discord and Moscow's diminishing role than on any promise of unity.

The Russians refused to stop trying, though. Finally they prevailed on eighteen of the nineteen to issue invitations to the eighty-one parties that had attended the 1960 conference to consult in Budapest at the end of February 1968. Only sixty-seven attended and the conclave was marked by a display of disunity that in Stalin's time would have been considered rank anarchy.

They could not agree on how to deal with China or West Germany, who to blame for the Mideast crisis and the key question of how much control Stalin's heirs still exert over his splintering empire.

Not only was the meeting marred by the dramatic walkout of Paul Niculescu-Mizil, the dapper and stocky chief of the Romanian delegation, but it took more than fifteen months finally to convene the full-scale summit conference that the Budapest meeting was supposed to prepare.

Those fifteen months were punctuated not only by constant bickering among what Moscow likes to call the "detachments of the Communist movement," but by the Soviet-led invasion of Czechoslovakia, the final obliteration of Alexander Dubcek's concept of "Communism with a human face," the emergence of Brezhnev's doctrine of "limited sovereignty" and the outbreak of fighting on the Sino-Soviet frontier.

When Moscow first began calling for the conference, it hoped to demonstrate that "more unites than divides us." By the time it opened, far more divided than united them.

Consider the state of the Communist movement in mid-1969. The invasion of Czechoslovakia had generated so much enmity toward Moscow that the Soviets were able to drum up statements of support from only thirty other parties, most of them minuscule client groups wholly dependent on the Kremlin. Leading Communist newspapers such as Italy's *L'Unità* and Great Britain's *Morning Star* had taken so critical a position that they were removed from sale on Soviet newsstands and banned from the open shelves of public libraries. The Soviets were calling leading Marxist philosophers and theoreticians such as France's Roger Garaudy and Austria's Ernst Fischer "renegades," "revisionists" and "traitors." At an anti-Soviet, pro-Czechoslovak rally in Peking the North Vietnamese ambassador applauded wildly when a Chinese speaker condemned the Soviet Union. Austria's Communist daily *Volksstimme* was comparing *Izvestia* with the Nazis' anti-Semitic sheet, *Der Stürmer*. The battles on the Ussuri had persuaded the Yugoslav and Romanian high commands to step up their defenses in anticipation of a Soviet invasion. The Romanians were even seriously refusing to sign the U.S.-Soviet-sponsored nuclear non-proliferation treaty.

In the light of these developments, why did the Russians push so hard for a public show that was sure to underscore the disagreements and obscure the areas of accord? The answers were never clearly given. Undoubtedly, both Brezhnev and Suslov, the architects of the conference, had personal ambitions of going down in the history of the Communist movement as men who accomplished what others had not. There was also a certain bureaucratic momentum which dictated that a policy, once formulated, should be pursued regardless of its irrelevance. But in the words of one Western expert, the conference had become a peak the Russians insisted on scaling simply because it was there.

By the time they reached the summit of what had begun as Khrushchev's mountain, however, it had turned into Brezhnev's foothill. To lure any meaningful number of parties to Moscow, the Soviets had been forced to reduce the discussion to the lowest common denominator on which all could agree. Even that was sometimes not low enough.

Moreover they had to pay the high price of the unprecedented openness of the conference itself. In sharp contrast to the secretiveness of the 1960 meeting, the 1969 conclave was a surprisingly public affair complete with press center, multi-lingual texts of almost all speeches and press conferences by most of the individual delegations that wanted to hold them.

The conference issued detailed daily summaries of all speeches, which, by the ground rules established at the outset, *Pravda* and other major Soviet papers were required to publish verbatim. As a result, Soviet citizens for the first time were able to read statements by important foreign Communist leaders who criticized the invasion of Czechoslovakia and Soviet leaders' views and policies. Some of what *Pravda* published in those two weeks was material as censorious of the Kremlin as that which had appeared in *samizdat* form by political dissenters.

No one in Moscow, of course, expected this open information policy to last a day longer than the conference itself. Nor had it been instituted by the Kremlin. On the contrary, the public character of the conference had been forced upon the Russians in weeks of behind-the-scenes squabbling between the Italian, U.S. and Romanian parties, which wanted an entirely open conference, and the Soviets, Poles and East Germans, who preferred to conduct the whole meeting *in camera.*

When it was over, cooler heads in the Kremlin must surely have asked whether it was all worth it.

Five ruling parties—the Chinese, Albanian, Yugoslav, North Korean and North Vietnamese—had boycotted the conclave. Another ruling party, the Cuban, had been arm-twisted into attending, but only as an observer delegation. Some of the world's largest non-ruling parties, such as the Japanese, had also stayed home.

Of the seventy-five that attended many were as minuscule as the Communist parties of Luxembourg, San Marino and Lesotho. Others were but subdivisions of larger national parties, such as Martinique and Réunion, both overseas *départements* of France. Many were parties so captive and dependent that they would report punctually to their own liquidation if Moscow ordained it. A half dozen were illegal parties whose delegates lived within a subway ride of the Kremlin's ornate Georgiyevsky Hall where the conference took place. A few were but minority wings of parties that have split into pro-Chinese and pro-Soviet factions, such as India's and Israel's.

And of these seventy-five only sixty-one ratified the basic conference document without equivocation. Five refused to sign at all. Nine others, including the world's largest non-governing party, the Italian, initialed only certain sections of the document, and those with grave reservations.

Despite the Kremlin's glowing reports that the Communist movement had never been more united, the conference left no doubt that there are now a number of "centers" of world Communism.

Moreover, besides focusing on disunity, the conference underlined the obsolescence and irrelevance of Soviet-style Communism in the modern world. Brezhnev's and Suslov's only answers to it were to whip up the spirit of good old religion and trot out the same old slogans and formulas, to call Leninism the "Marxism of our age."

As an influential Hungarian Communist told me some months before the conference opened: "There are many reasons why we should have a world council. We need to reassess the Marxist appraisal of capitalism in modern terms, to re-evaluate the Marxist response to the developing countries, analyze the meaning of the post-war power realignment to the Communist movement and examine how economic reforms affect Marxist theory and the socialist systems. And we must discuss Czechoslovakia. The Russians don't want to discuss any of those things. All they want to talk about is China, which no one else will let them talk about."

The theme song that the other parties are singing is "Unity Through Diversity and Autonomy." But Moscow has remained deaf to such atonal music, largely because it knows that "unity through obedience" is the only means for preserving its power.

Power is what it is all about. Power abroad and power at home.

Just as it invokes the words of Lenin to justify packing intellectual dissenters off to concentration camps, forcing its artists into a mold of mediocre conformity and giving lip service to economic reform, so the Kremlin calls upon Lenin to justify the invasion of Chechoslovakia, to threaten Romania and Yugoslavia and to polemicize against China.

The oligarchy ruling the Soviet Union today invaded Czechoslovakia primarily to protect its collective monopoly of power. Seen through Soviet eyes, the invasion was a defensive move against the specter of change. Change is a threat to the ruling establishment and it was pervasive fear of change that tipped the scales in favor of military intervention. No matter how insistently they attempted to justify the invasion retroactively, the men in the Kremlin knew that the real risk was not that Prague might break away but that it would infect the bloc, particularly the Soviet Union itself, with the virus of reform and reorientation. In the Ukraine the new climate across the border in Slovakia had already stimulated dangerous discussion among intellectuals. For the Ukrainians as well as other Soviet minorities and nationalities, the Czechoslovak formula of federation suddenly emerged as a panacea that they might apply to their own relations with Russia. Ukrainian party boss Pyotr Shelest was, understandably, one of the leading advocates of intervention.

Among the Soviet Union's dissidents, long in search of a positive alternative, Dubcek's Communism "with a human face" became a concept on which they could focus their energies and hopes.

And for the brighter, energetic younger men in Soviet industry and technology, Ota Sik's theories of economic reform crystallized as the cure-all that would free the Soviet economy from the fetters of top-heavy bureaucracy and inefficiency.

But these precisely are the currents that threaten the power structure in the Kremlin. It was to counter them that the Soviet leadership finally opted for armed intervention.

The Russians knew that the price of invasion would be high. For months preceding it they attempted to influence the course of events in Prague through other means: either by persuading the Dubcek leadership to alter its policies or to change that leadership with a coup d'état or some other ploy that would replace the liberals on the Czechoslovak party presidium with conservatives.

The final attempt was at the historic meeting between the Czechoslovak and Soviet leaderships at Cierna-nad-Tissou toward the end of July 1968, when Brezhnev presented a list of liberals to be purged from responsible party positions in Prague. The meeting ended in a compromise in which Dubcek gave general assurances designed to assuage the Russians. Among these were vague promises to curb freedom of the press in Czechoslovakia and halt Prague's headlong pace toward the sort of liberalization and political and economic reform that the Russians feared. These concessions, the Russians felt, were reaffirmed at the six-power conference held at Bratislava immediately after the Cierna meeting and were codified in the communiqué issued at the end of that parley.

Within a few days after the Bratislava conference it became clear that Dubcek was either incapable of fulfilling the promises he had given the Russians at Cierna or interpreted the results of the meetings differently, feeling he had made no concessions of substance.

What single factor, if any, persuaded the Soviets to move when they did is difficult to ascertain. One undoubtedly was the publication on August 10 of the draft of the new Czechoslovak Communist Party statutes to be presented to a special party congress, scheduled to meet in September. The draft provided for election of party officials by secret ballot, a policy which if adopted in the Soviet Union would jeopardize the entire party hierarchy. It also redefined "democratic centralism" to permit the continued propagation of minority views *after* a policy decision had been made. This constituted outright defiance of Leninist principles and would have had an explosively heretic impact in all other Communist countries, especially the U.S.S.R. Moreover, the special party congress itself was sure to result in the election of a new Czechoslovak Central Committee packed with men loyal to the Prague reformers.

What the optimists in Moscow were waiting for were signs of growing opposition to the reformers from within the Czechoslovak party. They had every reason to expect such signs, for the conservatives and dogmatists in Czechoslovakia had everything to lose if the new course was approved by the party congress in September.

Prague's hard-liners were virtually the only contacts that the Soviet ambassador, Stepan Chervonenko, had in the Czechoslovak capital. They readily assured him that discontent and anxiety over the Dubcek leadership were spreading rapidly within the party and that military intervention would be welcomed by a majority of the party membership, once the troops were in the country.

It was this false guidance that turned the invasion into a political fiasco from which the Soviet Union has not fully recovered. Moscow really had no intention of overthrowing the leadership of the Czechoslovak CP and government by naked force. But it did expect the Czechoslovak Central Committee, still dominated by conservatives and fence sitters, to change that leadership once the occupation was a *fait accompli.* Moreover it expected this change to take place within a very few days—three at the most, to judge from the logistic support which the occupying forces had. The Russians had been assured by Prague's hard-liners that a Quisling party and government leadership would be able to establish itself in power concomitantly with the arrival of the troops and legitimize their arrival with a call for "socialist assistance" from the fraternal Warsaw Pact countries. Technical failures in communication, as well as the absence of support on which the hard-liners had relied, foiled this gambit. After arresting Dubcek and Premier Oldrich Cernik, spiriting them to Moscow and branding them as traitors in public, the Soviets had to return them to Prague as the party's and government's legitimate leaders. The invasion itself, instead of a quick surgical excision of the reformers, turned into a long occupation.

Dubcek remained as first secretary of the Czechoslovak CP for another eight months and it was not until January 1970 that Cernik, the prime minister, was replaced by Lubomir Strougal, a man loyal to the Soviets.

But the invasion demonstrated that the Soviet Union will not countenance any other or new "models of the socialist society" than their own. It showed that the present Soviet leadership will not tolerate any domestic political policies among its allies when those policies become more liberal than those practiced in the Soviet Union and would, by cross-fertilization, threaten the Soviet power structure. The case of Czechoslovakia confirmed that the present leadership is reaching back to the Stalinist principle of control from a single center. It disabused those who believed that reform in Communist countries might be possible before there is reform in the Soviet Union itself.

The doctrine of limited sovereignty of the Communist countries, with which the Russians attempted to legitimize the invasion retroactively, had already been stipulated vaguely by the Bratislava communiqué. It contended that "the many-sided tasks of creating a socialist society in each of our countries are easier to solve with mutual help and support" and called for "fraternal mutual assistance and solidarity."

On September 26, 1968, Sergei Kovalev, a pseudonym behind which Kremlinologists suspect Soviet Deputy Foreign Minister Vladimir Semenov, wrote an article in *Pravda* which formulated that doctrine precisely.

The allegation that the invasion contradicted the Marxist-Leninist principle of sovereignty and the right to self-determination, Kovalev wrote,

> . . . is based on an abstract, non-class approach to the question of sovereignty.
>
> There is no doubt that the peoples of the socialist countries and the Communist parties have and must have freedom to determine their country's path of development. However, any decision of theirs must damage neither socialism in their own country nor the fundamental interests of the other socialist countries, nor the worldwide workers' movement which is waging a struggle for socialism. This means that every Communist Party is responsible not only to its own people but also to all the socialist countries and to the entire Communist movement . . .
>
> The weakening of any link in the world socialist system has a direct effect on all the socialist countries, which cannot remain indifferent . . .

Called the theory of the "qualified sovereignty of socialist countries" and the obligation of the U.S.S.R. to intervene where "socialism is imperiled," it became known as the "Brezhnev Doctrine" when Brezhnev formulated it more emphatically as a guest speaker during the November 1968 Polish Communist Party congress. Since then, hardliners, such as the chief of Soviet border troops, have elaborated it. In May 1970 he described the boundaries of the socialist countries as "borders of a new type."

The U.S.S.R. would, if it could, apply the doctrine to China. A pre-emptive military strike at Chinese nuclear research installations was seriously considered in 1969 following the Ussuri River clashes. Viktor Louis, ostensibly a Soviet journalist writing for Western publications, but in fact a high-ranking and privileged agent for the Soviet regime or some faction or organization within the regime, said as much in an article in the London *Evening News,* September 18, 1969. This implied threat to the Chinese apparently persuaded

Chou En-lai to meet with Kosygin in September 1969 and launch the Sino-Soviet river talks which augured the first thaw in frozen Russo-Chinese relations in almost a decade.

Since then the two Communist macropowers have escalated their diplomatic relations by exchanging ambassadors after a three-year hiatus. Trade between the two was expected to triple in 1971, after reaching a record low in 1970. But if it does, it will still be less than 8 per cent of what it was in 1960 when the Sino-Soviet rift became public.

What has changed in Chinese-Russian relations since the end of the Cultural Revolution in China and the border confrontations that brought them to the brink of war in 1969 is a slow, timid improvement in governmental relations at the expense, perhaps, of heightened ideological polemics.

It is a qualified improvement at best which promises no significant resolution of the basic conflict between the world's two largest Communist powers. What started as an ideological quarrel, rooted in the ambiguities of Soviet policy toward China's Communists in the 1920s and 1930s, is now a direct confrontation between two behemoths who share more than four thousand miles of common border.

In a clash of this sort it is difficult to say who is wrong, who is right, who is lying, who is not. Nor do I consider it in the purview of this book to do so. Moreover, as a correspondent in Moscow at the time when Sino-Soviet relations reached their most critical point, I had little choice but to accept the Soviet version of the dispute, though experience with Soviet propaganda justifies considerable skepticism about the Soviet role in Moscow's dealings with China.

Suffice it to say that a comparison of the record over the past decades leaves the Chinese with a far more pacific image than it does the Russians. Peking may have sounded belligerent, but Moscow has been so. Under the circumstances, publicized Chinese fears of Soviet aggression sound to me far more plausible than the Soviet phobia of the yellow Mongol terror.

And in the Soviet Union there is a phobia. The Russians are deeply and I believe irrationally frightened of China, in whom they see a potential repetition of the Tartar threat of the thirteenth century. In their fear and their irrationality, pre-emptive military moves against China cannot be ruled out.

In the weeks following the Ussuri clashes, of which I believe the first was started by Peking, the second by Moscow as a punitive action, the U.S.S.R. suffered a war psychosis that left more rational Western observers baffled. Remarks such as "Who knows, there could be war tomorrow" were heard everywhere.

In their own irrationality, or perhaps on instructions, famous writers and poets such as Konstantin Simonov and Yevgeny Yevtushenko did what they could to fan the psychosis.

Simonov, in a series of two *Pravda* articles about the Ussuri fighting, seemed to be deliberately preparing the Soviet people for the worst. "No, that is not a slip of the tongue," he wrote, "that is exactly what I wanted to say—war. War cannot always be prevented. History has taught us that . . . When we see a dangerous force arise which, were it allowed free rein, would mete out not scores, not hundreds, but tens and hundreds of millions of graves, that force must be made to feel that not a single one of its actions will go unpunished, that it will be countered from the very beginning, from the first step."

Yevtushenko contributed a poem in which he described Mao as a twentieth-century Ghengis Khan and the Chinese as savages.

True, Chinese phraseology is not exactly conducive to Soviet rationality. In March 1971 Peking accused "Brezhnev and his consorts" of being "social fascists" and of committing "treason to Marxism-Leninism." The Russians respond in kind. The exchange of millions of words of invective and vituperation reached a certain zenith when *Pravda* claimed that "Hitler's ravings about the need to 'save' the world from the 'Slavic threat' has been taken out of mothballs by the people in Peking, who have begun to emulate the ringleaders of the Nazi Reich."

Soviet propaganda about the atrocities committed by the Chinese during the Ussuri clashes, replete with photographs of multilated Russian soldiers and eyewitness reports of wounded border troops, were reminiscent of the Japanese atrocity propaganda churned up in the United States during World War II.

Soviet fears of China have been exacerbated by the specter of a *rapprochement* between Washington and Peking and by the extension of Chinese influence into the Balkans, where, in the summer of 1971, a Yugoslav-Romanian-Albanian coalition, based tentatively on Chinese support, was being formed.

Moscow responded to President Nixon's plans for visiting Peking with a flurry of diplomatic activity that included a hurriedly arranged friendship treaty with India, visits to Belgrade and Paris by Brezhnev, trips to Hanoi and Teheran by Podgorny and missions to Ottawa, Algiers, Copenhagen and Oslo by Kosygin—all within a period of a few months in the summer and fall of 1971.

It was also fear of China and the threat of eventual erosion of its East European empire through the extension of Chinese influence which induced the Russians to make saber-rattling moves against Romania in the summer of 1971 shortly after Ceausescu had returned from a triumphal tour of China, a $244 million credit line from Peking and Chinese promises to come to Romania's assistance in case of attack. The crisis months, just as three years earlier in the case of Czechoslovakia, were again July and August. During this period the Soviet Union attempted to intimidate the Romanians with military maneuvers along their borders and a virulent press campaign which accused Bucharest of forming "an anti-Soviet axis" with Yugoslavia and Albania. At the time of writing Soviet moves against Romania no longer seemed imminent. But the Soviet-Romanian confrontation is far from settled. For eight years Romania has striven to carve out a greater measure of independence from Moscow by exploiting the U.S.S.R.'s fear of Peking. How long the Soviet Union will countenance this remains to be seen.

Soviet policy seems to bank on a change of regime in Peking and relies on the hope that time is working in Moscow's favor. One of the calmer Russians, a journalist, with whom I discussed the problem, said: "For the next decade I do not see a likelihood of war, because Mao Tse-tung knows that we could finish him off in a few days. The Chinese will not be a military threat for at least a decade. By then, however, I hope that Mao and his clique will no longer be in power and relations will have become more moral."

Yet no Communist power in the world has shouted louder and expressed more apprehension about the Brezhnev Doctrine than Red China. Are the Chinese as irrational as the Russians or do they have more cogent reasons to be afraid?

Part Four

There is nothing more dangerous than a principle which appears in false and perverted form.

Ferdinand Lasalle, German socialist, 1862

*Up to now I believed that man could
no more live without truth for his
spirit than air and sun for his body.
My journey to Russia disabuses me.
Here, to lie is to protect the social
order, to speak the truth is to destroy
the state.*

Marquis de Custine, 1839

8 Horizons Lost, Dogmas Won

For twenty-five years Vladimir Ilyich Ulyanov-Lenin read, wrote and dreamed. He dreamed of a new kind of state, without a standing professional army, a state in which the people were not subordinated to an oppressive bureaucracy and a corrupt Church, a state in which there would be no secret police.

Lenin dreamed for twenty-five years but ruled for only five. In that shorter, second period he began to substitute the dictatorship of his party for the mass democracy of workers' councils, the so-called soviets, in which he once believed. Instead of the direct producer democracy he had once envisaged, the factories were placed under the control of state-appointed directors. The scores of nationalities and minorities were again subjected to Great Russian hegemony. And Lenin could be heard to say: "If Russia has gotten used to being run by 150,000 landowners why can't 240,000 Bolsheviks do the same job?"

When the Civil War was over and Bolshevik power established.

all that remained of Lenin's dreams was a lost horizon and a chimerical hope. There was a new professional army, a new secret
police. And even before he died a new bureaucracy and civil service
had emerged to oppress the people. Stalin, who succeeded him,
turned that bureaucracy into an instrument of unprecendented terror.
Under the men who have succeeded Stalin, it has become institutionalized.

The Church that Lenin scorned was largely destroyed. But in place
of it a new, even more doctrinaire eschatology has been established
and Lenin himself has been apotheosized.

"After their deaths," he once wrote about some of the world's
great revolutionaries, "people attempted to beatify them and to rob
their teachings of content and significance."

His own fate was the same.

Today his statue, in gypsum and bronze, plastic and granite, aluminum and marble, stands in squares, post offices, railway stations,
factories, cinemas, kindergartens, abandoned mosques, and kremlins.
The highest mountain, every fourth collective farm, 600 industrial
enterprises, 112 colleges and institutes and countless children's nurseries in the U.S.S.R. are named after him. There are Soviet towns
and cities called Leningrad, Leninka, Leninawan, Leninkent, Lenina-
bad, Leninakan, Leninopol, Leninogorsk and Lenino. His portrait,
like an icon, looks down on every factory and office worker, on every
student and pupil, on farmers, salesclerks, merchant seamen, airline
pilots and railroad conductors all over the Soviet Union. In Kiev I
have seen it as a permanent creation of grass and flowers in a public
park. In Novgorod it stared out at me, life-size, as a tattoo on a garage
mechanic's bare chest. It even follows Soviet cosmonauts into space
on the walls of their rocket ship cabins.

After his death in January 1924 Lenin lay in state for four days
in the Hall of Columns in Moscow's Trade Union House while a
temporary wooden mausoleum, the precursor for the present red
granite structure, was being built on Red Square. There the body was
taken during the funeral, only to be removed a few days later to
prepare it for the secret chemical process that has kept it lifelike
nearly fifty years.

Records of conversations and letters indicate that the *vozhd's*
widow, Nadeszhda Krupskaya, raised strong objections to Lenin's
deification, to a trend that presaged resurrection of a Byzantine
religious cult.

But the men in the Kremlin needed Lenin and need him still. They did deify him and in the absence of new ideas lean on his words and deeds. On the state's great festive occasions, when the Soviet Union's leaders review the masses in Red Square, they literally stand on him.

In need of a universal and durable ideal that the Soviet people, especially the youth, could be persuaded to emulate, the Kremlin has endowed Lenin with countless practical and moral virtues, any one of which can be trundled out, padded and reinterpreted to suit the needs of the moment.

His political views and theories have been drained of meaning, contorted to meet current needs, dogmatized, catechized and propagated, slogan-like, by the archimandrites and preachers of the new "religion." Recited by all but believed by none, Leninism, "the Marxism of our age," as it is called in Moscow, has become a cult, an ideology devoid of ideas, a congeries of outdated verbiage that has no relevance to the modern world but serves the U.S.S.R.'s ruling oligarchy as a justification and means to preserve its own power.

"The light of Lenin's ideas illuminates for all mankind the road ahead, the road leading to new victories, to new historical accomplishments, to the full abolition of exploitation and oppression," Leonid Ilyich Brezhnev says.

"It is fantastic and sometimes it surprises even us," Professor Mark Mitin, one of Moscow's most incorrigible dogmatists, once told me. "But take any problem or any important question in the world and you will find Leninist forecasts, explanations and answers for dealing with it."

The extent to which the name and image of Lenin are propagandized and inculcated into every facet of Soviet life is staggering. The Soviet press bristles wtih phrases such as "Lenin taught us," "as Lenin instructed us," "according to the immortal Lenin," "as Lenin saw it," "Lenin furnished proof that," "Lenin was the first to see that." In hundreds of thousands of offices, classrooms, laboratories and factories slogans exhort the multitudes to work, study and create "according to Leninist principles," or "in a Leninist way." Members of the Komsomol are told to "check your life according to Ilyich." Writers are reminded that their "adherence to the party principle is a knightly loyalty to a banner—and ours is the Leninist banner." Scientists are instructed that "Lenin's entire activity is inalienable from science," and that the leader had "profound scientific prevision."

Economists write essays and articles about "Lenin on Trade" and "Lenin and Modern Statistics." Scientists grind out books and articles entitled "Lenin and Philosophical Questions of Relative Physics" or "Lenin on Contemporary Natural Science." Lenin, to judge from the torrent of words poured out in the Soviet Union each year, had something to say about aeronautics, cosmonautics, electronics, fishing, potato growing, soccer, ice hockey, fashion, barbering and, of course, the arts.

Lenin, no doubt, would consider it all absurd. He was a plain man with plain tastes that bordered on the Spartan. He was scornful of the cult of his own personality even when he was already well at the peak of his power. And he would surely be frightened, as are many other people, by the quasi-religious trappings of the Lenin cult.

It is an ersatz religion which finds expression in the enshrinement of Lenin, in mass "pilgrimages" to places associated with him, in the exhortation to people to "offer up their work" to Ilyich and in the nationwide creation of Lenin museums and Lenin corners in the schools where children are expected to engage in spiritual communion with the dead leader.

In the houses he lived and worked in visitors are required to put on special felt overshoes. In the park surrounding the government mansion at Gorki where he died there are two paths: one for visitors and one on which his coffin was carried on January 23, 1924. In the house itself the stairways have two banisters: the original one which Lenin used, another for visitors.

Emblems and buttons produced by the Soviet souvenir industry show Lenin as a baby and child. In a square in Ulyanovsk (formerly Simbirsk) stands a white marble statue, cherub-like in appearance and proportions, of Lenin as a four-year-old. Near the house in which he was born a sculpture depicts Lenin as an infant with his mother, who, ironically enough, was named Maria.

A picture book for children about the places where Lenin lived includes a text by Sergei Mikhailkov that is chillingly reminiscent of the nativity story. It begins:

> In a quiet town a boy was born—
> In Simbirsk,
> Which stands on the Volga . . .

In Ulyanovsk, to commemorate the Lenin centennial, a vast memorial complex, containing a museum, library, concert hall and two cinemas, was built. In its atrium stands the little wooden house in which Lenin was born. The squat, modern structure also includes a shrinelike, chapel-like Lenin "memorial room" to be used, as a guide pointed out, "for solemn occasions such as giving out medals and awards." It contains a huge statue of the leader, flanked by a mosaic vaguely depicting a hammer and sickle and what appear to be rays of light reaching into infinity toward the ceiling, 60 feet high.

Asked his opinion of this "shrine," one non-Soviet Communist correspondent, with whom I visited it, said laconically: "I respect all religions."

The Ulyanovs of Simbirsk—a sleepy provincial town on the Volga that brought forth not just Lenin but his immediate predecessor, Alexander Kerensky, as well as Ivan Goncharov, one of Russia's most incisive nineteenth-century novelists and social critics—were indeed a remarkable family. Their son Vladimir Ilyich was cut from their phenomenal mold.

The comparison to the Kennedys of Boston is close at hand. Meals in the Ulyanov home, around a large dining room table, were intellectual affairs at which the children were required to recite verses upon verses of Nikolai Nekrasov's poetry. Every Saturday Lenin and his brothers and sisters contributed essays, poems and stories to a handwritten family magazine which was then read aloud at dinner. Young Volodya was a whiz at chess by the time he was eight. His mother had taught herself fluent French and English, in addition to her native German and Russian, and insisted on the use of all four languages in the house.

Vladimir Ilyich was valedictorian of his class with a straight "A" record except for one "B"—in logic. It was given him by his teacher and school principal, Fyodor Mikhailovich Kerensky, father of the man whose revolutionary provisional government Lenin overthrew exactly thirty years later. The elder Kerensky's explanation for the mark: "No adolescent is capable of receiving an excellent grade in logic."

But to the embarrassment of the proletarian hagiographers of today, the Ulyanovs were also very bourgeois. Their house on Ulitsa Moskovskaya, now renamed Lenin Street, has nine rooms. Compared to the hovels and huts in which the Russian peasantry lived, it was mansion-like. It exudes an air of gentility that no amount of propaganda by guides and curators can conceal. In their times and in their society the Ulyanovs were well to do and provided an unlikely background for the raising of two revolutionaries: one a young hothead, the other a brilliant strategist and tactician. Every effort is made to hide this background.

The other facts that are concealed are that Lenin's father, a self-made man, had risen to the hereditary service nobility with a civilian rank equivalent to major general as director of education in all of Simbirsk province; that Lenin's maternal grandfather was wealthy and landed; and that Vladimir Ilyich himself used his rightful title of "Nobleman Ulyanov" while a young lawyer in St. Petersburg.

Only a handful of Russians know that the Ulyanovs were so wealthy that even after the father's death in 1886, money was no problem and Lenin did not begin to earn a living until eleven years later, when he was twenty-seven. His mother supported him.

The nationalist content of Communism requires Lenin to be portrayed as an ethnically pure Great Russian. That he had non-Russian ancestors—his maternal grandfather was probably half Jewish, his father was half Kalmyk—is hidden from all but the most pertinacious investigators. A 602-page official biography of Lenin finds space for only eight words about his forebears.

In Kazan officials spare no effort to relate how in 1887, after Lenin's abortive university demonstration, he was exiled to the nearby village of Kokushkino, where he "began to study Marxism in earnest." What the guides neglect to tell visitors, however, is that Kokushkino was the estate of his maternal grandfather, who, until 1861, owned many serfs.

Much is made of Lenin's older brother Sasha, who was executed in 1887 for attempting to assassinate Tsar Alexander III. But it is not generally disclosed that Lenin would never have been enrolled at Kazan University, as the brother of an executed revolutionary, had it not been for the elder Kerensky's unrelenting efforts and excellent recommendation.

Lenin has become a manipulated symbol whose role is to serve the pragmatic aims of the present Soviet leadership. And never was the manipulation more evident than in 1970, when the U.S.S.R. celebrated his hundredth birthday.

The cacophonous hoopla began almost two years in advance of the day. It started with the predictable feverish production drive on the principle of "socialist emulation" that pledged thousands of enterprises and collective farms, shops and service organizations, hundreds of thousands of brigades and working collectives to celebrate the jubilee by overfulfilling their quotas or meeting the plan ahead of time.

Millions of words about the heritage of the great leader were uttered at thousands of scientific sessions, conferences, lectures and meetings. Poets waxed poetic, theorists propounded new theories and ideologues flooded a weary Soviet Union and a dumfounded world with yet more ideology. Every day, in every way, the people were inundated with Lenin.

To honor him the world's largest propaganda machine ran hot. His image and his name were emblazoned on hundreds of thousands of banners and signs. On radio, on television, on the movie screens, in theaters, at concerts, in art galleries and in the press the *vozhd* became the central theme.

Whole new libraries of Leniniana were churned out by the party and government press, though it hardly seemed possible that there was anything left to say. After all, UNESCO had already confirmed that Lenin was the world's most translated author. His works are available in 222 languages (though 64 of these, from Russian to Uigur, are peculiar to the U.S.S.R. itself). This places him well ahead of the runner-up, Georges Simenon, whose detective stories are available is only 143 languages, and of William Shakespeare, who is translated into only 111.

Soviet composers mass-produced an entire repertoire devoted to Lenin: choral works called *The Leader of the People, Our Lenin* and *The Nations Are Singing About Lenin;* a songbook for children; a chamber oratorio based on the reminiscences of a Red Guardsman and a woman worker who met Lenin personally; a cantata using poems of Mayakovsky, among them his "Last Page of the Civil War" and "Lenin Is With Us"; another oratorio entitled *Lenin—the Heart of the Earth;* and a vocal symphonic poem called *Singing About Lenin.*

The Union of Artists opened the floodgates, particularly, as a spokesman emphasized, "in the sphere of monumental sculpture."

Intourist, the Soviet travel agency, arranged "special jubilee itineraries" to one hundred cities and towns that included most, though not all, of the beds Lenin slept in. One notable exception: Samara, now named Kuibyshev, a city on the Volga where Lenin, his mother and sisters lived from 1889 to 1893. Kuibyshev is closed to foreigners.

The souvenir and gadgets industry worked overtime to produce buttons and emblems, china and glassware, pen and pencil sets, wall plaques and even hand-woven carpets with Lenin's name or Lenin's face. A meat-processing plant introduced a new sausage type called "Jubilee." A chocolate factory turned out a new candy named "The *Aurora*'s Gun Salvo" (an allusion to the cruiser *Aurora* whose forward battery signaled the storming of the Winter Palace). A group of schoolboys from Pskov recommended renaming the Zaporoshets automobile, made in the Ukraine, the VIL-100. A Moscow construction engineer suggested that every new building façade display Lenin's silhouette in brick. And a bakery trust designed a new cake whose chocolate icing depicted rays of light, the dates 1870–1970 and the words "Ilyich's Light" on the top.

These efforts obviously overshot their mark. "Have you heard about the new model bra they've made in honor of the centennial?" a Soviet acquaintance asked me one day. "It's going to be called 'The Lenin Hills.'"

Though April 22, 1970, was a regular working day, the streets of Moscow and other Soviet cities were hung with enough red flags and bunting to circle the earth in a crimson ribbon several times. In Moscow streets and squares were decorated in different themes: Gorky Street according to the theme "The Communist Party Is the Leading Force in Soviet Society"; Marx Avenue according to the slogan "Let the Immortal International Teaching of Marxism-Leninism Flower"; and Red Square itself with the motto "Leninism Is Our Banner, Communism Is Our Goal."

There were, as was to be expected, fireworks. And over downtown Moscow a World War II barrage balloon held aloft a 75-by-100-foot portrait of the leader, bathed from below in anti-aircraft searchlight beams.

While there was no parade, no flexing of military muscle, it was, as *Pravda* described it, "youth itself which filled the broad expanse of Red Square with a sea of smiling, jubilant faces." Thousands of children and teen-agers, accompanied by bugles, flags and choirs that sang songs from the Revolution and the time of the First Five-Year Plan, streamed into the square to be initiated into the young Pioneer organization or the Komsomol. They were met by military heroes, ace pilots, cosmonauts, Lenin's secretary Lydia Fotiyeva and Fyodor Petrov, the oldest living member of the Communist Party.

"We who worked with him," said Fotiyeva, "hope that you will always carry out the teachings of our dear Lenin unfailingly."

That exhortation to Moscow's young people embodied the dilemma of the Soviet leadership. For, notwithstanding the propaganda with which they are deluged daily, most young Soviet citizens remain impassive and immune to it. The reason is that the party strives for enthusiastic conformity from a youth and an intelligentsia that seems imbued with the *ohne mich*—without me—spirit. The goal in itself is contradictory. Moreover the party has chosen to reach it by demanding blind loyalty and rote recitation of Marxist-Leninist catechisms.

"Soviet youth," an American visitor to Moscow in the late 1960s remarked, "remind me of America's silent generation of the 1950s."

The comparison stands up well to closer scrutiny but with one modification. The silence of the Soviet Union's young generation is a two-way street.

Soviet students, it is true, do not picket the Kremlin to condemn the invasion of or demand the withdrawal of Soviet troops from Czecholovakia. None of them publicly demands an end to Soviet atomic testing or an explanation for Stalin's systematic rehabilitation. The ecology question does not drive them to the streets. Few of them openly protest the incarceration of General Grigorenko or the kangaroo trials of dissidents. No students burn draft documents, sign petitions demanding the right to travel abroad or stage Red Square sit-ins to achieve equal rights for Jews or Crimean Tartars.

The cost of such activity—loss of scholarships, expulsion from university, institute or job, prosecution and possibly imprisonment—is too high. Silence is the wiser part of valor.

On the other hand, young people in the U.S.S.R. are apathetic about the state, the regime, the party and Communism. Behind the backs of their elders and the official propagandists they break their silence only to laugh derisively about the system and the society they will someday inherit. Theirs is a silence of cynical contempt for all the values that are trumpeted at them day and night.

Discussion about a "generation gap" or a "fathers and sons" conflict, so the Communist Party claims, is all Western propaganda.

"Don't make me laugh," said the twenty-year-old son of a high-ranking party official. "You name it, and in our house you'll find two viewpoints on everything. The management's and mine." He then dropped the subject and went on to ask whether we couldn't help him get some of the latest record hits he had heard on Voice of America broadcasts.

"The young generation," said *Sovietskaya Rossiya* in one of its typically optimistic, never-look-back-except-to-study-Marx-and-Lenin editorials, "is loyal to the behests of its fathers and brothers and marches on confidently, scoring more and more achievements in labor, science, art and the defense of its country."

In fact, the majority of the Soviet Union's younger generation—those under thirty years of age account for half the total population—seem to be sitting on their haunches, saying adamantly: "Ask not what you can do for your country until your country does something for you."

Cynicism has replaced the enthusiasm that characterized the Soviet youth of the 1930s.

Sitting on a park bench along the banks of the Dvina in Riga, looking out over the river and toward the Baltic Sea, a student once grumbled to me:

"Here it isn't what but who you know," he said. "No matter how good an engineer I turn out to be, I won't get anywhere unless I join the party. That's where careers are made and they are all hypocrites.

"I can tell you now what my future is going to look like. Ten years after graduation I'll have a two-room flat, some flimsy furniture, maybe a refrigerator, a television set that will have cost me two to three months' salary, a one-room hut in the country which I'll call a dacha, and perhaps, if I have been lucky, very lucky, an old car.

"And that'll be it. *Vcyo*. Everything. I'll have settled into a routine as boring as my father's.

"Sure, I'm studying English. But where will I ever use it? Certainly not to travel abroad. That is beyond my wildest dreams—unless I were to join the party and become a careerist. That's not exactly my idea of living, either. So, for what I'm eventually going to get, why should I knock myself out?"

He was merely one of many who have become weary of the credibility gap between Soviet promise and reality.

By all the rules in the Marxist-Leninist book, no one should be building Communism more vigorously than the U.S.S.R.'s post-war generation. Guided virtually from the cradle, they have lived only under Communist Party rule. As no other generation before them they have been spared the horrors of war and the terror of despotism. They enjoy more freedom, benefits, educational opportunities, and a higher standard of living than Soviet citizens have ever known.

Yet this is the generation that is causing its leaders the most worry and the generation that least of all accepts the old standards and the old ways.

There was once a time when young Russians talked about *our* factory, *our* university, *our* party and *our* government. That was long ago when students, young intellectuals and the nation's working youth could feel that they *were* building Communism. But now *our* has been replaced by a very impersonal *the*. They know it is not theirs, for the young Russians of the 1960s and 1970s have a diminished sense of identification with their society at the roots of which are the party's clichéd and clumsy efforts to increase it.

"The main thing is to land yourself a good job with bonuses," a young civil engineering student told a *Sovietskaya Rossiya* interviewer in December 1969. "It's nonsense and an empty slogan to say that 'all forms of work are good.'"

"Materialistic" and "mercenary," as *Komsomolskaya Pravda* is wont to complain, young Russians, particularly the students, still go out in the summertime—during the so-called "third semester"—to work on collective farms, construction sites, dams and in factories. But they no longer do it, like their parents, to "build Communism," but to make money: plenty of money, as quickly and as easily as possible. A three months' stint in a remote area of Siberia can bring a Moscow student a thousand rubles—enough to supplement his university stipendium handsomely.

Officialdom and the elder generation are obviously concerned.

In his report to the Sixteenth Komsomol Congress in June 1970 Yevgeny M. Tyazhelnikov, the youth organization's forty-three-year-old first secretary, spoke of manifestations of "skepticism, an apolitical attitude, indifference to work, study and civic duty and a fawning on bourgeois morals and ways . . . The Komsomol must not tolerate this. It must improve the indoctrination of young people."

The congress itself was an assemblage similar to a moral rearmament meeting. When not listening to speeches that extolled the virtues of Soviet society, and urged to exhort their fellows to work harder for Communism or to attack "bourgeois ideology," the delegates waved signs in favor of Communism and chanted "Lenin is with us." But as an inspiration to the nation's youth, the congress was a total flop.

The Komsomol's paramount tasks, according to Leonid Brezhnev, are:

1. To bring up a generation of harmoniously developed, highly educated people, staunch and courageous fighters for the victory of Communism who will be capable of governing the affairs of the society and state;

2. To educate youth in the experience of the Communist Party and in the revolutionary, militant and laboring traditions of the people;

3. To inculcate in young men and women a Communist attitude toward work and socialist property, a lofty responsibility for the affairs of the collective and the society, to make them clearly realize the inseparable connection between personal ideals and the great aims of the people;

4. To educate the younger generation in the spirit of Communist morals and ethics.

These qualities are apparently lacking in today's Soviet youth. A 1968 survey of 17,000 young people by *Komsomolskaya Pravda* revealed that only 32 per cent could be called patriotic, only 22 per cent were faithful to the party and to the ideas of Communism and a mere 18 per cent believed in teamwork and principles of collectivity.

The Komsomol daily itself summed up the results of the survey laconically: "The process of bringing up young people in the spirit of Communism is not a quick and easy one."

It is doubtful whether the Komsomol is the right organization to do it. It only encompasses about one third of the Soviet youth eligible to join—the actual membership is 27 million but there are more than 50 million who do not belong—and its reputation among youth is low.

Most regard membership as a prerequisite for college or university admission and consider the "activists" in the organization as opportunists who use the Komsomol as a stepping stone to careers in the party and government.

Yuri Morozov, a young scientist, spoke for many former members when the senior class and Komsomol at his former high school in Kuibyshev asked him to contribute an essay or letter to the school's "museum of famous graduates."

"I am afraid that I cannot set a very good example or exhibit for your museum," Morozov wrote. "The period of Komsomol membership is supposed to be the period when a young person's character, convictions and moral qualities are formed. But fifteen years of membership in the Komsomol proved to me that in its present form this organization does not satisfy such requirements . . . In theory a member of the Komsomol is supposed to have the right to think or not to think, to learn or not to learn, to love or not to love, to decide which is better: physics or poetry. In practice the organization gives no one that right . . . It is demagogic, and a large proportion of my generation has developed a strong immunity to ideological demagogy."

The Komsomol is the only approved avenue of significant political activity for young Russians. But it is an activity that is tightly controlled and dictated from on high.

"Of course I'm a member," an engineering student in Kharkov in the Ukraine said to me over several drinks in a "youth cafe." "In fact, I am an activist, an official, so to speak, of my chapter. But you don't really think I believe in it? It's a useless organization except for getting ahead in life."

The main source of discontent and apathy among Soviet youth is in the general boredom and insufficiency of Soviet life and in the conformity demanded of its young generation. They express their discontent by doing the things that most horrify their elders and the puritanical ideologues of Communist doctrine.

They listen to foreign jazz and news broadcasts, in defiance of official disapproval, they wear their hair too long, their skirts too short, their pants too wide (or too narrow when wide pants were the official fashion), they pay black market prices for such status symbols as American cigarettes, chewing gum and whisky or gin from the foreign currency shops, they pass from hand to hand tape recordings of rock and other clandestine music, they devour typewritten manuscripts of forbidden books. Occasionally, when imported goods such as colored stockings or sixty-ruble ($66 at the official exchange rate) boots are available in Moscow department stores, the coeds are always at the head of the queue.

And it is officialdom's proscription of these fads and fashions that disaffects the youth.

"Don't the party and government have more important things to do than worry about whether we listen to the Beatles or not?" a young Soviet music fan told a Westerner in Moscow's Pechora youth cafe once.

"What really irritates us," a young Leningrad engineer and jazz fan told me a few days before the invasion of Czechoslovakia, "is that we have to fight so hard to hear good music. Czechoslovakia and all that is pretty far away. Whether or not we are going to have a jazz festival here is close."

When, the next day, he told me that the festival had indeed been canceled, I asked him why. He shrugged his shoulders and mumbled: "The authorities were against it." Later he added: "You know, if they sold good jazz records or allowed bands to play more pop and rock, no one would even bother to listen to foreign radio."

The young do not understand the party's interpretation of all such desires as symptoms of "ideological deviation." Just as the party cannot understand the teen-age girl who wrote to a youth paper and complained:

"The main enemy is boredom. You're bored, so you gallivant down the 'main drag.' You're bored, so you smell of wine (then things are more fun). You're bored, so you smoke a cigarette. You keep going and keep going—and you're sick to death of it all. Comrade adults! We want so very much to live a full life, not just exist. You were young once. Full of youth. Remember?"

The young are bored because they know that the U.S.S.R. is not the best of all possible worlds. The heavy increase in tourism and visitors from abroad, facilitated by mass media such as television and cinema, has confronted them with comparisons that their parents did not have.

They emulate Western styles and affect Western mannerisms. "Western" does not necessarily mean American but everything west of the Soviet border. Upbraided recently for his long hair, a Soviet high school senior said it was just like the hair styles "we saw on a program from Sopot on TV." Sopot, in Poland, is the scene of periodic jazz festivals and for young Russians everything that happens there is "in."

Soviet teen-agers have a hip, irreverent language of their own in which parents are *predki* (ancestors), their room or apartment is a *khata* (hut), friends are called *starik* (old man) or *starukha* (old woman) and anything good is *zhelezno* (iron). At the university level they enroll in a *fak* instead of a *fakultet*, and live in an *obshaga* instead of an *obshezhitnoye* (dormitory). They are scornful of *sots-realizm* (socialist realism) and plod cynically through their required courses in *diamat* (dialectical materialism).

They dream, like youth everywhere, of seeing the world.

"What I wouldn't give to be able to go to Paris," a married twenty-seven-year-old chemistry post-grad once told me. "Why do they treat us like children or criminals? Why can't we travel like anyone else? Do you know that one third of the students in one of my seminars are foreigners? How many of *us* get to study abroad?"

One manifestation of the resentments and frustrations is vagabondism, a copping out from society or a deliberate search for the adventure and challenges of which, they feel, they are deprived by official policy.

"Before we're even born," said seventeen-year-old Dimka Denisov, the main character in Vasily Aksyonov's novel *Ticket to the Stars,* "everything is worked out for us. Our whole future is all mapped out. That ain't for me. I'd rather be a tramp and suffer all sorts of setbacks than go through my whole life being a nice little boy doing what others tell me."

Said Dimka's girl friend, Galya, begging to be taken along: "I want to rough it too. I want to sleep under a tent too. I want to live on nothing but fish. I'm sick of this place where my mother wipes my lipstick off in front of everyone."

Normal teen-age attitudes? They would be considered so in most societies. But the U.S.S.R. lives by different yardsticks.

"These people are parasites," an editor of *Komsomolskaya Pravda* once told me. "They do not contribute constructively to society. We must take steps against them."

A Moscow police official said categorically: "A vagabond has to dress, eat and drink. If he has no job, that automatically makes him a potential criminal."

Many of the travelers are dropouts from society, not education. Quite a few, according to *Pravda,* which spearheaded a campaign against them in 1970, have college degrees. Often they have done nothing more criminal than refuse to work. But that is a serious enough crime in the Soviet Union.

Aksyonov's Dimka said:

"What's the hurry? You can enter a college any time before you're thirty-five, and we're only seventeen. That gives us a good eighteen years to make it in. And I could think of a few ways we could spend a year or two, fellows. We could go by train, hitchhike, walk, swim, whatever's available, and just keep moving on. We'd stop now and then, work for a few days and be on our way as soon as we felt that we'd had enough of a place. Just remember Maxim Gorky and Jack London . . . Anyway, what's the alternative? To spend the rest of our lives in this dump?"

"Aksyonov," a nineteen-year-old Russian once told me, "speaks for my generation. He writes the way we feel. He's our ideal."

But not the party's. For writing what he did Aksyonov was reprimanded and ostracized by the hacks and *apparatchiki* of the Writers' Union.

"Of course we understand that young people have to feel their oats and taste of life," the *Komsomolskaya Pravda* man said. "That's why we have summer work programs for college students. They go into the countryside and build dams, factories and plow new fields. We understand the pioneering spirit and the youthful thirst for travel. That is why we also have organizations for youth travel."

For those who conform, he should have added.

Most university students do. At least outwardly. They give the required Marxist-Leninist answers on exams, attend the required meetings and make the required speeches.

Regimentation of student life is strict. Moreover admission to a university, college or institute is difficult and the slightest displays of non-conformity can lead to expulsion and with it the destruction of all goals in life.

Even the malcontents among the students know it is essential to keep their noses clean.

"My greatest ambition is to travel and see the world, the real world outside the socialist bloc," a sophomore, majoring in architecture once told me. "I'll have to become an expert, so respected in my field that I'll be one of the privileged class who can leave this place, either as tourists, official emissaries or members of delegations. If I do something wrong now I'll never get my degree, my ticket. Call it selling your soul, if you want to, but that's the only way to get what you want in this society."

Official propaganda portrays the ideal student as an enthusiastic builder of Communism, the ideal university as his source of inspiration, a treasure house of science and culture. A disparate gap yawns between the ideal and reality.

Two aspects of Soviet higher education are rarely mentioned in public. First, the university and college are the surest road to material advancement; second, their doors are closed to a majority of Soviet youth.

According to Soviet statistics, about 3 million youths complete secondary schools each year. They compete for approximately 500,000 places in the day departments of universities, colleges and institutes of higher learning. One out of six thus has a chance of being admitted.

The majority of Soviet students are the children of white-collar workers and the new intelligentsia, although their parents represent a minority of 20 per cent of the population. Precise over-all statistics are not available, perhaps because they would disprove the claims of a social order based on the proletariat and the peasantry. But a 1969 survey in Leningrad region revealed that 73 per cent of children of the intelligentsia, only 50 per cent of workers' and 35 per cent of farm workers' children secure places for full-time study at universities and technical colleges. At Rostov-on-Don University some years ago 57.7 per cent of the students were sons and daughters of white-collar workers, 38 per cent were children of manual workers, only 4.3 per cent came from collective farm families. At higher schools in Sverdlovsk region in 1969 the ratio was 52, 44.5 and 3.5 per cent respectively.

Competition to get in is cutthroat for all applicants, regardless of social background. Aspiring students must either be exceptionally brilliant, have influential parents or possess an excellent recommendation from a Komsomol organization to stand a fair chance of passing the admissions barrier.

Students themselves talk cynically of the exams as the *konkurs roditelei*—the parents' competition—to get their offspring into college. "They lay siege to the examination and enrollment committees and take them by storm," one educator complained. "At first the fathers and the mothers phone, then the grandfathers and the grandmothers, eventually the uncles and aunts."

Often the *konkurs* is a simple question of which parents are willing to pay and which teachers and examiners are willing to accept the most in bribes to give young Ivan and Natasha the examination marks that will assure their matriculation.

One recent case of bribery involved five teachers and officials of Moscow's reputable Polygraphic Institute. Bribes totaling more than seven thousand rubles were received by some of the instructors. There was a fixed fee of five hundred rubles for each illegally admitted student with a hundred ruble rakeoff to the examiner who "improved" the grades of applicants whose parents had paid the fee. Prison sentences in the case ranged from one to fifteen years.

"To get their offspring into an institute of higher learning, at any price, is the dominating thought of some parents," said one of the school's convicted officials. "All moral principles are cast aside and the only thing that matters is to meet the entrance requirements."

In Moscow a "business" specializing in procuring places in institutes and colleges, operated by teachers and middlemen, was uncovered. This private enterprise, which levied between 1500 and 7000 rubles for its services, had placed dozens of students in thirteen separate universities and institutes in Moscow and Leningrad in the space of a few years. The fee represents twelve to fifty-eight times the *annual* average salary of skilled Soviet industrial workers.

Sometimes money isn't even involved. Instead there is a "timely telephone call from above" to the head of a college or examining board. In Armenia, for example, an investigation disclosed that a government minister's daughter had been admitted to the university under the "dean's quota" for favored applicants. The university examiners followed this example and admitted their own "favored applicants." Then the minister of education ordered the admission of another fifty students whose parents had approached him.

It is obvious that only the privileged can afford to bribe and the powerful to influence their children into university.

The competition to stay in is just as stiff. In this connection, the grades received in courses on Marxism-Leninism, political economy and dialectical materialism play a vital role. More than fifty years after the Revolution *diamat* has become a course of catechism, not one of ideas deserving critical inquiry. Taught by the department of political history, which students derisively call the *kafedra bogosloviya*—department of theology—courses like dialectical materialism, political economy and Marxism-Leninism are rigidly limited in horizons and students find it difficult if not impossible to venture beyond those limits. On the other hand they consider it dull and repetitive to confine their discussions to these narrow limits. The result is apolitical indifference, which, in the eyes of the authorities, may be even more dangerous than the few revolutionaries who have turned up at Soviet institutions of higher learning.

These rebels exist, of course. In Vladimir there was a Union of Independent Youth whose members were tried, convicted and imprisoned. In Saratov a group of six students founded a Party of True Communists. In Ryazan another group formed a Marxist Party of a New Type. Most were sentenced to labor camp terms of five to seven years.

The more prudent ones will discuss their political views only when they are absolutely certain of their partner. That was how an engineering student in a Soviet city apparently felt about me. So that his confidence in me was not in vain I will not identify him in greater detail. His views bordered on heresy.

"We will never catch up with the West economically," he said to me once, "because we lack the initiative and our people do not understand modern techniques. Nor will we really get anywhere as long as we spend 80 per cent of our budget on military hardware. Your country can still produce consumer goods despite the outlay for weapons, but we lack the know-how and the resources.

"The expenditures both here and in the U.S. are unnecessary, but in our country things will not change as long as the present crowd remains in power. They have no ideas. They're nothing but bureaucrats."

"It is not Pavel Litvinov's or Pyotr Grigorenko's type of protest that will make the difference," he said on another occasion. "Theirs are meaningless acts. Moreover they believe in the system.

"Why do you think we invaded Czechoslovakia? Because we were in danger of losing it. You see, it was becoming democratic. Democracy is not compatible with socialism. Only dictatorship is. Here we do not even have dictatorship, just an oligarchy of bureaucrats. That is why socialism does not work here either.

"The trouble with this country," he said, "is that 90 per cent of the people don't think and don't want to think. One per cent are trying to preserve their positions of power and privilege. The remaining 9 per cent think but are afraid to do anything about it.

"If I sound bitter, then it is because I am. At my age [he was twenty-one] it is a shame to be bitter. I consider my bitterness a reflection of the Soviet regime and its policies. Of course, I usually keep my ideas to myself. Where it counts I am a model of orthodoxy, for that way I'll get ahead in life. One day I will have the opportunity to travel abroad, to the West. Then good-bye, and maybe we shall meet."

It is doubtful whether my acquaintance represents any significant proportion of the student body. But even if there are many more like him, they would discuss their views only with friends whom they can trust completely. One can never know who in a dormitory or classroom might be a stool pigeon for the KGB or Komsomol. Every university has its own system of voluntary police run by the youth organization. Its purpose is to enforce conformity in taste and conduct by means that range from persuasion to outright intimidation. But even worse, they also act as *stukachi*—informers.

Theoretically students participate in running the universities. There are student councils which can make representations about the teaching. For example, Moscow University biology students some years ago asked for and got a well-known lecturer with a reputation of being interesting instead of one whom they considered dull.

But such cases are rare and there is no general feeling in Soviet universities that the students can influence either the curriculum or the choice of teaching staff. The system of student self-government is fatally undermined by its methods of cadre selection, identical to that in all Soviet political or public organizations. The candidates for office are trusties, selected by permanent officials of the party, or in this case the Komsomol, and formally elected without opposition. As a result the student Komsomol secretary and the student council leaders supervise the students on behalf of the authorities, rather than represent them to the faculty and administration.

No doubt, a large number of Soviet students are contemptuous of authority and resentful of the numerous restrictions on their lives. But the strictures of university life prevent these feelings from erupting into overt rebelliousness.

A few days before the Lenin centennial, I asked the rector of Kazan University what his and the faculty's reaction would be if a student today were to organize and lead a revolt of the type Lenin staged in 1887. My question caused consternation in the room and was at first met with baffled silence.

Finally he replied: "That is a completely abstract, theoretical question. The conditions that caused Lenin to revolt have been alleviated. A student demonstration today is an impossibility because there are no reasons for it. There are no conflicts with the students."

Were such a demonstration to occur it would be blamed on foreign influences, just as these are now blamed for all the manifestations of youthful non-conformity that cannot be explained by the tenets of ordinary Communist dogma. These influences against which the party continually warns originate not only in the West but in the East as well.

Herbert Marcuse, Danny Cohn-Bendit, Rudi Dutschke, American Yippies and student militants are as repugnant to the Kremlin leaders as dissidents at home and they pass up no opportunity to warn against them.

The party's efforts to immunize youth against influences from abroad is but part of a larger effort to isolate the entire Soviet population from foreign ideas. Such endeavors are almost as old as Russia itself but the present one, inaugurated by Brezhnev's ideological vigilance speech in 1968, is unusual both for its intensity and its length. Moreover it coincides with a tacitly approved wave of anti-intellectualism.

During the time I spent in the Soviet Union I observed five distinct campaigns against all foreign influences, each more intense than the other, which were aimed not only at the "bourgeois" West but at recreant Communists from other countries.

These insidious foreign influences, Soviet citizens were warned, come in a variety of shapes, forms and disguises:

Tourists who smuggle in reams of literature which "our vigilant customs officials" confiscate at the borders; diplomats who acquire a wide range of intellectual acquaintances in order to "subvert them"; journalists who "work hand in hand with the CIA and Western intelligence agencies"; exhibition personnel who visit Moscow for industrial or artistic displays; and foreign businessmen.

"The imperialists do not hesitate to falsify, to lie," the Soviet press warned. "A Soviet citizen must be capable of opposing the current of misinformation and slander on the Soviet way of life that pours from the pens of the bourgeois ideologists."

This subversion, in Soviet propaganda terms, is most devious because it "masquerades under the guise of 'friendship,' of 'building bridges' into the Socialist countries . . . Bourgeois propaganda relies on the revisionist, nationalist and politically immature elements which it praises and portrays as heroes. The aim is to erode socialism, to disintegrate it from within and, in the long run, to restore capitalism in the Socialist countries."

"Imperialist intelligence services, the clergy, international Zionism and right-wing social democratic leaders," one ideologist warned, "have joined forces to weaken every single detachment of the world revolutionary movement."

Brezhnev himself said: "Because imperialism cannot achieve its goals by openly proclaiming them, it relies on a whole system of ideological myths to obscure the meaning of its intentions and to blunt our vigilance."

Every Soviet citizen was called on to stand up and be counted, to "resist any manifestations of bourgeois influence . . . that fan nationalistic prejudices or poison the minds of some of our youth with nihilism . . . We cannot tolerate the attitude of non-involvement which some people adopt in the struggle against hostile ideology."

In the fall of 1970 the campaign reached heights that were frighteningly reminiscent of the Stalin years.

"Vigilance," the Soviet people were told, "is a patriotic duty." And citizens were called upon to assist the security agencies "in the struggle against the subversive work of capitalist intelligence services."

The press featured specific accounts of subversion:

Unsuspecting citizens allowed their internal passports, identity cards and even party membership cards to be photographed at foreign exhibits which were supposed to be demonstrating rapid copying devices.

A Muscovite, hunting mushrooms in the woods, met a stranger in the forest, whom he invited to his home. He drank heavily with him and a few days later noticed that his identification papers were missing.

A woman in Yerevan, Armenia, while strolling in the park, found a piece of paper "with foreign words on it. It turned out to be a copy of instructions issued by U.S. intelligence to agents sent in the guise of tourists."

"Speakers at conferences and meetings occasionally disclosed secrets, and scientists have sent their articles abroad in violation of the rules."

Scientists especially have been singled out for their ideological laxness and inadequate vigilance.

As a party official in Novosibirsk pointed out:

"It must be borne in mind that the science center here [Akademgorodok] has contacts with many foreign scientists. Last year about three thousand foreign specialists in various fields visited the center. We are pleased to have guests, but we should not forget that Academic City also attracts the attention of anti-Soviet centers abroad which would like to turn the scientific intelligentsia against the people, the working class and the Communist Party. Along with scientific literature, 'information' designed to serve the purposes of

psychological warfare occasionally reaches the scientific intelligentsia . . ."

This official, like others, struck the anti-intellectual tone that is
characteristic of the ideological vigilance campaign.

"Because of the youth of the team—the average age of scientific
personnel here is thirty-two—territorial isolation and the absence of
direct, daily ties with production," he said, "Akademgorodok has
a particular social climate that leads some of the young scientists
to hold an exaggerated opinion of their role in society. They see
the scientific and technological revolution as the exclusive province
of an 'intellectual elite.' This erroneous appraisal of their role has
been conditioned largely by the fact that these young scientists went
directly from school to the university and then to their jobs in
academic institutes. The absence of other experiences in their life
has given them a distorted outlook."

The formation of political consciousness among intellectuals,
Pravda once warned, cannot be allowed to go unguided. There are
too many cases of intellectuals who display individualism, indifference
to politics and who may be affected by ideological alien influences.

To prevent this the Communist Party has amassed an army of
200,000 agitators, 52,000 propagandists and thousands of lecturers
whose job it is to inundate the masses with more balderdash and
catechisms.

For the Soviet people today a Leninist maxim of pre-revolutionary days, rarely quoted today, would be highly pertinent:

"People have always been and will always be stupid victims of
deceit and self-deception in politics until they learn to seek out the
interests of this or that class or classes behind every kind of moral,
religious, political and social phrase, declaration or promise."

All history has been a history of class
struggles between dominated and
dominating classes at various stages of
social development.

Friedrich Engels, 1853

This new class . . . has all the
characteristics of previous classes, as
well as a few new ones which are
peculiar to it.

Milovan Djilas, 1957

9 *Life with the Beautiful People*

Mikhail Georgiyevich Motoriko, chairman of the executive committee of Kustanai *oblast,* a vast region of 75,000 square miles in northern Kazakhstan, rich in black soil and iron, turned fifty in November 1970. The Supreme Soviet of the U.S.S.R., *Pravda* announced, had honored him with the Order of Lenin, one of the Soviet Union's highest awards.

Such "birthday" honors for "meritorious service to the state" are usual for leading *apparatchiki.* But they follow a protocol which stipulates that chairmen of *oblast* executive committees at most may hope to receive the far less prestigious Order of the Red Labor Banner on their fiftieth—some may not get it even on their sixtieth —birthday.

Were Motoriko's services to the state that meritorious?

Well, hardly. Before he was named chairman of the provincial executive committee in 1963 he had been anything but a very skillful organizer. In fact, in the Zatobolsky district, where he had worked as production administrator, the plan for grain procurement had been underfulfilled by 66 per cent. Of the fifteen state farms under his administration, thirteen had finished the year 1962 with losses totaling 4.7 million rubles. During the same period, 1854 cows, 6190 hogs and 519 sheep had perished. Moreover, as an auditor's statement revealed, Motoriko was even a bit of a crook. In 1962, according to *Izvestia,* he had "illegally bought eight houses for dwelling purposes from private persons for a total amount of 29,300 rubles, paying for them from the accounts of state farms."

But Motoriko has other things going for him. Until 1962 he had been director of the Kustanai Stud Farm, whose special breed has been winning most of the horse races at Soviet tracks for the past decade or so.

Motoriko apparently knows not only his horses but his bettors, not to mention owners. Since horse racing, the only legal means of gambling in the Soviet Union, is a sport for gentlemen in a society where gentlemen have long ceased to exist—officially—Motoriko has connections to people high up in the Communist Party hierarchy in Moscow. They are links forged by common interests at the hippodrome, thanks to which he is now solidly ensconced in the privileged ranks of the new Soviet elite.

So is Jozas Shimalinus, deputy director of the district distribution center of the Lithuanian Consumers' Union in Vilnius.

Shimalinus is a *dachnik.* That is, he owns a dacha. Now, dachas can be many things. A wooden hut without water or electricity, like Andrei Amalrik's in Akulovo, or a villa like Shimalinus', a two-story house perched on concrete pillars beside a picturesque waterfall.

From the second-floor balcony Shimalinus can dive directly into the crystal-clear pool beneath, or just sit, fish and watch television —simultaneously. Although he does not hunt, the house boasts a den, the walls of which are hung with expensive shotguns from Tula, antlers, a bearskin and other trophies.

In this villa Shimalinus has made his reputation as one of the best, most gracious hosts of Vilnius. Here he entertains his friends and "business" contacts, his political and party associates. If Soviet newspapers published gossip columns, they would undoubtedly say that the blasts at Shimalinus' invariably include "the right people."

Viktor Louis also knows and invites the "right people." Louis, who identifies himself as "just a Soviet journalist," is Moscow correspondent for the London *Evening News*—the only Soviet citizen to work as a reporter for a foreign non-Communist newspaper. He does his job extremely well. He reported the fall of Nikita Khrushchev many hours before it was known to anyone else in Moscow except the Central Committee and the Politburo. And when he writes that certain circles in the Soviet regime are contemplating a pre-emptive strike against Chinese nuclear testing sites, the whole world listens.

Journalism, however, is not Louis' only profession. He has translated *My Fair Lady* into Russian and draws substantial royalties each time it is performed in a Soviet theater. When Svetlana Alliluyeva turned up in the United States with her memoirs, *Twenty Letters to a Friend,* Louis turned up in Hamburg, Germany, with another copy of the manuscript, which he sold to the German illustrated weekly *Stern,* thereby undermining the release plans of American, British and other German publishers. His role in the release of Khrushchev's "memoirs" remains a subject for considerable speculation.

Together with his British wife Jennifer, who is officially listed as Moscow representative for the London *Times Educational Supplement,* he has published a motorists' guidebook to the Soviet Union. Mrs. Louis also issues Information Moscow, a lucrative semi-annual telephone and address book of the foreign community that is printed in London and sent to its more than two thousand Moscow subscribers at a rate of $7.60 per year.

Most important, perhaps, Louis travels a great deal: to Taiwan, for example, to chat with Chiang Kai-shek's son-in-law, to Spain to deal with Spanish officials and to Israel to cure his lumbago and consult a physician who just happens to have been a former Israeli ambassador to the Soviet Union and to other unusual places where Soviet diplomacy cannot function through normal channels.

Louis lives in Peredelkino, Moscow's most exclusive dacha suburb, where he maintains a house that is more than just a modest home. An eleven room, three-story structure, which he bought from the widow of a Soviet Army general, it features an expansive dining wing, a den and bar, a sauna imported from Finland, a tennis court, a swimming pool, one of Moscow's better icon collections, paintings by avant-garde artists, antique furniture, West German hi-fi equipment and an intricate intercom network. There he maintains a staff of five, including a full-time cook, maid, nursemaid and chauffeur. The chauffeur looks after the Louises' three cars: a Mercedes, a Land-Rover and Moscow's only Porsche.

One of his next-door neighbors in Peredelkino, by the way, is General Sergei Shtemenko, chief of staff of Warsaw Pact Forces.

There are thousands of Motorikos, Shimalinuses, Louises and, of course, Shtemenkos in the Soviet Union, many of them bigger, richer, better connected and more privileged, many of them smaller, but all in their way members of the classless society's upper classless, the new bourgeoisie, the new elite.

Members of the party hierarchy, top government bureaucrats, managers of big industrial enterprises, high-ranking military officers, scientists, university professors, academicians, establishment writers, socialist-realist artists, composers, musicians, performers, entertainers —they flash around in chauffeur-driven cars and wear the latest clothes from abroad. They take pride in drinking and offering scotch whisky and in smoking American cigarettes. They move in a tight, private little world of suburban dachas, downtown co-operative apartments and exclusive clubs. They all know each other. Their sons and daughters attend the same schools and eventually intermarry.

The high society of a professed egalitarian world, they are blessed with money and/or privileges that create a greater gap between them and Ivan Ivanov, Russia's Mr. Average, than the one between the John D. Rockefellers and the John Does of the United States. They are the living proof that Communism works—for those who know how to make it work for themselves.

The crowded communal flats, persistent shortages, endless queues, shoddy workmanship, battles with bureaucracy, collectivized vacation resorts and drabness bordering on poverty which are the bane of millions—these are not for the new elite.

As one iconoclastic but idealistic Soviet journalist once told me: "The men on the Politburo as well as the *apparatchiki* on several power echelons below them are more isolated from the people of this country than were any of the tsars and boyars. Entitled to enormous perquisites, they haven't the faintest notion how the country really lives. No *apparatchik,* once he has reached a certain echelon of power, even on local party levels, ever stands in a queue, is ever face to face with a sullen clerk and never has to fight his way into a bus or the metro."

Money is one though not the chief reason the elite can escape these realities of Soviet life.

By now it is admitted, reluctantly, even in the U.S.S.R., that there are ruble millionaires: mostly the big-name authors, composers, screenwriters and playwrights, movie stars, musicians and performers, who benefit from a liberal system of royalties on massive circulations of popular books, films or records. These don't have to be the big names known in the West: Shostakovich, Khachaturian, Sholokhov, Oistrakh, Richter or Rostropovich. Some have made their fortunes writing pop music, children's books, popular verses and the dozens of B-rated films that flicker across Soviet movie and television screens every day.

Perhaps not quite as rich but still comfortably wealthy are scientists, particularly members of the august Soviet Academy of Sciences, and Lenin Prize winners of every description. Top government officials, military officers and industrial managers rank right behind them.

In 1970 the statistical average monthly wage of skilled blue- and white-collar workers in the U.S.S.R. was 122 rubles.

But the director of a factory will earn from 500 to 1500 rubles a month, depending on the size of the plant and the bonuses he receives. In addition he is entitled to such emoluments as a chauffeur-driven car for his constant use, two or three personal secretaries and usually two personal assistants.

A full professor's base salary is around 450 rubles per month. The majority earn two to three times that much from lecturing, writing and consultation fees. Extra salaries, frequently double the base, are paid to directors of institutes and laboratories engaged in important research.

Important scientists whose discoveries are recognized internationally may be earning as much as 9000 rubles monthly from royalties, special fees and bonuses.

The Soviet armed forces have 350,000 to 400,000 active officers on the rolls, nearly each of whom, starting with senior lieutenants, earn more than the statistical national average. Colonels are in the 450–500-ruble category. A one-star general earns from 650 to 750, although some, such as Grigorenko, who taught cybernetics at Frunze Military Academy and drew additional pay in that capacity, receive even more. Four-star generals earn up to 1300 and marshals as much as 2000 rubles a month. And there are, according to Western estimates, approximately ten thousand active general and flag officers in the Soviet armed forces today. Like the military anywhere, Soviet officers are catered to and cared for by a special network of military stores and housing, and high-ranking officers have such privileges as chauffeured automobiles, special rest centers and sanatoria at their disposal.

As in many Western countries, there is less to be gained from government service. Full ministers may be drawing as little as 800 rubles per month. But they have privileges that go with their jobs: government dachas (with swimming pools, of course), limousines (a fleet of luxurious cars is available to the Kremlin hierarchy and Brezhnev prefers a Rolls-Royce, in which he speeds down Kutuzovsky Prospect—from his apartment to the Kremlin—each day just before 9 A.M.) and a bevy of servants for their private use—until they are either dismissed or resign.

Many members of the elite receive a second wage—from the Communist Party—for performing certain full- or part-time executive party functions. The vast army of party *apparatchiki* has a pay scale of its own, about which virtually nothing is known outside its ranks. At the very highest level, however, such as the Politburo, pay is not even an issue. The top functionaries have "open accounts" at their disposal from which they may draw and spend as much as they wish.

Unlike the rich and superrich in other countries, the Soviet Union's elite can keep most of what they earn. Communist propaganda and Marxist principles notwithstanding, Soviet income and other tax laws benefit the wealthy to the detriment of the poor. Even Soviet millionaires pay only the legal maximum in income tax: 13 per cent. Many capitalist countries tax inheritance as high as 91 per cent. The Soviet Union has no inheritance tax at all. But it does have a high hidden sales and turnover tax. Included in the price of all consumer goods, it disadvantages lower-income groups and benefits the wealthied elite.

Money income, particularly if it is mostly in rubles, is, however, the least important advantage of making it in the U.S.S.R. The real boons derive from a compendium of tangible and intangible privileges: greater freedom, better medical care, the opportunity to travel abroad and the right to shop in special stores where goods, at cut-rate prices, are available which the average citizen may not see in his lifetime. Caviar, never sold in ordinary Soviet shops, is but one example.

Playing the system has had its material rewards in the U.S.S.R.

since the Revolution and it is not coincidental that a Communist Party membership card has been known since the earliest days of Soviet power as a "bread card."

"To understand our country," a friend once told me, "you must learn that there are two ways of Soviet life. One is the official way, reflected in *Pravda*. It portrays a life of glowing statistics, rigidly controlled prices and wages and the interminable promises of a better tomorrow. But this is also the life of shortages, queues, waiting lists, low-quality goods at sky-high prices and compliance with stupid rules enforced by mask-faced cretinous bureaucrats.

"Then there is the real life," by which he meant the gray and black markets which thrive on corruption, bribery, influence peddling, theft and the traditional Russian adage that it is infinitely better to have a hundred friends than a hundred rubles. "This," he added, "is the life most of us lead part of the time, some of us most of the time."

It is a way of life that depends on human ingenuity to overcome the inefficacy that human minds built into the Soviet system. It has turned the U.S.S.R. into a nation of merchants and hypocrites who distribute and redistribute goods according to need, not government plan, with sometimes legal, frequently semi-legal and usually illegal means: the Georgian farmers who fly tomatoes, cucumbers, lemons and gladioli to Moscow and other Central Russian cities where they sell them at twice to ten times what they would cost in state shops —if the state shops stocked them; the worker who filches nuts and bolts from his shop, bags of cement from a construction site or water faucets from a half-completed apartment house to sell to friends and acquaintances; the *kombinator* (a smart operator) who can supply underground artists with good canvas, aspiring dacha owners with lumber and even a state-owned motor pool with spare parts to put its trucks and cars on the road again.

But then there is also a third way of life—for the privileged. It is the only Soviet way of life that is both legal and free of material worries and wants. It encompasses a whole network of closed shops, hotels and other facilities, to which only certain members of the elite have access, where the highest-quality goods are sold at very reasonable (sometimes nominal) prices and service is excellent. Once called "Central Committee stores," they now cater to a somewhat larger group than the narrow circle of top-echelon party bureaucrats to which they used to be restricted: government and party professionals of second-echelon rank, as well as diplomats from Communist countries who do not have access to hard Western currencies.

These "closed shops," which sell luxury, high-quality and imported merchandise—for rubles—are but one aspect of the good life. Another is the system of so-called *valutniye magaziny,* or foreign currency shops, where export-quality Soviet merchandise, never available in Russian stores, and imported goods are sold for foreign currency or currency certificates. Here American cigarettes cost 19 cents, twelve-year Scotch whiskies only $2.60 a fifth, fresh caviar $44 per kilogram, Soviet television sets one fourth their ruble value at the official exchange rate and Russian furs as little as a fifth of the price in state fur shops.

The circle of the privileged who may shop here includes foreign tourists, diplomats, businessmen and correspondents; Soviet citizens who receive money from relatives in the West; those who have earned foreign exchange—writers, composers, artists and performers; Soviet diplomats, journalists, government bureaucrats and commercial agents; and finally a small elite of high-level party people who have been given foreign currency certificates as bonuses for work well done.

Moscow even boasts a foreign currency supermarket, the *valutny gastronom,* where foreign residents rub shoulders at the checkout lines with Soviet officers, diplomats, the widow of Sergei Prokofiev, Yevgeny Yevtushenko and leading scientists.

Red-armband-wearing guards stand at the doors of most of these outlets to keep away the masses of average Russians who have no *valuta* (foreign currency) but press their noses to the windows to see what is inside. *"U vas yest tserifikaty* (Do you have certificates)?" the guards ask every Russian who attempts to enter. For certificates —of varying colors and value, exchanged under varying conditions —are the only legal tender in these emporiums of relative luxury and plenitude.

I have seen *valuta* shop bouncers turn away countless Soviet citizens, who could then be heard grumbling loudly: "What kind of a country is this, where our money is no good in a shop that belongs to the people?"

The class system extends even to the quality of free medicine and medical attention that members of the elite enjoy. Many members of the upper and middle class can afford to pay high fees for private treatment by the most competent doctors and dentists, whose semi-legal practice is infinitely better than the distinctly poor medical service provided the general public. But those who are really in have something even better than private practice: a network of free poly-clinics and hospitals more modern and elegant than any open to the general public.

"I didn't know anything like that existed in our country," said one acquaintance after visiting a friend in one of these institutions. "There are more doctors than patients and they provide personal care. It's just like somewhere in the West."

Having been in the West, this Russian had already met one of the key criteria of having "arrived." To have traveled abroad, even more, of course, than to have access to foreign currency, is an unmistakable sign of being "in." And those who are in make the most of it. When she was still alive it used to be said of Kosygin's wife that when she accompanied her husband abroad she spent nearly all her time shopping. In Helsinki, for example, she passed her days in Stockmann's Department Store, the Finnish capital's emporium of plenty where the shelves bend with goods most Russians have never seen.

Soviet society is still too new to have established an elite within the elite based on heritage and parentage. But who doubts that the children of today's privileged will become the privileged of tomor-row? Money, bribes, political influence and pressure, as I pointed out earlier, are paving their way to a better education, better con-nections and a better job.

Most high school students, according to a survey conducted in Leningrad in 1969, want to go to college, university or technical institutes to become physicists, medical researchers, geologists, chemists, mathematicians or radio specialists. They list as the least desirable occupations: turner, milling machine operator, store clerk, bookkeeper and agricultural worker. And the reasons for their choice invariably are prestige and the material benefits that accrue to the professions and members of the technical intelligentsia.

For children of industrial workers and farmers, a higher education is a guarantee of social advancement. For the children of the in-telligentsia and the privileged, it will ensure continuation of the privileges they enjoy by virtue of their parents' social position.

While attitudes are changing, wealth and privilege are still a sufficient source of embarrassment to those who have them that they prefer discretion and quiet. Of course members of the elite show up at fashionable premieres in the Bolshoi Theater in their latest acquisitions from Paris, London or New York. But when they whiz off afterward in black Volgas, Chaikas and Zim limousines, it is not to mingle with the proletariat in popular Moscow restaurants but to private parties at their fenced-off dachas in Peredelkino, Kuntsevo and Zhukovo or their respective clubs—the House of Journalists, Writers, Composers, Cinema Workers, Actors or Architects.

They have usually read the latest Western books—brought home by friends and passed surreptitiously from hand to hand. They have seen in their clubs or the Dom Kino, the House of Cinema Workers, the latest Western movies and even proscribed Soviet movies (such as *Andrei Rublyov,* the fictionalized biography of the master icon painter, which has been hailed as an outstanding film abroad but will never be cleared by Glavlit for general release in the U.S.S.R.), which are never shown to the public at large, but serve to keep Soviet cineasts and technicians up to date.

If they are following the latest snobbism among Moscow's intelligentsia they have switched from modern to antique furniture, energetically hunted among descendants of the old bourgeoisie or bought in the secondhand shops run by the government. And they may have been more than a little worried when the director of the largest of these shops in Moscow was imprisoned in April 1971 for accepting bribes from wealthy customers.

Clannish and disinclined to flaunt their wealth in a society where the worker remains the eulogized paradigm of virtue, the elite tend to vacation together—in *modniye* spots such as Bakuriani in the Caucasus for winter skiing or Tallin on the Baltic Sea for summer swimming.

The creative unions maintain not only their own rest homes and country houses where members can relax but some have their own kindergartens and summer camps for members' children with the best equipment, teachers and counselors that rubles and influence can buy. There the offspring of the privileged are free from the prying eyes of nosy Communist do-gooders who might wonder why little Pyotr or Katya are dressed from head to toe in foreign clothes.

The advantage of all this is not only that the elite are among themselves, and presumably more at ease, but succeed in living free from the public's prying eye. The limousines in which they ride have the rear and side windows curtained and in the suburbs there is not a dacha without a ten-foot board fence around it—invariably painted green.

The wives of the upper classless have their own clique of hairdressers, manicurists and dressmakers who are remunerated for their discreet, speedy and meticulous service by occasional small gifts from abroad, tickets to important theater premieres or, even more valuable, appearances in Moscow by foreign ensembles such as the Paris Opera ballet or the Berlin Philharmonic with Herbert von Karajan conducting. For the latter, a total of 600 tickets were sold publicly for three performances. All remaining seats in the Moscow Conservatory—4800 for the three nights—went to members of the privileged elite. The audience was so stellar that even Veronika Duderova, conductor of the Moscow City Symphony, had to sit in the fifth to the last row of the orchestra.

With all its money, stature and influence, however, the Soviet elite live in a luxury that could, at best, be called upper middle class by American standards. Even a Viktor Louis with his sauna, swimming pool and three cars would cause hardly a ripple in Westchester. But in the Soviet context he is a manifestation of the lip service that the regime gives to the egalitarian principles on which it stakes its claim to power.

Even if the Soviet elite seem merely upper middle class by Western standards, compared to the Soviet average, their style of life and their privileges are palatial. To understand that one must experience the average Russia.

I will never forget the reaction of a Soviet acquaintance to whom I showed a *Newsweek* special report on poverty in the U.S.A. Leafing through the magazine and glancing cursorily at the pictures of hungry and bedraggled children in Appalachia and the big city slums of Chicago and New York, he turned to me and said: "You call this poverty? Well, you had better look around Russia to see what poverty is all about."

Crime is a product of social excess.

V. I. Lenin

Alcoholism is a disease of capitalism.

Friedrich Engels

10 *The Imperfect Society*

"The Russians," Adam Olearius wrote in 1647, "are more addicted to drunkenness than any nation in the world . . . The vice of drunkenness is prevalent among this people in all classes, both secular and ecclesiastical, high and low, men and women, young and old. To see them lying here and there in the streets, wallowing in filth, is so common that no notice is taken of it."

Two centuries later Custine wrote:

"The greatest pleasure of these people is drunkenness. Poor people! They have to dream to be happy."

Communism, it was promised, would change all that.

In the heady days of the 1920s, the Large Soviet Encyclopedia pontificated that in the U.S.S.R., "where class exploitation has been finally liquidated and where the material well-being of the people has been improving constantly, the social roots of alcoholism have been destroyed."

Yet today, fifty-four years after the Revolution, more than three hundred since Olearius wrote his observations, the Russians still seem more addicted to drunkenness than any nation in the world and the picture of drunks staggering on the streets and wallowing in the dirt is as much a part of modern Moscow as it was three centuries ago.

In fact, to judge from Soviet figures, Russians today are drinking more than at any time in their history. The sale of alcoholic beverages, primarily vodka, has more than doubled during the past decade, and increased fivefold since 1940, although the population has grown by only 20 per cent.

Alcohol, according to the deputy minister of internal affairs, Boris T. Shumilin, accounts for more than two thirds of all crimes committed in the Soviet Union, is involved in 98 per cent of all murders, is the cause for 40 per cent of the divorces, 50 per cent of all accidents and 63 per cent of the drownings. Moreover, 90 per cent of the inmates of juvenile correction colonies are serving sentences for crimes committed while intoxicated.

The losses incurred by Soviet industry from alcoholism are probably incalculable, but by early 1970 they had reached such proportions that drunkenness became one of the chief targets of a nationwide labor discipline campaign. In fact, the "demon vodka" had grown to such menacing proportions that the Politburo was seriously considering prohibition. A debate on the subject in January 1970 reportedly lasted almost ten days. Too many persuasive arguments, however, were finally raised against that idea. The loss of revenues from vodka, a state monopoly since tsarist days, would have a debilitating effect on the economy. Moreover Russians—as they have on past occasion when partial prohibition was introduced or the price of vodka raised prohibitively—would merely turn to moonshining.

Instead the Soviet leadership decided to compromise. The restaurant price of vodka was doubled. The over-the-counter price was surreptitiously increased from 3.07 to 4.12 rubles per half-liter bottle by introducing a "new and better" vodka on the market: the same beverage with a different label. The price of Armenian and Georgian brandies was doubled. The sale of spirits in shops and kiosks near factories, schools, institutes and other public places was halted. The number of points of sale were reduced and the hours of selling spirits restricted to the period between 11 A.M. and 8 P.M.

Like many of the Politburo's compromise solutions, this one soon proved a failure. The price increase had virtually no effect on vodka sales in restaurants, though even affluent customers boycotted brandies, of which medium-quality labels were selling for 16 rubles per bottle. Moonshining increased perceptibly. And the only effect of restrictions on sales hours has been to stimulate the black market. By early afternoon it is now virtually impossible to buy a bottle of vodka in a Moscow shop. *Kombinatory* have bought up most of the day's supply. It reaches prospective customers again through taxi drivers at eight rubles—twice its official price—per half-liter bottle as soon as the Kremlin chimes strike 8 P.M.

Frequently Russians will quote an old saying, ruefully or proudly depending on the point of view, that "the joy of Russia is drinking," and hardly a traveler to Russia has neglected to mention the effect of alcohol on the people.

If it was not the cold, inhospitable climate that provided the need for strong, warming drinks in Russian history, then it was the tribulation of despotism and abject poverty. As Baron August von Haxthausen, a German traveler to Russia in the mid-nineteenth century, observed, the tavern and the cup were the only refuge for the *muzhik,* the only place and the only way he could escape his griefs. And then as now, the government pontificated against this evil but continued to encourage it, for liquor has been one of its chief sources of revenue—either through taxation or through the establishment of monopolies—since the days of Ivan the Terrible.

Describing the condition of the English working class in the nineteenth century, Friedrich Engels wrote: "When the tired and exhausted worker returns home, he enters his uncomfortable damp, cheerless dirty dwelling. He is urgently in need of recreation. He needs something to make working worthwhile, something that may alleviate for him the prospects of a hard day tomorrow." So he drank. And he drinks in Communist Russia because a half century after the Revolution the life of the Russian working man fits Engels' description as aptly as did the life of English workers a hundred years ago.

There is no cocktail hour refinement to divert attention from the glass to the conversation or the gentle sound of dreamy background music. There are no bars and taverns, in the Western sense, where conviviality is as important as what goes down the hatch. Most drinking is done in the home and few Russians could call their home their castle. It is cheerless and bare. There seems little else to do but open a bottle, set it on the kitchen table, bring out the water tumblers and proceed to attack it.

Restaurants, the closest thing in the Soviet Union to a night club in the West, are always overcrowded, hard to get into and usually devoid of ambiance, elegance or coziness. Even in metropolitan centers such as Moscow the best restaurants are often not better than second-rate cafeterias in Western cities. Entertainment is limited to a tired, off-tune band playing the hits of yesteryear. By 11 P.M., when most of them close, the tables groan with the weight of empty bottles and the shutdown scene is invariably a drunken Bedlam.

One of the most pernicious influences is the pride that Russians place in their capacity for alcohol. "I can drink a whole liter and still walk without difficulty," one acquaintance used to say. And he wasn't exaggerating.

A good deal of Russian intemperance is also due to the style of drinking. They make no compromises about imbibing. The long drink that the Westerner tends to nurse for a good part of an evening is just unknown. Whether he drinks to toast a friend, to wash down food, to impress a guest with his hospitality, to celebrate a wedding, a funeral or the acquisition of a car, apartment, refrigerator or new job, the Russian approach is singularly destined to produce quick results: *do dna*—bottoms up—and down the hatch.

Moreover, vodka drinking represents a Soviet style of machismo. Fifteen- and sixteen-year-olds prove their manhood by getting inebriated. The initiation of young apprentices in factories and workshops ineluctably calls for getting these teen-agers drunk. Foreigners who fail to empty their glasses in one gurgle, no matter how often in the course of a dinner or banquet, are scoffed at as weaklings.

As long ago as the sixteenth century Sigismund zu Herberstein observed that the "Russians go to great lengths to make their guests drunk . . . When they have no reason for a toast they look for one. They will drink to the health of the tsar, his brothers, and all the other princes and boyars . . . One must empty the cup and turn it upside down over one's head to prove that it is really empty . . . He who does not want to drink so much must either feign drunkenness or act as if he were full of wine or drowsy, or he must attempt to get the others drunk and the convince them that he has had enough, for the Russians believe they have not received and entertained their guests properly until all the guests are drunken . . ."

"Mistaken notions of manhood and pseudo-national customs," Dr.

Lydia Bogdanovich, a Soviet physician, lamented in *Izvestia* once, "are responsible for much unnecessary drinking."

But while mistaken notions may be the cause of unnecessary drinking, they do not explain satisfactorily the recent increase in consumption. One reason appears to be that Russians earn more money than ever before but have virtually no consumer durables to spend it on.

Another factor is additional leisure time and the introduction of the five-day week in 1968. The two-day weekend's potential effect was predicted in January 1968 by *Krokodil,* the Soviet humor magazine, which published a cover-page cartoon showing a thoroughly soused Russian returning from work on a Friday night, triumphantly holding a bottle of vodka in *each* hand and proclaiming loudly to his waiting wife: "Look, Natasha, now I have *two* free days a week."

The measures introduced in the spring of 1970 were not the first Soviet efforts at temperance. All have been to little avail. In the 1920s there was the All-Union Council of Anti-Alcohol societies whose only significant achievement seems to have been to increase the production of *samogon*—moonshine. Dispensation by the glass disappeared in the 1950s as part of a moderation drive. The result was that two and three Russians will double and triple up to polish off a whole bottle and drink more than if they could buy a shot or two at a kiosk or tavern counter.

Until the price went up in 1970, one could frequently see a customer, his fist across his chest and thumb pointing upward, somewhere near the liquor counter of a grocery store. It meant: "I have a ruble toward a bottle of vodka, who's sharing?" Eventually a second tippler would join him and the finger signs changed to two digits, which meant: "Two rubles in the kitty, one to go." A third volunteer was never far away and then the three would buy a bottle and adjourn to a dark doorway or a quiet corner of a park.

Probably a second bottle would follow the first before the night was over and the three went their separate ways to stagger across dimly lit thoroughfares or, even worse, drop off in a stupor on the sidewalk—in subzero temperatures. If a militiaman found them they would end up in a "sobering-up station" where a night's "cure" now costs 25 rubles. Moscow alone has more than twenty of these.

Now that the price has increased from 3.07 to 4.12 per half-liter bottle the three-on-a-bottle routine has changed to two, with the net effect that consumption has increased.

"It is good that we have declared war on drunkenness," a high-ranking police officer said in the spring of 1970.

But the war has been waged for many years. When will, or can, Russia win it? "Never," a Moscow friend told me emphatically. "If they decided to stop the sale of vodka or greatly reduce it, there would be a bigger revolution than in 1917."

* * *

Drunkenness has been a Russian curse for centuries. Drugs, on the other hand, are a recent phenomenon. And while it has not reached Western proportions, the problem exists, is getting worse, and to deal with it Soviet authorities have increased the penalties.

I never met any Russians who claimed or admitted to be pot users, although I have encountered some youngsters who said that they had "a lot of friends" who smoke hashish, while insisting that they did not do so themselves.

"There is very little of that," a Komsomol activist and post-graduate student in mathematical analysis at Kazan University told me. "I won't deny that we have some hashish smokers in the school, but I'm sure they represent less than 1 per cent of the student body."

According to prevalent grapevine information, 100 grams of hashish in Moscow costs around ten rubles. The price is three to five times higher in other cities, though considerably less in the Central Asian republics, where Moslem tradition has made hashish a part of life. Visitors to Uzbekistan, Tadzhikistan, Kirghizia and other Central Asian areas have all observed men taking a drag or two from a "joint" in public, then throwing it away.

The main problem area in the U.S.S.R. seems to be Georgia. In June 1969 the Georgian Supreme Soviet passed an anti-narcotics law that imposed penalties twice as severe as those in any other Soviet republic. Moreover the new law made use of drugs an offense for the first time in the U.S.S.R.

Under the Georgian edict, users will be detained for ten to fifteen days' compulsory treatment, if they are first offenders. Repeaters may be committed for six to twelve months to special camps for drug victims. Procuring or selling drugs was made an offense punishable by a maximum of ten years, and growers or processors of narcotics may be imprisoned for up to fifteen years.

Since the new law went into effect, Georgian officials have mounted an intensive propaganda campaign against narcotics. In Tbilisi billboards warning against the use of drugs have been posted on main streets. One sign on Rustaveli Avenue showed photographs and gave the names and addresses of several convicted addicts.

Soviet officials have never provided any explanation for why addiction should be so much greater a problem in Georgia than in other republics. True, it borders on Turkey, one of the chief opium-growing and -exporting countries of the world, but then so does Armenia, where drug addiction apparently is not a problem.

More severe penalties and intensified propaganda notwithstanding, usage and addiction continue to proliferate in Georgia. Vasily Mzhavanadze, the Georgian Communist Party's first secretary, has inveighed against drug addiction on at least three public occasions since the new law was passed in the summer of 1969.

As with so many other phenomena in Soviet life, authorities make little or no attempt to discover the real causes of drug addiction but prefer to call it a "remnant of the past" or a "bourgeois infection."

"Narcomania is a national tragedy in many countries of the capitalist world," said *Vercherny Tbilisi,* the Georgian capital's evening daily. "Unfortunately here and there we too have a few young people who blindly follow the bourgeois example, have lost their human feelings, have substituted idleness and drug taking for socially useful work, thus harming themselves, their families and the interests of the whole nation. It is clear to all that drug taking is not characteristic of the Soviet way of life and is a foreign bacteria that has penetrated the healthy body of our society . . ."

*   *   *

The bacteria that seems to have penetrated deepest in "the healthy body" of Soviet society is crime, although most Soviet officials are reluctant to admit it. They prefer, instead, to see crime in Soviet society as a remnant from pre-revolutionary times.

Crime, reported a panel of Soviet experts in *Izvestia* in 1968, "is a phenomenon that is socially and historically conditioned. It started at a certain stage of society's development with the appearance of private property and division of society into classes . . . The victory of socialism has liquidated the cardinal causes that generate crime, though crimes and offenses continue to be committed in socialist society. They are not a creation of socialism but followed into socialism from the exploitatory society that preceded it."

It was at about the same time that General Nikolai Shchelokov, the minister of internal affairs, boasted that "we have been successful in fighting crime because we have eliminated its basic social source: private ownership of the means of production and exploitation of man by man. Our socialist way of life, our moral and political unity, our mass education have ensured this success."

More than two years later, in an interview with a reporter from *Ogonyok* magazine, Shchelokov was singing a slightly different tune.

"One cannot fail to note the high level of crime in our daily life," he said. "There is a large proportion of murders and assaults . . . A merciless and uncompromising struggle must be carried on against thieves and hooligans."

Like accident figures, crime figures are not published in the Soviet Union and newspaper reportage on individual crimes is sharply curtailed. The only trend statistic that Soviet officials will disclose is that crime has decreased to 30 per cent of the 1928 level. The last time a breakdown was published in the U.S.S.R. was in 1966. It revealed that 25 per cent of all crime in the Soviet Union was misappropriation of state property; 15 per cent was theft of personal property; 12 per cent was crime against persons; 20 per cent hooliganism (a Soviet euphemism for every kind of asocial behavior from drunkenness to petty theft and unarmed robberies); 15 per cent "personal crimes" such as brawls, slander and insult; 5 per cent automotive crimes, presumably accidents involving criminal negligence; and 8 per cent "others."

But notwithstanding the exiguity of statistical information, other indicators point to an increase, particularly in misappropriation of state property and theft of personal property.

The evidence can be found between the lines of carefully worded proclamations of concern by Soviet officials. Burglaries, for example, have become so prevalent in Moscow that in 1968 the militia began advertising an alarm system with which private citizens could protect their apartments for an installation charge of 13.50 rubles and a monthly service charge of less than 3 rubles. The system, based on an electronic connection between apartment doors, windows and the telephone, has "thousands" of subscribers, according to Moscow militia colonel Pyotr Moskalkov.

Anyone who has lived in Moscow for a few years can attest that some system is necessary. In the thirty-two months that I spent in the Soviet capital, the *Newsweek* office was burglarized three times. A fourth break-in occurred shortly before I arrived. I did not even count how often side mirrors and other accessories were stolen from my car. It was pilfered once in Yaroslavl by an as yet unidentified adolescent who stole a camera, several lenses, a light meter and other items and left a handwritten calling card, signed "Fantomas": a French underworld character whose crime series has run on Soviet television.

Not only is the crime rate climbing, despite socialism, the abolition of private enterprise and all those other factors that Soviet theorists claim should render crime obsolete in Soviet society, but Russian sociologists, psychologists and criminologists have begun to recognize that the causes in Soviet society are virtually the same as in capitalist countries. It is the industrialization and urbanization of life with all the pressures this entails: crowded living conditions, nervous tension, excessive drinking, broken homes, rising expectations and wants, social inequality and a degree of boredom.

By New York or Washington standards, of course, Moscow and Leningrad are still very safe cities in which to live—a fact that Soviet propagandists never fail to mention when they gloat about the high crime rate in the United States.

"You mean," an incredulous New Yorker asked me on her first visit to Moscow, "that you can really ride the subway at night and a woman can walk the streets alone after dark?"

Yes, on the whole, one can. But Moscow, too, has street thugs and muggers.

Muscovites still talk about Yuri Zemtsov and his girl friend Ala Demina, sentenced to thirteen and eight years respectively for a series of Moscow assaults. Ala played decoy, propositioning men in the vicinity of the three largest Moscow railway stations around Komsomol Square. Inviting them to her apartment nearby, she led them down dimly lighted streets and into dark alleys where Zemtsov and some of his accomplices waited to rob them.

Another case involved a gang of sixteen, led by a Georgian named Mamiya Vasadze, who drugged victims with doctored wine and vodka before robbing them. In several months of operation in Central Russia they raked in 250,000 rubles and left two corpses—victims to whom they had given an overdose. Vasadze was sentenced to death, the others to terms of five to fifteen years in labor camps.

The case of Valentin Samoilov, sentenced to death in December 1970 for five attempted murders, could have been taken from the police blotter in Boston as easily as in Voronezh. Samoilov had been out drinking with friends when he boarded a streetcar, slumped into a seat and started cracking sunflower seeds with his teeth and spitting the husks on the floor. Two passengers standing near him told him "this streetcar is not a garbage can." He lunged at each of the passengers, a man and a woman, with a switchblade knife, stabbing both of them, dashed for the center exit and knifed a woman standing in his way, then rushed toward the rear platform, where he cut up two students who tried to grab and detain him. Samoilov jumped from the moving car and was caught a short time later by *militsionery*.

But even if one can walk the streets of Mosow in relative safety, there are many other things one cannot do. It is difficult, for example, to travel to Sochi on the Black Sea without encountering swindlers on the train. An evening at even the most expensive and exclusive Moscow restaurant is likely to end with a drunken melee that would make a saloon battle in a B-grade Western movie seem tame. The Russian industrial manager who leaves his warehouses or parts and machinery stocks unguarded is likely to find them empty within a few weeks, due to pilferage.

The militia in Baku, capital of Azerbaidzhan, are reputed to be so corrupt that Moscow's best-known comic, Arkady Raikin, brings the house down with a line in one of his skits suggesting that anyone planning a murder should commit it in Baku—where the police can be bought off to look the other way.

And obviously it is no longer safe to leave one's apartment unguarded.

One gang of burglars in Moscow specialized in furs which they stole from apartments, mostly on "fashionable" Leningradsky Prospect and Prospect Mira, reselling them for thousands of rubles in Siberia. The four men and a woman worked out a system of studying apartment windows and looking for expensive curtains, which, they believed, indicated that the occupant also owned other expensive things. When they saw the type of window they were looking for, they kept watch on it for several days. If it never opened, they assumed the occupants were out of town. They entered with skeleton keys and looked only for fur coats, spurning everything else of value. The ringleader then left Moscow by plane with a coat—or two or three if it had been a profitable day—to sell his merchandise in the far north or Siberia, where quality goods are in even shorter supply than in Moscow and the police less efficient.

The thieves who broke into David Oistrakh's apartment several years ago were apparently less discriminating than the fur coat gang, but therefore more avaricious. They allegedly stole about a million rubles' worth of cash, paintings, *objets d'art* and antiques from the musician's flat while he was out of the country on a concert tour.

In many apartment houses residents have chipped in to pay for an elevator woman who screens all people coming into the building and locks the front door at midnight. In other buildings elevators are locked and only tenants have keys.

General Shchelokov boasted several years ago that there has been no bank robbery in the Soviet Union in decades. One reason may be that there are so few banks. But if bank robbery has indeed been abolished, the Soviet Union still has almost every other kind of crime committed in capitalist countries, including some rather gruesome murders.

One of the grisliest in Moscow in recent years was the rape-murder of two coeds whose bodies were found hidden in the attic of the Moscow Power Engineering Institute. Their confessed killer turned out to be a thirty-year-old professional photographer who allegedly lured them to a secluded spot in the building with the intention of taking pornographic pictures.

Cop killings, while undoubtedly not as numerous as in the United States, also occur. Soviet newspapers periodically report posthumous awards for militiamen killed in the line of duty.

However, the majority of slayings—Soviet sources have indicated to me that 250 to 300 are committed in Moscow each year—are not premeditated and involve alcohol. Husbands kill wives, fathers, sons and sons, fathers because, as the brief report of one such case explained, "vodka destroyed and burned out everything that was alive and decent in this man."

Confidence crimes and fraud are prevalent and usually mirror those shortcomings of the Soviet economy on which bunko men and swindlers capitalize.

Thus, a Moscow woman was convicted for having defrauded dozens of people of a total of more than 38,000 rubles by pretending to be an official of the city council taking down payments on co-operative apartments.

Restrictions on the population growth of large cities prohibit anyone from moving to Moscow unless he has a guaranteed job or apartment, or happens to marry a legal Moscow resident. Leonid Kasakevich turned the latter requirement into a lucrative undertaking. For a fee of a thousand rubles he agreed to become a temporary legal husband to a half-dozen young women eager to move to the capital.

One gang preyed on Armenian and Georgian demands for private automobiles at inflated black market prices. They plied their victims with drugged champagne, then robbed them of the cash they were carrying. Three of the "customers" died for their gullibility.

Some prosperous Georgian and Armenian farmers are willing to pay fabulous premiums for cars. In January 1971 *Izvestia* reported on the case of a lottery ticket, good for a Volga sedan, which a woman in Kazakhstan had exchanged for the official cash price of the car: 5602 rubles. Many months later the ticket surfaced in Yerevan, where it was worth 19,000 rubles. A half-dozen people had made profits of 1000 and 2000 rubles on it en route from the town of Rudny, east of the Ural Mountains, to its ultimate purchaser in the Armenian capital.

Although Soviet authorities have divulged little about the scope, Russian sociologists are now making public information about the shape and nature of juvenile delinquency. Vandalism, rowdyism and petty larceny account for most of it. The crimes parallel those committed by youths in other countries, with disemboweling of pay phones and vending machines high on the list.

Seventy-five per cent of juvenile crimes, according to one Moscow University survey, are committed by youths acting in groups of twos and threes, rarely larger. Only 15 per cent of the crimes by minors are committed by children under sixteen years of age. Forty per cent of the offenders come from homes where at least one parent drinks heavily or leads what the researchers consider an immoral way of life. More than three fourths of all juvenile offenders are urban youths. Hooliganism accounts for 36 per cent of the crimes committed by them, theft of state and public property represents 20 per cent, theft of property 13 per cent and robbery 13 per cent.

Although Soviet officials express concern both about the increment of juvenile crime as well as crimes of violence under the influence of alcohol and the climbing personal theft rate, their greatest worry is misappropriation of state property and the Hydra-like phenomenon of "economic crime."

This term is a convenient misnomer to cover a wide range of economic and social offenses: petty larceny of state property, profiteering, illegal private enterprise, black-marketing, influence peddling, bribery and corruption.

As a genre of crime it is at least as old as the Tartar occupation and in seven centuries it has almost become a Russian way of life.

Who knows what really makes other societies and other economies function? But in Russia, it seems, the lubricant and impetus are easy enough to find. It is the greased palm. And to judge from the observations of earlier travelers, it has always been that way.

"Money from other cities and districts was paid and weighed in the Court Treasury," Heinrich von Staden, no paragon of honesty himself, wrote in 1578. "One fiftieth of it always went astray before being reckoned and when the money was paid out by the chancellory, one tenth of it was always missing."

No one seemed to care.

Three centuries later Alexandre Dumas visited Russia and wrote: "Everyone from the emperor down to the humblest *dvornik* is forever urging that corrupt practices must cease. But they go on just the same."

Today everyone still urges that the fight against corruption must be stepped up. But in practice everyone expects the other *tovarishch* to do the fighting.

For decades Soviet authorities have tried to inculcate in Russians the idea that when they steal from the state, which owns just about everything, they are merely stealing from themselves. That concept has failed to take roots. On the contrary, the prevalent belief appears to be that since public property is everyone's property, it is also no one's property and therefore free for the taking.

Soviet newspapers are forever wagging an admonitory finger at construction workers who build their dachas with pilfered building materials, bus drivers who pocket most of the day's receipts, factory employees who steal 2 to 3 per cent of the total production.

No one seems embarrassed. In 1963 Nikita Khrushchev asked the artist Ernest Neizvestny where he got the bronze with which to make the figures and sculptures of which the premier had disapproved. Neizvestny replied laconically: "I steal it."

Many of the practices that are considered crimes in the Soviet Union would not be thought of as offenses elsewhere. They are the outgrowth of an economy that proscribes any kind of private enterprise and in which demand chases supply like a greyhound pursues the mechanical hare around the track. Often they are the consequence of a welter of bureaucratic regulations, ponderous planning and the inefficiency that seems to be endemic to the Soviet economic system.

The U.S.S.R. permits only one type of private business undertaking: the sale of produce from kitchen gardens and farmers' private plots in the free peasant markets of the large cities. Thus, a Georgian farmer may take his tomatoes, cucumbers or lemons to Moscow to sell in the peasant market, at a rate of profit that borders on usurious extortion. He is merely taking legal advantage of the economy's failure to produce tomatoes, cucumbers and lemons in sufficient quantity to meet demand at the prices established for state stores.

The Armenian who once flew two suitcases of gladioli to frozen Kamchatka, where he sold them in one day for a net profit of eight thousand rubles, was also a legal operator. He grew the gladioli on land around his country cottage and they were rightfully his.

But the Muscovite who bought up batches of flowers from state shops at low prices early one morning, then resold them at a profit on the street and in the peasant market later in the day, was committing, by Soviet standards, a major economic crime.

So was the Georgian who once boasted that he could obtain trucks, railway cars and even airline seats within a few hours to ship scarce luxury goods such as Georgian grapes, flowers, wines and brandies, all bought on the black market, to anywhere in the Soviet Union. In a capitalist country he would be considered a shrewd entrepreneur. In the Soviet Union his acumen is punishable with death.

Nearly every Soviet city and town has a black market. Tbilisi's, with typical Georgian braggadocio, claims to be the best of them all. It operates from 10 A.M. to 7 P.M. and its operators can provide, at very high prices, Dacron fabrics, Japanese bikini bathing suits, artificial and real fur coats, American dentures, French perfumes, scarce medicaments and pharmaceutical products, imported sweaters, pullovers and shoes, Pop and rock records, English textiles and almost anything else discriminating customers may want.

Located in back alleys and dead-end lanes, it conducts business right under the noses of the law. One Soviet journalist hunting for a sport coat made of a specific synthetic fiber and cut to meet certain style requirements was led to a "businessman" in a certain Tbilisi street. There was nothing surreptitious about it. The customer stood on the pavement, the dealer on a second-story balcony, and they conducted their transaction at the tops of their voices and with plenty of gesticulation as scores of people passed by.

In the United States it might be called the "I can get it for you wholesale" syndrome. In the U.S.S.R. it is illegal and were it not for the leniency of the Georgian militia, or the greased palm that bought their silence, sport coat buyer and sport coat seller would both be in a labor camp. Yet it is illegal only because the state decrees it so, just as the market is black only because Soviet officialdom calls it black. The same entrepreneur could have sold the coat to a state-run *komissiony magazin*—secondhand store—where the same journalist could have bought it—at approximately the same price—and the transaction would have been considered completely lawful.

Although the Soviet Union is a land of chronic shortages and insufficient supply, there is nothing one cannot get—provided one has the connections, the money, the savvy and the patience to obtain it.

This postulate applies to private citizens as much as it does to state enterprises, which frequently employ the same illegal or extra-legal methods to obtain raw materials or spare parts to meet their production quotas as a Soviet housewife might use to put dinner on the table or a toothless *babushka* to put porcelain dentures in her mouth.

In Kiev the public prosecutor's office has published a report summing up a two-year investigation on why some institutions, enterprises, government agencies and apartment houses managed to have telephones installed almost overnight while others had to wait for months, sometimes years. The answer, of course, is bribery and juggling of the books to conceal the payoffs. Thus the administrative section of the Central Bureau for Scientific and Technical Information of the Ukrainian Ministry for the Chemical Industry paid an official bill of 18.45 rubles to postal authorities and 550 rubles in bribes to two technicians and two installation mechanics to get the phone that the Ministry of Communications said would not be available for months. For the 550-ruble "tip" numbers were redistributed mysteriously from other exchanges and bureaucratic regulations ignored. To cover the expenditure of 550 rubles the Chemical Ministry's phoneless department brought an unemployed man named Ponomarenko into the act. A fictitious contract, stipulating a "salary" of 550 rubles, was signed with him. After the money had been "earned" Ponomarenko was dismissed and he, the two technicians and the two mechanics divided the sum.

"Additional fees" such as this are paid by enterprise directors who want and need the machinery that the ministry above them has failed to allocate or deliver, by taxi drivers who need spare parts to keep their cabs running, collective farm chairmen who require an extra tractor or harvester and housewives who want a faucet repaired.

As a researcher for the All-Union Crime Research Institute lamented some years ago: "Chronic mismanagement in the economy plays an important role. It provides fertile soil and has the psychological effect of creating an asocial attitude."

What is an asocial attitude?

By Soviet standards it is the desire, first of all, to obtain and perform quality service *bez kvitantsii,* that is, without a receipt. The repair shop won't fix a tape recorder because it doesn't have the spare parts? Scrape up a three-ruble bill and the parts will be found. The galvanizer says it will take a month to put a coat of brass on the old nickel samovar? Tell him to do it *bez kvitantsii* and it'll be ready tomorrow. The shop says there is such a backlog of work that it'll take two to three weeks to mount the bindings on a new pair of cross-country skis? Dig up a bottle of vodka or cognac and they'll be ready "later today." The doorman at the restaurant says, "absolutely, there are no empty tables and besides we are closing for the day"? Slip him a fiver and he'll tell the maître d'hôtel to clear the best table in the house.

"Not only are bribes detrimental to society in a material sense," says *Pravda,* "but they inflict great moral damage as well. In selling their soul for a ruble and letting their respect go at a discount, some people grow accustomed to living beyond their means and sneering at the generally accepted rules and standards of life. Bribery leads to drunkenness, depravity, personal corruption. The struggle against the briber and the extortionist is the concern of all society."

But everybody does it, because social conditions encourage it.

The case of a Moscow construction enterprise, mismanaged for years, is typical. Orders placed for materials and supplies always overstated the needs and the surplus was allowed to deteriorate and go to waste. A worker there who saw perfectly good wire being written off as scrap and no one punished for it reasoned logically: "Why shouldn't I take it for myself?" He did and was convicted for theft. His attitude, the court judged, was asocial.

Workers at a factory producing women's synthetic raincoats in Suchumi, Georgia, played a variation on the same theme. According to the specifications the raincoats should have been packed in bags of the identical synthetic material and a kerchief should have been included in each. The workers decided the kerchief wasn't needed and the coat could be packed in a bag of cheaper material. They overfulfilled the plan by saving on materials and pocketed bonus payments.

Engaging in any private enterprise is automatically an economic crime.

For example, in Baku, the Azerbaidzhanian Choral Society asked authorities for permission to form a company to produce costumes for the group. The request was approved and with the help of a few arrangements and a bit of bribery, plant space comprising 2000 square yards was found and the factory began production. But instead of choral society costumes, it produced ready-to-wear items that are in short supply in the U.S.S.R. To keep the workers quiet, above-average salaries and extremely high premiums were paid. The plant practiced genuine socialist codetermination and profit sharing. Immediately upon closing a profitable deal, bonuses were paid out. Functionaries from various official institutes, including the state bank and the republic's Central Planning Commission, were involved in the operation. Eventually it was forced to shut down.

It would be misleading to suggest that all "economic" crimes are "innocent" misdemeanors. Graft is graft, even under Communism, and there is no dearth of examples of it.

From 1965 to 1967, for example, party officials in the district of Agdash in Azerbaidzhan set aside 65,000 rubles to build a kindergarten for twenty-five children. When all the money had been collected, the district party chief, A. S. Ragimov, decided that his own house should be converted into the kindergarten, and in exchange he would receive a "replacement" house to be furnished and outfitted with part of the money for the kindergarten. Some 10,000 rubles were spent on converting Ragimov's old place into the pre-school, although conditions were so unsatisfactory that the children had to take their noontime naps on the floor and there were insufficient sanitary facilities. The balance of the money, including 16,000 spent on original paintings and other ornamentation, went into Ragimov's "replacement" house. Ragimov was expelled from the Communist Party. A lesser personage would have been sent to prison.

In Azerbaidzhan, in fact, a massive purge has swept the party and government since July 1969, when the Azerbaidzhanian CP's first secretary was sacked and replaced by Geidar Aliev, the republic's former KGB chief.

Inveighing against "amoral behavior, the dissolute lives of some officials, the troublemakers, slanderers, intriguers and careerists who bring harm to our cause," Aliev has dismissed scores of functionaries, including the president of the republic, its prime minister, the minister of health (for falsification of accounts), the chief of the militia and various province and city party chiefs. The charges against them ranged from "dishonesty, insincerity and deceiving the party" to "giving responsible posts to close friends and relatives . . . and for allowing speculation in private houses and cars."

In Poltava in the Ukraine, on the other hand, militia officials have tried for three years to crack a bribery and misappropriation case dealing with several trucks full of grain and more than 20,000 rubles in payoffs. Because the principals are leading local party officials, the Ukrainian Central Committee, apparently acting directly on orders of party chief Pyotr Shelest, first secretary of the Ukrainian CP, has ordered the investigation closed and the charges quashed.

Even the Soviet Art Fund, the Artists' Union agency which distributes orders and assignments to the members, has been named in a major scandal. Fund officials were accused of swindling, theft and taking bribes and giving the most lucrative assignments to their friends, while younger, less protected artists were left without work. The fund set exorbitantly high prices for artwork and used the revenue to pay kickbacks and juggle the salaries of fund employees.

One artist earned 4000 rubles for three days' work setting up a display stand in a park in Frunze, Kirghizia. A sculptor was paid 23,000 rubles for five months' work on a monumental sculpture at a collective farm.

The petty crook, the black marketeer, the worker who filches the wiring, the sculptor who steals the bronze, the plant manager who finagles the books to get bigger deliveries of raw materials which then may go to waste, the farmer who sells his produce for exorbitant prices in the peasant market, the choirmaster who goes into the production of ready-to-wear clothes—they are all the products of the Soviet economic system and its deficiencies. They may be amoral by Soviet standards, but they are also human. They are the living proof that human nature does not change, no matter how often or how loudly Soviet propagandists proclaim the era of the new Soviet man. The Revolution, the Russians and the downtrodden of the world were promised, would mark the start of a new millennium, an era of total justice and equality, without poverty, without crime, without classes. It remains a noble goal. No one can deny that. But like so many human dreams before it, as yet it remains unfulfilled.

Part Five

Ivan Vasilyevich Ivanov, a Moscow worker and loyal Communist Party member, had been hoping and waiting for a new apartment for years. Finally, losing patience, he wrote his party organization, but got no reply. Then he wrote the Central Committee. It did not answer. Finally he fired off an angry letter to Lenin, who also didn't respond. In desperation, Ivanov went to the Central Committee and asked the guard on duty to speak to Lenin. "But Comrade," the guard replied, "Vladimir Ilyich died in 1924, more than forty-six years ago." Angrily Ivanov shot back: "That's it. Whenever the party needs Lenin, it says he is alive and will always live. But when I happen to need him, they say he's dead."

A widely retold Moscow anecdote of 1970

*It was the year 2000 and Communism
had at last been built in the U.S.S.R.
Inquisitive little Sasha, aged seven, and
eager to learn about the past, asked
his father one day: "Daddy, what was
socialism?" The father stopped to
contemplate a moment, searching for
a way to explain something so
complicated to a child, then replied:
"Well, socialism was when you needed
money for things instead of everything
being distributed free, according to our
needs, the way it's done now. For
example, if you wanted some butter,
you had to stand in a queue at the
cashier's desk, pay for it, then take
the receipt to the sales counter and
give it to the clerk who would hand
you the amount you had paid for."
Sasha was silent for a minute,
obviously in deep thought. Then he
asked: "Daddy, what's butter?"*

A Soviet anecdote of the late 1960s

11 Paradise Lost

The "must" sights of Moscow used to be the Kremlin, Red Square,
the magnificent subway and the gingerbread thirty-two-story sky-
scraper of the university, a neo-Byzantine version of New York's
Woolworth Building. But since 1967, when construction workers
rushed the façades to completion in time for the fiftieth anniversary of
the Revolution, there has been another marvel to which enthusiastic
Intourist guides drag their foreign charges: Kalinin Prospect. A wide,
modern avenue, flanked by high-rise office buildings and apartment

houses, lined by gleaming shops, cafes and restaurants, it is Moscow's first architectural step into the twentieth century, and, according to Soviet propagandists, typical of life in the U.S.S.R.

No travel brochure appears without a photograph of this gleaming new thoroughfare. Nearly every day some film crew is at work on Kalinin Prospect: either to make a propaganda movie, to use the sleek façades as backdrops of a thriller or its cafe and store fronts as settings for a musical. Foreign TV correspondents who receive permission to make documentaries on the life of the average Russian are invariably required to shoot on Kalinin Prospect.

But Moscow's Park Avenue, as Muscovites have begun to call it, is about as typical and representative of life in the U.S.S.R. as Prince Grigory Potemkin's fake villages were in 1787. West German TV correspondent Lothar Loewe, introducing a film about "life in Moscow" made entirely on Kalinin Prospect, sardonically described it as "the most modern avenue between Brest-Litovsk and Vladivostok."

Behind the face of this contemporary Potemkinism is the real U.S.S.R.: inadequate, inefficient, ugly, shabby, shoddy, jerry-built, chipped-off, flaked-off, often dusty, frequently muddy, usually drab and cheerless.

As one bitter Russian friend described it: "The essential element of our system and society is that it is *protiv chelovechestvo*—against humanity."

Those who are tired of the consumer-conscious society with its overabundance, weary of keeping ahead of the Joneses, bored by the pink plastic veneer of affluency or the excessive cornucopia of choice at the supermarket should try it.

The Soviet Union is the place to get away from it all. There one can experience the frustration of spending days in search of the right size nails or buttons, hunting for pencils or an iron skillet, for water tumblers or coffee cups, for mittens with which to brave the subzero cold or a bathroom towel, spend a few hours queuing at counters for merchandise sold out before one reaches the head of the line, or listen to the sound of a dozen sullen nyets grunted by shop clerks who resent being asked for something unusual like men's shoes size ten.

It is a country where flower shops usually have no flowers and butcher shops usually no meat, where queues and shortages are the rule. It is a land where portraits of Lenin and Brezhnev and yards of red bunting substitute for merchandise in shop windows, when stores either have nothing worth buying or are closed—"for repair," "for inventory," "for lunch," "for sanitation" or "for the day" simply because the staff has already overfulfilled its trade quota and sees no reason for continuing to work. There restaurants display little signs in their windows that read "Closed" on one side and "No Seats Left" on the other, but never one reading "Welcome." It is a country whose economy produces envelopes without gum, elevators that don't elevate, locks that don't lock, doors that don't close, windows that don't open, refrigerators that don't refrigerate and new apartment houses that are instant slums before the first tenants even move in.

To convey the flavor of life in the U.S.S.R. to someone who has never been there is next to impossible because of the lack of familiar reference points. But I hope that the following random excerpts from notes collected over several years will provide a hint.

Kiev—summer of 1970. As usual the lobby of the hotel is filled with kiosks and sales counters, but most of the shelves and displays are empty. A sign reading *"Zakrit* (closed)" hangs on a piece of limp string in front of most of them.

Near the Intourist service counter I overheard an American tourist with a crippled wife in a wheelchair ask the girl for a taxi. She told him that none would be available for three hours—4:30 P.M. At six-thirty, I saw him and his wife on the sidewalk outside the hotel, still waiting for that cab.

Later at the same counter an American woman shouted angrily at one of the clerks: "I gave you six dollars for theater tickets this morning and now you say there are no seats tonight. There are never any seats. I'd like for one thing to go right on this trip."

Odessa—several days later. A huge sign in English in the hotel lobby reads: "You may try delicious Russian-Crimean dry, luscious, medium sweet and dessert wines at the Scientific Institute for Grape Testing. Ask your guide for details." But in this wine-growing center of Russia, not a drop of wine was available in a single restaurant.

We decided to have dinner at one of the Intourist hotels, the best in town. The service and food were abominable. By 6 P.M. there was no meat of any kind left. The waiter said they ran out five minutes before we arrived and blamed it on "too many foreign tourists yesterday." We ordered blinis with strawberry jam for dessert but they arrived before the soup. When I complained that they would turn cold he shrugged and suggested we eat them as hors d'oeuvres.

We strolled on the main street and checked the largest produce shop, whose total stock consisted of cabbages (with leaves starting to turn black), shriveled carrots, some mud-covered potatoes, dried fruit, one box of wrinkled and bruised apricots. No cucumbers, no lettuce, no tomatoes, although a sign on one counter said tomatoes were selling for 1 ruble per kilogram (cheap). The salesgirl mumbled "nyet" when I asked for some.

The sign on the hotel bar read "Open from 8 P.M. to midnight." It was closed. The porter, in a rumpled, wrinkled uniform, rushed up to explain that the bar operates from 8 A.M. to noon. "That's the sign from last year," he explained. "It was open in the evenings then, but now only during the day." Why? He merely shrugged.

At the famous Potemkin steps, an escalator has been installed. It was not working. Our guide said it wasn't quite ready yet, but the sign read: "Being repaired."

Yaroslavl—spring of 1970. Three women sat behind the hotel reception desk, chewed sunflower seeds, conversed energetically and eyed us suspiciously as we came in. They were visibly irritated when I interrupted them, placed our passports on the counter and explained that we had reservations. After settling into the room—an interior decorator's atrocity painted purple (most hotel rooms seem to have either purple, chartreuse, mint green or ochre walls)—we asked for a map or guidebook of the city. "Nyet," said one of the women, still chewing on her sunflower seeds. "Go into the center to buy one." I asked her for directions, she pointed out the door.

Yaroslavl has a population of 500,000, yet it is so sleepy, so lethargic, that Sinclair Lewis' Gopher Prairie seems like St. Paul in comparison: like all Soviet provincial towns, no matter how large. What do people do in them—besides work? Restaurants are all shut tight by 11 P.M. with the usual collection of drunks around them. Movies? But there's always a queue. Whenever there is something unusual or different there's a blocks-long line trying to get in. No wonder everyone wants to go to Moscow, "a gleaming metropolis."

Ulyanovsk—March 1970. So this is where Lenin was born. The countryside is reminiscent of the Kansas prairie: flat, flat, flat. Ivan Goncharov was also born here and in his *Oblomov*—whose title character was symbolic of Russian indolence—Ulyanovsk was the setting. Little has changed since the nineteenth century.

Our group was taken to the Hotel Volga, but told that we could not eat there—the dining room was being renovated and repaired.

Everything is always being repaired. The elevator too. It didn't work and a sign on it said . . . *"Na Remont* (being repaired)."

To feed us they took over the entire Rossiya Hotel, where we were taken by bus, and closed it to the public. At last a new sign on a door: "Closed for Use by a Delegation." The hallway leading to the dining room was dreary, dingy, shabby. One fluorescent lamp on the high ceiling cast a blue shimmer over it. Drunks, a few sullen spivs, a couple of peroxide-blond girls and police crowded the lobby and hallway, all either watching us foreigners or watching each other.

Kazan—several days later. Practically all municipal deliveries seem to be made with horse carts. Nowhere have I seen as many horses and wagons as here.

I also discovered a new type of queue: dozens of people lined up with pails and canisters at a tank truck selling kerosene: for lamps or stoves?

On the highway between Moscow and Vladimir—fall of 1969: All the trucks, buses and cars seem to lean perilously to one side or the other. Invariably they have at least one wheel that wobbles dangerously as they trundle along. Many of the open trucks transport kolkhoz workers. Buses are a rare sight.

The villages are picturesque in their dilapidated fashion. The wooden houses all sag in one direction or the other. They have no foundations and in the winter, I suppose, the weight of the snow eventually makes them cave in. Apparently none of them have running water. All had wells or pumps by the roadside and we saw dozens of people carrying water in pails hung on a yoke. There is electricity, however. The naked light bulb is almost a symbol of Russian interior decorating.

Valadimir. The picture in shops is the same as everywhere: acres of floor space, a few counters and virtually no merchandise. The fixtures invariably have a scratched, chipped, synthetic veneer.

Many new apartment houses are rising on the outskirts of the town. But the façades are cracked, pieces of mosaic are missing from the panel tiles and the front doors all seem to be coming off their hinges. Most of these places look as if they should be condemned, yet some aren't even ready for occupancy and others have just been made available.

Bukhara—spring of 1969. While sitting in the restaurant I could observe the doorman. Although half the tables were empty, he let no one in. And each time a guest left he unlocked the door, argued with customers waiting outside, bolted the door again, then sank back down on a rickety chair and dozed off. Well, what's a doorman for but to keep doors closed?

I have slept in better army barracks and flophouses than the Hotel Bukhara. Yet our guide described it as the "new" hotel, the best, built in 1964. The bathroom tells it all: crooked and broken tiles on the wall and floor, globs of dirty oil paint where the tiles stop, a rusty tub with a corroded faucet that sputtered out a thin stream of grimy cold water, a cracked mirror whose silver coating was peeling off in the corners, a naked light bulb and a broken wooden toilet set. On the door was a sign—in English, of all things —which read: "Please do not stand on the toilet seat."

Moscow—summer 1970. Driving to a dinner party at a diplomatic dacha in Serebryany Bor (a wooded district on the outskirts) we noticed a queue of about a hundred people at a furniture store on Novokhoroshevskoye Chausse. Only the fact that the store was obviously closed—it was about 8 P.M.—and not likely to reopen that late in the day struck us as strange. When we returned the same way around midnight a crowd of at least three hundred Muscovites had gathered near the darkened shop on the dimly lit street. Some had brought folding cots, others air mattresses, a few had come equipped with chairs and blankets. Those in the crowd not jostling for better positions had bedded down for the night on the sidewalk and a small patch of grass. We parked our car several blocks away and walked back to mingle with the crowd.

"What's everybody queuing for?" I asked a man near the end of the line. "Don't you know?" he replied surprised and probably recognizing me immediately as a foreigner. "They're opening the new list for orders on kitchen furniture tomorrow morning."

Only several days later, when a Russian acquaintance explained the system to us, did we fully comprehend. It was not the furniture itself that these patient nighttime suppliants had been waiting for, but the chance to get their names on the list for furniture that would be delivered. When? In several monhs if they were lucky; in a year if things followed their normal course; in two years if, as is often the case, furniture makers failed to fulfill their production quotas.

* * *

More than thirty years ago, twenty years after the Revolution, André Gide observed similar queues. "What do they gain by standing there?" he asked himself. "Only the firstcomers are served."

"The needs," he said, "are so great and the public so numerous that the demand for a long time to come will be greater than the supply—much greater." Little could Gide have guessed that more than three decades after he wrote his elegy of disillusionment, *Retour de l'U.R.S.S.,* supply would still be chasing demand. He wrote:

> The goods are hardly less than repulsive. You might think that textiles and other objects were deliberately made as unattractive as possible in order to put people off so that they shall only buy out of extreme necessity and never because they are tempted . . . Everything is frightful. And yet, for some months past, great efforts have been made—efforts directed towards an improvement of quality; and by looking carefully and devoting the necessary time to it, one can manage to discover here and there some recent articles which are quite pleasing and of some promise for the future . . . Here you are obliged to choose what is offered you. Take it or leave it.

It could have been written yesterday. Today there are just as many queues, needs exceed supply, quantity is wanting, quality atrocious, choice is non-existent, great efforts are being made to improve and those who have the necessary time and money will "here and there" discover "some recent articles which are quite pleasing and of some promise for the future." What's more, to judge from the torrent of words unleashed by Leonid Brezhnev and Aleksei Kosygin at the XXIVth Party Congress in April 1971, the future sounds as promising as it did in Gide's day thirty-five years ago.

Yet if Gide could see Russia today, he would notice tremendous improvements.

In 1970 every third Soviet family owned a refrigerator, more than half had television sets and 52 per cent possessed washing machines. Every twelfth family now owns a motorcycle or motorbike, every third a camera, every tenth a vacuum cleaner and nearly every family possesses a radio or phonograph. During the past five years alone 11 million apartments were built or renovated and modernized.

Statistics indicate progress, visual observation confirms it. Women look better dressed, men better tailored. Each year more Russians drive private automobiles, move into new apartments and eat better.

Russians are also becoming more selective and more demanding. Economists point to two phenomena as proof: the spiraling personal savings, which rose by 21 per cent in 1970 to an all-time high of more than 49 billion rubles, or approximately 205 rubles per person, and the rising inventory of unwanted, unsalable goods in Soviet warehouses.

Both the increase in savings, despite the high cost of living, and the steady decline in credit purchases indicate that the volume and quality of available goods and services have trailed behind disposable money incomes. Rising inventories of unsold goods consist largely of products that are either defective or unappealing and no longer meet present-day Soviet consumer criteria.

In just one republic, Uzbekistan, the inventory of unsold goods in Ministry of Trade warehouses reached 68 million rubles by October 1970.

To whittle down this mountain of white elephants, Soviet trade authorities exploit the continuing shortages of many other goods. Oilcloth, for example, has been scarce for years. When it does reach the market, customers must also buy an otherwise unsalable plastic child's handbag with each meter or two of oilcloth they are permitted to purchase. In 1970 when Moscow stores received an allocation of a scarce type of synthetic-fiber blouse, the blouses were sold only to shoppers who also agreed to buy a bottle of a perfume that had been produced in excess.

But progress is all relative. It has been inchlike while demand, aspirations, expectations and criteria for both quality and quantity have surged ahead by yards. Moreover other societies and countries have advanced by miles.

A typical example of this is the washing machine situation. According to Soviet statistics, every other family now has a washer. But what kind? Eighty-five per cent of these machines have hand wringers, 15 per cent are semi-automatic. None are automatic. The very best of them, the Aurika-2, according to Yuri Solovyev, director of the Technical Aesthetics Research Institute, can wash only cotton or linen items, no synthetics or knitwear. To wash 2 kilograms of laundry eighty different operations, most of them manual, are necessary on this machine.

By and large the standard of living in Moscow and other cities of the Soviet Union today is similar to that of West European countries in the early 1950s. A Swiss economist, Jovan Pavlevski, has estimated that it was not until 1963 that average real wages of workers in the U.S.S.R. reached their 1913 level. And while they have been rising perceptibly since then, the growth rate in the U.S.S.R. has been slower than in many Western countries.

Notwithstanding palpable improvements and the promise of more improvements to come, the U.S.S.R. remains a society where shortages are the rule and the customer is invariably wrong. Undoubtedly, essential needs, or what would be considered essential in Russia, have been and are being met. But most other commodities seem either momentarily out of stock, out of season, available yesterday but no longer today or exorbitantly expensive.

The reasons are a compendium of bad planning, poor distribution, ideological hang-ups and lack of the proper incentives.

No Russian would go anywhere without a shopping net, called an *avoska*—which, translated literally, means "just in case" or "perhaps." It will come in handy "just in case" Vegetable Store No. 66 has tomatoes today or Shoe Store No. 79 happens to have the size boots he needs. "Perhaps" Sporting Goods Store No. 16 has received a consignment of tennis balls, Stationery Shop No. 11 now has a supply of pencils or TsUM Department Store might just be selling winter gloves.

The queue, called an *ochered* in Russian, is ubiquitous and the smart shopper will automatically line up at the end of the longest, for that is the one where something "scarce" or "unusual" is being sold: oranges in winter or bathing suits in summer, for example. Or for the more discriminating customers: knitwear from England, stylish shoes from Italy, men's suits from Holland or toy cars from France.

When it happens, all of Moscow, Leningrad, Kiev or Novosibirsk is sure to know within hours, usually long before the stores open.

If what Natasha Ivanova stood in line for turns out to be something she couldn't possibly use, she'll buy it anyway, certain in the knowledge that Galya Petrovna or Nina Alexova will be only too glad to have it and offer to exchange something she bought, and could not use, after standing in a different queue.

Products that Americans or West Europeans take for granted are often unknown or unavailable and when they do go on sale, many customers do not know their purpose.

"What is it?" asked dozens of shoppers in Moscow's Leipzig Magazin, a store that features goods imported from East Germany.

"It" in this case was a hand-held electric food mixer selling for fifteen rubles. Many of those who didn't know its purpose bought several in the conviction that the consignment would be sold out in a day or so if not hours.

Shortages and the sporadic nature of supply and distribution make any shopping expedition in the Soviet Union a test of stamina, will and nerves. If it is washcloths or winter gloves that are not available today, then it will be razor blades and electric irons tomorrow. Next week it may be dishpans and 60-watt light bulbs, just as it was 75-watt bulbs a month ago. What TsUM Department Store sells today may be gone tomorrow and no Russian is naïve enough to believe he'll then find it in GUM.

A Soviet shopper is guided by certain conditioned reflexes. If he wants a specific type of cap, size eight, and discovers it in Hat Store No. 21, but only in sizes seven and nine, he will not look elsewhere but buy the larger size and let his hair grow until it fits.

"Today I went around the shops again looking for a bathroom towel," a Moscow housewife wrote to *Pravda* in August 1970. "There are none, and there haven't been any for years. And now there aren't any kitchen towels either. They've all been bought up because of the lack of bathroom towels. It's difficult to believe that it could take so long to get to grips with the towel problem. Could you please interview the responsible person and trace the cause?"

In September 1970 *Pravda* reported a nationwide shortage, not only of towels, but dishes, cutlery, blankets, oilcloth and hardware. There was a deficiency of 40 million drinking glasses because the Ministry of Building Materials (responsible for manufacturing glassware) had failed to meet its production quotas. Moreover the glasses on sale proved to be defective: they cracked in hot water. The output of knives and forks had fallen short by 20 million pieces because new manufacturing facilities, planned by the Ministry of Ferrous Metallurgy, which supervises cutlery production, had not been completed.

Before the start of the 1970 school year, a shortage of exercise books, drawing pads, rulers, paints, erasers and plain and colored pencils was reported in the Krasnodar area. Although 1,860,000 pencils had been ordered, only 285,000 had been allocated to this region and not all of these were delivered. Only 2.6 per cent of the amount of required and allocated drawing paper had been supplied. *Pravda* reporters pursued the pencil mystery and discovered not only the reasons for the shortage, but that it was nationwide. Besides a lack of cedar wood, from which pencils are made, the U.S.S.R.'s *entire* pencil production is concentrated in one workshop of a factory, in Tomsk, Siberia, "whose equipment is housed in a dilapidated, hutlike building."

In the summer of 1971 *Nedelya, Izvestia*'s weekly magazine supplement, reported a nationwide shortage of men's suspenders because production of the old model had dropped to 500,000 a year and new production facilities, scheduled to produce 3 million pairs of a more stylish model by 1973, have not been completed.

The national pillow shortage has gotten so serious, according to *Pravda,* that in some towns in the summer of 1971 newlyweds, along with a marriage certificate, are given a coupon entitling them to buy a pillow.

According to an official of the Ministry of the Medical Industry, it will be 1975 before all the near- and farsighted people in the Soviet Union will have eyeglasses. The demand for glasses, explained Y. G. Logacheva, a department chief in the ministry, has been growing too rapidly and at present only 82.2 per cent of the need can be met. In the meantime, she recommended, people with bad eyesight should do less reading and watching of TV.

The production of enamelware, particularly teapots, coffeepots and cooking pots, has not increased for six years, primarily because of maladroit planning by the Ministry of Ferrous Metallurgy, whose enterprises are assigned the manufacture of pots and pans from waste materials and by-products. Because production assignments were expressed in tons, rather than units and categories, large and heavy saucepans and buckets, which can be made faster and more cheaply, were overproduced to meet tonnage obligations while cooking pots and tea kettles disappeared from the stores. As one plant director in the Ukraine lamented: "A teapot requires twenty more production operations than a pan." Ministry of Trade officials hope that in the current five-year plan the chronic shortage of enamelware will be alleviated because "trade organizations have now been given the right to order in terms of numbers of pieces, not tons."

The meat grinder problem is a "whirligig," to quote a December 1970 article in *Izvestia.* "No one can say how many times the meat grinder has been overproduced, how many times it has been in short supply." For a number of years meat grinder production has been a specialty of automotive equipment plants such as Kuibyshev's Automobile and Tractor Electrical Equipment and Carburetor Factory. Years ago that plant, and others, undertook the production of meat grinders on such a broad scale that soon all local warehouses overflowed with meat grinders.

Understandably, the plant halted production and turned instead to iron grills: for so long that these too filled warehouses to bursting and meat grinders were again in such demand that the factory reverted to meat grinder manufacturing. But in the meantime the Ministry of the Automotive Industry had decided that all other factories should cease making meat grinders. The Kuibyshev plant is now the only one in the Soviet Union producing this item, but its facilities are too small. The result is a nationwide shortage of meat grinders.

Electric iron production has experienced similar vicissitudes. A few years ago, according to a deputy minister of the electrical equipment industry, 8,500,000 electric irons were produced annually in the Soviet Union. That was considered excessive and production was "sharply curtailed." So sharply, in fact, that a national shortage of irons set in.

The total absence of market factors and a top-heavy bureaucratic superstructure account for many of these deficiencies. In a November 1970 interview Yuri Vinogradsky, the Latvian Republic's minister of local industries, provided some insight with the case of the aluminum pan. "Its fate," he explained, "is decided by the U.S.S.R. Ministry of the Aviation Industry. If it is a new type of pan, it must pass inspection by the Institute of Technical Aesthetics. It must also be submitted for approval to trade and sanitary inspection agencies, the State Committee on Prices and a whole series of republican organizations. Frequently, a new item will become obsolete during the approval process, not even reaching the assembly line, and sometimes even the need for its production will disappear."

Shortages in one field are likely to affect others. Thus the lack of textiles and the refusal of metal plants to produce unprofitable furniture locks has resulted in a dearth of upholstery and case goods. The absence of door locks in hardware stores is attributed to a shortage of screws. The output of quality dairy produce is hampered because "year in, year out, requests by dairy farms for pasteurizers, churns, refrigerators and disinfection equipment are not met."

Some shortages, such as flowers, a perennial non-starter, are endemic.

"Try to buy flowers in Moscow," *Literary Gazette* complained once. "In winter there are none at all in the state shops, only on the streets and in the markets [where they are sold by private entrepreneurs] at prices no one can afford. A skilled worker's daily salary is what it takes to buy two or three gladioli . . . It should be easy to deliver flowers from the south through state-owned channels on a contract basis with the southern collective farms. If private entrepreneurs can use the Aeroflot facilities [to bring flowers to the north in suitcases] why can't the state-owned trade sector do likewise?"

The vagaries and built-in disincentives of the centralized planning system are major causes of the shortcomings.

"To this day," I. M. Khrekin, director of the All-Union Research Institute for the Study of the Population's Demands for Consumer Goods and the Conditions of Trade, told a *Pravda* interviewer in May 1971, "our country has no unified state service for the study of demand. Separate enterprises and even research groups work in isolation [which leads] to duplication of effort, unjustified expenditure and losses of time."

Everything is done according to plan, and fulfilling the quotas stipulated by the plan remains the main goal of production and trade. *Trud,* the labor union daily, described the effect of this on the consumer when it printed an overheard conversation between a housewife and a clerk in a Moscow grocery store.

"Do you have eggs?" the woman asked.

"Of course. Pay at the cashier."

The customer paid, then returned to the counter and handed the clerk her receipt.

"Wait," said the clerk.

"For what?"

"Until the hens have laid the eggs."

"How long?"

"A week, maybe longer," replied the salesgirl.

"But why did you make me pay for them?" asked the bewildered customer.

"So that we can fulfill our plan. Today is the thirty-first of the month and we haven't fulfilled our plan for exchange of goods yet."

Fortunately, the month's-end *shturmovchina,* which compels retail stores to meet their quotas in turnover, does not always work out to the disadvantage of the customer. "The end of the month," a Soviet acquaintance advised me shortly after arriving in Moscow, "is always the best time to do your shopping. That's when they bring out the goods they have held back in the stockrooms, just to meet the turnover quota. The selection in quality and quantity is usually better."

Nor are all queues the result of shortages. The queue is endemic to the Soviet retail trade system, which has far too few outlets to meet demands and is barely on the threshold of self-service and pre-packaging techniques. A confoundingly bureaucratic sales and service technique, seemingly predicated on the assumption that every customer is either a suppliant or a thief, makes shopping an ordeal.

To go through her grocery list at the average *gastronom* or *pro-dovolstvenny magazin,* a Soviet housewife will have to queue at each counter just to see what is on sale, compute the amount by converting the per kilogram price into the quantity she wants to buy, then line up at the cashier's cage, tell the cashier to ring up individual chits for each item, rejoin the queue at the proper counter to turn in the receipt and wait for the merchandise to be weighed and (if there is paper) wrapped. Milk products must, of course, be bought in dairy food shops, bread in bakery stores, where the queuing process is likely to be the same.

The result, as one working Moscow housewife computed, is that she and her mother-in-law, who stays at home to look after the children, each put in an average of two hours daily just to shop for the day's meals.

Neither the management nor the clerks care whether or not or how long customers have to stand in line. They have nothing to gain from reducing the length of a queue, nothing to lose from its getting longer. No one is answerable for their formation, no one rewarded for eliminating them.

By the fall of 1970, according to Soviet Ministry of Trade statistics, only one out of ten Soviet food stores operated on a self-service basis and the majority of these were bakeries. Pre-packaging, which would speed up transactions in all types of stores, not just self-service outlets, is virtually non-existent. By the end of 1970, for example, only 6 per cent of the candy and 16 per cent of the macaroni and noodle products sold in the Ukraine were pre-packaged. Retail stores were still receiving yeast in 1-kilogram blocks, jam and tomato paste in 3- and 10-kilogram jars, tomatoes and pickles in 3-quart jars and virtually all of their sugar in 100-pound bags.

Meanwhile Soviet trade publications bristle with interministerial bickering over who has responsibility for packaging. Once the arguments are resolved, there will still be the problem of manufacturing and distributing packaging equipment.

In 1970 an enterprising Italian sold the Soviet government on the idea of setting up fifteen American-style supermarkets in Leningrad, Moscow, Sochi, Volgograd, Irkutsk and Vladivostok. The first of these, on an experimental basis, was established in Moscow in 1970 only for sale of goods in hard-currency coupons. Two more large Moscow *universamy*, as they are called, selling goods for rubles, went into operation in April 1971. They were an immediate and sensational success.

Self-service will solve only part of the problem, however. More retail outlets of all kinds are needed everywhere, particularly in the provinces.

Frunze, capital of Kirghizia, a city of 431,000 population, seems to be typical for what is a nationwide dilemma. It has a total of 257 retail stores of all types, including a two-story central department store where an estimated 40,000 people shop each day. Only 26 of the retail outlets were self-service by the end of 1970. A new six-story building to house the central department store had been under construction for five years and was still not completed. It was not an exception. Local authorities complained that not a single trade enterprise had been opened on schedule.

There are countless exhortations to do better.

"It is high time," said a front-page *Izvestia* editorial in August 1970, "for all industrial executives to realize that the customer who wants to buy a box of matches costing one kopek enjoys equal attention from the socialist state as a factory wanting to acquire a rolling mill costing millions of rubles."

Officials and propagandists are forever urging enterprises, workers, executives and "all those engaged in every branch of trade" to use "every opportunity to increase considerably the market stocks of fruit and vegetable products," "to promote a more extensive output of goods such as garments, cotton, mittens and woolen socks," to assure "that everything designed for the Soviet citizen is of good quality, handsome and convenient," "to increase sharply the output of foods prepared with groats, flour, macaroni, milk, fish and sea products," "to enable the clients to purchase what they need without queuing" and "to develop in every tradesman the sense of personal responsibility for the achievements in raising the people's well-being."

The results are likely to be meager, despite the promises made by Brezhnev during the XXIVth Party Congress. "The Central Committee," he said, "considers it important to draw the attention of plan and economic agencies, party, soviet and professional organizations to the necessity of a serious change in the very approach to the production of consumer goods."

But even before the congress ended, two vital passages of Brezhnev's speech were excised from the version printed in *Pravda,* according to some observers, on the behest of the military and heavy industrial lobbies.

A torrent of publicity has pointed to plans for a faster growth of consumer goods production than heavy industry by 1975. But in fact, the growth rate for consumer goods production has not been accelerated; the growth rate for heavy industry has merely been slowed down.

The plan calls for a 44 to 48 per cent increase in consumer goods production but only 41 to 45 per cent in industrial goods production. But who is to say that by 1975 consumer goods production will not have grown by the smaller rate, that is 44 per cent, while producer goods output will have increased by the larger rate of 45 per cent?

Percentages or promised rates of increase, moreover, tell an incomplete story. For example, the current five-year plan calls for doubling the volume of consumer *services* in urban areas, trebling them in rural areas by 1975. Yet the total value of consumer services in 1970 was a mere 4.1 billion rubles, the equivalent of 17 rubles per person in urban areas, or the dry cleaning of seven overcoats, and only 1.70 rubles per capita in rural areas, the equivalent of four haircuts.

More than 130 years ago the Marquis de Custine complained to his readers: "How can I give you a true idea of Russia without contradicting myself at every word?"

The same quandary confronts me, particularly when I attempt to correlate what I have just written about rising consumer demands, expectations and criteria and increasing individual savings, on the one hand, with the low average incomes of Soviet workers, not even to mention kolkhoz farmers, on the other. Where does the average Soviet citizen get the 205 rubles that he is now reported to have in his savings account?

There are no easy answers to this.

Obviously the more than 49 billion rubles earning 2 to 3 per cent interest in Soviet *sberegatelniye kassy* (savings banks) are not evenly distributed. Most of this hoard belongs to members of the upper and upper-middle classes who live in the largest, most cosmopolitan cities where scientists, *apparatchiki* and highly paid intellectuals, executives and artists are concentrated. If a David Oistrakh has a million rubles' worth of cash and valuables for burglars to steal from his apartment, there must be millions of Ivan Ivanovs who cannot afford washing machines or television sets.

A satisfactory explanation may never be offered for either the statistical contradictions and those any visitor can observe by walking through a Moscow grocery or department store and comparing prices with incomes. There seems to be no logical relationship between the cost of living and the way of life, between prices and incomes.

"We don't have a penny in the bank," an upper-middle-class couple, earning more than five hundred rubles a month, told me. "Yet somebody must be stashing it away. Just don't ask us how."

Food consumes half the average middle-class and upper-middle-class urban paycheck, and the cost of many consumer items such as clothing, appliances and furniture is exorbitant by any society's standards.

One important compensation, of course, is that many expenses such as rent, medical treatment and medication, education, entertainment and vacations, which absorb large proportions of family budgets in Western countries, account for only a small fraction of Soviet living costs. The quality of these emoluments and services may range from substandard to mediocre, but medical care is free, education is free for the vast majority of Soviet youth, vacations cost little and rent rarely exceeds 10 per cent of a family's income; usually it is as low as 6 to 7 per cent.

Under the circumstances an attempt to describe the standard of living is fraught with imponderables. Suffice it to say that mounting savings notwithstanding, the average Soviet blue- or white-collar worker must be living just at the border of what Soviet economists themselves have described as the "minimum of material well-being," a Soviet euphemism for "poverty level." This minimum, according to Moscow's Scientific Research Institute on Labor, is (in 1965 prices) 51.50 rubles net income per month per capita, or 206 rubles for a family of four.

One group of Soviet economists has calculated, but not published, an even higher per capita income of 81.40 rubles as necessary for a decent minimum standard of living for Soviet urban families.

In 1970 the average monthly wage of Soviet factory and office workers was 122 rubles, leaving a take-home pay of around 112 rubles, or $124.32 at the official exchange rate. (By comparison, the average take-home pay of skilled factory workers in the U.S. was $502.34, in the United Kingdom $208.66, in West Germany $248.44 and in France $182.23.) Because nearly 77 per cent of all Soviet women between twenty and the legal retirement age of fifty-five have at least a part-time job, it is estimated that the average Soviet family has 1.6 wage earners, which should bring family income to around 200 rubles per month, or 50 rubles per capita if there are two non-working children.

Half that amount is required just to feed the family, half to buy a man's suit, a week of work to pay for a reasonably attractive pair of women's shoes, a whole month's income to outfit the children for one season, two months' income to buy a large-screen black and white television set and half a month's work to purchase a washing machine with a hand wringer.

Clearly, that makes budgeting a problem, and the largest problem of all is food.

One Western economist, Keith Bush, has calculated that the cost of a weekly median American-style food basket for a family of four, at April 1969 Moscow prices, would cost a Soviet worker more than 50 rubles or eighty-two hours of work time, expressed in take-home pay. Perhaps the greatest boon to a Soviet worker is that the eight most expensive items on Bush's weekly shopping list are either never or rarely available in the U.S.S.R.

A British dietician, on the other hand, has proposed an adequate, balanced and economic food budget for a family of two adults and two school-age children that, at Soviet prices, would come to slightly more than 40 rubles per month per capita—sixty rubles more per month than the average Soviet family can now be expected to spend. This diet calls for one pint of milk or milk product per day, one egg or one ounce of cheese, a half pound of vegetables (cabbage, beets, carrots or onions), a half pound of bread (either white or dark) and buckwheat porridge or potatoes, one ounce of butter or margarine, one ounce of sugar or jam, a quarter pound of meat or fish, some tea, salt flavorings and herbs. The cost would be 1.35 rubles per day per person.

According to Soviet statistics per capita consumption of meat, lard and fish is only 62 kilograms per year and less than one egg every other day (144 per year). The average Soviet citizen consumes only 79 kilograms of vegetables and fruit compared to the 91 kilos of vegetables prescribed in the model diet, but eats 280 kilograms of cereals and potatoes per year, more than three times the amount prescribed in the British dietician's menu.

This is an imbalanced diet, despite the fact that the daily Soviet calorie intake is equal to that in most other developed countries. Stanford University's Food Research Institute has estimated that if a nation's diet is composed of more than 70 per cent cereal-potato calories or less than 35 per cent from animal products, it is deficient. The Soviet Union is near to that deficiency criterion. Potato-cereal calories account for 57 per cent of the diet, animal products for only 25 per cent.

The absence of certain vital foodstuffs in the Soviet diet is due both to their high cost in the market and to the vagaries of supply.

"As soon as the procurement level of some farm product decreases, due to crop failure or some other problem caused by poor weather," said Soviet trade minister Alexander Struyev, "a chain reaction takes place, purchases of substitute products increase and new problems come to the fore."

The meat and poultry shortage that has afflicted the Soviet Union since 1969 can be ascribed only in part to weather, however. The primary cause, besides an unfavorable price relationship for meat vis-à-vis grain, seems to be an ill-fated attempt to switch from small livestock farms to large-scale factory farms: the former were liquidated before the latter had been properly organized. Consequently livestock holdings (except in pigs) decreased and in 1969 were lower on a per capita basis than in 1916, the year before the Revolution. In fact, since the Bolshevik take-over, per capita holdings of cattle, cows, sheep and goats have been higher than the 1916 level in only one year: 1928.

Today, more than forty years after forced collectivization of agriculture in the U.S.S.R., private plots and holdings—limited by law to about one acre, one calf, one cow and one pig with sucklings —account for 38 per cent of the total Soviet meat output. And meat sold by farmers from their privately owned livestock in the peasant markets is correspondingly expensive.

Although the official state store price for "first category" beef (comparable to soup meat) is 2 rubles per kilogram, free market prices for similar cuts can be as high as 4.50 and 5 rubles.

The compilation of a food price list is complicated by regional and seasonal differences, which can range from a few to more than 1000 per cent. Moreover state store prices for most products become meaningless when the merchandise is not available but is sold much more expensively in the kolkhoz and peasant markets. Thus in May 1969, for example, Moscow state shops listed tomatoes at 50 cents per pound but didn't have a single tomato for sale. At the Centralny Rinok (Central Market), however, tomatoes cost $6 (converted at the official exchange rate) per pound, and in Riga, in the U.S.S.R.'s first and largest peasant market, the price was $10 per pound.

The following list, while not aspiring to completion, should provide some idea of what a Soviet housewife must spend to put dinner on the table. The prices are quoted in rubles. For quick conversion into dollars, 11 per cent should be added. All prices are for 1 kilo (2.2 U.S. pounds) or 1 liter (approximately 1 quart) unless otherwise specified:

White bread	0.56
Dark bread (unwrapped, unsliced)	0.48
Rice (polished)	0.88
Beef (with bones, fat, soup or stew quality)	2.00
(similar quality, free market)	2.50–5.00
Mutton (best available, state price)	1.90
Pork (chops, state store prices)	2.10
(similar quality, free market)	3.00
Chicken (one small, state store, frozen)	2.75
(one small, free market)	4.00–6.00
Minced beef meat (state store)	2.00
Sausage (cheapest kind)	3.00
Herring (fresh)	0.94
Cod (frozen, fillet)	0.77
Fish fingers (frozen)	1.35
Sardines (canned)	4.13

Sugar (granulated, white)	0.94
Cocoa	5.10
Chocolate (100 grams)	1.20–2.30
Boiled sweets (assorted flavors)	2.00
Ice cream (vanilla, one quart)	1.80
Butter (unsalted, best kind)	3.60
Margarine	1.80
Vegetable oil	1.98
Lard	2.00
Milk (cheapest kind, one liter)	0.32
(best kind, one liter)	0.36
Yoghurt (depending on type, one liter)	0.30–0.47
Sour cream (best kind)	1.70
Cottage cheese (state stores)	0.70–0.88
(free markets)	2.50
Cheese (local types, state store)	2.60–3.90
Eggs (depending on size, season and where available, one dozen)	1.08–2.04
Potatoes (old, state stores)	0.10–0.14
(old, free markets)	0.20–1.00
(new, state stores)	0.20
(new, free markets)	1.20–2.00
Cabbage (state stores)	0.50
(free markets)	0.30–1.50
Lettuce (free market) up to	4.00
Onions (free market)	1.00
Beets (state store)	0.10
(free market)	0.30–0.60
Cucumbers (state stores)	1.20
(free markets)	2.00–8.00
Radishes (free market, average per bunch)	0.50
Dried mushrooms	15.00–22.00
Green peppers (free market)	1.30–1.50
Apples (state stores, bruised)	1.30–1.50
(free market, depending on quality)	1.30–3.50
Oranges (Moroccan, state stores)	1.40
Lemon (one piece, state stores)	0.35
Cherries (free market)	2.00–5.00
Strawberries (state stores and free market)	2.00–7.00
Preserved peaches (state)	1.20

Strawberry jam	1.41
Honey	3.04
Coffee (ground, state stores)	4.50
Wine (red or white, 0.7 liter)	1.80–2.90
Vodka (half liter)	4.12
Soda pop (half liter)	0.27

In May 1970, the following items were being sold in Moscow markets but not in state stores: veal, large chickens, cottage cheese, new potatoes, lettuce, onions, spring onions, garlic, radishes, pepper, cherries, red currants, mushrooms, dried mushrooms.

Once a Soviet family has fed itself, it must cope with high prices for other consumer goods, from clothing, cosmetics, drugs to durables. The following list is representative.

Toilet soap, small bar	0.25
Detergent, imported, one-pound box	0.66
Toothpaste (regular-size tube)	0.35
Rador blades, ten (bad steel)	0.25
Toilet paper, one roll (rough paper, rare find)	0.25
Aspirin, 100 (cheapest)	0.64
Lipstick, one	1.50
Nail polish, half-ounce bottle	0.40
Eye shadow	1.50
Nylon stockings, one pair, cheapest	2.00
Hair lacquer, spray, one can	4.00
Girdle	10.00
Woman's fall coat, imported from Belgium	130.00
Children's knitted wool cap and mittens	23.00
Women's shoes, imported	40.00–60.00
Women's shoes, Soviet-made	20.00–40.00
Diapers, ten, cotton	10.00
Men's shirt, white cotton, cheapest	7.00
Men's socks, colored, nylon	3.00
Men's suit, Soviet made, cheapest	75.00
Men's suit, imported, medium quality	150.00
Woman's negligee, imported (East Germany), nylon	60.00
Tea service, six cups, pot, sugar bowl, creamer, cheapest porcelain quality	62.50
Tea or coffee cup, one, cheapest porcelain	16.00

Vase, glass, portrait of Lenin engraved	42.50
Electric shaver, depending on quality	14.20–40.00
Serviceable ball point pen	0.77
Refrigerator, small (125 liters) with up to five-year waiting period	210.00
Refrigerator, large (240 liters) also up to five-year waiting period	310.00
Washing machine, with hand wringer	90.00
Washing machine, semi-automatic, separate spin-dry bin, hand draining	144.40
Television, 23-inch screen, black-white	423.00
Living room couch, cheapest kind	160.00
Bicycle, man's cheapest	50.00
Motor scooter (approximate)	460.00
Motorcycle, light	280.00
Automobile, Fiat-124	5500.00
Automobile, Moskvich	5090.00
Automobile, Zaporozhets (cheapest)	3950.00
Automobile, Volga (newest model)	9150.00

On the other hand, not only are rents low but telephone and postal rates (two kopeks from a call box, four kopeks for a domestic letter) and public transportation (a subway ride costs five kopeks, the bus four and a streetcar only three) are also cheap.

Certain consumer services, such as haircuts and beauty treatment, are also surprisingly inexpensive, although the advent of tipping is driving prices up. The meter on a taxi cab rings up only ten kopeks per kilometer, but any Muscovite knows that even to obtain a cab late at night he will have to pay two to three times what the meter reads. A tip rounding out the price to the nearest ruble or half-ruble is considered standard.

A celebration in a restaurant—something the average Russian is not likely to do more than once a year, to celebrate a wedding, graduation, birthday or anniversary—can easily run to 10 rubles per person. On the other hand, an evening seat in a downtown Moscow movie costs only 80 kopeks and the most expensive seat at the Bolshoi is 3.50 rubles. But the problem with theaters and movies, as with most other things in the U.S.S.R., is not being able to afford them but getting in.

The two consumer items for which Soviet citizens have been

waiting longest are housing and automobiles. And while the regime has made gargantuan efforts and invested huge amounts in both the construction and automotive industries, there is little prospect that demand will be met in the foreseeable future.

* * *

The tens of thousands of construction cranes that typify the urban Soviet landscape today have been there only fifteen years—since 1956 when Nikita Khrushchev opened the floodgates for mass, low-cost apartments.

In that relatively brief period more than 44 billion square feet of new urban housing have been built annually and the Soviet way of life has altered beyond recognition. In the next decade, by which Soviet authorities hope to "solve" the housing problem, it is bound to change even more.

But the "solution" is a mixed blessing, for it is designed to provide each Soviet city dweller with only 9 square meters of living space— the minimum sanitary norm established in 1922, and 3 square meters less than the West German Humane Society recommends for an Alsatian dog. Moreover the "solution" will be merely temporary, for most of the new housing is so shoddy, so jerry-built that it is substandard on completion and usually in need of major repairs and renovations within half a decade.

But, as a Soviet fitter moving into his new apartment declared: "Everything is relative." When he came to Moscow with his parents as a child, he shared his bed with two brothers and seventeen people lived in one room. Later, after marrying, he and his wife had a bed to themselves in the same communal room and they considered it a great luxury. After the birth of their first child they received a separate room, and only after twenty years of married life did they acquire an apartment.

It seems minuscule by Western standards: two rooms measuring not more than 9 by 12 feet each, a cubicle-sized bathroom, an even smaller separate toilet, a kitchen barely large enough to cook in and some corridor space: for two adults and two adolescents. Yet, compared to the past, it is palatial.

In 1956, before the building boom began, more than 90 per cent of Moscow's population lived in so-called *kommunalniye kvartiry* —communal apartments: large flats of three to seven rooms in which one family, regardless of size, occupied one room and all shared the apartment's single bathroom and kitchen. Today that percentage of communal apartment dwellers has been whittled to 40 per cent and the aim is to eliminate communal living, not only in Moscow but in other large cities, by 1980.

Most likely, the goal will not be reached. Since the Revolution housing construction targets have been met in only two five-year-plan periods: from 1951 to 1955, and again from 1956 to 1960. The 1969 plan called for construction of 121 million square meters, but only 102.5 million were built. In 1970 a scaled-down plan foresaw construction of 116 million square meters; only 106 million were completed. In the Russian Republic, a five-story brick apartment house is supposed to be built in 265 days. The average construction period, however, is 467 days. A pre-fab, large-panel apartment should take 207 days to build; the average is 295. In Azerbaidzhan the same structure takes 900 days to complete.

Furthermore, although approximately 2 million urban apartments may be built annually by 1975, the urban population has been increasing at a rate of 3,500,000 people per year for the last decade, and predictions are that this growth pattern will continue. Also, demolition of old housing must be deducted from the gross total of new construction.

In 1923 the average living space available to a Soviet citizen was 6.45 square meters. By 1950, as a result of population shifts and wartime destruction, there were only 4.67 square meters, or roughly 50 square feet. By the end of 1970 the figure had increased to 7.4 square meters, or approximately 77 square feet. But even if the 1922 sanitary minimum can be reached by 1980, every Soviet urban dweller still will have an area to himself measuring not more than 10 by 10 feet.

Comprehensive figures for the entire Soviet Union are not available, but in Moscow less than 70 per cent of all dwellings now have piped water, less than 65 per cent have central heating, 60 per cent have piped-in gas.

Because the construction industry is exhorted to fulfill a quantitative plan, all considerations for quality are eschewed. Complaints about jerry-built new housing fill the Soviet press.

Because of the end-of-the-year *shturmovshchina,* the last-minute rush to meet targets that is endemic to all Soviet industry, 40 per cent of all new flats are completed in December, when climatic conditions in most of the U.S.S.R. inadvertently prevent high standards in roofing, finishing work and application of façades. Just as examples: building inspection committees in the cities of Ufa, Elista, Magadan, Togliatti, Vladivostok and Belgorod complained about unsatisfactory brick laying, slipshod joining of pre-fab panels, substandard materials, tasteless finishes or poor interior decoration in 90 per cent of new housing.

A letter to the editor of *Sovietskaya Rossiya* by a woman occupant of one of these instant slums expresses the problem in human terms:

"Four years ago I received a separate one-room flat in a new five-story building. You can imagine how happy I was. But my delight washed away with the first rain: the walls let in the water because the builders had not filled in the joints between the edges of the panels. They just flung things together and departed. I have put up with it for four years. In wet weather it is damp and in winter I freeze, because the room temperature never rises above 50 degrees [Fahrenheit]."

The chief inspector of the Russian Republic's Architectural and Construction Control Commission, Mikhail Gerashchenko, reported in 1969 that in the town of Kirov the panel joints of 1762 apartments in 44 new buildings leaked, while the occupants of 285 top-floor apartments complained of water dripping through the roof.

All too frequently, Gerashchenko complained, "the wood products used in new construction are of low-grade, insufficiently dried lumber. Reinforced concrete elements arrive at construction sites with deviations from state standards, with holes and cracks and with chipped corners and edges and inexact in dimensions . . . Many construction jobs are submitted to and accepted by inspection committees without such amenities as access roads, sidewalks, landscaping, completed façades or built-in closets, [even] without hot water, with temporary heating, plumbing and sewage systems as well as many other defects and unfinished details.

"A new building should last from forty to fifty years without capital repair, but our experience shows that the need for such repair work sometimes arises within three or four years."

On the other hand, as minuscule and shoddy as new apartments may be, they are private—*odyelny*—and for Russians plagued by decades of communal living, that is an improvement. The Moscow chauffeur who shared a 15-by-15-foot room with his wife, mother-in-law and two children until he was allocated a self-contained two-room apartment in a new building obviously believes he is in a palace.

Anyone who doubts that a dwarf-sized *odyelny kvartir* is a blessing need merely look at a communal one. The kitchens in these "universities of life" are uniformly dank, dark and malodorous. They have a sink and one or two gas ranges, depending on the size of the apartment and how many people live in it. Space is taken up by the separate cupboard that each family maintains—and usually the doors to these are heavily padlocked, because no one really trusts all his neighbors. Potato sacks overflow on the floor and strings of old vegetables—onions and garlic cloves—hang from the ceiling. Inevitably these kitchens are the scenes of constant squabbles and frequent marathon drinking bouts.

Bathrooms (provided there is one) and toilets are murky and fetid. Many older buildings have no bathrooms and tenants must use the public baths. Toilet paper is frequently unavailable and piles of *Izvestias* or *Pravdas,* which serve as a substitute, litter the floor.

The rooms are invariably overcrowded with bulky, ugly furniture and the possessions accumulated by two or three generations of occupants. They serve to eat, sleep, live, relax, work, study, argue, quarrel, get drunk and make love in, and no one is ever alone.

One Muscovite remembers how she used to go to sleep with a pillow over her ear so as not to "hear my mother and father in the bed next to me." In these apartments the young hear and see too much and the grinding enforced togetherness has a harrowing effect on marriage.

The problems are by no means solved. A 1969 poll at Leningrad's Wedding Palace revealed that more than half of the newly wed couples expected to begin married life by moving in with parents, or into workers' dormitories.

But those Soviet citizens lucky enough to have a private apartment are already evincing changes in their living patterns and attitudes. They spend more time at home and tend to avoid civic and political meetings, they have become more acquisitive and more bourgeois in their outlook and more conscious of the need for privacy as opposed to collectivism.

Private apartments have become status symbols. While the majority of *kvartiry* are assigned by municipal councils, many come with the job, the buildings having been erected by the enterprises or organizations for which the tenants work. The bigger and more important the job, the larger the apartment is going to be.

The biggest status symbol of all is a co-operative apartment for which a down payment of 40 per cent must be made, with the balance due over a period of fifteen years. Prices range from 3000 rubles for a one-room, self-contained utility flat to as much as 10,000 rubles for a three- or four-room apartment. Expensive as they are by Soviet standards, they are the ultimate escape. Such buildings are easily distinguished from ordinary state or enterprise housing by better construction, more colorful balconies, smoother façades and improved interior decorating and workmanship.

To join a co-operative, however, takes influences and pull, for most of them are organized by large agencies such as the foreign ministry, newspapers and the creative unions. Money in the bank is never the sole criterion and even the wealthiest Muscovite must prove that he has the right credentials: that is, that he belongs to the right organization and that he needs a larger apartment.

For the mass, therefore, the road to a better life leads through the municipal housing offices into one of the huge blocks being erected by the state.

So what if the newly relocated Muscovite finds himself a long way from the center of town amid a wasteland without stores, adequate transportation, telephone and sometimes water and proper sewage outlets? So what if the elevator in the new building rattles like a tank and never works beyond the eighth floor? Who cares whether the walls leak, the plaster is already chipping off, the toilet has been hooked to the hot water and the radiators to the cold or that the door handles have been installed on the wrong side of the door? "We finally have a place of our own," said one housewarming host. "And that's what counts."

* * *

Just as he knows his own and Lenin's birth date, the date of the Revolution, the targeted growth rate for consumer goods production in the current five-year plan, any Russian knows the facts and figures of the Zhiguli by heart. From memory he can recite its horsepower, gas consumption, top speed and acceleration rate, for the Zhiguli, Moscow's name for the Fiat-124, is the U.S.S.R.'s entrance ticket to the automotive age.

Automania has infected Ivan Ivanov like a fever and next to an apartment of his own, a car has become his greatest dream. But as with most other Soviet dreams, this one is far from being fulfilled.

In 1970 the Soviet automobile industry produced only 344,000 passenger cars, a mere 50,000 more than the year before and approximately 400,000 less than originally planned. Of these only about 120,000 were retailed to private citizens.

By 1975, according to the current five-year plan, the output of passenger cars in the U.S.S.R. will have reached 1.2 to 1.3 million annually, of which 800,000 are expected to be sold to the public. It is a goal based largely on hopes for which past performance provides inauspicious prospects. Most of these cars are to come from the Fiat-Zhiguli plant in Togliatti, a factory that is two years behind schedule. In 1970 it manufactured only 22,000 automobiles— less than half the production originally targeted. The Moskvich plant in Moscow, which has been expanded and re-equipped with the help of France's Renault Company, is also behind schedule. In 1970 it was to produce 280,000 units, but turned out only 100,000. By 1971 output was to reach 350,000 cars, but the factory will be lucky if it produces two thirds that many.

Assuming the 1975 target can be met, the U.S.S.R. will still be making only as many cars as the United States produced in 1916, and the availability of private automobiles will be extended to only a further 1 per cent of the Soviet population each year. Thus, even if he has the money, Ivan Ivanov's chances of buying a car in 1975 will be only one in twenty.

At least, however, he can dream. Five years ago he could not have done even that, for the Kremlin considered the automobile a symbol inimical to Soviet ideology. The decision to start mass-producing cars and to invest hundreds of millions of rubles followed years of ideological bickering and endless interpretations and reinterpretations of Lenin.

Until 1966 the notion prevailed that a private car, except of course in the possession of the privileged elite, was synonymous with capitalistic ownership and unsocialistic affluence. Nikita Khrushchev, who proposed a nationwide car rental and taxi system instead of private ownership of automobiles, once said: "People are not vagabonds. They work, and when people work, the automobile stands idle. But while it stands it still gets old. Therefore we consider it unwise to have many unnecessary cars." Khrushchev, who had been frightened by the traffic nightmares witnessed in the United States, raised the question of our epoch: "Why should a man have to worry about where to park his car?"

However, Russians, like most people in the world, apparently want to worry about it, and as an *Izvestia* editorial said shortly after Khrushchev's fall: "The desire of the people for automobiles is as irresistible as the technical progress of mankind itself."

In 1966 the U.S.S.R. signed an agreement with Fiat which called for an entirely new plant in Togliatti, where the Soviet Union has now started producing a slightly modified version of the Fiat-124, a model that was six years old by the time the first samples rolled off the Togliatti assembly line.

It will cost Ivan Ivanov 5500 rubles—or the equivalent of 50 months' take-home wages of a skilled industrial worker. The same automobile, on sale in West Germany and United States, costs a German worker seven and an American four months' wages.

Expensive or not, outdated or not, and notwithstanding the paucity of usable roads or the facts that gasoline stations are often more than a hundred miles apart, that Moscow has a total of seven repair garages and that spare parts are usually available only through pilferage, the average Soviet citizen now feels he is on the threshold of motorized bliss.

Presently, any Russian able to pay for a car must queue to get on the order list and make a substantial down payment. The list is so short that it is filled within a day. Four years later, if the pace of production has continued, the car may be delivered. Moscow, a city of 7 million population, has only 100,000 privately owned cars. By 1980 the list may be longer, delivery times shorter and Moscow's streets as nightmarish as New York's.

But voices can still be heard warning against the moral harm to the Soviet way of life which the automobile portends. In the fall of 1970 *Literaturnaya Gazeta* published letters and essays about the perils and advantages of private auto ownership. One author propagated a nationwide taxi rental system as an alternative. Readers rejoindered with the contention that his scheme would require a taxi fleet of 14 to 15 million vehicles and 25 to 30 million professional chauffeurs.

When the automobile age dawns in the U.S.S.R., Soviet motorists will find the physical environment for their Moskviches and Zhigulis hostile for decades to come.

Soviet roads and highways are so few and used by so many trucks that the average speed attainable on all highways in the Russian Federation was less than twenty miles per hour in 1970.

"Two hundred years ago," quipped the weekly *Economic Gazette*, "our grandfathers traveled in troikas from Petersburg to Moscow at approximately the same speed."

No one doubts the story about the engineer who required three days to motor from Kazan, on the Volga, to Perm in the Urals, a distance of 360 miles. The road was so bad that this car was forced into a garage for repairs after the ordeal. And he was lucky to find a garage. In the entire Soviet Union there are approximately 150 of them, euphemistically referred to as "maintenance centers."

Those who find a repair shop have little hope of getting the work done. Delivery time for a Moskvich fender, for example, is five to six months. Of Moscow's estimated 10,000 taxicabs, only 6000 are in service at any given time. The remainder are in motor pool garages waiting for spare parts.

Gas and service stations are so scarce that every Soviet motorist carries a spare can of gasoline Since gas stations provide neither water nor air, it is best also to keep a water canister and a hand pump in the trunk.

In 1968 an organization with the promising name of Avtotekhob-sluzhevaniye (Automobile Technical Service) was established to provide the lacking services and build a network of gas stations, garages, parts depots, car wash points, motels and parking lots. By the time I left the U.S.S.R. two years later its efforts had not produced a shimmer of progress.

"The question of our ability to handle cars is worrying," an official of the State Automobile Inspection Administration admitted. "I think we are not yet ready."

Undoubtedly it will be the 1980s before the real impact of the automotive age will be felt in the Soviet Union. But that impact is destined to be profound. As the experience of other countries, particularly the West European ones, has shown, nothing changes the character of a society (not to mention the environment) as much as mass ownership of automobiles. Just as it has in other countries, the private car is certain to force a revolution in attitudes, and it will drag behind it a whole new industry of services and ancillary enterprises. A motorized Russia will be a different Russia from the one we know today.

* * *

"In tsarist days," Nikita Khrushchev once proclaimed, "when a man married you he would say: 'I will love you like my safe, I will beat you like my fur coat.' Today you are no longer an object to be bought and it is you women who beat the men. Therein lies the proof that we are on the road to Communism."

Many Soviet women would not have agreed with Khrushchev, but none can deny that in the more than five decades since the Bolsheviks stormed the Winter Palace, a remarkable transformation has taken place in the life of the women of Russia and what was once the tsarist empire.

Not only do women in the U.S.S.R. outnumber men by 130 to 111 million, but they represent 72 per cent of the Soviet Union's physicians, 83 per cent of the dentists, 52 per cent of the hospital directors, 32 per cent of the judges, 35 per cent of the lawyers, 40 per cent of the agronomists, 32 per cent of the college instructors and 6 per cent of the factory directors.

On the other hand, they also account for 91 per cent of the pig breeders, 90 per cent of the textile workers, 57 per cent of the streetcar, trolley and bus operators, 20 per cent of the construction workers and 54 per cent of those employed in the building materials industry.

The one profession in which women are critically underrepresented is the running of the state. Only 21 per cent of the party members are women and they represent less than 30 per cent of the membership of the Supreme Soviet. In the power centers that really count they are a minuscule minority. Of 396 full and alternate members of the Central Committee, only 11 are women. There is but one woman, Yekaterina Furtseva, in the Council of Ministers and none in either the Politburo or the Central Committee secretariat.

"What do we care about politics, the Chinese or intercontinental missiles," said one Moscow woman. "Hunger, poetry and love—those are the important things in life."

She reflects the changing mood of Soviet womanhood in the second half century of the Communist era. They have begun to reassert themselves as women, not just as dam builders and tractor drivers. They have started—slowly, of course, by the criteria of other industrialized societies—to become fashion- and beauty-conscious and hungry for the feminine frills of life. They are growing audibly impatient with a form of emancipation that entitles them to work and earn like men but also requires them to do all the traditional chores of womanhood.

It is Natasha, not Ivan, who is most furious about the lack of household conveniences, the crowded living conditions, the constant shortages and the long queues. And above all she is angry that she has to hold down two jobs, her husband only one.

"All my married life I have carried my *muzh* [husband] like this," complained a forty-year-old Moscow woman who works an eight-hour day. To illustrate what she meant, she stooped and patted her back to show that she has carried him like a burden on her shoulders. "Most of the time he comes home from work like this," and she tilted her head slightly to one side, flicked a thumb and forefinger to the jawbone in her silent demonstration of his drunkenness. "Frankly I'm sick of it."

"A new type of woman has developed in our country," said a female Moscow lawyer acrimoniously. "But the development of a new type of man is taking much longer."

Ada Baskina, a contributor to *Literaturnaya Gazeta,* asked: "Have women gained the right to work, only to lose the right to leisure?"

Almost all of them work and few things leave a more indelible impression on foreigners than the ubiquity of working women. They refuel the planes at Sheremetyevo airport, inspect arrivals' luggage, drive the taxis taking them into town, run the hotel desk and hand out the keys on the floor. When we had our Moscow apartment renovated, the painters and plasterers were women, so was the tile layer in the bathroom, and a woman repaired and sanded the flooring. Women shovel the millions of cubic feet of snow that fall on Moscow streets each season, and empty the garbage containers. They seem to do most of the road construction work, while idle male supervisors look on. They garden and landscape Moscow parkways, deliver the mail and newspapers, announce the news on radio and television, drive railway engines and, despite the fact that there is a law against it, mine coal in the Ukraine.

Yet the propagandistic picture of the buxom, kerchiefed and coveralled lass riding a bulldozer, operating a crane or supervising the construction of a new hydroelectric dam is more cliché than reality, for women complain, and male sociologists agree, that most women are left with the far more menial and unattractive jobs.

A representative survey at a construction enterprise in Saratov disclosed that 87 per cent of the diggers, 62 per cent of the steel erectors, 98 per cent of the insulators and 88 per cent of the plasterers and painters were women, who in turn accounted for only 2 per cent of the excavator operators, 5 per cent of the gas welders, 4 per cent of the compressor and 6.5 per cent of the crane operators—all jobs requiring skills and qualifications.

Most married women, despite emancipation, work primarily to supplement family income and have neither the time nor the inclination to obtain the training needed for better-paying and less strenuous work. Nevertheless the majority seem to have become so accustomed to working that they cannot imagine themselves without a job or profession.

"You can't just sit and look at four walls all day," an eighteen-year-old told one Western correspondent. She works eight hours daily in a textile plant and spends four evenings a week studying to become a chemical researcher.

Although Soviet sociological surveys show that up to 80 per cent of working women would not want to be without their jobs, 70 per cent of their husbands would prefer them to stay home. And that statistical analysis hints at the dichotomous situation that has arisen in Soviet male-female relationships.

Aside from the biological disadvantages that women have—they bear and suckle the children—fifty years of Communism have apparently failed to efface the traditional male view that women's role is to keep the house. As a result, Soviet women continue to do the cooking, washing, sewing and cleaning, in addition to holding down a job. Statistical analyses show that while the average Soviet man works eight hours daily, his working wife puts in a thirteen- to fourteen-hour day.

As long ago as 1923 Leon Trotsky wrote that the simplest task of all is to establish political equality. Equality in the factory, he warned, would be more difficult to accomplish. To bring about equality between man and woman in the family, however, "will be the most difficult task of all."

How difficult was revealed by a survey in Pskov that indicated that married men spend twice as much time reading, two and a half hours more on entertainment and five hours more seeing their friends each month than their working wives.

One young Moscow housewife, living with her husband and three-year-old son in one room of a communal four-family apartment, has described her day as a harried grind that begins at six in the morning and usually ends with complete exhaustion at 10 P.M. In between she cleans the apartment, makes the breakfasts, takes the boy to a crèche, rushes to her job, uses her half-hour lunch hour to queue for some of the supper groceries, hurries to stand in more lines after work, picks up the child, starts preparing supper, sews and mends, puts the child to bed, washes the dishes, does some laundry, irons some clothes and then plops into bed.

At that, she is lucky to have a place in a crèche for her little Sasha. Notwithstanding the auspicious picture of a nation of day nurseries and kindergartens, *Literary Gazette* has disclosed that there are only enough day-care centers for 23 per cent of the U.S.S.R.'s preschool children. The majority either are cared for by babushkas or their mothers cannot work.

If the problem looms large in Russia, it is even greater in Central Asia and other regions where old traditions and viewpoints prevail more persistently.

One woman sociologist has described the causes for the male-female conflict in Soviet society as a product of the changing roles of the sexes. "There was a time," she said, "when the man was the undisputed head of the family because he was the breadwinner. Today many women earn as much or more than their husbands. They may be better educated too. All too frequently men react by saying: 'If I am not the head of the family, then you get on with it.' They deliberately do nothing to help in the house."

Yet there is a hint of change in the air, particularly among the very young, the third post-revolutionary generation.

The U.S.S.R. is unquestionably entering an era of feminization of its women, despite their continuing appreciable role in production. It reflects itself in new attitudes toward beauty, female appearance, sex, marriage, divorce and children.

"We can work like men," one young science student said. "However, we don't want to be looked upon as *tovarishchi,* but as women."

The matronly *apparatchik* with a heaving bosom full of medals is no longer the Soviet standard of beauty, no matter how many such portraits *Pravda* insists on printing on its front page. Elderly women, who associate slimness with the hunger of the post-revolutionary and war years, plumpness with the relative cornucopia of food since the early 1950s, still shake their heads sympathetically when they see photographs of Galya Milovskaya, "the U.S.S.R.'s Twiggy" and probably its best-paid model. "The poor child looks so sickly. Why doesn't she eat?" they say. But among the majority of younger girls Bardot-like figures are now the aim, even if diet and anatomy conditioned by centuries of peasant traditions do not always make them attainable.

Given the limited means at her disposal, the young Soviet girl does what she can to make herself look attractive, though confused notions about style and fashion often produce unflattering extremes of either too little or too much. The Soviet girl who strikes a happy make-up medium is rare. And bleaching one's hair a shocking canary color seems to be a national pastime.

Just as standards of fashion and beauty are changing, so are criteria of morality and the attitudes toward sex.

Since the Revolution Soviet moral standards have undergone vicissitudinal changes that ranged from the unbridled libertinism advocated by the Bolsheviks' most outspoken "feminist," Alexandra Kollontai, to the Victorian prudery of the Stalin era; from the free-love concepts of 1918, when enthusiastic Bolsheviks in the town of Vladimir suggested that all girls of eighteen or over should be declared state property, to Stalin's maxim that "the sexual question can be decided only through steadfast and lasting marriage founded on love."

Today Russians are still publicly puritanical, but behind a façade of morality, the Soviet Union may well be one of the least inhibited societies in the West. What distinguishes the Soviet from most contemporary Western societies is that there is very little talk about sex, and even less guilt. Lovemaking, like liaisons and—to the dismay of sociologists—even marriages, is extraordinarily casual: emotionally as well as physically.

Although there is virtually no public education about birth control and the pill is still rejected by Soviet physicians as potentially harmful, there are few unwanted births in the European republics. The answer is abortion, which is legal and either free or so inexpensive that the average city girl has had several before marriage.

Single women, of whom there are millions because of the disproportions in the population balance caused by wartime losses and a continuing but inexplicable higher male mortality rate, have no reservations about having children, when they want them, out of wedlock, and many of them do. The stigma of illegitimacy has been virtually erased.

If moral standards have been subjected to oscillatory changes since 1917, attitudes toward marriage and divorce, not to mention the laws regulating both, have run the gamut from licentiousness to extreme rigidity. At the moment the pendulum has again swung toward greater freedom, as a result of which the U.S.S.R. has one of the highest divorce rates in the world, officially given at 2.75 divorces per 1000 population but probably running closer to 3.2 per 1000 because of the perfunctory registration requirements.

Immediately following the Revolution, in an attempt to give men and women equal rights and break the grip of the Church and bourgeois morality, divorce and marriage requirements were trimmed to a minimum. A couple simply went to the neighborhood registration office, signed the book, paid three rubles and they were married. Divorce was equally simple. All it required was a three-ruble note and another notation in the registry book. Often the husband or wife didn't even know until—if they were lucky—their former mate wrote them about it. The era is still referred to as that of "postcard divorces."

Some couples, facing fifty-ruble fines for having failed to change the names in their passports within the required ten-day period after marriage, simply got divorced and remarried: total cost six rubles—a net saving of forty-four over the fine they would have had to pay.

The simplicity of marriage and divorce, however, was having a disastrous effect on family life in a war-crippled nation, and in 1944 the policy shifted instantaneously from permissiveness to one of the strictest divorce laws in Europe. It was not relaxed until 1965, and in 1967 was subjected to several more liberalizing changes. These produced the initial increment in the Soviet divorce rate, which has soared during the past six years. Soviet sociologists at first attributed the increase to a closing of the hiatus between reality and legal requirements. Those people who had either not attempted divorce or simply separated because the procedure was too costly and bureaucratic under the old law hurried to legalize the status quo retroactively. But once the initial rush was over, Soviet authorities expected a leveling off. It has not come about.

Moreover Soviet citizens seem to be marrying at an ever younger age and after having known each other for less and less time.

The attitude toward marriage is becoming more flippant and some young people regard marriage as a form of lottery. "If you draw the right ticket, you're lucky," one girl wrote to *Komsomolskaya Pravda*. "But if you don't get a winner, you get a divorce."

The chief of one Moscow registry office, Zoya Kuzina, has observed that for the 400 marriages she registers each month, she also records 250 to 300 divorces. The pattern, she said, is depressingly familiar. "Before the wedding they hardly knew each other." She has recommended extending the mandatory waiting time between declaration of intent and the marriage ceremony from one month to six.

Evdokia Voroshilova, director of Moscow's main Palace of Weddings, feels that would be going from one extreme to another. She told me that out of every hundred who hand in their applications to marry, ten to fifteen on the average fail to turn up on the big day. "But I think a three-month period would suffice. Six is too long."

Like increasing consumer consciousness and the embourgeoisie-ment of Soviet society, the current attitude toward love, marriage and divorce does not satisfy the Soviet ideal.

"Under socialism," said one doctrinaire ideologist, "all manner of objective social reasons for the instability of marriages will disappear and genuinely human relations founded on love, mutual respect, common interests, views and spiritual requirements will develop between husband and wife, parents and children."

If that is really the case, then many Russians have not been reading their Marx and Lenin lately.

Part Six

The party has set itself the task of transforming our country into the world's foremost industrial power and of surpassing the U.S.A. in both absolute and per capita volume of production during the next decade. By approximately the same date the U.S.S.R. will exceed the present level of per capita agricultural production in the U.S.A. by one and a half times.

Nikita S. Khrushchev, October 19, 1961

*Did you know there is a basic
difference not only between Communist
and capitalist ideology, but between
Communist and capitalist fairy tales?
A capitalist fairy tale usually begins
with "Once upon a time there
was . . ." A Communist story starts
with the words "Someday there will
be . . ."*

Overheard in Moscow, 1970

12 *Someday There Will Be . . .*

Rostov-on-Don, with nearly 800,000 population, is one of the Soviet Union's most important industrial and commercial centers. Besides agricultural machinery, aircraft, textiles and ships, it also produces gravel. Each year the Rostov gravel plants send approximately 5000 railway cars of gravel to Stavropol, 180 miles to the southeast. Stavropol, a city of 200,000 population, is an important industrial center in the foothills of the Caucasus. Among other things, it produces a great deal of gravel. Each year the Stavropol gravel industry ships about 5000 railway cars of gravel to Rostov, an important industrial and commercial center, 180 miles to the northwest.

For many years Dyushambe, the capital of Tadzhikistan, could not be considered an industrial center. It had only a few textile and food processing plants. But in 1964 it acquired a factory making refrigerators. Because Dyushambe is situated in the Gissar Valley at the foot of the Pamirs, the U.S.S.R.'s highest mountains, whose eternally snow-and-ice-covered peaks tower 20,000 feet and more over the hot

Central Asian plains, the refrigerator was appropriately called the "Pamir." The name, unfortunately, is all it has in common with ice. In fact, by 1968 dissatisfaction with the Pamir's performance had reached the staggering proportion of 28,000 letters of complaint and a queue of 12,000 disappointed customers demanding a replacement. There are, the plant's management insists, explanations for this. The shop that makes the freezing compartments works at 25 per cent, the galvanizing shop at 100 per cent over capacity. They do this by so-called "telescoping of technology." Also, the plant does not produce its own compressors. These are imported—by air, because of the lack of rail and road facilities—from Odessa, 2500 miles to the west. Approximately 10 per cent of the compressors arrive in an unserviceable condition and many others are so deficient in their performance that many Pamirs do not work.

In the fall of 1968 a new petrochemical plant, designed to produce polystyrol, was completed in Angarsk, Siberia. Almost nine months later it had not yet turned out a single ounce of it, because no raw materials had been delivered. Nevertheless, during all those months, all the employees showed up punctually and faithfully for work each day, stood at the switches and levers of machines and instruments that were not operating and, of course, drew their pay.

The Voskresens Chemical Combine near Moscow has more than three hundred instruments in its "automated system of management." Unfortunately, manufacture of this equipment has been discontinued. So has the production of spare parts for these instruments and machines. As a result, 50,000 rubles' worth of equipment stands idle.

The U.S.S.R. has the world's largest seagoing fishing fleet, which brings in a catch of almost 8 million tons, yet provides Soviet consumers with less than half that amount because it lacks the cold chain and the canning equipment to process it. Moreover Soviet-made fishing trawlers require twice the crew for the same catch as competitive ships from Poland and East Germany.

Exaggerations? Canards? Soviet economists, business executives and government and party officials probably wish they were. But all of these examples—selected from the Soviet press—are true, and in a nutshell, they are what the Soviet economy is all about.

It makes refrigerators that don't refrigerate, cars that drive and ride like trucks, trucks that drive and ride like tanks. It turns out clothing that is either out of style or doesn't fit and airplanes so crudely appointed that the foreign Communist airlines, which buy them, have the interiors restyled in Western Europe.

It has hosiery plants that are idle because of the shortage of elastic band, enterprises that have halted production of kitchen ranges because they are out of sheet metal, shoe factories that are out of leather and ornaments, furniture plants that have no wood, textile mills that have no thread, state and collective farms that fail to bring the harvest in because they have received no gasoline or diesel oil for their tractors and combines, breweries and bottling plants that have no bottles or caps, food processing enterprises whose lines stand idle because they are out of jars or tops, mineral and mining complexes that have been built three hundred miles from the nearest rail line and so far from power sources that they must truck in coal to supply their own steam generators.

It produces machinery for factories that are not even built and builds factories for which there is no machinery. It has 2500 machine tool plants whose metal-cutting equipment works at 40 per cent capacity. It has one engineering enterprise that in 1969 systematically turned 18,000 of the 40,000 tons of metal delivered to it into scrap. Its cement industry annually loses more than 10 million tons of its output—about 11 per cent of the total—because of improper storage, waste or pilferage.

Undeniably, the Soviet economy faces unique geographical and meteorological problems. Vast distances and extreme weather conditions debilitate the effect of even the most strenuous efforts and make progress more expensive than elsewhere.

In March 1970 Galiyer Usmanov, premier of the Tartar Autonomous Republic, told a group of foreign correspondents in Kazan: "Last year [1969] we had only forty-five days without frost. As early as August 8 it was 17 degrees [Fahrenheit] in Kazan." True, as Usmanov explained, a year that cold comes but once every half century. But even in an average one there are only 120 days when the thermometer does not drop below freezing part of the time.

Yet, to judge merely from the Soviet press, climate and distances are not the greatest banes of the Soviet economy. The papers burgeon with reports of maladroit planning, mismanagement, theft and waste of materials, of machines delivered but no longer needed, of equipment delivered too early or too late which is then left to rust in front of factory gates or to be slowly slaughtered by workers who eviscerate the machines and sell the parts on the black market.

The disproportions and losses caused by desultory planning and organization are staggering.

Ten years ago, for example, the value of uninstalled equipment in the Ukraine totaled 478 million rubles. By 1971 this had increased to 987 million. An official of the Ukrainian People's Control Committee explained to a reporter from *Sotsialisticheskaya Industriya* how this "frozen capital" has accumulated.

A plant will receive an order, two or three years in advance, for equipment to be installed in a new factory or one that is being enlarged. The plant completes its preparatory work and starts to produce the equipment. But then it turns out that the new factory was not included in annual construction plans and is therefore not ready to utilize the machinery. The supplier, however, is geared for production and delivers the equipment to the "client," who then leaves it on the construction site for a year or two until it has either rusted or simply disappeared, component by component.

"Planners," the official explained, "tacitly assume that all construction plans will be fulfilled and all projects will be completed on time. But, to put it mildly, this does not always happen."

Waste, labor indiscipline, built-in disincentives, mismanagement and egregious mistakes in planning are among the chief reasons why the Soviet economy has been decelerating perceptibly since 1968.

By all criteria the eighth *pyatiletka*—five-year plan period—from 1966 to 1970 was one of the worst in post-war Soviet history. Instead of a planned 47 per cent, investments increased by only 43 per cent over the 1961–65 period, labor productivity by only 25 per cent, although real per capita income increased by 26 per cent. Soviet statistics claim that gross industrial output and national income grew by their planned targets of 50 and 41 per cent respectively, but every major index in heavy industry, except oil, was substantially below plan, leaving Western economists with the justified suspicion that the figures were manipulated.

During the 1966–70 period the Soviets increased the annual output of electrical energy to only 740 billion kilowatt-hours instead of the planned 845 billion, natural gas to only 200 instead of the planned 225 to 240 billion cubic meters and coal to only 624 instead of the targeted 670 million tons.

By 1970 Soviet industry hoped to produce 124 to 129 million tons of steel, but turned out only 116 million; 95 to 99 million tons of rolled metal, but delivered only 92.4 million; 62 to 65 million tons of fertilizer, but produced only 55.4 million. Instead of a planned 800,000 tons of chemical fibers, 623,000 were produced; instead of 2,200,000 tons of plastics and synthetic resins, 1,672,000 were turned out. In 1970 the engineering industry was to make 600,000 to 625,-000 tractors, but manufactured only 459,000; 2.5 billion rubles' worth of agricultural machinery, but delivered only 2.1 billion rubles' worth; 600,000 to 650,000 trucks, but produced only 525,000; and instead of a planned 700,000 to 800,000 passenger cars, made only 344,000. The plan for paper was underfulfilled by about 1 million tons—about 20 per cent—and instead of 100 to 105 million tons of cement, only 95.2 million were produced.

In fact, besides oil, of which 353 million tons instead of a planned 350 million were pumped, only the furniture, footwear and sugar refining industries fulfilled or exceeded their quotas.

The planned 1971 increase in the national income is only 6.1 per cent—less than the average annual growth of 6.3 per cent during the period of 1961 to 1965. Industrial output was scheduled to increase by only 6.9 per cent in 1971, the most modest growth in almost two decades, although Soviet sources reported an 8.2 per cent growth for the first nine months of 1971—a good enough performance to persuade Kosygin to revise upward some of the targets for the current five-year plan when he addressed the Supreme Soviet in November 1971.

Despite initially good results, prospects by 1975 do not look propitious. When the 1971–75 *pyatiletka* was first unveiled, it called for a 42 to 46 per cent increase in gross industrial output. In November 1971 Kosygin set a target of 47 per cent. But even this revised figure would still represent 3 per cent less than the claimed increase during the previous (1966–70) *pyatiletka*. The national income is to increase by 37 to 40 per cent, as against a claimed 41 per cent increase during the 1966–70 period. Capital investments are scheduled to increase by 41 per cent. Labor productivity, the index figure that shows the greatest lag in the Soviet economy, is also to increase by 36 to 40 per cent during the current five-year plan and is scheduled to account for 87 to 90 per cent of the rise in industrial output, an indication of the continuing scarcity of investment funds.

Actual output targets by 1975 are modest—despite Kosygin's claim that by that year the U.S.S.R.'s physical output would match 1970–71 American production—and in some categories barely exceed what Soviet industry had been *scheduled* to produce by 1970. There is, in fact, no prospect whatsoever that the U.S.S.R. will catch up with the U.S.A. in the foreseeable future.

The current plan was unveiled in February 1971, more than thirty months after Soviet media had said it would be ready, and it is striking for its relatively modest goals and the delays that preceded its introduction. Moreover, for an economic plan that prides itself on being "scientific," it is remarkably vague. For example, it discloses nothing about the distribution of capital investment funds to the various branches of the economy. Western economists see this as clear indication that the debate over allocations and priorities, which preceded publication of the plan, has not been resolved.

That debate has obviously been going on since the summer of 1968, for in May of that year the weekly *Ekonomicheskaya Gazeta* announced that the plan would be made public and submitted to discussion in August 1968. By December 1970, when the *1971* plan was disclosed, the vital *five-year* targets were still shrouded by a veil of silence.

Discussion of the plan was an essential item on the agendas of all fourteen republican party congresses that preceded the XXIVth Congress of the CPSU. But ten of these congresses, originally scheduled to be held in late January and early February 1971, had to be postponed—because of the delay in publication of the plan until February 15.

The crucial argument had undoubtedly been whether consumer goods production should grow faster than industrial goods and which branches of the economy should receive how large a slice of the cake.

Until June 1970 the "metal eaters" of Soviet heavy industry and the military-industrial complex were apparently still presenting the more persuasive arguments. In a speech to workers in Moscow's Bauman district, before the national elections to the Supreme Soviet, Brezhnev said that heavy industry would enjoy a slight predominance over the consumer goods sector in 1971–75 growth rates. But eight months later when the plan was made public, the announced priorities were reversed. What had happened? Most observers ascribe the shift in emphasis to two factors: repressed inflation in the U.S.S.R. and the strikes and riots in Poland in December 1970.

Inflationary pressures are clearly having a deleterious effect on incentives and productivity in the Soviet Union. For several years, as wages rose steadily, total household disposable income has grown faster than the supply of available and desirable goods and services.

With little or nothing to spend their accrescent incomes on, Soviet workers either drank more—resulting in reduced productivity, increased absenteeism and a higher accident rate—or deposited their money in savings accounts. During the first half of 1970, in fact, absolute increases in net savings were greater than the absolute increases in disposable money incomes. Because of the lack of incentive to spend additional money, productivity growth has decelerated.

Perspicacious Soviet economists contended that to increase productivity and to assure a healthier growth of the economy, wage increases would have to be kept at a minimum and the flow of consumer goods would have to swell. This, precisely, is the thrust of the five-year plan, which has made the fight against inflationary trends in the U.S.S.R. a top priority.

Most likely, this general direction had been determined by the fall of 1970. But the uprisings in Poland, which the Soviet leadership justifiably read as a tocsin for the U.S.S.R., served to lard the plan with propagandistic promises of a consumer goods cornucopia just a half decade away. Many aspects of the plan, including the exuberant pronouncement that its "main task . . . is to ensure a considerable growth of the people's living and cultural standards," were undoubtedly written into it at the last minute, between December 1970 and final publication in February 1971.

These last-minute alterations, designed to assuage the masses with propagandistic promises, apparently ran into stiff opposition from the heavy industry interests.

By the time the XXIVth Party Congress convened in April, the metal-eating lobby, as the heavy industry interests are called, had regained so much influence that, according to some Kremlinologists, it effected the censorship of two important passages relating to the production of consumer goods from the printed version of Brezhnev's report to the congress.

Clearly, the Stalinist or neo-Stalinist bosses of heavy industry, the prophets of central planning, and the orthodox Communist ideologues prefer the stick of tightened discipline, exhortation, moral incentives and appeals to patriotism over the carrot of more consumer goods and a higher standard of living as a means to spur production.

It is difficult to ascertain precisely where Brezhnev really stands in this debate between the doctrinaire prophets of the command type of economy, who think in the clichés and tenets laid down by Stalin forty years ago, and the pragmatic liberal economists, who propagate the levers of economic incentive. But in December 1969, when the Soviet economy had reached its most recessionary level since World War II, it was Brezhnev who set the repressive tone that signaled the drive for labor discipline, economic frugality and austerity.

The year 1969 was undeniably catastrophic, and bad weather was a vital factor. Soviet statisticians padded the figures, but the grain harvest, according to Western experts, was down to around 152 million tons. Instead of increasing as planned by 6.1 per cent, gross agricultural production had decreased by 3 per cent. Gross industrial production had increased by only 7 per cent, the worst peacetime rate since 1928. National income had grown by only 6.1 per cent and labor productivity by only 4.4 per cent, one of the worst performances on the Soviet record.

The year was so poor that the 1966–70 plan targets would not be met. Planners performed the sort of economic black magic for which the U.S.S.R. is infamous. They dropped the earlier target figures down a convenient memory hole and revised the plan downward so that in 1970, the year of the Lenin centennial, it would look as if the Soviet economy had overfulfilled its quotas.

But, far more important, in a secret meeting of the Central Committee, details of which began leaking out only weeks and months later, Brezhnev called for a tightening of discipline and inveighed against waste of raw materials and money, shirkers and loafers, drunkards and spongers and "frequent job changers" and "production spoilers."

Sovietologists believe that the essence of his December 1969 speech was contained in a January 13, 1970, *Pravda* editorial which called for a "thrifty attitude to every minute of working time, every machine, every mechanism and each gram of raw materials and fuel."

The paper stressed the necessity of measuring "expenses against results" and warned that every invested ruble must be used with maximum efficiency.

"Particular attention," the editorial stressed, "should be paid to strengthening labor and production discipline and stepping up the struggle against such anti-social practices as misappropriation of public property, loafing and alcoholic overindulgence."

Ranking party officials went on the hustings to deliver the message. Politburo member Alexander Shelepin, the chief of the Soviet federation of trade unions, told a plenary session of the union council of the need to "resolutely increase discipline and responsibility at all levels, intensify the struggle against . . . the rolling stones [people who shift from job to job], the absentees and the drunkards." All of them, in his words, were "anti-social elements." Gennady Voronov, at that time also a Politburo member and premier of the Russian Republic, flatly told one audience to stop blaming the weather. "In our century of rapid development, science and technology, one cannot blame the weather for everything."

In the most delinquent republics—Turkmenia, Azerbaidzhan and Kazakhstan—top party officials were summarily dismissed. In Alma-Ata it was the premier, in Turkmenia and Azerbaidzhan the party first secretaries. Tougher *apparatchiki* were appointed to replace them. In Azerbaidzhan, for example, the chief of the KGB became the new first secretary.

New laws to deal with shirkers and shiftless workers were passed, the anti-alcohol drive was stepped up and vodka and cognac prices increased. "Idlers" were exhorted to go to work. One article in *Pravda* suggested that the "labor shortage" in Azerbaidzhan should be solved by requiring "several thousand" students in correspondence and night schools to go to work, by sending "healthy young lads, now working as store clerks, to the production lines," and filling their places with "women who are now sitting at home because of the shortage of child-care centers."

Draconian as these measures and recommendations sound, there was a certain justification for them. The indolence, inefficiency and obvious apathy of Soviet workers has to be seen to be believed.

Because the Soviet system has failed to produce zealous and conscientious workers it has tried to substitute quantity for quality of labor force.

On the basis of a paradoxical principle of the Soviet constitution which stipulates that every citizen has both the right and the duty to work, the Soviet economy has for decades operated on the premise that two (or more) people should do the work of one. As a consequence, featherbedding, absenteeism, slothfulness and clock watching have reached proportions unmatched by any other industrialized country.

In every room or hall of each museum in the Soviet Union there is one old woman who spends an eight-hour day doing nothing but sitting on a rickety chair watching the visitors pass to and fro, even if there are no visitors for hours. Presumably these babushkas are hired to prevent anyone from touching or stealing the exhibits.

On each floor of every hotel in the U.S.S.R. at least one *dezhurnaya* —a woman who hands out room keys, takes orders for morning wake-up calls and other services—is on duty twenty-four hours each day, seven days a week. This requires three women, who work eight-hour shifts, and a fourth to substitute for weekend duty for each floor. In Moscow's thirty-story Ukraina Hotel, for example, one can assume that at least 120 women are employed to do the work of a dozen desk clerks and a few switchboard operators in New York's Waldorf Astoria.

At Moscow's new Italian-designed Universam (supermarket) No. 1 in Lyublino, 240 employees and 15 check-out counters serve 8000 to 10,000 shoppers. The sales area is 12,840 square feet. But the assistant manager, Lyudmilla N. Vorobyeva, feels she needs an even larger staff.

Playing chess, checkers, dominoes or cards, writing private letters, solving crossword puzzles, calling friends and relatives, going shopping and to the barbershop or beauty parlor during working time, complained *Pravda,* is the rule, not the exception.

In 1969 a team of People's Control Committee reporters conducted a spot check at a factory in Perm, observing the working habits of one three-man team. Their day ran as follows:

Starting time is 7:45 A.M., though only one of the three reported for work punctually. Work continued until 9:20, when a twenty-minute smoke break was called. From 9:40 to 9:55 work was resumed, then there was another smoke break until 10:20. From 10:20 until 11:20 there was a lunch break. From 11:05 to 11:20 the inspector observed aimless standing around and strolling through the plant area. From 11:20 to 11:40 the machines were readjusted. Relatively intensive work was performed between 11:40 and 1 P.M. From 1 to 2 o'clock another smoke break was called, followed by more aimless wandering about. From 2 until 2:30 machines and tools were cleaned. At 2:30 the team quit for the day.

Pravda reported that at another plant only 96 out of 280 employees were at their place of work the entire day. The remaining 184 either came late, left early or did not show up at all.

And who can calculate how much paid working time is spent by the average Russian moonlighting on the side?

Despite legions of people who are being paid to do little or nothing, the Soviet Union complains of a labor shortage. Konstantin Novikov, chairman of the Russian Federation's Committee for Utilization of Labor Resources, has mentioned a million open jobs and suggested that the problem in some other republics is proportionally worse.

On the other hand, economic reformers, such as Professor Alexander Birman, scoff at the notion of a labor shortage. The problem, according to Birman, is one of excess bureaucracy, outdated equipment, outdated thinking and inefficient use of labor. "We have enough manpower," he says. "What we should discuss is more efficient use of it." Excessive labor losses result from the use of old equipment, insufficient mechanization, inadequate specialization. Just as an example, some light bulb and vacuum tube factories employ three to four times as many people as foreign plants with a similar output. The reason: an outdated production line.

Under the influence of the decelerating economic situation in 1969, Soviet authorities resorted not only to the tested lever of exhortation and tightened discipline but decided on a surprisingly radical solution. The Central Committee formally endorsed the so-called Shchekino experiment and recommended its wider application.

Shchekino is a chemical combine in Tula, a hundred miles south of Moscow. In 1967 it introduced a revolutionary pilot program calling for increased output with a reduced labor force. Under the terms of the experiment, the combine's wage fund—that is, the amount of money available annually for wage payments—was frozen at 1967 levels. Within three years the enterprise was to lay off a thousand workers but increase output by 73 per cent. The earnings of the redundant workers were to accrue to the remaining labor force as a reward for increased productivity.

Such a scheme is pregnant with implicit political heresies. Committed to the principle of full employment and proletarian welfare, the U.S.S.R. has always forsworn rationalization programs that demand layoffs or—Marx forbid!—such capitalist machinations as closing down unprofitable enterprises.

Yet the Shchekino experiment was enormously successful. Although a thousand workers were dismissed, productivity increased by 87 per cent, actual output by 80 per cent and the remaining workers augmented their wages by an average of 30.7 per cent.

Inadvertently a Soviet economist revealed how overstaffed the Shchekino enterprise was—and presumably still is. He pointed out that whereas the Dutch and Italian designers of the ammonia, methanol and carbamide plants at Shchekino had specified a crew of 278, the actual number employed totaled 806.

At any rate, by 1971 the Shchekino method, or some variant of it, was being applied in 107 enterprises throughout the U.S.S.R.

The political and ideological problems it raised were staggering, and Soviet officials were understandably reluctant to explain what happened to the redundant workers. Under the original terms of the Shchekino experiment, they were to be assigned to new jobs in other sections and plants of what is a rapidly expanding chemical complex. When details of the experiment were made public, *Pravda* claimed that this is what happened to them. Subsequent reports, however, indicated that nearly five hundred workers had been transferred to construction jobs in the Moscow region and most of the others had been retrained and reassigned within the combine or to a new artificial-fiber plant under construction nearby.

The Shchekino experiment, as well as an October 1969 decree requiring governmental and industrial administrations to pare their white-collar staffs by an estimated 200,000 in 1970 and again in 1971, has raised the question of unemployment and unemployment benefits for the first time in forty years. In early 1971 the journal *Voprosy Ekonomikii* (Problems of Economics) revealed that such benefits were being paid (albeit only to engineering, technical and supervisory employees) under provisions of a February 27, 1970, edict that had been kept secret for almost a year.

Since unemployment is allegedly a capitalist phenomenon, Soviet economists must be careful in their use of terms. They refer instead to "material allowances" for workers "freed" from enterprises. But according to *Voprosy Ekonomikii* white-collar workers dismissed under the efficiency program receive up to three months' full pay while being retrained for production jobs. Those relocated in other parts of the country are assured preferential placement on lists for housing and day-care centers for their children.

Unfortunately for the Soviet economy, the Shchekino experiment is virtually the only element of reform, incentives and rationalization that enjoys active official support. In fact, if anything typifies the regime's response to the deceleration of the economy, then it is abandonment of liberal, innovative tenets and renewed reliance on traditional, command-type panaceas.

Officials still talk volubly about economic reform, and Nikolai

Baibakov, head of Gosplan, the State Planning Committee, rarely fails to boast about the number of enterprises "now working according to the new methods." By the end of 1970 the figure was 41,000, representing 83 per cent of the total, and 93 per cent of the volume of profit. Yet such pronouncements are little more than lip service.

Whereas once discussions focused on the independence of managers, the current five-year plan places the stress on their responsibilities. From economic pragmatism the Kremlin is moving toward Communist moral rearmament. Under the pretext of making adjustments in the reform and in its application, centralism is being reestablished and *apparatchiki* are replacing the technicians, who have been made to bear the burden of the reform's alleged failures.

If the reform has failed, it was because it was a diluted concept of reform and, stymied in its application from the outset, has been eroded in practice since then. As a consequence, today the conservatives and traditionalists point accusing fingers at the reformers and gleefully assert that "we told you so." They fill the trade and professional journals with warnings about the dangers of "Philistinism," raise the specter of "enterprises floundering in the anarchy of market conditions" and ring the tocsin against "departures from central planning."

Today the old-line prophets of central planning, exhortations and emulation drives, not the reformers, have the Politburo's ear, and calls for a return to Stalinist economic principles have become increasingly insistent.

In the spring of 1970 Ivan Bachurin, one of Baibakov's deputies, openly attacked reformers, notably Professor Nikolai Fedorenko, and accused them of being market economists. One need only recall the fate of Ota Sik, Czechoslovakia's chief reform economist and former deputy prime minister, to appreciate the seriousness of such a charge.

At a Moscow press conference Bachurin stressed that the 1971–75 five-year plan would emphasize more, not less, centralization of the economy. The economic decline of 1969, he said, "showed graphically where the illusions spread by some theoreticians can lead."

The best-known reform economist, Kharkov University professor Yevsei Liberman, has virtually been forced to recant. In a book published in January 1971, he wrote that "it was a mistake to state that profitability was the only criterion of the work of an enterprise." He expressed preference for central planning and said, "after an experience of ten years it has become clear that an investment is profitable only if it is socially useful." The new work is critical of too much reliance on economic incentives and describes orientation toward market factors as "a socialism of skeptics who do not believe in the power of planning."

Although by no means the only reform economist, it was Liberman whose 1962 *Pravda* article, personally approved by Khrushchev, set out the principles of what became known as economic reform in the entire Communist bloc.

He called for the introduction of profit and profitability as the chief criteria of economic success instead of simple plan fulfillment of dozens of meaningless indicators under which managers of factories had been turned into bureaucrats. They were told by their ministries specifically not only how many pieces of a given product or how many tons of it they were to manufacture, but how many producer goods, how many workers, how much in wages and how much in investment they were to put into producing it. They literally received instructions on the number of nuts and bolts they could use to put together a tractor, how many buttons to sew on a shirt, how many nails to hammer into a packing crate.

As reform was envisioned in 1962, enterprises should be freed from the nearly total external planning and control to which they were subject. Instead of thirty to fifty mandatory plan indexes which used to be dictated to them, only two—total production in terms of numbers, and fulfillment of delivery dates—should be stipulated. The only criterion of efficiency was to be profitability, which would determine premiums and wage increases for both labor and management. Reinvestment funds, instead of being budgeted and allocated by the state, were to derive from profits. Suppliers and producers were to deal directly with each other instead of channeling deliveries and procurements through their ministries to exchange goods on the basis of pre-planned indexes.

The basic principle of socialist ownership of the means of production, however, was to remain sacrosanct.

Within this general theoretical framework there can be many variations of reform, ranging from a true "socialist market" economy, based on supply, demand, profit and flexible prices, as envisaged by Sik, to the timid approach finally adopted in the U.S.S.R. which accorded enterprises just a little more autonomy, provided for fewer compulsory plan indicators and prescribed profitability as the basic criterion.

In 1964, with Khrushchev's blessings, two textile plants shifted to "Libermanism" on a trial basis. Subsequently four hundred other light industrial enterprises adopted the system and all showed an appreciable increase in efficiency.

In September 1965, at a plenary meeting of the Central Committee, Kosygin's "New System of Planning and Economic Stimuli" was adopted and its implementation ordained for all Soviet industry. But the Kosygin reform was an adulterated version of the original concept and prescribed only a modicum of decentralization. Instead of the two mandatory plan indexes recommended by Liberman, enterprises had to fulfill seven. Each year they were to be told their volume of sold production, the assortment of products, the size of their wage funds, to how much they would be entitled in centrally allocated investment funds and when they could start new production capacities, how much new technology they were to introduce, what their profits should be and how much technical and material supply would be at their disposal. In a sense this nailed down the coffin lid on reform before it was even born.

The Soviet approach represented a compromise between the reformers versus the formidable bureaucrat-managers, the *apparatchiki* of the huge Gosplan machinery and the vested interests of the ministries and industrial branch committees whose roots were anchored and mentalities forged by thirty-five years of Stalinist command planning, the principle of strict obedience and the idea of production for the sake of production.

Concomitantly with the inauguration of the reform the industrial ministries—there are more than forty of them on the all-union level —which had been abolished by Khrushchev in 1957, were re-established. Around 25 per cent of the "new" ministers turned out to be men who had held the same posts eight years previously. All of these were old-line central planners of the Stalinist school.

Nor were many of the managers enthusiastic about the greater degree of autonomy to which the reform entitled them. Raised and trained in the Stalin era, inadequately qualified for the jobs they are supposed to perform, these complacent bureaucrat-executives, of whom there are thousands, do not understand and are lukewarm to the reform principle.

Whereas the party leadership may have been convinced of the need for change in 1965, the lower and middle echelons were opposed to it. After the September 1965 Central Committee plenum, which had provided for "broadening economic independence of the enterprises," the various vested interests mounted an offensive to channel as much of that new autonomy as possible either to party organizations within factories or to the "collectives" of the plant, which are, of course, wholly under party control.

By 1968 the implementation of what had been a conceptually modest reform was beginning to falter and grind to a halt in the face of growing opposition from conservatives who reign in the centers of economic power.

Those executives who wanted to use their greater autonomy have been deprived of their legal privileges in practice and those who abhorred the prospect of decision making have been protected in their complacency by the combination and interaction of sheer bureaucratic inertia and institutional opposition.

Ministries arbitrarily limit the size of development funds. Fines for contract violations have been kept so low and irrational that they do not serve to deter violations. Under the original provisions of the reform, there were to be only seven mandatory plan indexes. Two more have been added and the nine cover such a broad spectrum of a factory's inputs and outputs that autonomy of management remains largely theoretical.

One of the criteria for determining how far an economy has moved from central planning is the degree to which wholesale and producer prices have been adjusted to real cost factors and are determined by market forces. A massive revision of the 9 million or so wholesale prices throughout the Soviet economy was completed by July 1967. Because they were calculated on the basis of 1964 and 1965 prime costs, they were in effect obsolescent before they were introduced. Moreover the new prices remain administered, cost-plus prices: they do not reflect need, scarcity or abundance, supply and demand. And as Vladimir Sitnin, the chairman of the State Committee on Prices, has pointed out, they do not encourage the production of new and improved products or discourage the manufacture of old ones.

By May 1971 it appeared that a stepped, three-tier price system might shortly be introduced. This would provide for the highest price for new products—to encourage development and to compensate the producer for investment costs—the main price when the item is produced in quantity, and a lower price when the product is out-dated—to penalize enterprises that continue to produce outmoded goods. If and when this system is introduced it will bring about improvements although it will still represent a compromise with the solution that Soviet economic circumstances demand: market conditions for the exchange of producer goods.

Despite official abjuration of the old tonnage ideology, weight still plays a vital role in the Soviet economy. A chemical industry trade journal in 1969 complained that prices for chemical equipment are often fixed according to the weight of the product. These tonnage prices "naturally lead to the creation of excessively heavy designs."

In 1965 Kosygin spoke of direct contractual links and the gradual conversion of administrative allocation into wholesale trade, which would provide for greater flexibility in distribution of producer goods. Little has been accomplished. Central allocation through administrative rationing of virtually all producer goods and supplies persists.

The *tolkach*—that wheeler and dealer of the Soviet economy who provides a plant director with the supplies and producer goods he needs to keep the assembly line moving and the quotas fulfilled—remains an essential figure on the Soviet economic scene. The *tolkach* is complementary to the planner, and any Soviet manager needs both of them. The planner tells him what and how much to produce, the *tolkach* provides him with the resources to produce it. An extroverted, effervescent type, the *tolkach* would be a salesman in any capitalist society. But in the Soviet economy, where there is nothing to sell, his job is to buy: raw materials and parts, semi-finished products and producer goods that will enable his factory to meet its commitments. Savvy in the ways of the Soviet business world, he has innumerable connections, is a master of *blat*—influence peddling—and knows how to circumvent both the bottlenecks of bureaucracy and shortages.

"Do you think I enjoy knocking on doors with a briefcase full of letters and orders and begging for supplies and equipment?" one of these expediters asked in *Izvestia*. "But it has to be done to avoid paralysis of the factory's work."

Boris Rakitsky, a young economist, has spelled out the dilemma in

day-to-day terms, as it applied to the Motor of the Revolution diesel
engine factory in Gorky:

> Some of the petty regulation that hinders development of ini-
> tiative was eliminated and rejected at the time of the change to
> the new system of planning and incentives. It was assumed that
> this trend would continue as the reform developed. But things
> turned out differently. Before the reform the plant received eighteen
> sets of instructions "from above." In 1966 this was decreased to
> four. In 1967 it was increased to nine. By 1968 it was twenty-
> three.
>
> The ministry now even fixes prices and quotas on expenditures
> for travel and the use of the plant's cars . . . The factory must
> go to great lengths to justify overexpenditures on the travel budget,
> although without them it would be unable to market its output.

Many of the factory's products are outdated, largely because they
are stationary diesel engines for which demand has waned as the
nationwide electric power grid has expanded. But ministerial instructions and fund allocations make it impossible for the plant to develop
new, more marketable items.

The ministry shackles the factory to suppliers and subcontractors
who are incapable of meeting their obligations. Conversely, the factory must deliver its diesel engines to ministries whose supply functionaries don't want them or don't know what to do with them. The
Ministry of Timber, Cellulose, Paper and Wood-Processing Industries, for example, was unable to dispose of the twenty Motor of the
Revolution diesel engines that had been allocated to it. Yet during
one six-month period a Krasnoyarsk lumber plant's *tolkach* bought
seven, and six other lumber enterprises each bought one of the
factory's engines directly from the Gorky plant. Occasionally the plant
produces more engines than the plan calls for and sells them through
crude advertising or uses its own *tolkachi* to trade them off against
needed equipment and supplies. Such transactions, however, are illegal and could cause the *tolkachi* and the management to end up in
Siberia.

Frequently ministerial production plans are late and the plant produces without knowing whether it is authorized to do so or not. In
1968 it turned out 70,000 rubles' worth of spare parts before having any central orders for them. To get rid of these parts simply by
advertising them or selling them through its *tolkachi* to enterprises that

might need them is also illegal. "A case for the public prosecutor's office," as Yevgeny Smelev, one of the factory's executives, put it. How does the management avoid being prosecuted? It arranges the sale of spare parts through direct contacts, but then waits until the customer has put in an order for them through the central bureaucracy in Moscow. Once the order arrives in Gorky, the parts are delivered —but in the meantime two to three months have gone by and the customer's diesel engine has been standing idle.

It is a tale of woe that could have been told by thousands of Soviet executives. According to a 1970 survey of 241 enterprises in Siberia and the Far East, 56 per cent of the queried managers believed that the economic reform had extended the independence of the plant and the rights of the director insufficiently. Some 79 per cent said that they had experienced no improvement in the supply system, while 74 per cent said the production development fund is inadequate.

"It is naïve to think," Professor Birman once wrote, "that the reform should have rid us at once, as if by a magic wand, of all our difficulties, of all the accumulated disproportions, incompetence and other weaknesses. In reality, even an ideal economic system requires time to eliminate bottlenecks."

He called for less interference from the center, expansion of direct contact between enterprises, more autonomy for managers in the use of their manpower and wage funds, a higher rate of profit for enterprises with a lower contribution (tax) to the state treasury and the expansion of wholesale trade to adjust machinery and material supplies. He blamed the central planners and ministries for tinkering too much with the production quotas so that individual managers never know what they may be asked to do at short notice and consequently protect themselves by concealing their true capacities and operate on minimal quotas.

But Birman's is a voice in the wilderness of an economy moving backward, not forward. No matter how many enterprises may be converted to the "new system of management and economic stimuli" by 1975, the reform is dead. It was killed by the halfhearted implementation of a halfhearted program which, as was predictable, brought halfhearted results.

As the British economist Keith Bush put it: "The men who took over from Khrushchev sought to compromise and to implement their goals as cautiously as possible in order to reduce the risk of their own positions. In this they were aided by the conservative officials who abound in the planning, supply and ministerial offices—time servers who pay lip service to the need for reform while backpedalling stubbornly and effectively sabotaging those few changes which were introduced."

And could it have been otherwise?

Real economic reform would require not only political reform but a sense of active participation at all social levels. As such it would bring about a gradual shift to what could loosely be defined as a "participatory semi-authoritarian system."

Inevitably, a more participatory system would create new special interest groups, some of which would evolve into new elites with powerful vested interests of their own and would become, eventually, contenders for political power and a threat to the vaunted supremacy of the Communist Party.

But this the party cannot allow.

Economic reform, as conceived by Khrushchev, was a further stage of de-Stalinization, and in those terms it is easy to understand why the Soviet leadership and extant vested interests have now had second thoughts about it.

Implicitly, the original reform concept demanded a gradual transfer of economic decision-making powers from the party establishment and the central administrative apparatus to the new managerial class and, perhaps eventually through the market mechanism, to the consumers themselves. Inevitably this would weaken the position of the party oligarchy and the administrative bureaucracy by striking at the economic roots of their political power.

The men now ruling the U.S.S.R. would never countenance this. They may be perspicacious enough to recognize the economic need for reform, but the political arguments against it will outweigh the need.

Yet, having set out on a mini-reform, they have opened a Pandora's box of imponderables. Today the argument in the Soviet Union reduces to a simple one between those who contend that only reversion to the Stalinist principles of a command economy will save the nation and those who assert that only "real" reform can provide a solution. The leadership attempts to walk a narrow wire between them.

The situation is ominously reminiscent of the one in Czechoslovakia in 1967, just a few months before Antonin Novotny was brought to fall. Obviously Moscow is not Prague, but the analogy is striking.

By 1937 the Soviet Union will be the
most advanced country in the world
so that all the toilers can see with their
own eyes what the working class can
achieve . . .

Valerian Kuibyshev,
the chairman of Gosplan,
at the XVIIth Party Congress
in 1932

13 *In Another Epoch*

On October 4, 1957, earth awoke to the startling news that it had a second moon—a brightly polished, 184-pound sphere with the unfamiliar name of Sputnik I. As it circled the globe every one and a half hours, its slender antennas transmitted an intermittent beep-beep that sent tremors of fear and alarm through the capitals of the Western world.

The Soviet Union was first in space with an orbiting artificial satellite. In quick succession it followed up on that initial triumph with a series of other "cosmic victories": the first dog in space, the first physical contact with the moon, the first photographs of the lunar far side, the first man to orbit the earth, the first man to spend a full day in space, the first launch of two spacecraft, the first near rendezvous, the first woman in orbit and the first man to leave a spacecraft in flight.

Russians and Westerners alike tended to see the Soviet scientific-technological complex as a juggernaut moving inexorably from one spectacular success to another. But only a decade after Western scientists and politicians publicly expressed their fears and privately voiced their grudging admiration for the Soviet accomplishments, that view began to change drastically.

Today, some of its impressive achievements notwithstanding, the U.S.S.R. must be regarded as a technologically backward power. Except for its triumphs in a few specific fields, it has barely passed the threshold into the "technotronic" age. What is more, the technological gap between the Soviet Union and its Western rivals is widening, not narrowing.

No one has spelled out the magnitude of the problem more succinctly and with more authority than the eminent Soviet physicist Andrei D. Sakharov.

"In the course of the past decade," he wrote in a highly unorthodox letter to Leonid Brezhnev, Aleksei Kosygin and Nikolai Podgorny, "menacing signs of breakdown and stagnation have been discovered in the economy of our country."

The letter, co-signed by Valentin Turchin, another physicist, and Roy Medvedev, a historian and the twin brother of the geneticist Zhores Medvedev, was dated March 19, 1970, and reached Western correspondents in Moscow several days later through *samizdat* channels.

Sakharov wrote:

> At the end of the 1950s our country was the first to launch a sputnik and it was the first to send a man into space. By the end of the 1960s we had lost our lead and the first men to land on the moon were Americans. This fact is just one of many that shows the growing gap between the extent of research in our country and the developed nations of the West.
>
> In the 1920s and 1930s the capitalist world was hit by crises and depressions. Our motto at that time was to catch up with America and overtake it. We were in the process of doing that for several decades. Then the situation changed. The second industrial revolution began and now, at the beginning of the 1970s, we can see that we have not even caught up with America but that the gap between the two countries is becoming greater and greater.
>
> The growth rate of our national income is dropping steadily . . . There is a chronically grave situation in agriculture . . . The number of goods in short supply is increasing . . . Productivity of labor remains many times lower than in the developed countries . . . And

when you compare our economy with that of the United States, you see that ours lags not only in quantitative but in qualitative respects.

In fact, the newer and more revolutionary an aspect of the economy, the greater is the gap between us and America . . .

The extent of the gap—not only between the U.S.S.R. and the U.S.A., but between the Soviet Union and the other developed capitalist countries such as Japan, West Germany, Britain, France and Italy—is staggering.

Soviet per capita production of steel, cement and mineral fertilizers, for example, is less than that of the six Common Market countries. In 1970 the Soviet Union produced less than half as much electric power, 40 per cent as much natural gas, 25 per cent as much in plastics and chemical fibers, one third as many trucks and buses and one thirtieth as many passenger cars as the United States did in 1968. It also fell short of the 1968 U.S. production of steel, oil and fertilizers. By 1975, if quotas are met, targeted Soviet production will still be critically below the 1968 American output of electrical power, natural gas, chemical fibers, plastics and synthetics, and trucks and buses, not even to mention passenger cars, of course.

Technologically the Soviet Union is not a pacesetter but a follower: a borrower and buyer of foreign ideas and techniques. In the 1940s and 1950s Soviet officials did not even try to conceal the fact that they stole patents, designs and know-how. One camera plant executive told a visiting East European in 1958: "Just think how much human energy is wasted in countries such as the U.S.A., where hundreds and thousands of companies, competing factories, construction firms, inventors and scientists work for the sole purpose of bringing out new models . . . We let them do it for us. My job . . . is to pick out the models best suited to our needs from the hundreds of types of cameras appearing in the world, to select the easiest and comparatively cheapest to manufacture and to put it into production here." Those days are clearly over. The Soviet Union rarely steals and, in fact, is trying hard to sell its own patents and designs abroad. The effort, however, remains ineffectual. In 1966 the United States, the United Kingdom and France applied for 163,000 and were granted 107,000 foreign patents on new products and processes. The Soviet Union, by comparison, applied for only 2268 and was granted a mere 1032.

Although some 94 per cent of all Soviet railway locomotives are now either electric or diesel-powered, the vast majority of them were built not in the U.S.S.R. but in more technologically advanced countries such as East Germany and Czechoslovakia.

The Soviet merchant and fishing fleet is one of the largest in the world, but nearly all its ships come from Polish, Finnish, French and East German shipyards.

True, its Tupolev-104 was the world's first commercial jet and the Tupolev-144 will not only be the first supersonic transport to go into service, but may corner the world market for such planes in view of the American decision not to build its SST.

However, since the first test flight in 1969 the TU-144 has been equipped with French and British navigational and generating instruments, because Soviet counterparts were too imprecise and unreliable, and in the spring of 1971 the Russians began shopping around Europe for seats and interiors for the TU-144 so that the craft will meet Western standards. And when it made its debut at the 1971 Paris air show all observers noted that each one of its twenty-six tires was either bald or threadbare.

The U.S.S.R. produced about 210,000 metal-cutting machine tools in 1970, and a British industrialist, visiting a Soviet trade show, acknowledged that "the Russians have, in effect, done for machine tools what the Italians did for washing machines. They turn out runs of thousands where we would have to be content with hundreds. But," he added, "as with most other Soviet goods, design and finish leave much to be desired. Safety glass is often badly scarred, rough edges are left and there is an appearance of yesterday's design. The Russians are good at turning out a big, powerful, efficient machine. But over a period of a week I saw no more than one, possibly two models that would cause any surprise in British industry. And this at a time when they were obviously showing off their best equipment to potential buyers."

The Soviet Union pioneered the use of oxygen conversion for Steel production. Yet pioneering is about all it did. In 1968 only 10 per cent of Soviet steel output came from oxygen converters, compared to 25 per cent in Western Europe.

By volume of output the Soviet Union is often a behemoth. Its chemical industry is now second only to that of the United States, though even as runner-up its volume output is only one fourth as great as the American. But the range of plastics produced is narrow and the synthetic fiber industry lacks diversification. Output is still mainly of cellulose rather than fully synthetic fibers and the quality of viscose rayon as well as capron (the Soviet equivalent of nylon) is well below Western standards. The chemical fertilizer industry is far behind schedule and Soviet medicine still depends largely on imported pharmaceuticals from Poland, Hungary and East Germany.

The greatest Soviet deficiency is in the field of computers, where the gap between the U.S.S.R. and the United States is so wide, according to Sakharov, "that it is impossible to measure. We simply live in another epoch."

The effect of this is often crippling. At Serpukhov, for example, the U.S.S.R. has the world's largest and most modern particle accelerator. But West European scientists doing research there must fly their daily readings to the C.E.R.N. nuclear research center in Geneva via a regular Swissair flight because the Soviet computers are incapable of digesting and analyzing the material.

Western experts can only estimate the scope of the computer gap. A 1970 RAND report said the U.S.S.R. had 6000 computers, other sources give a figure as low as 4000. By comparison, in 1970 the United States had approximately 70,000 computers in use, the six Common Market countries around 18,000. There is little prospect that the Soviet Union can close the gap in the next decade or two. In 1969 and 1970 the Soviet computer park grew by an estimated thousand units annually. At the XXIVth Party Congress Kosygin announced that computer production would increase 160 per cent by 1975. If the Soviet electronics industry achieves that goal, the park will be growing by 2600 units annually at the end of the current five-year plan. But the U.S. stock is already increasing at a rate of 13,000 units a year.

Numbers, moreover, tell only part of the story. Production of fourth-generation computers started in the United States and United Kingdom in 1970, whereas Soviet output concentrated on the Minsk-22, a second-generation variety. The U.S.S.R.'s third-generation computer, a prototype, is barely off the drawing boards and Western estimates place Soviet data processing technology seven to twelve years behind that of the West.

There is also a critical lack of software and peripherals. Systems control as such is still in its infancy. The causes are to be found in the typical miscalculation and inefficient planning that is endemic to Soviet industry. Western producers of computer hardware also provide the peripherals and software. But in the U.S.S.R., for example, the enterprise that produces the BESM-6, the Soviet Union's largest computer, does not deliver the additional equipment and programs.

The previous five-year plan called for the introduction of twenty central computer systems and automated systems control programs with which an entire plant—administration as well as production—can be computer-directed. By mid-1970, however, such complete systems had been installed in only three Moscow plants, one Leningrad factory, a television factory in Lvov and the Minsk tractor plant.

Ideology was at fault for the Soviet computer lag. Stalin considered cybernetics "a capitalist ploy for increasing the exploitation of the working class by creating artificial redundancy and loosening the revolutionary tie between the worker and the means of production . . ." As a young computer specialist said to me: "Back in 1948 we were told that cybernetics is a bourgeois pseudo-science."

By the time the Russians realized Stalin had been wrong, it was already late. And they were slow in catching up. First-generation computers appeared in the United States in 1953, the second generation in 1957, the third in 1964. The U.S.S.R.'s first-generation machines were not put into production until 1959, the third has just entered the experimental stage.

On the other hand, when they did recognize the importance of the computer, the Soviets first turned it into a panacea for all the ills that beset the economy in the post-Stalin era, then into the *deus ex machina* which was supposed to serve Communism as it could never serve capitalism. The cyberneticization of the Soviet economy became one of the ideological sacred cows of the Khrushchev era. Soviet ideologists produced quotations from Lenin's collected works to prove the need for computers and the scientific organization of society became the party's paramount task. High-ranking *apparatchiki* held wordy speeches and wrote lengthy dissertations to prove that they had always stood for this principle and promised the party's full support of cyberneticization.

It was a perfect demonstration of a Soviet "campaign" in which a basically sound idea is taken up by party leaders in a current five-year plan and becomes ideologized and mythologized into something far greater than its real potentials: such as Khrushchev's corn-on-the-cob effort.

The picture that resulted is the familiar one of overconfidence, concentration on the most obvious points—in this case production of computers but neglect of the details such as software, programmers, systems and preparatory work—with the effect that practical benefits are sporadic and isolated.

The situation of the Tomsk manometer plant typifies that throughout Soviet industry. In 1970 a computer center was completed and the plant received a Minsk-22 and a full array of peripheral devices, as well as a calculating station with dozens of keyboard machines and other equipment. One year later the computer and the center were still standing idle. No programs have been written and the center's staff consists of seventeen people, who, though young and enthusiastic, have no experience and no special training: they are mathematics graduates of universities and teachers' training colleges and the Minsk-22 at the Tomsk plant is the first computer they have ever seen.

Soviet authorities today would, if they could, computerize the whole country. But the obstacles are overwhelming.

"You cannot just dump a computer in the midst of an existing system," said a British specialist who spent a year in Moscow installing data processing equipment. "You must reinterpret the system in terms of the computer and that's difficult for anyone with ingrained habits and a job to protect."

To fill the gap the Soviets are shopping anxiously abroad. Britain's International Computers Ltd. (ICL) has already installed $10 million worth of equipment and has orders in hand for $24 million more. Thomas Watson, president of International Business Machines, was in Moscow in 1970, at Soviet invitation, to explore how "some type of relationship might be worked out." Thus far none has, because the problem is one of both money and the regulations established by a Paris-based organization called Cocom, made up of all the NATO countries plus Japan, which has the authority to bar trade in war-potential goods with the Communist countries. Sophisticated computer equipment falls into this category. The embargo was partially lifted in the summer of 1971 when ICL received permission from Cocom to sell two of its big 1906-A computers to the U.S.S.R. for use at Serpukhov. But even without the trade embargo, would the Russians be able to pay for what they need? Invariably the Soviets look for credit or barter deals, which do not appeal to all foreign suppliers. ICL was once offered birth control pills in exchange for computer hardware. Since the U.S.S.R.

does not produce oral contraceptives, it was assumed that the Soviets had obtained them in a different barter agreement. ICL did not want the pills but accepted a delivery of tractors instead.

Until the gap can be filled, the U.S.S.R. presumably will continue to rely on what foreigners jokingly call "wood electronics": the ubiquitous abacus which seems to be a permanent fixture of the Soviet scene.

If the lack of computers is the Soviet Union's greatest problem, the state of transportation runs a close second.

True, the rail network with some 80,000 miles of track and 94 per cent electrification and/or diesel power is good. But then, it always was—even under the tsars. In the forty-two years preceding the Revolution 927 miles of new track were laid annually, giving the Bolsheviks a solid network on which to expand. They have not quite matched the tsars' zeal, building only 630 miles annually, enough, however, to double the pre-revolutionary system.

Road transportation, however, is in a critical state.

By the end of 1970 the Soviet Union had only 930,000 miles of roads of which less than one third were surfaced. By comparison, the United States has more than 3.7 million miles, of which more than three fourths are surfaced.

In 1961 Soviet truck production was 381,617. By 1965 it was supposed to reach 600,000, a figure that now will not be met until 1972 or 1973—*if* plans are fulfilled.

Some 3 million trucks are registered. Most of them are of low and medium capacity, nearly all of them are outdated in design and performance. One model, still in production, has not been changed for twenty years. Moreover an estimated one third of these vehicles are in repair at any given time.

Roads that are not paved are impassable for more than half the year. Those that are paved are too narrow and cannot handle the traffic. Soviet experts have estimated that whereas the average speed for automobiles on Soviet highways is twenty miles per hour, for trucks it is only eighteen. At that speed, it has been suggested, it will take a truck fifty-two hours to deliver a load of tomatoes from the village of Lipkany in Moldavia to Moscow, a distance of 930 miles.

The losses to the economy that result from these conditions are almost incalculable. All over the U.S.S.R. thousands of factories, shops, construction sites, laboratories and institutes, each dependent on the other, wait for supplies that are stuck somewhere. *Sovietskaya Rossiya* once estimated that the annual monetary loss due merely to poor *urban* roads cost the economy 500 million rubles in delays, damage to vehicles and increased fuel consumption.

The prospects for alleviating this situation soon are inauspicious. The U.S.S.R. lacks the resources and the equipment with which to modernize its road network. Moreover climatic conditions in some parts of the country would dissipate the effects of any construction efforts in a year or two. Nevertheless, the current five-year plan calls for almost 70,000 miles of new surfaced roads by 1975. If this target is met, the Soviet network of surfaced roads will approximate that of the states of Illinois, Iowa, Michigan and Ohio—combined.

The U.S.S.R. was a pioneer in atomic power generation and the reactor at Obninsk was the first in the world to go into operation. At the 1964 Atoms for Peace conference in Geneva, the Russians talked bravely of their long-range ambitions for portable nuclear power plants which would trundle electricity into the backwoods, and fusion reactors which, once built, would cost almost nothing to run.

In the meantime, however, the U.S.S.R. has lost its lead. It is still talking bravely, but its share of the world's installed nuclear power capacity has declined steadily. Today it is not only less than that of the United States but has been surpassed by such countries as Britain, France and West Germany. Given targeted increases, Soviet capacity will soon be below that of Canada and Japan as well.

In 1968 the U.S.S.R. had thirteen atomic power stations in operation, compared to eighty-eight in the United States and seventy in Western Europe. Its share of the total world nuclear power capacity was around 11 per cent. Between 1971 and 1975 it will build only twelve more stations with a total capacity of around 7 million kilowatts, bringing its total share of world nuclear power capacity to around 4 per cent by the middle of the decade. In fact, a single power unit planned for the state of New York will reach about 50 per cent of the Soviet Union's targeted nuclear capacity for the year 1975.

And yet, as in so many other fields, Soviet nuclear *research* is excellent. The Russians are ahead of the United States in plasma physics. The accelerator at Serpukhov is not only the largest but most sophisticated in the world. The Soviets also lead in the study of transuranium elements. One physicist, Georgy N. Flyorov, has discovered an "island of stability" beyond uranium and believes that

Element 116 exists in nature. If it could be synthesized it would open new vistas in atomic power. Moreover the U.S.S.R. is still trying to domesticate energy produced by thermonuclear fusion. If research on this at the Kurchatov Institute in Moscow proves successful, it will have significant meaning for the production of cheap electric power. But *research* is all it is for the time being.

And that is the Soviet malady.

Despite the brilliance of some of its scientists and the sophistication of some of its most advanced laboratories, research remains uneven and a hierarchical, bureaucratic structure hampers its timely application in practice.

Professor Vadim Trapeznikov, director of the Institute of Automation and Telemechanics and a deputy chairman (minister) of the government's Committee for Science and Technology, has estimated that 98 per cent of Soviet researchers work in institutes and universities, while more than half of American scientists are employed directly in relevant industries.

One Soviet scientist has calculated that "five to six years elapse from the moment a new idea is off the drawing boards until it is embodied in a model for series production." At a meeting of Soviet scientists and industrialists in Akademgorodok, the director of an electrical equipment plant complained that the agreements of sixteen different bureaus and agencies had to be obtained to approve the technical specifications of a new hydroelectric generator. The time required to obtain these approvals, he explained, is longer than the preparation and manufacture of the generator itself. *Pravda* has disclosed that in the 1920s Soviet researchers developed a technique for food dehydration that was then the most advanced in the world. More than forty years later it was still not being used in the Soviet food processing industry although other countries had adopted it long ago.

A compendium of factors, rooted deeply in Russian tradition and the nature of the Communist system, interacts to keep the U.S.S.R. behind: secrecy, bureaucracy, inefficiency, poor labor discipline, lack of a traditional class of craftsmen and artisans, a propensity for bigness to a degree of unprofitable return, and built-in disincentives to modernize and improve.

Obviously, the Soviets have an advanced technology. Without it, they would not have scored their space success or been able to create a viable military machine, whose equipment, according to experts who have examined it, is excellent. But there is no spin-off from the space-military program to benefit the civilian economy. In fact, the entire military-industrial complex runs on a parallel track with its own factories, labor force, executives, bureaucratic hierarchy and sources of supply.

The purpose of secrecy is to conceal military developments from foreigners, but it is so unbelievably thorough that the average Soviet industrialist is as poorly informed as any foreign ambassador. Little is published in the technical press about space developments and even the identities of scientists working on projects are concealed. The Lenin Prizes to space scientists in 1970, for example, were awarded anonymously. And it was not until he died in June 1971 that the world first heard of Aleksei M. Isayev, the unknown and unheralded rocket designer who was the Wernher von Braun of the Soviet space program. His obituary was the first public acknowledgment of his enormous contribution.

Secrecy is maintained to such a degree that certain cities are not even identified. During national and regional elections, for example, when Soviet papers publish the names of candidates from all districts, the existence of these secret towns—most of which appear to be located in Central Asia and Siberia—is inadvertently admitted. But they are identified only by the numbers of their election districts, not by name, and their location is never specified.

Most of the advances that benefit the military and space establishment simply have to be rediscovered and redeveloped by the civilian economy. NASA, on the other hand, has established a service that provides computerized retrieval of more than 200,000 technical developments and inventions in the space field to any applicant for a small fee.

Another fundamental problem is censorship and the restriction on information and travel that surrounds the Soviet scientific community and prevents researchers from learning about developments in the West and sharing their experiences with Western colleagues.

Even a man of the stature of Gury Marchuk, deputy director of the Akademgorodok complex and head of its famous computer center, seems to experience difficulties in going abroad. Asked by German TV correspondent Ulrich Schiller in the summer of 1970 why he favored an improvement of relations between the U.S.S.R. and the Federal Republic of Germany, Marchuk replied: "The better our relations are the greater the scientific exchange will be. I would love to see your nuclear reactor in Karlsruhe."

Soviet statistics indicate that only one in ten of Soviet scientists (and even that may be an inflated figure) has ever traveled abroad, and then primarily to the other Communist countries. When they are permitted to go it is usually in the accompaniment of a KGB watchdog—either an official escort or a colleague who operates as an informer under secret police pressure.

As Zhores Medvedev put it: "Can we imagine a European scientist, fifty to sixty years old, who has never once traveled beyond the limits of his own country, nor even taken part in an international meeting abroad, nor ever once visited a foreign laboratory, even in neighboring countries? Of course we cannot imagine it; it would be impossible in England, France or Belgium. But in the U.S.S.R. this is still true of most scientists."

Medvedev's refusal to report for the KGB prevented him from making a number of trips abroad. The most notable case was his inability to go to Sheffield, England, to deliver the traditional annual lecture on the problem of aging at the 1966 meeting of the Ciba Foundation. To be invited to deliver that lecture is one of the highest honors in Medvedev's field of science. His abortive efforts to reach Sheffield sound almost as Kafkaesque as his odyssey through the Kaluga insane asylum in the spring of 1970.

On the morning when he should have been in England, the U.S.S.R.'s leading gerontologist was on a state farm, eighteen miles away from his Obninsk laboratory, picking potatoes. "In the autumn," Medvedev has explained, "all urban organizations must take part for a couple of months in the potato harvest. It just happened that on precisely that morning it was the turn of our section, radiobiology and genetics, to go potato picking."

When a scientist anywhere in the world is invited to deliver a paper at a congress abroad he will make every effort to send a copy of his manuscript in advance and as early as possible. For a Soviet scientist to comply with this standard of professional conduct he must run a bureaucratic obstacle course. As a private individual he is not permitted to send manuscripts abroad and the post office is not allowed to accept them from him. Only state or public organizations may send such scripts, provided each one is accompanied by Form No. 103-A in triplicate.

Form No. 103-A, Medvedev has explained, is considered "completed" if three experts have declared that the manuscript material is not of a secret nature, if the paper has been reviewed by the academic council and the director of the author's institute and by the foreign section of the ministry to which the institute is attached. Finally it must be approved by Glavlit. In the event that it is a translation into a foreign language, Glavlit reviews both the Russian original and the translation to assure that there are no deviations.

"Only after this," said Medvedev, "can the [manuscript] start out on its journey."

But not yet its author, who needs a passport, exit visa and an exit dossier called a *vyyesdny akt.* This is a catalogue of documents and questionnaires, accompanied by "two copies of a detailed autobiography, twelve photographs, two copies of the birth certificates of [the applicant's] children and a copy of one's marriage certificate, as well as a health certificate." The application must be approved by a whole series of departments, organizations and superiors, including borough, town and provincial Communist Party committees, the applicant's ministry, the KGB, the "Exit Commission" of the Central Committee of the Communist Party of the Soviet Union and, in some cases, the Central Committee's Section of Science and Higher Education.

Assuming the scientist has cleared through all these organs and echelons, his chances are good. But before he receives a passport and travel permit, he will undoubtedly be visited by KGB agents who will ask him to report to them.

The U.S.S.R. obviously needs foreign help to overcome its technological backwardness. But how can it obtain Western know-how without scientific contacts? Sovietologists believe that two schools of thought on this question emerged in the Kremlin in late 1970. One holds that the potential advantage of economic and scientific co-operation with the West outweighs the ideological disadvantages that derive from greater contacts. The other view appears to be that economic and technological backwardness is less harmful than exchanges of people, and with people, the introduction of subversive ideas. Which view will prevail remains to be seen.

Because Glavlit assumes that scientific journals from abroad may contain anti-Soviet ideas, they are subjected to excruciating censorship and held up, sometimes for months, before they go to translation bureaus of institutes and research laboratories. To save foreign currency and to meet censorship requirements many institute and city libraries are sent photocopy or photo-offset copies of foreign journals. Produced in Moscow by the All-Union Institute of Scientific and Technical Information, these reprints frequently have advertisements and controversial articles excised from them by Glavlit. According to Medvedev, about five hundred foreign scientific and technical journals are copied in this manner and distributed to institutes and laboratories.

Until a few years ago, when "objectionable" articles had been excised from them, these photocopies of foreign journals went to libraries with the pages missing. But in 1968, according to Medvedev, the producers of these reproductions began inserting articles and reviews from earlier issues so that the order of pages would not be disrupted and readers would not notice the omissions. *Nature,* the British scientific journal, is frequently subjected to this kind of Soviet censorship and the American journal *Science* has an article or two missing from almost every issue of its Moscow-produced version.

The delay caused by this adulteration of foreign journals is six to seven months, a tremendous time lag in this age of rapidly developing science and technology.

In 1969 two researchers on the "science of science," V. Nalimov and Z. Mulchenko, published a book entitled *Naukometriya (Sociometry)* which pointed out many of these obstacles of information, among them the fact that Soviet libraries order only about half the scientific books published in the world each year and subscribe to only about one third as many scientific and technical journals as Western libraries do.

The major problem, according to Nalimov and Mulchenko, is the absence of direct, regular exchanges with foreign scientists, most of whom meet with each other frequently and discuss, or exchange through correspondence, information on important advances and discoveries long before they are published in journals.

"We are already encountering difficulty comprehending some of the foreign publications we receive because we are not familiar with all the long discussions that preceded articles in them," Nalimov and Mulchenko wrote. "Such articles have to be deciphered and summarized in a form accessible to our readers and then published. All this may take several years."

The isolation of the Soviet scientist under such conditions has a crippling effect on technological and scientific progress. Moreover it results in considerable duplication of effort and no small amount of self-adulation when a Soviet researcher reports something that he or the regime believes is new.

In 1966 another Soviet author, G. M. Dobrov, in a book called *The Science of Science,* estimated that in the United States repetition and duplication of scientific work constituted 10 to 20 per cent while in the U.S.S.R., in a number of branches, it was as high as 85 per cent. Only one out of every four claims of inventions in the U.S.S.R. does not duplicate earlier solutions.

Restrictions similar to those imposed on scientists apply to Soviet industrialists and technical experts.

"There has been endless discussion as to whether our products are up to world standards," a foreign trade executive complained. "But to match them we must know what these standards are. Yet whenever the question is raised of sending specialists abroad to trade fairs and exhibitions, we are told that it is too expensive or unproductive. We will send fifteen or twenty experts to a show abroad to look at what other countries are producing. The other countries send hundreds and thousands of specialists . . ."

Concepts of management and consultation that Western industrialists take for granted are still in their infancy in the U.S.S.R. Kosygin's son-in-law, Dzherman Gvishiani, a deputy chairman of the State Committee for Science and Technology, once pointed out that the United States has more than six hundred university-level business schools and business administration colleges which carry on widespread research into production organization and management. In the Soviet Union the first management training school was not started until 1969.

No discussion of Soviet backwardness can overlook the rank inefficiency, the top-heavy bureaucracy and the built-in disincentives to modernize that plague the Soviet economy.

As an Akademgorodok chemist put it:

"In our country it is easier to discover a new element than to shut down a useless laboratory."

The same thing is true for industry. It is easier to add more workers and produce heavier equipment in order to fulfill the plan than to halt production, retool and increase efficiency. In fact, the manager who does retool and who does introduce new technology will be penalized in the form of reduced bonuses for failing to meet his quotas during the transition period.

The provisions of the economic reform itself are inimical to innovation. Because bonuses are geared to profits and return on capital, executives must pay more attention to production costs, including the costs of capital. Since success still depends on fulfillment of annual plans, managerial decision is biased toward short-run gains over possible long-run benefits. Managers are reluctant to add new capital or to undertake equipment changes: to do so would disrupt production and adversely affect the level of profitability.

The present wholesale price structure tends to reward continued production of outmoded products and penalize those who make innovations.

A factory producing radio and TV vacuum tubes provides a typical example. It developed a new and better tube whose life was increased from an average one thousand to three thousand hours playing time and managed to reduce the unit cost of the tube. The plant was compelled to reduce the price of the tube by 10 per cent because the unit cost had been lowered.

The Siberian Heavy Electrical Machine-Building Plant in Novosibirsk can tell a similar tale of woe. Its TVM-300 turbogenerator saves any user almost 200,000 rubles a year in comparison with the performance of other units with similar capacity, and its new frequency transformers save the national economy 4 million rubles annually. Yet developing this equipment has reduced the plant's profits, because of the complicated cost-plus price structure and bureaucratic regulations. It could earn more by turning out two hundred outmoded generators than two hundred new ones.

It remains to be seen whether the three-tier price system, if and when it is introduced, will alleviate and ameliorate the situation. Another factor retarding technological progress is that the Soviet labor force is recruited largely from a population that was almost exclusively peasant two generations ago. The economy is plagued by hamfistedness to a degree that defies description. As one Western economic expert told me, "Anything that cannot be assembled or repaired by banging on it with a hammer is just left outside to rust. It is incredible how things are just smashed here. I have seen crates containing sophisticated machinery and imported computers dropped off the back of stake trucks for no other reason than the fact there was no crane or forklift to move them with."

Occasionally Soviet officials even sound proud of this nonchalance toward refined technology.

Interviewed by *Ogonyok,* the Soviet illustrated weekly, in June

1970, N. N. Smelyakov, the deputy minister of foreign trade, boasted that an Oslo, Norway, cab driver who owned a Soviet-made Volga taxi called it "the world's fastest tractor." Discussing why, previously, Soviet aircraft had found no market in the West, Smelyakov said: "Our aircraft designers failed to take into account . . . such trifles as tail and fuselage signal lights, which, apparently, are required by international rules."

Such "trifles" may be one reason why in 1969, for example, finished goods represented only 2 per cent of the total Soviet exports to the United Kingdom.

Is there anything the Russians make that is up to world standards or competitive on world markets? Western experts usually find it a challenge to produce examples. Electrical turbines, rugged tractors, cheap cameras, cheap watches and . . . and . . . then the list usually ends.

Another difficulty facing the U.S.S.R. is what some Western economists describe as a "monomaniac" approach. "They always do everything on such an enormous scale that it takes too long to complete and the project is outdated before it is even in operation," a British technical adviser told me in Moscow. "Moreover, preoccupied with doing things big, the Soviets have completely forgotten that bigness too is governed by the laws of diminishing returns."

The Soviet answer to the technology gap seems to be a buying spree of foreign know-how. Since early 1970 West European corporation board rooms have been electrified by the prospects of ever bigger deals with the U.S.S.R. The pace is dizzying, the size of the projects staggering and the hoped-for profits lucrative enough to excite even the most blasé capitalist. But no matter how great the benefits to Western economies, the Russians are ill advised in treating the purchase of foreign know-how as the panacea for their difficulties.

More often than not, the foreign plant, equipment, designs or know-how that the U.S.S.R. purchases will be out of date by the time they are ready for use in the Soviet Union—a consequence of Soviet bureaucracy, inefficiency and long lead times.

"Sure, they can buy the technology," one Western businessman visiting Moscow told me. "But the basic organizational problems and the built-in disincentives remain. The real gap is in application of the technology and that will never be bridged unless the Soviet Union is prepared to change its entire social, economic and political system."

*If we could only provide agriculture
with 100,000 tractors—you realize
what a fantasy that is at this time—
then the peasants would say: "We are
for Communism."*

V. I. Lenin at the VIIIth
Congress of the CPSU,
March 23, 1919

14 *Tractors, Where Art Thou?*

A variegated representation of the Soviet Union's nationalities filled
the six thousand softly upholstered crimson seats of the Kremlin's
modern Palace of Congresses: Uzbeks, fierce-looking Kazakh herdsmen, mustachioed Georgians and Armenians, ruddy-faced Russians,
pug-nosed Ukrainians, kerchiefed babushkas and sturdy peasant
women whose matronly bosoms glittered brightly with rows of "hero"
and "motherhood" medals.

On stage was the usual "presidium": a familiar three-row cast of
characters that included the Politburo, the Central Committee secretariat, members of the government and a corps of honored and
meritorious citizens, peasants and workers. Among them were such
perennial stalwarts as Anastas Mikoyan, the novelist Mikhail Sholokhov and Fyodor Petrov, the Communist Party's nonagenarian
veteran. Behind them rose the traditional backdrop: a huge plastic
and metal screen bearing a portrait of Lenin on a red background.

But the gathering on this November day in 1969 was an unusual one. The All-Union Congress of Collective Farmers was the first such conclave to be held in thirty-four years and the third in the entire history of the U.S.S.R. The main issue on its agenda was the discussion and ratification of a new "model charter" for the Soviet Union's 34,200 collective farms to replace the one adopted in 1935 when the last All-Union kolkhoz congress had been held.

The charter, a nineteen-page document with sixty-one subsections, is a model contract and set of bylaws which determines how a collective farm is to be organized and operated and stipulates the relationship between the kolkhoz and its individual peasant members. Its various paragraphs and subparagraphs spell out the rules for the selection of officers and management; prescribe the amount of private livestock and the size of personal plots allowed each member; set out wage rates and regulate auditing procedures. They specify the amount of maternity leave to which women *kolkhozniki* are entitled, which medals and rewards may be given members for what type of accomplishments and what kind of penalties may be meted out for which violations of work discipline or damage to common farm property.

More than merely a model labor contract or constitution for the organization of collective farms, the charter is a document that will influence and affect the lives of at least one fourth of the U.S.S.R.'s population—those who work, live and are raised on the kolkhozes— for decades to come.

A high-powered commission of 149 members, chaired by Leonid Brezhnev himself, had worked three years to produce it. And when the draft was made public in April 1969, propagandists hailed it as "new proof of the party's concern . . . for the working people on the farms."

But as a purported milestone in the history of Soviet agriculture, originally intended to produce fundamental reforms, it was a disappointing compromise that fell far short of initial expectations.

When the previous kolkhoz charter was adopted by the Second All-Union Congress of Collective Farmers in 1935, the Stalinist wave of "de-kulakization" and forced collectivization had just swept the Soviet countryside. The land lay fallow; countless cattle, pigs, sheep and goats had been deliberately slaughtered by rebellious and intractable farmers. Millions of peasants had died of starvation and millions more had been deported to Siberia and imprisoned in labor camps. In the charter itself the emphasis was upon the duties and obligations, not upon the rights and privileges, of the *kolkhozniki*.

Slightly amended in 1938, this charter was considered out of date by the mid-1950s. Khrushchev conceded that it was obsolete, although he attempted no revision.

One of the first acts of his successors, however, was the March 1965 Central Committee plenum at which agricultural reform was promulgated. Brezhnev implied that a new draft would be prepared and submitted to a Third All-Union Congress of *Kolkhozniki* by 1966.

Euphoria pervaded the countryside and a broad and relatively frank discussion of possible changes was aired by the Soviet press: until early 1966 when the names of the charter commission were made public. More than one third were high-ranking *apparatchiki,* including Brezhnev, Mikhail Suslov, Alexander Shelepin and that conservative's conservative, Sergei Trapeznikov, chief of the Central Committee's Department of Science and Education. Another third were kolkhoz chairmen of whom few, if any, were known for their controversial or independent viewpoints. The commission included few of the better-known agricultural reformers.

Three years passed before the draft was completed and instead of 1966, as originally promised, the congress did not convene until 1969 to approve the new charter. It was a document of contestable value.

True, the Stalinist crudities of the 1935 charter had been replaced by less objectionable phraseology. Pilferage, for example, was no longer defined as "betrayal of the kolkhoz cause" and "assistance rendered to the enemies of the people."

It provided an improved social security scheme and certain minimum pay guarantees, although these were not on the level of *sovkhoz* (state farm) scales. It reiterated the right to maintain small private plots and personal livestock and officially approved, for the first time, ancillary kolkhoz industries such as canning, brick and cinder-block making, carpentry and handicrafts production. It also provided for the establishment of kolkhoz soviets, which were acclaimed as "another step toward democratization" of society in the U.S.S.R. In practice these councils soon saw their principal function as the approbation and enforcement of party and government decisions. They have become just one more extension of the transmission belt for political and economic policies set from above.

However, of the many proposals aired after the 1965 Central Committee plenum, six of those most vital to any basic reform of Soviet agriculture and peasant life were significantly not incorporated into the new charter.

The kolkhoz is not yet protected by a "bill of rights" in its dealings with higher organs. There is no provision for secret balloting during the election of the kolkhoz chairman and assembly. Members of the collective have no meaningful defense against arbitrary decisions of their chairman and are not entitled to take labor and wage disputes to court. The right of a *kolkhoznik* to leave the farm after giving reasonable notice remains disputed and theoretically collective farmers are tied—serflike—to the land for their entire lives. They are not even entitled to internal passports, which would give them the same legal rights of movement as other Soviet citizens, including the salaried employees of sovkhozes. The passport entitles Soviet urban residents and sovkhoz employees to freedom of movement and the right to settle in other towns or to visit and vacation in places away from their legal residence. Anyone going to another city or town with the intention of remaining there longer than three days must present his passport to the police in the new locale within twenty-four hours after arrival and apply for a temporary or permanent residence permit. Onerous as this may seem to Americans who are not accustomed to carrying official identity papers, the internal passport in the U.S.S.R. is a prerequisite for full citizenship. The *kolkhoznik* is denied it. To leave the kolkhoz a collective farmer must obtain certificates of permission from the farm chairman's office and the local soviet. These are not always given. And while they would be honored by police elsewhere when applying for a temporary residence permit, for example to visit relatives in Moscow, these certificates would never be valid when applying for a permanent permit in another community.

If these omissions seemed significant to some progressive elements in the U.S.S.R., they apparently meant little to Brezhnev and the party leadership. Addressing the opening session of the farm congress with a ninety-minute televised speech, Brezhnev described the new charter as "an important landmark in the development of our entire socialist democracy, new proof of its profound popular nature, its irrefutable advantages . . . The new model rules are expected to play an enormous role in the future growth of agriculture and in the development of the collective farm system."

Such exuberant pronouncements notwithstanding, the general secretary knows that Soviet agriculture is far from proving either its profound popular nature or its irrefutable advantages. Nine months after the congress, at a Central Committee meeting, he admitted as much.

"It is clear," he said, "that new enormous tasks in the field of agriculture remain to be solved . . . If we look at the accomplishments we must also look at the remaining problems. The need for produce grows all the time and cannot be put off until we have finished rebuilding the material-technical base of our agriculture. If we do this, we will lose time, new shortages will develop and new difficulties will arise."

Shortages, difficulties and crises seem to be endemic to Soviet farming. Although the world's first workers' and peasants' state has developed an appreciable albeit inefficient and technologically retarded industrial potential, its agriculture remains incredibly backward and ineffectual. It lags not only behind the major Western and some Asian powers, but behind most of the Communist countries as well.

Among the eight countries of Comecon, the Communist equivalent of the Common Market, the Soviet Union is unquestionably the major agricultural producer—thanks to sheer size and mass of output. But its per-acre yields of key crops, its degree of mechanization and its state of agricultural chemicalization are below those of all the other nations with the exception of Mongolia. In 1969, according to the Comecon Statistical Yearbook, only barren Mongolia, with 3 quintals per hectare, had a lower yield of grains and pulses than the Soviet one of 13 quintals. By comparison in Romania the yield was 19, in Poland 21, in Bulgaria 27, in Hungary and East Germany 29 and in Czechoslovakia 30 quintals per hectare. Only Mongolia and Poland had fewer tractors in use per thousand acres of arable land and only Mongolia—whose nomads use none at all—applied less fertilizer per acre than the U.S.S.R.

Fifty-four years after the Revolution, more than forty after the start of the bitter and costly battle to collectivize the countryside, Soviet agriculture remains largely dependent on vast hordes of manpower. Despite tangible improvements during the past decade, it is the hortatory stick of discipline, rather than the incentive carrot of rationalization and mechanization, on which the regime relies for progress in farming.

When the first Russian census was taken in 1897, some 106 million people lived in villages and only 19 million in towns. Today the urban population has grown to 136 million but the rural population, after some fluctuations due to war, deportation and famine, is still virtually as large as it was more than seventy years ago: 105.7 million. The disparities between city and village life are almost as great as they were six decades ago.

Until the early 1960s it was still essential for some member of a kolkhoz family to "marry money," that is, someone working for money wages, because collective farmers were paid mostly in kind. Old-age pensions for *kolkhozniki* were only introduced in 1965.

Since then conditions have improved palpably. Pensions in 1966 averaged 16 rubles per month and in July 1971 were increased again to a minimum of 20 rubles monthly, though they are still far below the average 60 rubles paid to retired urban blue- and white-collar workers or the minimum of 45 rubles guaranteed to salaried sovkhoz workers. Average pay for collective farmers rose by 43 per cent during the last five-year plan to 3.60 rubles for a day's kolkhoz work and the current *pyatiletka* calls for another increase of 30 to 35 per cent by 1975. But the enormous discrepancies between the incomes of farm chairmen, whose estimated average monthly base salary is 300 rubles, and the unskilled horse and hand workers, who are the backbone of Soviet agriculture, will remain.

The agricultural economy comprises 34,200 kolkhozes, which have an average area of 15,000 acres, 1156 cattle and 420 families in which an average of 1.6 adults are working members of the collective. There are also 14,300 sovkhozes with an average of 70,000 acres, 2000 cattle and 600 salaried farm workers.

About 30 million adults are engaged in agriculture—a third of the labor force. They produce to the point of scant sufficiency for a growing population. In the United States about 3.4 million adults are engaged as farmers, farm managers, foremen and agricultural laborers —approximately 4.5 per cent of the gainfully employed labor force. They produce to the point of gluttonous superfluity for a population that is burgeoning. Stated in slightly different terms, one American farm worker provides high-quality products for sixty people in addition to exporting 20 per cent of what he produces. One Soviet farm worker provides low-quality products for approximately eight people and manages to export around 2 per cent of his production.

Despite forty years of intensive efforts to collectivize and nationalize agriculture, private farming—restricted to dwarf-sized personal plots of slightly more than one acre, the possession of one cow and calf, one pig with sucklings, and ten sheep or goats—is still what keeps the Soviet Union fed. Private plots account for only 3 per cent of the cultivated land, personally owned livestock for less than one fourth of the animal population. Yet they provide Soviet consumers with 63 per cent of their potatoes, 41 per cent of available vegetables, almost 40 per cent of the meat and milk products, 63 per cent of their eggs and 30 per cent of their wool.

The urban housewife who queues two hours daily, never forgets her *avoska* and spends half the family income to put inferior and vitamin-deficient meals on the table can have but one terse assessment for the state of Soviet agriculture. It is insufficient.

The numerous and complicated reasons for this are strikingly similar to those which have impeded the development of Soviet industry: inefficiency, lack of and poorly applied incentives, maladroit planning, overcentralization and excessive bureaucratization, poor organization, inadequate mechanization and technology, vast distances, poor transport, political, social and economic discrimination against the bulk of the agricultural work force and extremes of climate. Frequently they concatenate to produce calamity. In 1969 weather interacted with equipment shortages and lack of transport resulting in a 3 per cent decrease in agricultural output instead of the 6 per cent growth the plan had called for.

The spontaneous response of Russians, when supply breaks down, is to blame it on the *kolkhozniki*. Western observers instinctively single out forced collectivization as the cause of all the Soviet Union's agricultural difficulties. Both are oversimplifications.

For one thing, the U.S.S.R. *does* face problems of climate and geography unmatched by any other country. To take but one example: the Soviet Union's most southern cotton-growing regions are on a plane with the northernmost cotton lands of the United States.

The vast distances between the nation's most fertile and its most populous regions would impede deliveries of produce even under optimal conditions. Equipment shortages and poor roads exacerbate the problem. Nearly every kolkhoz chairman will say, as did one to me in Kazakhstan: "We produce plenty but cannot get it all to market because the transport system is too thin, the bureaucracy too thick."

While on a group trip to Moldavia, the U.S.S.R.'s fruit and vegetable basket, I was taken to a model collective farm near Kishinev. On acres upon acres of apple orchards it grew the reddest, juiciest Jonathan apples I have ever seen.

"Lovely," I told the mustachioed, bemedaled sexagenarian agronomist of the kolkhoz. "But why don't we ever see apples like that in Moscow?"

"Moscow," he said with a shrug of the shoulders, "is very far away."

In 1969 Sergei F. Antonov, the minister of the meat and dairy industry, deplored that the capacity for livestock and milk processing had grown more slowly than the supply of produce because the specialized construction ministries are behind schedule in their building plans.

Collective farms perennially complain of shortages of materials and machinery for their ancillary industries.

"We are putting the first line of our vegetable processing plant into operation," said an official from a kolkhoz near Ternopol two years ago. "But we may have to quench the flames under our boilers in a couple of months . . . because we have no glass jars or lids. Our people must travel to distant towns to find tin plate from which we punch out covers. And then there's the problem of labels. Where, in what printing shop, can a collective farm order attractive labels?"

Undoubtedly, one of the greatest obstacles to efficiency and increased productivity in Soviet agriculture is the low degree of mechanization and the bureaucratic obstacles raised against proper distribution and application of machinery when it becomes available.

In 1970 more than half the milking operations, 91 per cent of livestock feeding, 74 per cent of stall and pigsty cleaning and 30 per cent of cattle watering in the U.S.S.R. were still performed by hand.

Fyodor Kulakov, a member of the Politburo and head of the Central Committee's department of agriculture, once pointed out that spring plowing should take twenty days but because of the scarcity of machinery and general inefficiency, twice the time is usually required. Fall plowing usually requires fifty to sixty days.

The motor vehicle industry's failure to expand and produce according to plan has had a deleterious effect on agriculture, where, according to one Soviet estimate, 40 per cent of the human and motor power are preoccupied with transport of one type or another during peak periods of the year.

American agriculture has an estimated 3.3 million trucks in use and various Soviet estimates have suggested an "optimal" agricultural truck park for the U.S.S.R. containing 2 to 2.7 million vehicles. By the beginning of 1970, that Soviet pool consisted of only 1,153,000 trucks. At the rate with which the industry is expanding, allowing for retirement of existing trucks through wear and tear or obsolescence, the optimal figure will not be reached until 1985 or 1990. Meanwhile tens of thousands of trucks will continue to be commandeered from industry to help out on the farms during the harvest season. In 1970 this was an estimated 120,000 vehicles in the Russian Federation alone.

In the fertile grain region of the Don basin, for example, 29,500 additional trucks were brought in for the 1970 harvest: not merely from surrounding cities and industrial centers but from as far away as Moscow and Kostroma—distances of more than a thousand miles.

This annual *shturmovshchina* of trucks might not even be necessary if Soviet authorities abandoned the Stalin-era policy of requiring kolkhozes to transport their grain to central state procurement points as soon as it is harvested. Initially dictated by Stalin's suspicion that the recalcitrant *kolkhozniki* would steal the grain if they were allowed to dry and store it on the farms, this policy led to a nationwide dearth of on-site drying and storage facilities.

Those farms which now have such installations apparently still use them inefficiently. Mechanized threshing floors, for example, have been installed in twenty-one strategically placed areas in the Vozvyshensky district of the North Kazakhstan province. Grain-receiving points and branch offices have been established in five state farms. But, as a district official complained, they are not being fully utilized.

"At the height of the harvest season," he said, "some state farm threshing floors receive more than 1000 tons of grain daily. Trucks waiting their turn create traffic jams at the threshing points. Half an hour is spent unloading each vehicle and drawing up the necessary documents—a task that should require only ten to fifteen minutes. In the fields the combines grind to a halt while workers wait for the trucks to return. When the overflow pits are full, the grain must be removed manually [from the trucks] to the threshing floors, where townspeople, students and housewives are put on round-the-clock duty.

"Meanwhile scales, power dumpers and high-output cleaning installations at the grain-receiving points, which may be located across the road from the threshing floor or at the other end of the settlement, stand practically idle during the day. Many people, specially enlisted to help with the harvest, mill about with nothing to do. But after dark, lines of lorries begin to back up at the receiving points."

The tractor shortage is even more critical. The United States had an optimal park of 4,820,000 medium- and large-sized tractors at the end of 1967, plus 5.1 million small garden tractors which would be ideal for private plot farming in the U.S.S.R. The optimal Soviet park, depending on which Soviet expert's figures one employs, should have been 3.2 to 4.2 million tractors. At the beginning of 1971 this tractor park consisted of some two million units. Delivery plans for the 1966–70 period were underfulfilled by almost 20 per cent and planned deliveries for the current five-year plan are lower than the quotas set for the previous *pyatiletka*.

At present, the Soviet ratio is 150 acres per 15-horsepower unit of tractor and it will probably take two decades before the optimal relationship of 62 acres is reached. The current rate of tractor deliveries virtually offsets normal wear and tear.

The problem entails more than sheer numbers. Tractors lack auxiliary implements. For every ruble of tractor, according to Soviet experts, there should be 2.50 rubles' worth of agricultural implements. Actually there is only one third that amount.

Tractor design must be standardized and quality improved. One sovkhoz chief engineer complained that his farm utilized sixteen different types of tractors. In one province thirty different types with a total of 50,000 uninterchangeable parts were in operation.

Approximately 50 per cent of all tractors and other agricultural machines are idle because of the scarcity of replacement parts. It was a figure I had heard but refused to believe until the engineer of a sovkhoz near Alma-Ata once told me: "We have seventy-five tractors. Between thirty-five and forty of them are in the shop for repair at any given time. We just can't obtain the parts." The dismantling of newly delivered machines to obtain spares for others is an everyday occurrence.

Efforts to produce newer, more efficient equipment are frequently entangled in bureaucratic red tape. At the Minsk tractor plant in Byelorussia, one of the largest in the country, designers developed a new model whose productivity, depending on the job being performed, is 12 to 58 per cent higher than that of the currently produced MTZ-50 tractor. Tests disclosed that it would yield an annual saving of more than a thousand rubles per machine when used in the non-black earth regions. Its projected over-all savings to agriculture would amount to approximately 55 million rubles annually. The state testing committee recommended that it go into serial production no later than 1972, but the Ministry of Tractor and Farm Machinery, for reasons that left even a *Pravda* correspondent baffled, has postponed the start of production until 1974. By then the new model will already be obsolete.

When equipment is produced it is frequently of inferior quality or unsuited for the conditions in the area to which it is delivered.

The chairman of the New Life kolkhoz in Tula province has a complaint about the SK-4 combine. He loses two to four quintals of grain per hectare because the machine, built for dry climates, cannot handle the wheat in his region when it is moist. Because of morning dew and evening mist on the fields, operators of the SK-4 on this farm are limited to the hours between 10 or 11 A.M. and 5 to 6 P.M. Because of the peculiarities of the equipment, a great deal of grain remains in unthreshed ears and among the chaff.

"Moreover," he said, "the combines arrive from the factory without having been tightened and with parts attached indiscriminately. We have to take them from the railroad siding to the repair shop to finish what the factory failed to do. [In 1970] we received two combines and had to spend five days on each one in order to tighten the fastenings . . . If new machinery is not sent immediately to the shop on receipt, it will stop working in the field."

Less diligent farm chairmen do end up with their equipment stalled in the fields. And as a Western agricultural expert once told me: "There's hardly a district where you don't see an expensive machine or two sitting out in the open, rusting away."

Breakdowns may not be the only reason for this. Frequently the sporadic supply system, which directs machinery to where it is not needed, leaving other districts short, is at fault. In 1968, for example, authorities in Krasnodar province ordered 374 new rice harvesters but received only 200. Instead 850 grain harvesters were delivered, although only 300 had been ordered.

Besides machinery, chemical fertilizer is in short supply and of poor quality.

Originally the last five-year plan called for the annual production of 62 million tons of mineral fertilizer by 1970. This was revised downward to 58 million, but only 55.3 million were actually produced, of which 46 million were delivered to Soviet farms.

Because fertilizer output is measured quantitatively, quality suffers. According to no less authoritative a source than Brezhnev, only 6 per cent of the total produced is in the form of concentrated compound fertilizer. The nutrient content is appreciably below that produced in the West. Even if qualitative goals for 1975 are reached, the nutrient content of Soviet fertilizer will still be 10 per cent less than that of the U.S. varieties.

Thus far fertilizer is used mostly for commercial crops. Only 25 per cent of the Soviet grain area is treated, although even Soviet agronomists admitted that the record 1970 grain harvest took as much nutrient out of the soil as would be contained in 110 million tons of standard fertilizer—more than twice what the Soviet chemical industry produced.

The problem is not only one of insufficient production but of improper transport and application. According to reports in the Soviet press, mountains of fertilizer are left at railroad sidings or at farms, packaging is poor and fertilizer is often transported in open railway cars so that great hardened blocks of it must be drilled or blasted out of the rolling stock.

In 1969 the U.S.S.R. used merely 17 kilograms of fertilizer, expressed in nutrient content, per hectare, compared to 238 kilograms in East Germany, 159 in Czechoslovakia, 115 in Bulgaria, 110 in Poland, 101 in Hungary and 37 in Romania.

Lack of supply may be only one reason for this. Farmers are probably apathetic toward its use because of a lack of direct incentive. Theoretically farms should order certain quantities of specific types for delivery at given times to correspond to soil charts and crop rotation schedules. In practice, they must take what they are sent and whenever it suits the supply organs.

Besides fresh vegetables and fruit, meat is in chronically short supply. A series of complex factors, beginning with a traditional European concentration on dual-purpose cattle, appears to be the cause.

The U.S.S.R. has failed to diversify into beef production by using distinct types of cattle, although it has large areas of steppe land where a beef cattle-grazing industry would be more suitable than growing wheat—particularly in Kazakhstan, the lower Volga regions and West Siberia.

To increase range pasturing in the eastern regions, more herdsmen or fences would be needed. The former appear to be unavailable and the construction of fences would draw on otherwise scarce material resources. Extensive road building would also be required to get animals to slaughter and to various seasonal pastures.

Moreover distinct types of meat cattle would have to be bred. In 1970 a team of Soviet agricultural experts toured the United States, reportedly with $15 million to spend on 30,000 head of beef cattle with which the U.S.S.R. hopes to crossbreed and improve the meat quality of its livestock. Western experts have suggested that it would be infinitely cheaper and more practical to fly frozen semen for artificial insemination to the U.S.S.R.

To raise the quality of both beef and milk products from extant stocks, the U.S.S.R. would have to adopt a radically different approach to grain. In 1969, according to Western analyses, 67 per cent of all grains in the U.S.S.R. were food grains, compared to 21 per cent in the United States. Conversely, feed grains comprised only 33 per cent of the Soviet harvest, 79 per cent of the American output. This is the main reason why the U.S.S.R. ordered $136 million worth of feed grain from the United States in 1971. Even more critical deficiencies have been noted in the high-protein feed sector which balances out the ration of carbohydrates so as to promote fast and economical growth in productive animals.

As one Western agricultural expert put it: "It is hard to make an encouraging projection as to when the Soviet meat crisis will be resolved."

Despite the obvious excess of manpower in agriculture, Soviet authorities complain of a dearth of personnel and the exodus of youth from the villages has been viewed as a national calamity. No doubt it is, considering the low level of mechanization on Soviet farms and the continuing requirement—at least during the next two decades—for vast armies of "horse and hand workers."

The flight from the land involves primarily the skilled and the very young, leaving a rural population that is overaged, unskilled and untrained for dealing with new equipment or implementing new agricultural practices. From 1965 to 1968, for example, the tractor park grew by 18 per cent but the number of trained "mechanizers" by only 8 per cent.

In 1964 and again in 1970 *Izvestia* conducted a survey among high school seniors in the Smolensk region. Of the group of 401 interviewed in 1964, only 27 wanted to stay and work on a collective or state farm and 56 intended to enroll in an agricultural school or technicum. The others hoped to work in industry or offices, go to technical colleges and universities or enter the professions. In 1970, in the same school, 458 graduates were interviewed. Of these

47 expressed a desire to work on farms, 61 to obtain a specialized agricultural education.

The retention rate for the agricultural sector, *Izvestia* pointed out with satisfaction, had improved from 20 per cent in 1964 to 22 per cent in 1970. The paper attributed this to improved living, working and income conditions in the Soviet countryside.

Conditions have improved. From 1960 to 1968 the pay of *kolkhozniki,* in both cash and kind, has increased by 150 per cent (compared to a 71 per cent increase for state farm workers and 33 per cent for industrial workers). As one of the interviewed youths put it: "Formerly one never saw television sets and refrigerators. People lived in shacks, not houses. Now almost every family has a TV set and other appliances. The people have begun to dress attractively and fashionably. Our parents' earnings have risen. They now have free days and vacations."

But the improvements are relative. Of the interviewed pupils who wanted to go to the cities, 6 per cent gave low earnings, 30 per cent unsatisfactory conditions in farm work, 39 per cent listed poor housing and inadequate services, 30 per cent mentioned bad roads and lack of transportation, 14 per cent the lack of cafes and shopping difficulties, 24 per cent the absence or inferior condition of clubs, libraries and art circles, 18 per cent the infrequency of films and touring performances, 37 per cent the lack of sports facilities and 40 per cent boredom as the causes for their wanting to leave.

To understand how these young people feel one must know the Soviet villages. They are inaccessible to most foreigners because of travel restrictions and because officials invariably steer visitors to model state and collective farms. Even these are aeons removed from village life in the industrialized countries of Western Europe. After excursions to the Soviet provinces I was always surprised by the cosmopolitan and metropolitan impression that Moscow made on me immediately upon my return.

Entering Moscow by road after driving along bumpy, potholed roads crowded with lopsided trucks and buses and lined by rows of villages that had no running water leaves an indelible impression. The roads and streets suddenly widen and become smoother. Even on the outskirts, tall apartment houses, broad avenues, the heavy flow of traffic, shiny cars and brightly lit stores convey a sense of "civilization," of a glossy, elegant, lively, vibrant metropolis. Such trips vicariously gave me the peasant's point of view. I began to understand why hundreds of thousands of them stream into Moscow each day to shop in GUM or TsUM, not just for consumer durables and clothes but even for some of the same food products that they produce but cannot obtain in the countryside. I started to see why the platforms of the Byelorussian, Kiev, Kazan and Yaroslavl railway stations in Moscow are inevitably crowded with masses of peasants lugging huge baskets of eggs, canned goods and sweets or whatever else happens to be in short supply in their villages.

Western experts estimate that even today approximately half of the U.S.S.R.'s farm communities, particularly those far from railways or main highways, are without electricity, except perhaps for small gasoline-operated generators. Running water, gas, plumbing or a paved street are the exception rather than the rule. The only brick or concrete buildings are the farm's administration center and Communist Party headquarters. The "dwarf" or one-room school prevails.

Of the 6395 rural settlements in Smolensk province in 1970, 376 had five or fewer inhabitants, another 376 had six to ten inhabitants, 1070 had a population between eleven and twenty-five, and the remainder above twenty-six. As *Izvestia*'s survey team said: "Can one build a club, store, school and service facilities in each? Of course not. This is why the inhabitants of these hamlets, including the young, must trudge through mud and snow for kilometers to reach a store, a movie or a schoolhouse."

Even larger communities or administrative centers are islands of desolation in a sea of incredible backwardness. Andrei Amalrik, in his poignant report of exile to a collective farm in Siberia, described Krivoshcheino, the county seat, as a primitive frontier town with two main dirt roads, board sidewalks, deserts of dust in the summer, lakes of mud in the spring.

In the village of Gurzhevka where he lived and worked, *kolkhozniki* kept newborn calves, pigs and poultry in their houses. Two dynamos in the farm's administrative center provided the kolkhoz's entire supply of electricity. Usually they worked only early in the mornings, at noon and late at night for milking. The abandoned house into which Andrei moved was "one of four or five in the village which had an outhouse. The majority of inhabitants simply squatted wherever and whenever nature demanded it." Medical assistance consisted of a "feldsher," that is, a corpsman, who lived in the neighboring hamlet and visited Gurzhevka once a week in the summer, once monthly in the winter.

Gurzhevka also boasted a club—an empty room measuring 40 square yards with four wooden benches—where old movies were shown once weekly in the winter. A dance usually followed the movie. There being neither a record player nor any records, Gurzhevka's accordion player did the honors and he seemed to know only three numbers: a waltz, a Charleston and a folk dance.

Under such conditions it is little wonder that productivity is low and no one seems to care. Andrei once said:

> The *kolkhoznik* is a hybrid. He is no longer a farmer but he is not yet a worker and he doesn't give a damn about anything. The only objective seems to be to fulfill a plan. If the plan calls for digging holes and putting in fence posts, although the posts have not been impregnated and are sure to decay in the soil within a year or two, the holes are dug and the posts put in. And if there is no wire for the fence, what difference does it make?
>
> A year or so before I arrived, they had started a garage for the tractors and got as far as the framework. Nothing else was ever done and bit by bit the frame collapsed as *kolkhozniki* hacked it away to burn in their stoves during winter. Once there was a board loose in the barn. Everybody stumbled over it or broke through with his horse, but no one ever troubled to repair it. Why should they? After all, the barn doesn't belong to anyone and who'd get paid for nailing down the board?

Obviously Soviet authorities are making efforts to ameliorate such conditions but these endeavors are fraught with new problems and raise new obstacles to increasing agricultural productivity and to keeping a skilled labor force on the farms. Typical of this is the drive to build multi-family brick or pre-fab concrete houses, to pave the roads and to urbanize the villages. *Kolkhozniki* who move into such buildings are unavoidably deprived of their kitchen gardens and have no place to keep their personal livestock. Yet, as one Soviet economist said: "If only one fifth of the rural population were to abandon keeping private livestock, the country would suffer the loss of 6 to 8 per cent of its annual output of milk and meat and 12 to 14 per cent of its egg production."

One possible solution to the farm drain as well as to the indifference and low productivity of *kolkhozniki* would be widespread adoption of the so-called *zveno* (link system), which is based on a "masters of the land" concept. This scheme, which is backed by a vociferous and active lobby but has won only grudging lip service from the party hierarchy, calls for a radically different approach to collective farming in the U.S.S.R. At present kolkhoz's "hand and horse workers," who represent approximately two thirds of the membership, are divided into brigades which are assigned to one plot of ground one day, another the next, doing one job today, performing a different function tomorrow. They are, in practice, nothing but field laborers who have lost all sense of attachment to the soil. Under the *zveno* system small groups of *kolkhozniki*—the proponents say the smaller the group the better—would have mechanical equipment at their disposal and be assigned specific areas of kolkhoz land to till and cultivate over a period of many years. Their incomes would depend largely on the yield of that particular parcel and on their productivity. They would be economically accountable for losses and crop failures but would also derive the benefits from heightened productivity.

In theory the system provides direct incentives and should reimbue in farmers a feeling of kinship with and greater responsibility for the land and for the equipment used.

Zveno's advocates, the most prominent of whom is Politburo member Gennady Voronov, until July 1971 the premier of the Russian Federation, were heartened by the April 1969 draft of the new kolkhoz charter, which seemed to provide considerable support for the idea. But by the time the kolkhoz congress convened, seven months later, official enthusiasm had waned. The final version of the charter contained a highly diluted article that barely gave lip service to the *zvenos*.

The advantages of the system are obvious. But its critics are more influential and powerful than its supporters. "Where is the additional equipment to come from?" they ask. "How are land and the available machinery to be apportioned between the subunits? What will happen to the millions of elderly, unskilled women kolkhoz workers who would be left out of the links and become unemployed?" These arguments, while persuasive, merely hide far more fundamental objections. The critics of *zveno* reason, probably correctly, that the independent team, with its own mechanical equipment, operating almost autonomously, would undermine party control over agriculture, obviate the staffs of the parent farms and, in time, might even supplant the sacrosanct kolkhoz.

The *zveno* scheme is to agriculture what meaningful economic reform is to industry. Consequently doctrinaire ideologues, vested party interests and hard-liners oppose it. The present standing of the *zveno*'s most intrepid champion, Voronov, is dangerously weak. He was not awarded the customary accolade of Hero of Socialist Labor on his sixtieth birthday and when Brezhnev announced the new Politburo at the XXIVth Party Congress, Voronov was tenth on the list—just a rung above Alexander Shelepin. Four months later he was eased out of the premiership of the RSFSR and given the unimportant chairmanship of the People's Control Committee. Most Kremlinologists believe that his days in the top leadership are numbered. The minister of agriculture, Vladimir Matsekivich, an agricultural traditionalist with strong Stalinist proclivities, is clearly against widespread introduction of the *zveno* system. So, from all indications, is Brezhnev. In his speech on agriculture to the July 1970 plenum of the Central Committee he ignored *zveno* completely.

Agriculture, more or less, has been the cross that every Soviet leader since Lenin has had to bear. Brezhnev has virtually staked his reputation on success in the agricultural sector. And to everyone's astonishment, he has scored relatively well.

During the last five-year plan, it is true, many goals were not reached. Instead of the targeted 25 per cent, agricultural production increased by only 21 per cent; production of tractors, combines, trucks, agricultural machinery and fertilizer all fell short of planned goals. Instead of an average of 169,400,000 tons, only 167,200,000 tons of grain were harvested annually, although in the final reports the original plan figures were reduced to make it appear as if the plan had been overfulfilled.

But the present leadership can also take credit for some remarkable achievements. The 1970 grain harvest of 186 million tons set an all-time record; the increase in agricultural production, though less than planned, is one of the highest for any five-year period since the Revolution; acreage yields rose from around 10 to 13 quintals of grain per hectare; and Soviet farmers earn more money and live better today than at any time since collectivization.

Luck has been Brezhnev's companion, however. Russians say that the weather usually causes two very poor harvest years in every five-year plan period. The 1966–70 *pyatiletka* had only one such year.

Nonetheless, even Western experts now believe that, on the whole, agricultural production in the U.S.S.R. has been stabilized. Because of the growth and improvements since 1965 it seems unlikely that the tremendous fluctuations in harvests and production that characterized the 1950s and 1960s will be repeated. But despite stability, the U.S.S.R. remains decades away from a breakthrough to abundance. For the remainder of this century investments in agriculture seem destined to exceed by far increases in production. The current five-year plan admits this. It calls for a 60 per cent increase in investments over 1966–70: a total of 129 billion rubles which represents nearly 26 per cent of the entire state investment budget. Yet agricultural production is expected to increase by only 20 to 22 per cent. The ratio is not likely to improve perceptibly before 1990.

By then, perhaps, the "scientifically determined norm" of 1969, calling for per capita consumption of 120 kilograms of bread and grain products, 97 kilograms of potatoes, 146 kilos of vegetables and melons, 82 kilograms of meat and meat products, 43 kilograms of milk and milk products and 292 eggs per year, will have been reached. To achieve this norm present productive capital assets in agriculture will have to be doubled, possibly trebled. And even then the average Soviet citizen's diet will not be as nutritious as was that of the average American in 1967.

"The Soviet economy," says Carl Zoerb, an American agronomist with extensive theoretical and practical exposure to Soviet agriculture, "is geared to cereal grains and carbohydrate crops. It is the world's leading producer of wheat, potatoes and sugar beets. In an advanced industrial order, however, these crops are becoming marginally important. From the viewpoint of modern nutritional standards centering on livestock products, fruits and vegetables, the Soviet preoccupation with relatively obsolescent crops precludes any breakthrough in improving either animal or human nutrition above present levels."

Part Seven

The present Grand Prince has managed so that in all of Russia there is one faith, one weight, one measure. He alone rules. Everything he orders is done and everything he prohibits is not done. No one, neither cleric nor layman, stands against him. How long such a government can continue only the Almighty God knows.

Heinrich von Staden, 1579

*This is what I want to do but I
cannot yet say when I shall do it.
I must have the agreement of the
others. I am not all-powerful. Such
matters have to be discussed.*

Nikita Khrushchev to
Hans Kroll, West German
ambassador, in Moscow—1960

15 *Battles Under the Blanket*

It was the week of the "Moscow epidemics." Colds, influenza and other vaguely defined illnesses kept four of the Soviet Union's most prominent leaders—Aleksei Kosygin, Nikolai Podgorny, Mikhail Suslov and Alexander Shelepin—out of public view. Four other senior government and party officials had been suddenly and inexplicably dismissed. Contagious gossip spread virus-like through the capital's foreign community and kept diplomats and correspondents traveling the cocktail party circuit.

The tension had been mounting for days and an intimation of portentous changes in the Kremlin hierarchy had charged the atmosphere with the electricity of something momentous about to occur.

It being a Thursday, the only night of the week when it is open to resident foreign correspondents, I decided to go to the House of Journalists, Moscow's press club.

The restaurant and bar were more crowded than usual—my colleagues were obviously searching for the same thing: information with which to shore up their tenuous theses that the Kremlin was being buffeted by a serious leadership crisis. As I searched for an empty seat or a worthwhile conversation to butt into, a senior official of the Foreign Ministry's press department, sitting alone at a table, caught my attention and invited me to join him.

"Well, what have you been writing these days?" he asked.

"Nothing but rumors and speculation," I replied half jokingly. "I am reshuffling the membership of the Politburo."

"Ah," he said, suddenly very serious and giving me a penetrating glance, "that is a very dangerous thing to do. You must understand that there are only eleven people in this city, in the country, in the whole world, in fact, who know what is happening or is about to happen in the Politburo: the eleven members."

What could sum up more succinctly the nearly impossible task of reporting on what takes place behind the Kremlin's crenelated walls? It is like watching a wrestling match under a blanket. The observer sees the movement and hears the occasional grunts and groans, but can have no idea of who is doing what to whom.

The problem is epitomized by a conversation I had with an American diplomat shortly after arriving in Moscow.

"Have you heard the latest?" he asked me one day in the street near the embassy, whispering conspiratorially so as to create the impression that his information was hot off an unimpeachable source's lips. "Number Two is supposed to be resigning." "How interesting," I stammered in my wide-eyed naïveté. "Thanks for the tip." Then he said with a faint smile: "You're welcome. But now tell me something. Who's Number Two?"

In a regime where rank and station must be tenuously deduced from the order in which the oligarchs' portraits hang on a building façade or the sequence in which their names appear on a communiqué, his question was more justified than jocular.

Predicting Kremlin politics is next to impossible for outsiders and perilous even for those on the inside. On the day he was toppled from power, not even Nikita Khrushchev knew that his political demise was imminent. On the morning of October 13, 1964, in his dacha near Sochi, he chatted amicably with France's minister of science and space, Gaston Palewski, discussed his plans for visiting West Germany and was waiting to congratulate the U.S.S.R.'s three newest cosmonauts, whose landing was expected momentarily.

Suddenly he left on a plane for Moscow and by evening he was virtually an "unperson."

Unlike most other leaders in Russia's long history of secretive, autocratic and Byzantine politics, loquacious Nikita Sergeyevich Khrushchev used to provide an occasional insight into the mysteries of the Kremlin. But with his fall that murky political labyrinth again became a "riddle wrapped in a mystery inside an enigma."

Soviet politics have again become so arcane that frequently the only hint of a Central Committee meeting is an increase in the number of cars parked outside the Central Committee building on Staraya Ploshad. Even that may mean nothing, for some experts contend that the plenary hall in the old gray stone structure is no longer large enough to accommodate the present committee of 241 full and 155 alternate members and that it convenes in the Kremlin instead.

Russia's leaders speak with what amounts to virtually one voice to the outside world. Yet logic suggests that they must have differences of opinion and are constantly maneuvering for position and power. An exiguity of information allows foreign observers to *postulate* that hawks and doves, conservatives and liberals, progressives and reactionaries exist in the Politburo; spurious leaks merely permit them to *hypothesize* who the protagonists may be.

The art of making assumptions, drawing conclusions, establishing postulates and proposing hypotheses about disagreements and power struggles in the Soviet hierarchy is called "Kremlinology." As a "science" it is about as precise as alchemy. As a tool for predicting the future it is as trustworthy as star-gazing or reading tea leaves. At best it can interpret and analyze the past, at worst it can make educated guesses about who is up and who is down, who is in and who is out of the Kremlin sweepstakes. Yet, inadequate as the Kremlinological art may be, unreliable as it has proved in the past, it is the only means at the disposal of foreign observers and allows the following suppositions to be made.

1. There was a leadership crisis in the spring of 1970 that was papered over, albeit not resolved, by mid-July of that year. The enlargement of the Politburo from eleven to fifteen full members at the XXIVth Congress of the CPSU in April 1971 suggests that this crisis could flare up anew in the not too distant future with potentially convulsive results, for Soviet experience teaches that this ruling body of the party has always been augmented in advance of a

sweeping purge of its membership. The same technique was used by Stalin in 1952 and by Khrushchev in 1957, and it has been adopted by other Communist countries. The coming year could be a climacteric and the demotion of Gennady Voronov from the premiership of the Russian Federation in July 1971 may have been the first hint of it.

2. In the wake of the purge that may sweep the Politburo, four of its present members could be dismissed. The two most plausible candidates are Shelepin and Voronov. Both are in disgrace and on the political skids. Two others—Suslov and Arvid Pelshe, aged sixty-nine and seventy-two respectively—might be honorably retired for reasons of health and age. The political future of Pyotr Shelest, the sixty-three-year-old first secretary of the Ukrainian CP, must also be considered, if only because he exposed himself as an antagonist and opponent of Brezhnev at the XXIVth Party Congress. Finally, there is Kosygin, by far the most intelligent, astute and able of the fifteen, whose imminent resignation was a persistent Moscow rumor long before I arrived there and is still just as assiduously rumored today.

3. By the very nature of his position, the party's first secretary is *primus inter pares*. But since ascending to the post in October 1964 Brezhnev has systematically widened his power base, reinforced his authority, arrogated political privileges and aggrandized the cult of his own personality to become the undisputed ruler of the U.S.S.R. Even if this was not entirely the case before the XXIVth Congress when Brezhnev had to depend on narrow, fluctuating majorities and may, at times, have been overruled within the Politburo, that body's enlargement augurs the strengthening of his position. Of the four additional members, two are unquestionably his protégés and the other two are probably loyal to him. It can be assumed that in a future purge he would seek to oust his opponents and change the power balance in his favor.

4. Brezhnev has ascended largely at the expense of three other men: Kosygin, Podgorny and Shelepin. He has encroached systematically on Kosygin's preserve as head of the government and usurped many of his functions. Since the XXIVth Party Congress, when he was demoted from second to third place in the hierarchy, Kosygin's position seems to have eroded steadily. Brezhnev and/or Podgorny have performed numerous duties which in previous years would have been Kosygin's responsibility. Podgorny, who was Brezh-

nev's chief rival during Khrushchev's last year, has been largely deprived of any effective power base and plays a primarily honorific role, despite the fact that he moved from third to second place in the ranks at the XXIVth Party Congress. Shelepin, the primary challenger and, despite its new additions, still the Politburo's youngest member, has been neutralized and his political annihilation seems preordained.

5. Brezhnev is probably seeking not only to usurp more of Kosygin's functions but also his office and title to become head of both the government and party as Lenin, Stalin and Khrushchev were before him. The question remains whether and how he will achieve that goal.

6. Regardless of changes that may take place at the apex and barring unforeseeable circumstances and events, the essential characteristics of the U.S.S.R.'s ruling elite—colorlessness, blandness and senescence—will remain unchanged at least to the middle of the present decade. The next party congress, which might be expected to provide for a larger proportion of younger men in the party's leading bodies—the Central Committee, the Central Auditing Commission and the Politburo—is not scheduled until 1976. Thus the Soviet leadership will continue to comprise primarily that age group which is least representative of the party membership at large.

More than half of the Communist Party's 14.4 million members are under forty years of age. Yet this generation constitutes the disenfranchised and unrepresented majority of the party, whose leaders—even on the provincial level—are mostly men in their fifties and sixties.

Even after the infusion of new blood in April 1971, the average age of the Politburo is sixty-one and its fledgling, Shelepin, has turned fifty-three. The Soviet leadership, with the exception of Bulgaria's, is the oldest, most conservative, orthodox and catatonic in Eastern Europe, although hoariness is hardly a Soviet tradition. The members of the Politburo with whom Lenin staged the October Revolution averaged thirty-five and Lenin himself was a mere forty-seven years old. The Politburo with which Stalin began his era was, on the average, a little over forty and Stalin himself was merely fifty.

Sexagenarians and quinquagenarians account for less than one third of the party, yet they comprise more than two thirds of the Central Committee membership—the body from which the next group of Soviet leaders will emerge. A similar bias toward venerability exists at the republican and provincial level. The average age of the 148 provincial party chiefs reconfirmed in their positions in the spring of 1971 was fifty-two. Only fifty were younger than forty-nine and of these only one was under forty.

Of the nearly five thousand delegates to the XXIVth Party Congress, less than one third were forty or younger. The overwhelming majority were between forty-one and sixty.

The CPSU is a three-generation party with a two-generation leadership. It can be compared to an ecclesiastical hierarchy whose inability to find a workable solution to the "succession problem" has led to an increasingly inflexible system of advancement based on seniority rather than aptitude or ability. The leadership is comprised of two archetypes: the pre-1933 party joiner, now in his sixties, and the World War II initiate, now in his mid-fifties. Both represent "party generations" whose careers were determined largely in the Stalin era. Conservative men, they are ill-prepared for coping with the psychological and ideological problems of modernization that the U.S.S.R. will face in the coming years.

As one Soviet acquaintance phrased it: "Until those who were the accomplices or beneficiaries of Stalin's rule pass from the scene, there will be no real change in our country." Real change is thus a long way off, for it is precisely from the narrow base of "accomplices and beneficiaries" that the current leadership is drawn and the leaders for the rest of this decade will emerge.

The discrepancy between the generations has become so large and the imbalance in representation has been allowed to grow to such a degree that a normal, evolutionary turnover of membership of the Central Committee would have to assume drastic house-cleaning proportions to make the Central Committee a representative mirror of the generational distribution of party membership.

Of course, no such house cleaning took place at the XXIVth Party Congress. On the contrary, of the old Central Committee's 195 full members, only 37 were not re-elected and the younger generation of functionaries appears to be the one that was penalized the most. Of the 37 at least 8 were linked to Shelepin's circle of "Young Turks" whose drive for power ran out of steam in 1967. Among them were such men as Nikolai Yegorichev, fifty-one, the former first secretary of the Moscow party organization, now ambassador to Denmark; Vladimir Semichastny, forty-seven, former chief of the KGB; Sergei Pavlov, forty-two, former first secretary of the Komsomol; Nikolai Mesyatsev, fifty-one, former head of the State Committee for Sound and TV Broadcasting, now Soviet ambassador to Australia. Others were Khrushchevites. Of the 88 new members, 42 had been alternates to the previous Central Committee.

True, there has been a change, but not of generations. The government apparat increased its representation both numerically and relatively. The KGB succeeded in quadrupling its representation in the leading CPSU organs. But the essential character of those bodies remains unaltered. Of the 241 full members of the Central Committee 105 are professional *apparatchiki,* 75 are government ministers and officials, 20 are marshals and generals, 13 are ambassadors.

Thus it will be at least 1976 before any significant change becomes feasible, though it is not likely to occur even then. The type of housecleaning that would make it possible is practically precluded by the existing mechanism for selecting Central Committee members.

No one can predict when the generational imbalance may become the epicenter of conflict in the party. But the potential grows with each year that the old guard clings to power.

Of the twenty-five men who rule the U.S.S.R. today—the twenty-two members and candidates of the Politburo and the three secretaries of the Central Committee who are not represented on the bureau—only one, Konstantin Katushev, is under fifty. Now forty-five, he is the only man who cannot trace his career in either government or party work back to the days of Stalin's rule.

Although he was not co-opted into the Politburo at the XXIVth Congress, as many observers had predicted, he is one of a half-dozen top officials who deserve closer scrutiny as potential party or government chiefs of the future.

Except for the people in crucial Gorky *oblast* east of Moscow, only a handful of Russians in the upper echelons of the Soviet power structure even knew his name before April 10, 1968. His face was indistinguishable from the hundreds one saw buried behind newspapers and hidden by curtains in the back seats of shiny black Chaika limousines. A high forehead, a bit on the fleshy side, cold eyes framed by gold-rimmed spectacles, a neatly cut suit with a carefully Windsor-knotted tie—he could have been any of a thousand *apparatchiki*—anonymous in a collective crowd, as quickly forgettable as the car in which he rides. But on that spring day when his picture appeared next to a twenty-five-line biographical notice at the bottom left-hand corner of *Pravda,* Katushev, an engineer by education, became one of the twenty-five most powerful men in the U.S.S.R. and the fifth new face to join the Soviet leadership since Khrushchev's fall.

His appointment as Central Committee secretary in charge of relations with ruling Communist parties—a position that made him the *de facto* foreign minister in dealings with the world's other Communist powers—baffled the experts at first. True enough, the job had been vacant since May 1967 when Yuri Andropov was transferred from it to head the KGB. But Katushev, one of the youngest men to penetrate the inner sanctum of power since Aleksei Kosygin himself became a candidate member of the Politburo in 1946 at the age of forty-two, hardly seemed the man to fill the slot.

From the time he was twenty-four years old, Katushev had worked as an engineer and designer in Gorky's automobile industry and he met the description of the perfect technocrat. He joined the party in 1952 and five years later switched from designing to become first secretary of the party committee in the Gorky plant. By 1963 he was first secretary of the Gorky city party committee and two years later, in 1965, thanks to the personal support and intervention of Brezhnev, who traveled to Gorky to promote him at a plenary meeting of the provincial committee, Katushev became political boss of Gorky *oblast;* baron of the fifth largest province in the U.S.S.R. One year later, at the XXIIIrd Party Congress, he was elected to the Central Committee.

In his current role as a Central Committee secretary, Katushev was instrumental in crushing Alexander Dubcek and the Czechoslovak experiment in "Communism with a human face." For all practical purposes he was the man who "normalized" the situation in Prague.

"A tough negotiator with a steel-trap mind," as one East European diplomat described him, Katushev, by Soviet standards, has had a sensational career and it is far from its zenith. Linked inextricably with Brezhnev, his future looks promising as long as the general secretary remains in power.

Another Brezhnevite is Andrei P. Kirilenko, the general secretary's elder by three months. His status has been generally scandent since 1967 and for most of the time since then he has ranked fifth in the Politburo's order of precedence right behind Brezhnev, Kosygin, Podgorny and Suslov.

Chunky, gray-haired, bespectacled, with an *apparatchik* record that dates back to 1939, Kirilenko is so little known outside higher party circles that many Russians cannot identify his portrait when it hangs out on festive occasions. Among the top leadership he appears to be the epitome of blandness.

Born into a family of craftsmen in the town of Alekseeva in Voronezh *oblast,* three hundred miles south of Moscow, Kirilenko has been a member of the CPSU since 1931. He graduated from the Rybinsk Aviation Institute and worked as an aviation engineer until he went into full-time party work in 1939. Since then he has climbed the ladder of the apparatus, succeeding Brezhnev, with whom he had served in the Eighteenth Army on the southern front, as first secretary of the Dnepropetrovsk *oblast* committee in 1950. He was in that post until 1955, then was named first secretary of Sverdlovsk *oblast.* In 1959, at the XXth Congress, he was elected to the Central Committee. One year later, in the wake of Khrushchev's victory over the anti-party group, Kirilenko entered the Politburo as a candidate member. In 1962 he was promoted to full membership.

As a Central Committee secretary in charge of general questions, party affairs and party activity in Russia, he is *de facto* first secretary of the party in the Soviet Union's largest republic which has no separate party organization.

Listed sixth in order of precedence at the XXIIIrd Party Congress in 1966 and fifth at the April 1971 Congress, portrait order has occasionally even placed him fourth in the hierarchy over Suslov.

Not even his occasional speeches reveal much about him though. One that he gave in July 1968 to a group of Italian Communists in Bologna was remarkable for its appeal to variegated views and the specific audience. It disclosed nothing about his character or personal opinions. Kirilenko, in fact, is so gray, his behavioral patterns and views are so obscured from public scrutiny, that Kremlinologists have identified him as a conservative one day, a liberal the next, a hawk one week, a dove in another.

One thing does seem certain. He has become Brezhnev's closest confidant and most trusted lieutenant. Age alone precludes his succeeding Brezhnev except in the case of unforeseeable circumstances such as death. In that case I would consider him a good caretaker candidate for succession. He cannot, however, be ruled out to fill either Kosygin's or Podgorny's posts at some future date.

No discussion of potential successors to Kosygin seems possible without examining the career of Kirill Mazurov, one of the premier's two "first deputies."

Mazurov has the distinction of being the first and only Byelorussian to sit on the Politburo as a full member. In the intricate balance of national representation on that powerful body, the distinction is an important one. Some experts believe that his birthplace categorically excludes him from rising higher, although he is the second-ranking man in the Soviet government today.

Mazurov seems to have been a major beneficiary of Khrushchev's fall and Kosygin's rise. Stocky and ruggedly handsome, with black hair and chiseled features, he has been a candidate member of the Politburo since 1957, was raised to full membership in March 1965 and named a first deputy chairman of the council of ministers to Kosygin, a job that places him in charge of the industrial ministries and of implementation of the economic reform. Since the spring of 1970 Mazurov has also been exposed increasingly to foreign affairs and has frequently been Kosygin's surrogate.

Born in 1914 in White Russia, of peasant stock, he started in the party through the Komsomol and became first secretary of the Byelorussian Central Committee in 1956, a post he held until 1965, when he was promoted to his present position.

During World War II Mazurov distinguished himself as a guerrilla fighter and partisan organizer behind the German lines. He was one of the leaders of the Byelorussian resistance movement, an organization that was far too independent for Stalin, who attempted to purge it after the war.

Thus far Mazurov has been either too prudent or has had too little opportunity to carve out a special identity. He has traveled little, but diplomats who have met and conversed with him at receptions describe him as alert, confident, energetic and "as open-minded on economic questions as can be expected from a member of this collegium."

One Western embassy's economic counselor once told me: "Mazurov struck me as a man who is both interested and interesting. He is definitely an expert in his field and as an economist I found a common language with him, which is more than one can say for some Soviet economic experts. He seems to know exactly what he wants and is working toward it. I consider him a politician who must be watched, although his national and geographic background poses a considerable hurdle for a leap to the top."

No such handicap impedes Viktor Grishin, the Moscow party chief who joined the Politburo as a full member in April 1971. The hypothetical qualifications for Brezhnev's successor require him to be a Great Russian, to have spent most of his career as a party—not a government—*apparatchik* and to be healthy enough at the time of his nomination to serve at least five years. Grishin certainly fits that description. Moreover among the ascending quinquagenarians in the Politburo he is the man with the most diversified party experience.

Born in 1914 in Serpukhov, sixty miles southwest of Moscow, Grishin graduated from the Locomotive Trade School in 1937 and went to work as a marine and railway machinist, returning for a while to his home town as assistant chief of the local engine depot. He joined the party in 1938, held various small party jobs until 1950, when he moved to Moscow to become chief of the machine-building department of the Moscow city party committee. Two years later he was elected a secretary of the Moscow city committee and to the Central Committee. In 1956 he was named chairman of the All-Union Council of Trade Unions, a post he held until Shelepin, already on the skids, replaced him in June 1967. Grishin moved up to become first secretary of the Moscow city party committee, replacing Shelepin's protégé Nikolai Yegorichev.

Incontrovertibly the Moscow post is one of the most important in the country. With 824,000 CPSU members in its ranks, Moscow is larger than the republican organizations of Kazakhstan, Kirghizia, Tadzhikistan and Turkmenistan *combined*. Khrushchev launched his career from the same position, which he filled from 1935 to 1938. It provides for a degree of public exposure that only the first secretary and premier enjoy, and next to them Grishin may well be the best-known *apparatchik* in the U.S.S.R. He is the official greeter at virtually every function and his face is frequently flashed to TV screens around the country.

Other than a tightening up on the arts and intellectuals, Grishin has not exposed himself politically, and he is just as much an enigma as the rest of the collective leadership. Dark-haired, sallow-complexioned, he seems to be a man of great drive and energy. As long ago as 1968 a Soviet source described him to me as a man "with a bright future." His 1971 promotion from candidate to full Politburo membership seems to justify that prognosis.

Whereas Grishin's promotion seemed almost a foregone conclusion, the sudden rise of Fyodor Davydovich Kulakov took every expert by surprise. Unlike the other three Politburo members elected for the first time at the XXIVth Party Congress, Kulakov skipped a rung, moving directly into that inner circle of power without serving a candidature in the anteroom.

Kulakov, fifty-three, seems to be a paradigm of the gray party functionary and his background is probably too specialized to include him as a serious contender in the game of Russian power roulette. Yet, precisely because the game is predicated on so many imponderables, his bid cannot be ignored.

A graduate of a correspondence course at the All-Union Agricultural Institute, Kulakov has been an agronomist most of his adult life. From 1938 to 1941 he was a section manager of a sugar refinery and from 1941 to 1955 served in various full-time party positions until he was named deputy minister of agriculture of the Russian Federation, a post he held until 1959. Then he was appointed Russian minister of grain production. In 1960 he became first secretary of Stavropol *krai,* one of the U.S.S.R.'s chief agricultural regions. He remained there, according to official biographies, until 1962. There is a gap in his career from 1962 to 1965, when he was named Central Committee secretary in charge of agriculture, a function he continues to fulfill now in addition to being a member of the Politburo.

Alexander Shelepin has for years been the *Wunderkind* of Kremlin politics. No one has risen faster and fallen more quickly than this former Komsomol and KGB chief who, despite his apodictic state of disgrace, still keeps the wheels of Moscow's gossip machinery oiled. Perhaps that is because Shelepin, next to Brezhnev, seems like the man with the greatest will to power.

Yet, for all the excitement and speculation he has aroused, Shelepin continues to be a mystery man about whom most people know nothing, a few just a little.

Shelepin's star faded soon after Khrushchev's fall, probably because he was too much in a hurry. But no one knows whether he was an upstart of the liberal or conservative stripe, a Russian Dubcek in waiting or a tough-minded new Stalin.

Born the son of a railway man in Voronezh in 1918, Shelepin is a typical member of the war generation of Communists. He joined the party in 1940, specialized in working with the Komsomol and became head of the youth organization in 1952 while Stalin was still alive. Later he directed the "volunteer" program that sent hundreds of thousands of *Komsomoly* to the virgin lands and proved so efficient that Khrushchev chose him in 1958 to head the KGB. He was forty years old at the time.

In 1961 he was rewarded with a Central Committee secretaryship and the following year was named a deputy chairman of the Council of Ministers under Khrushchev. As a new broom at the top, Shelepin apparently swept too clean. One day he called in Khrushchev's son-in-law, Aleksei Adzhubei, then the editor-in-chief of *Izvestia,* and remonstrated him for heavy drinking and womanizing. Whether this was what cooled the ardor between Shelepin and Khrushchev remains open to speculation, but by October 1964 Shelepin had clearly sided with Khrushchev's opponents. He supported the coup and lined up the KGB with the new leadership. In November he entered the Politburo as a full member and ranked fifth in the power ratings behind the troika and Suslov. In addition, he retained his deputy premiership and Central Committee secretaryship as head of the Party-Government Control Committee, giving him the widest power base in the hierarchy.

Shelepin was patently too ambitious and posed too much of a challenge to Brezhnev. Gradually his feathers were plucked until by 1967, though still a full member of the Politburo, his only other position was the chairmanship of the Trade Union Council. Protégés and mentors provide the props of power in the Soviet Union. Shelepin's were the Young Turks of the so-called Komsomol group. They have all been demoted: Semichastny; Yegorichev; Dmitry Goryunov, the former director-general of Tass; Sergei Romanovsky, former chairman of the Committee for Cultural Relations; and Sergei Pavlov, the former head of the Komsomol.

Most of these "Shelepinites" were transferred to sinecures outside of Moscow between the summer of 1967 and mid-1969. In April 1970 the purge of Shelepin's group entered a second round. His erstwhile mentor and predecessor in the leadership of the Komsomol, Nikolai Mikhailov, was dismissed as chairman of the State Press Committee and retired. Mesyatsev, the broadcasting tsar, was sent to Australia as ambassador.

Concomitantly Shelepin's position as trade union chief was emasculated. Traditionally, since 1937, the trade union leader had served as chairman of the quadrennial central election commission, which supervises the election to the Supreme Soviet. In 1970, for the first time, that tradition was ignored and a shock worker was named to play the role.

At the XXIVth Party Congress, true enough, Shelepin was re-elected to the Politburo. But when Brezhnev read out the names of the members, he mentioned Shelepin in eleventh place—last on the list of incumbents. It was an unmistakable sign that Shelepin was down for the count. Yet until he is actually demoted out of the inner circle he cannot be counted out. He has bounced back before and as one of the U.S.S.R.'s wiliest and most resilient politicians, he could bounce back again.

Dark-haired but balding, blue-eyed, well groomed and well educated (he has a degree in history), Shelepin is one of the collective's brightest members and has established a reputation as an intelligent, competent, tough administrator with a sharp political nose.

That, however, is the extent of Western knowledge about him or his leanings. His role during the Czechoslovak crisis remains obscure, although in September 1968 Shelepin dared to do what no other Soviet leader had done. In Pyongyang, North Korea, he unequivocally told an audience that the U.S.S.R. had been compelled to invade because Soviet national interests were at stake.

As Komsomol chief he cracked down on the dissidents and revisionists in that organization. And a Soviet acquaintance once told me: "The greatest and only blow the present leadership has struck for democracy was the demotion of Shelepin." Yet, despite his reputation as a neo-Stalinist, Shelepin did more than any other Soviet official to weed Stalinists out of the secret police. On the other hand, he sounds tough and is known to have once advocated prison sentences for bureaucrats "who fail to carry out major decisions of the party and government."

As my Soviet source phrased it: "Shelepin is neither a hawk nor a dove, neither a hard- nor a soft-liner. He is a 'Shelepinist.'"

Although he has never been a contender for power, no decision about power is likely to be made without the voice of Mikhail Suslov, the aging ideologist and éminence grise of the Soviet leadership. Suslov is reported to have abandoned his usual modesty on only one occasion when he said: "I have merely to cough in the Kremlin to start the whole Western world guessing about my state of health."

Judging from the political and physical resilience that Suslov has shown in the past, it seems to be better than its reputation.

Whenever an important decision is made in the Kremlin, the emaciated and disheveled-looking Suslov is sure to be in on it. His role is a prominent one and on occasion even decisive. In Moscow it was frequently said that if something were to happen to Brezhnev or Kosygin, or both, they could easily be replaced by others with similar capabilities. But the disappearance of Suslov would present greater problems.

He is not remarkable for any outstanding theoretical faculty or for a profound knowledge of Marxism: such attributes are not in high demand these days. But he has an uncanny ability to interpret pragmatically the party line, whatever it happens to be, and to provide an ideological justification for putting it into practice.

At sixty-nine he is merely four years older than Brezhnev. But he joined the party ten years earlier—in 1921 at age nineteen—during the period when Lenin and Trotsky, having triumphed in the Civil War, established Soviet power. Stalin was not yet the party's secretary-general. In fact, as Khrushchev was to remark thirty-five years later: "At that time Stalin's name was known to perhaps 1 per cent of the party members."

Suslov, one can assume, was among that 1 per cent, for he was one of those Communists who not only found in Stalin their idol but saw in him the only possible successor to Lenin. He sided with the dictator in his struggle for power against the left and right opposition movements.

Suslov had a brilliant Communist academic career. In 1928 he graduated from Moscow's Plekhanov Institute of Economics, then went on to do post-graduate work at the Institute of Economics of the Communist Academy, also known as the "Institute of Red Professors." Later he taught there.

In 1931 he became an inspector of the Party Control Commission, which performed secret police functions within the party, and he played a major role in the purges of the 1930s in various provinces. By 1941 he was a member of the Central Committee and in 1946 Stalin appointed him chairman of the Bureau for Lithuanian Affairs with plenipotentiary powers to purge the Baltic republics. The next year he was named a secretary of the Central Committee, in charge of agitation and propaganda, and allowing for certain divisions of labor, he has been doing that ever since.

From 1946 to 1948 he shared the ideological responsibilities with Andrei Zhdanov. The 1946–48 campaign against "cosmopolitans and toadies," although referred to as the *Zhdanovshchina,* was the "achievement" of both men. After Zhdanov's death in 1948 the entire ideological apparatus was concentrated in Suslov's hands and the campaign widened in scope to include not only literature and art but the natural and social sciences as well. In 1949 and 1950 he also took over the editorship of *Pravda,* and in 1950 he joined the Politburo.

An important milestone in Suslov's career was the XIXth Party Congress in 1952—the last during Stalin's lifetime—at which he delivered a panegyric, eulogizing Stalin's theoretical work as "an inexhaustible fund of creative Marxist-Leninist thought." He said that "it would be difficult to name a branch of science, culture or art, a sector on the ideological front, where one does not feel the inspiring and guiding role of our great leader and teacher and the beneficial influence of his genius."

After Stalin's death the enlarged Politburo which he had created in 1952 was purged of its younger members: Kosygin, Brezhnev, Suslov and Semyon Ignatiev. Suslov, however, stayed on as a Central Committee secretary. Two years later he was back as a Politburo member, soon performing what must have been for him and his new mentor, Khrushchev, a strange task: unmasking Stalin. Khrushchev assigned Suslov the responsibility of justifying the measure ideologically. He has not looked back since then.

The part Suslov played in de-Stalinization largely escaped notice because Khrushchev managed to keep him in the shadows. But some Kremlinologists contend that it was Suslov who, more or less, wrote the theoretical parts of Khrushchev's historic "secret speech."

At the time, Suslov's approach was the "two Stalins" theory, which held that the dictator had been an orthodox and faithful pupil of Lenin until 1934. After that, he erred in theory and was guilty of distortions in practice: not a criminal, just an erring Leninist.

By Suslov's reasoning, Stalin's body could remain next to Lenin's in the mausoleum and the names of streets and cities would not have to be changed. As long as Khrushchev hewed to this Suslovian interpretation, Suslov supported him, even providing the ideological justification for some of his wilder schemes. But in 1961, when Khrushchev declared Stalin a criminal and sinner and arranged the removal from the mausoleum, Suslov abandoned the first secretary. By October 1964, when it appeared that Khrushchev was about to mount another purge of the leadership, especially of its old Stalinists,

Suslov, it is believed, led the conspiracy against him and played a crucial role in organizing the coup.

Because of his age, health and perhaps because of his nature, most Kremlinologists believe that Suslov never aspired to be king. But he has long been the U.S.S.R.'s wiliest kingmaker. He has exploited the concept of "collective leadership" and taken advantage of the fact that in any ideocratic party the tone is set by the chief theoretician. It has been Suslov who has determined the party's tone on everything from foreign policy to the Sino-Soviet rift, from economic reform to the repression of intellectuals, from unity of the Communist movement to the rehabilitation of Stalin since Khrushchev's fall. And when it is time to choose a successor for either Brezhnev or Kosygin, if he is still around, Suslov will surely play a major role in the decision-making process.

The decision to replace Kosygin, Sovietologists believe, was probably reached in the spring of 1970. To judge from rumor and Kremlinological analysis, the man who failed to receive the nod—probably by just a few Central Committee votes—was Dmitry Polyansky, the "other" first deputy premier.

Polyansky is a genuine child of the Revolution. He was born on November 7, 1917. The son of Ukrainian peasants in Slavyanoserbsk in the Donets basin, Polyansky joined the Komsomol at fourteen, the party at twenty-two in 1939, and has more than a quarter century of party work behind him. In 1958, when only forty-one but already one of Khrushchev's "golden boys" like Shelepin, he was vaulted from the first secretaryship of Krasnodar *oblast* to the premiership of the Russian Federation and into the Politburo as a candidate member. Two years later, in 1960, he was admitted as a full member. Today, as first deputy chairman of the Council of Ministers, he is charged primarily with responsibility for agriculture.

The most extroverted and Western in manner of all the Soviet leaders, Polyansky has traveled extensively abroad and seems to be the only member of the Politburo to play to the crowds in the old Khrushchevian manner. He dresses nattily and would, in the words of one Western observer, "make a good handshaking, baby-kissing American politician."

This provides no real clue, however, to Polyansky's political and ideological proclivities. There is, for example, no evidence to indicate whether he was a hawk or a dove on the Czechoslovak question.

On the other hand, his views on agriculture are known. By Soviet

criteria he is liberal and progressive. He favors increased investment, mechanization, modernization and less centrally directed med-
dling in the farm economy. Clearly much of the credit for the
improvement in agriculture during the past five years must go to
Polyansky. But if performance on the agricultural sector makes Polyansky shine, his inextricable identification with farming is also
his political Achilles' heel. It has won him the enmity of powerful
Central Committee interests: the military-industrial bloc and the
"metal eaters," who, it is believed, blocked his ascension to the
premiership during the leadership crisis in 1970.

The full story of that crisis may never be told and Kremlin watchers
are by no means unanimous in their analyses and opinions about
what actually occurred. One version has described it as an attempt
to topple Brezhnev, another as an attempt by Brezhnev to establish
his unquestioned predominance over both the government and party
apparatus. Besides the secretary-general Kosygin, Shelepin, Suslov,
Mazurov and Polyansky have been ascribed various roles in it.

The point of departure, most observers agree, was the December
5, 1969, Central Committee plenum at which Brezhnev delivered
the "secret report" that was violently critical of the state of the
economy.

The fate of the economic reform, to which Brezhnev has long paid
little more than lip service, and the role of the party in state enterprises were visibly among the crucial aspects of the debate as it unfolded in the Soviet press. Brezhnev presumably demanded a reinforcement of the role of the party in enterprises, and to judge from
the attacks against the state administration, his criticism focused
mainly on the institutions of the government, its ministries and their
chief, Kosygin.

While calls for labor discipline thundered across the country and
party officials fulminated against the economic reform as the root
cause of the nation's troubles, a strange rumor, soon circulating
widely in the Western press, originated in two East European capitals: Prague and Belgrade. It hinted that three members of the
Politburo—Suslov, Shelepin and Mazurov—had addressed a mem-
orandum to the Central Committee openly questioning the administration of both Kosygin and Brezhnev.

The style—several members of the top leadership addressing the
largely ineffectual Central Committee—is without precedent in Soviet politics and most Kremlinologists discounted the rumor as base-

less. But it was, nevertheless, a wisp of smoke to indicate that trouble in the collective was smoldering somewhere. Further evidence of a crisis was presented by the inexplicable disappearance of Kosygin, Podgorny, Suslov and Shelepin in late March. In the first week of April all four were reported ill. This epidemic of colds and unspecified ailments was soon followed by the sacking of four key media and propaganda officials: Mikhailov and Mesyatsev, both Shelepin men; Vladimir Stepakov, the chief of the Central Committee's department for Propaganda and Agitation, a Kosygin man; and Aleksei Romanov, the chairman of the State Committee for Cinematography, believed to be a Suslov protégé.

Moreover in Moscow the diplomatic grapevine, fed by obscure confidants with spurious leaks, buzzed with the rumor that a major reshuffle of the collective leadership was imminent and that Kosygin as well as the collegium's oldest member, Arvid Pelshe, would be honorably retired.

There was but one logical counterargument to oppose the theories and rumors. The long-planned Lenin centennial celebration was due in two weeks and it seemed implausible that the leadership would undertake a purge before that momentous event.

What probably happened is that the basic decision to replace Kosygin was reached in this crucial period but that the leadership also decided to postpone the choice and announcement of a successor until a more propitious period following the anniversary: June or July. At any rate on April 21, the eve of Lenin's birthday, the entire leadership appeared on the podium of the Palace of Congresses and none looked the worse for their "illnesses."

The crisis thus was shelved for a while.

One can only speculate that the key figure was Kosygin. There is no evidence, of course. Moreover the reasons for the hypothetical "Kosygin crisis" remain obscure. Had he become the scapegoat for the economic debacle of 1969 and the alleged failure of the reforms? Was his health really as precarious as some KGB tipsters intimated to foreign correspondents and diplomats in Moscow? Had he challenged Brezhnev's visible ascendancy and intrusiveness and suffered a political defeat? Or had he, as some sources suggested, merely grown weary. It was often suggested in Moscow that Kosygin was tired of pulling Brezhnev's chestnuts out of the fire.

Although in April various sources had suggested that a decision had been reached and that it would become public in late June or

July, the crisis built up again. The reason may have been that while the question of Kosygin's successor had been settled with the choice of Polyansky in April, by June another candidate—Brezhnev—had thrown his hat into the ring.

Presumably the plan was to retire Kosygin honorably at the first session of the newly elected Supreme Soviet in mid-July. His government would have had to submit its formal resignation anyway and his successor could thus have been named in a most democratic, parliamentary fashion. Probably in late June the question of succession came up at the Politburo meeting. The Politburo deadlocked —possibly because of the additional candidacy—and decided to throw it to a vote in the Central Committee, which was scheduled to meet July 2–3. When the committee met, a Munich-based Kremlinologist, Christian Dueval, has theorized, the principal candidate was Polyansky. He was blackballed, probably by the heavy industry lobby, which objected to his investment and development schemes for agriculture.

The result of this political impasse was that Kosygin stayed on, although Dueval does not rule out the possibility that wrangling over his succession continued until shortly before the Central Committee met again on July 13, on the eve of the convocation of the Supreme Soviet.

Since Kosygin had not anticipated being entrusted with the formation of the new government at that session of the Soviet parliament, he was virtually unprepared. He took the unprecedented step of not replacing a single member of his government—the Council of Ministers—and did not deliver a major policy statement as he had done four years previously upon his re-election as premier.

This would also explain the mysterious postponement of the XXIVth Party Congress. As late as mid-June no less authoritative a source than Brezhnev said emphatically that the congress would be held in 1970. On July 13, following the Central Committee plenum, it was announced that the congress would be held in 1971, and the agenda specified that Kosygin would deliver the main economic report. This announcement could only have been made after it was certain that Kosygin would still be in office when the congress was to be held.

The congress, it was assumed, would change the balance of power in both the Politburo and the Central Committee so that when the question of Kosygin's succession arose again there would not be another deadlock. At the time of writing this does not seem to be the case and there are persuasive arguments for the theory that in the summer and autumn of 1971 there was yet another stalemate.

That theory is based on the assumption that the style of the present leadership precludes the sudden political deaths that characterized the Stalin and Khrushchev eras. Everything points to their penchant for orderly, democratic fig leaves. Under those circumstances Kosygin's political withdrawal could be expected to take place at a session of the Supreme Soviet to which he would tender his resignation as head of the government, although the real decision concerning his succession would have been reached beforehand in the Politburo and Central Committee.

The Supreme Soviet usually meets for only a few days each time—invariably preceded by a Central Committee plenum—twice annually: in mid-summer and mid-December. The 1971 summer session was not held and, instead, the Supreme Soviet's only session for 1971 was in late November—a highly arbitrary, most unusual and unconstitutional step. One reason for the odd postponement of the session from the summer to November was undoubtedly continuing debate and confusion over the current five-year plan which the Supreme Soviet is supposed to ratify. But another explanation could be a continuing stalemate on personnel matters. There are several indications of this. For one thing, Voronov was not demoted from the Politburo as most Kremlinologists expected. Instead, in a move that is highly suggestive of compromise, Voronov's successor as premier of the Russian Federation, Mikhail Solomentsev, previously the Central Committee secretary in charge of heavy industry, was named a *candidate* member of the Politburo, enlarging the group of candidate members from six to seven.

All of the preceding scenario, I would like to stress, is based on circumstantial evidence and constitutes a hypothesis of what happened. It is a retrospective attempt, so to speak, to peek under the blanket.

What is not circumstantial but demonstrable, however, is Brezhnev's rise to pre-eminence over the members of the collective and the development of his personality cult.

An experienced, shrewd politician, he wasted little time after being named first secretary in building up his personal power base. Methodically he brought cronies and protégés from his home town of Dneprodzerzhinsk and his period as a *politruk* officer in the war, from his stints as party chief on Dnepropetrovsk *oblast,* Moldavia and Kazakhstan into key party and government positions: Kirilenko; Katushev; Sergei Trapeznikov; General Shchelokov, the interior minister and chief of the militia; Defense Minister Marshal Grechko; Vladimir Matskevich, the minister of agriculture; Viktor Chebrikov, the deputy chairman of the KGB who is Brezhnev's watchdog in the secret police; Dinmukhamed Kunayev, Vladimir Shcherbitsky and Fyodor Kulakov—the three newest members of the Politburo—to mention just a few. Of course, this is a universal political technique. But in the Soviet Union patronage has been developed into a fine art and Brezhnev is clearly a master of it.

Conversely, he has struck at his rivals by neutralizing them, purged the props who supported them and gerrymandered districts in the republics so as to obtain a more favorable alignment in the Central Committee. He systematically moved old Khrushchevites out of key positions, decimated the Shelepin team, cleansed the provinces of Podgorny's supporters. In September 1970 he even manged to eliminate one of his most formidable rivals, Vassily Tolstikov, the party chief of Leningrad, by exiling him to Peking as the U.S.S.R.'s new ambassador. Tolstikov had been one of three speakers at the XXIIIrd Party Congress in March 1966 who more or less subtly criticized Brezhnev's style of leadership.

He has systematically encroached on Kosygin's sphere as the head of the government by making important speeches and pronouncements on domestic and foreign affairs, has engaged in personal diplomacy and has used the party apparatus to force the government administration into a subordinate role. The major breakthrough in this connection came at the December 1969 Central Committee plenum when he delivered his obloquial attack on the administration.

Brezhnev, it must be remembered, has no authoritative government and state title, other than being a deputy to the Supreme Soviet and one of the thirty-six members of its presidium. Yet in March 1970, unaccompanied by other Politburo members or senior government officials with the exception of Marshal Grechko, he journeyed to Minsk to review the important Dvina military maneuver, an act that cast him in the role of supreme commander of the Soviet Army.

In June of that year he set a noteworthy precedent by attending a meeting of the Council of Ministers, of which he is not even a member, and delivering what *Pravda* called a "major speech" that presumably dealt with the new five-year plan and the state of the economy. Several days later Brezhnev intervened with another major address at a meeting of the Council of Ministers of the Russian Federation, of which he is also not a member. *Pravda*'s reports of both sessions created the impression that they had been held under the *de facto* chairmanship of Brezhnev.

The December 7, 1970, plenum of the Central Committee, convened to approve the draft economic plan and budget for 1971, adopted a unique semantic formula that seemed intended to create the impression that the Council of Ministers was subordinate to the Central Committee of the party, which "empowered" the government to submit the draft to the legislature.

In February 1971, when the draft of the new five-year plan was published, the Central Committee decree approving it was signed by but one man: Brezhnev. It was the first time since Stalin's death that a Central Committee decree had been published with only the personal signature of the senior secretary. Not even Khrushchev had gone so far and Stalin used this technique of demonstrating his pre-eminence sparingly.

Those foreign observers who still believed that a triumvirate or duumvirate ruled the Soviet Union were disabused of their notion at the XXIVth Party Congress.

Brezhnev's marathon speech—six hours not counting the smoke and lunch breaks—was televised live. Later during the conclave, when Kosygin delivered his report, only excerpts were videotaped. In fact, while Kosygin was speaking, Soviet TV rebroadcast Brezhnev's address. Observers who studied the clips of Kosygin's talk noticed that as he spoke, Brezhnev could be seen reading correspondence, Pyotr Shelest was engrossed in a magazine and Matislav Keldysh, the president of the Academy of Sciences, was sucking his thumb with an expression of total boredom.

Since the Congress there has been virtually no stopping him. Even without the title, Brezhnev began acting very much like the head of the Soviet government and state. In September 1971 he invited West German Chancellor Willy Brandt for a meeting in the Crimea. Kosygin was nowhere around. In October, unaccompanied by either Kosygin or Podgorny, he journeyed to France where he was welcomed with a 101-gun salute and treated like a head of state by President Georges Pompidou. It was a remarkable and unprecedented performance—particularly when compared to how Khrushchev used the fig leaf of Nikolai Bulganin's premiership in the mid-1950s during the period when Khrushchev was already master of the country but without the title to prove it to the world.

Brezhnev obviously wants the title. How and when he will get it is another question. In the late summer and early fall of 1971 an interesting "esoteric" debate, suggesting that Brezhnev had mobilized forces outside the Politburo to help him become premier, unfolded in the more obscure and specialized party journals such as *Kommunist* and *Partiinaya Zhizn*. The thrust of the discussion, which involved Suslov, Pyotr N. Fedoseyev, the director of the Institute of Marxism-Leninism and lesser known theoreticians centered on the question of whether or not the party *and* government leadership ought to be recombined under Brezhnev. Of course, as is typical for such debates, the issue was never spelled out in those words but rather in the convoluted, coded language which only cognoscenti and Kremlinologists understand. To them, however, the meaning was clear: Brezhnev still lacked the majority in the Politburo to back him in this and had turned, instead, to powerful supporters in the Central Committee and elsewhere. In the days preceding the November 1971 Supreme Soviet session Moscow and the East European capitals were rife with rumors about an impending constitutional change that would establish a state council—a collective presidency on the model of the one in East Germany and Romania—with Brezhnev as its chairman. Such a change would make Brezhnev titular head of state. There is enough evidence to suggest that the scheme was debated at the Central Committee plenum preceding the Supreme Soviet meeting but that the proposal was rejected. On the eve of the Supreme Soviet session "tipsters" were telling newsmen in Moscow that rumors about such a constitutional change were "premature."

Brezhnev may be powerful, but he is far from popular. In fact, since they conspired jointly to bring Khrushchev to fall, Kosygin's popular image has shone far brighter than Brezhnev's. Whispered political jokes convey the public mood.

"What is the difference between Brezhnev and Stalin?" goes one such tale. "The mustache has slipped over the eyebrows."

Another is in the form of a question to an agitprop official. "Is it really vital to Soviet interests to send the first man to Mars?" "Yes," the speaker replies. "The first man in the U.S.S.R. is Leonid Brezhnev."

One anecdote that made the rounds behind cupped hands shortly after the December 1969 death of Marshal Kliment Voroshilov, the

Civil War hero famed for his cavalry exploits, is trenchantly anti-Brezhnev. It depicts Kosygin taking a constitutional along the Kremlin wall when he suddenly hears a voice calling him by his sobriquet: Alyosha. It seems to be coming from Voroshilov's grave nearby and as Kosygin approaches it the call becomes louder. Kosygin, barely believing it, bends down and asks: "Is that you, Kliment?" Voroshilov's ghost replies: "Yes. Alyosha, it's so boring here. For God's sake bring me a horse so I can at least go riding again." Kosygin, shaken and trembling, rushes back into the Kremlin to tell Brezhnev, who, understandably, thinks the premier has lost his mind. Finally Kosygin prevails on Brezhnev to accompany him to prove that he is sane. As they approach Voroshilov's grave, the voice can again be heard: "But Alyosha, Alyosha. What's the matter with your hearing? I said a horse, not an ass."

By comparison, jokes about Kosygin are benign. In one, a party member asks an *apparatchik:* "Is it really necessary to guard Comrade Kosygin so closely?" The official replies: "But of course. Someone could steal him from us."

Whether or not such stories reach the Kremlin, Brezhnev appears determined to change his public image and he is assiduously building up his own personality cult. His photographs and speeches dominate the party press. During one two-week tour of Central Asia he placed his picture on the front page of *Pravda* six times—an achievement unequaled since the Khrushchev era. In the space of two months Brezhnev's name appeared in fifteen of *Pravda*'s front-page editorials.

Increasingly he takes the opportunity to travel to the provinces and to deliver major speeches. Invariably they are telecast live. In the month or so preceding the Lenin centennial, when the rest of the leadership was "ill," Brezhnev dominated the scene.

Brezhnev, who seems to have an *idée fixe* about anniversaries and birthdays, even tried to change his own to January 1 so that it would fall on a public holiday.

In 1966 Brezhnev persuaded the Supreme Soviet to award him the gold star of a Hero of the Soviet Union, the U.S.S.R.'s highest award for valor. Since then the press has burgeoned with reports of his military exploits as a *politruk* officer during the war. At the front, said one eulogy in *Ogonyok,* the weekly illustrated magazine, Comrade Brezhnev "made the impossible possible . . . The men of the Eighteenth Army knew him well . . . he was their favorite. He knew their moods and thoughts and was able to imbue in them the thirst for victory . . . At the most critical moments in battle he would find stirring words which had a rapid and powerful effect . . . He repeatedly showed personal bravery and iron coolness."

The nature of the Soviet Union's ideocratic system demands that the maximum leader also be a major exponent of Marxist-Leninist theory. Stalin did it. Khrushchev did too, by publishing eight volumes of his speeches and articles. Brezhnev has finally been elevated to authorship as well. A two-volume edition of his collected works was published—presumably as a trial run—in Bulgaria in 1969. An updated version called *Along the Leninist Course* appeared in Soviet bookshops in the summer of 1970. Critics immediately waxed enthusiastic with adulatory praise. "The collection of L. Brezhnev's speeches and statements," wrote one reviewer, "will help readers gain a deeper insight into the topical questions of Marxist-Leninist theory." The monthly *Voprosy Istorii KPSS* (Problems of History of the CPSU) gushed that Brezhnev's style is characterized by "calm efficiency, all-around validity of the theses propounded, by a Leninist method of persuasion, by the scientific objectivity of evaluations, and its most profound conviction which is passed on to the reader [sic]."

Just as in the case of Khrushchev's works, Brezhnev's speeches and articles *before* his election as first secretary were unfit to print. Khrushchev's collected works had to begin with 1953, for his earlier articles and speeches were saturated with sycophantic praise of Stalin. Similarly, Brezhnev's pre-1964 pronouncements overflow with the tribute he paid to Khrushchev's wisdom and insight. The collection thus begins with his pronouncements since October 1964.

Now it is time for Brezhnev's sagacity to be praised and the XXIVth Party Congress set the tone for it as speaker after speaker moved to the platform to panegyrize the general secretary in the same style in which Khrushchev had once been extolled.

A milkmaid from the "Dawn of Peace" kolkhoz in Orel *oblast* told the delegates: "I won't hide the fact that tears of joy and pride came to my eyes when Leonid Ilyich, himself a former front-line soldier who went through the flames of war, told in his reports so warmly and sincerely of the labor exploits of soldiers at the front." The new first secretary of Azerbaidzhan said: "In all the work that was accomplished by the Central Committee, the general secretary of the CC, Leonid I. Brezhnev, played an enormous role, earning general love and respect through his tireless acitivity and his constant concern for the welfare of the people." The party chief of Gorky *oblast* said that Brezhnev's "meetings and conversations with workers" had an "enormous mobilizing and organizational effect." Kirghizia's first secretary eulogized Brezhnev's "simplicity and humanity" and put Brezhnev's report to the congress "into the ranks of the most important documents of creative Marxism-Leninism." The first secretary of the Komsomol, E. M. Tyazhelnikov, and the party chief of Novosibirsk shared the record of referring to Brezhnev eight times in their speeches. The Soviet minister of ferrous metallurgy and the first secretaries of Latvia and Tadzhikistan ran close seconds with seven mentions.

What he cannot achieve through praise from the deferential *apparatchiki* Brezhnev seeks to obtain by direct appeal to the masses. New Year's 1971 he took the unprecedented step of going on nationwide television and radio at midnight, when millions of people turned in to hear the Kremlin chimes to launch a round of heavy toasts, wished the Soviet people a happy new year and exhorted them to "new milestones in Communist construction." The ten-minute videotaped address also set a milestone in personality cults.

Since 1964 Soviet history has moved a long way toward a full circle. Kremlin roulette is a game that demands a fast draw. As Khrushchev's case proved, this morning's maximum leader can be tonight's unperson. But for the moment one thing seems certain. While there may be genuine doubts about the identity of Moscow's Number Two, Number One is there for all to see.

16 *The Legacy of a Millennium*

When a Russian says that this year he plans to spend his vacation abroad—*za granitsei*—it does not necessarily mean that he is one of the fortunate few who receive permission to leave the country. On the contrary, he will probably be one of the many who visit what has become known as *Sovietskaya zagranitsa*—the three Baltic republics of Estonia, Latvia and Lithuania.

Wrested by Russia from the Poles and the Swedes in the eighteenth century, independent from 1918 until 1940, when the Red Army reoccupied them, the Baltic republics are where the Muscovite smart set goes to enjoy a whiff of the West, a breath of Europe, an illusion of high life and luxury without having to obtain either exit visas or foreign exchange.

In baroque and Catholic Vilnius, capital of Lithuania, miniskirted girls and long-haired boys, wearing local versions of Cardin-cut suits, stroll down the linden-lined boulevards, while away hours drinking espresso in cafes such as the Neringa, Palanga or Vilnius and dance to restaurant bands that play the slop, the monkey, Israeli horas and a German beer-hall tune called *"In München Steht ein Hofbräuhaus."*

In Latvia's capital of Riga, where even officials claim there are still forty-four "working" churches, immaculately but conservatively dressed citizens spend their Sunday afternoons strolling leisurely past the variegated flower beds of the Vermanya Garden, watch the swans on the pond in front of the old university building or drink coffee and munch creamy cakes under the vermilion umbrellas of the Vecriga Cafe.

From the medieval ramparts and towers of Tallin, formerly Reval, one can see all the way to Helsinki, across the bay, and "Finnish antennas," at a cost of only thirty to fifty rubles, afford Estonians a television peephole to the West. Here bars, restaurants and nightclubs remain open until the early morning hours, some as late as 4 A.M. The men wear carefully tailored suits, no woman would go out without a hat, private houses—a startling number of them—are equipped with the highest of all Soviet status symbols, a garage, and per capita income in 1970 was more than 1500 rubles.

In the Baltics clothes are more fashionable in cut and the explanation is that some 800,000 Lithuanians, 120,000 Latvians and 100,-000 Estonians live abroad and keep their relatives supplied with gift packages.

Restaurants are tastefully decorated with an eye on *ambiance* and they specialize in carefully prepared cuisine and waiters who care. One, in Tallin's Astoria nightclub, a subterranean *variété* relic from the 1920s, actually asked: "Would you care for some roasted almonds with your drink, sir?"

Stores are better stocked and managed with consumer convenience in mind. Houses are better built, with the stress on permanence and attractive design.

Here the propaganda is less obtuse and less ubiquitous, and the arts and literature are less constricted. The city streets and parks look less run-down, the kolkhoz fields less neglected. And the European soul feels again at home.

But most important of all, the economy functions more smoothly and more efficiently than anywhere in the Soviet Union. With but 1 per cent of the U.S.S.R.'s territory and less than 3 per cent of the population, the Baltic republics produce 8 per cent of the Soviet Union's metal-cutting machine tools, 12 per cent of its washing machines, 20 per cent of all railway passenger cars, 47 per cent of all automatic telephone exchanges, 20 per cent of all radios and television sets, 65 per cent of all shale oil, 30 per cent of the large electric transformers and 33 per cent of the electric welding instruments.

With almost predictable consistency, the indicators for economic growth—industrial and agricultural production, labor productivity, national income, wages and retail trade turnover—show better results in the Baltics than in the U.S.S.R. as a whole and most of the other republics. In 1969, for example, when labor productivity in the Soviet Union registered a growth of only 4.4 per cent—the lowest since World War II—Estonia reported a rate of 8, Lithuania 7 and Latvia 6 per cent.

These showcase results raise the unavoidable question whether the deficiencies of Soviet society are due to the built-in peccancies of Communism or, perhaps, to something traditionally Russian.

"To understand this country," a colleague advised me several months after arriving in Moscow, "you really should read the journals of the Marquis de Custine."

It is a remarkable document, written more than 130 years ago, from which many commentators about the Soviet Union have drawn to demonstrate that little, if anything, has changed in Russia since tsarist days. In fact, Phyllis Penn Kohler, the wife of a former U.S. ambassador to Moscow, appropriately called her translation of the nineteenth-century Frenchman's book *Journey for Our Time*. In a sense Custine's report is exactly that: a sociopolitical Baedeker to the U.S.S.R., particularly the Russia, of today.

Yet even more astonishing than the contemporaneity of Custine's observations is the fact that the Marquis himself came to Russia in 1839 armed with the reports of earlier travelers. Concealed in the pocket of his steamer coat, where he hoped they would escape the vigilant scrutiny of the St. Petersburg police and customs, were excerpts from the book by Sigismund zu Herberstein, written in the sixteenth century. Just as we turn to Custine today, so Custine turned to the writings of a man who predated him by three hundred years.

For nearly a millennium Russia's intelligentsia and its ruling elite have been engaged in a protracted debate over how the country should be run. Xenophobia, incontrovertibly a Russian syndrome nurtured by the Mongol conquest and the doctrinaire isolationism of the Orthodox Church, is as pervasive today as it was centuries ago. Suppression of those who think differently has been a way of life at least since Ivan the Terrible came to power. Apathetic lethargy and indolence have been characteristics of the Russian muzhiks since the earliest records, and the real question to raise today may well be whether or not Communism, with its command economy and lack of incentives, has contributed to and exacerbated this inherent spirit of the Russians.

Few documents attest more convincingly to the immutability of Russia and the Russians than the travel reports, journals, diaries and letters of foreign visitors during the past 450 years.

Germans, Englishmen, Scots, Frenchmen, Italians, Dutchmen and Americans, they represent a wide spectrum of interests and backgrounds. Some, such as Alexandre Dumas and Giovanni Casanova, were professional writers and adventurers. Others, such as Herberstein, Giles Fletcher, Adam Olearius and John Quincy Adams, were ambassadors and diplomats. A few—Heinrich von Staden, for example—were mercenaries. Madame de Staël came as a political refugee. Others—Captain John Perry and the Quaker Daniel Wheeler —went in the service of the tsars to render what today we would call development aid. Some, like Custine and Gide, traveled to Russia in search of confirmation for their political views but returned disillusioned.

They do not necessarily agree with each other. On the contrary. Taken together, their reports often seem contradictory. Some thought the Russians dull-witted and melancholy, others considered them joyful and acute of mind. While they all agreed, for example, that the Russians are more addicted to drink than any other people they had encountered, their views did not coincide on the effect of inebriation: some described them as cheerful and good-natured when in their cups, others wicked and violent. But despite differences of opinion and interpretation, a broad band of continuity runs through all these documents and conveys a picture of a Russia that has remained remarkably unchanged from the sixteenth century to the twentieth.

It is a Russia in which for centuries secrecy, police surveillance, rewriting of history, the omnipotence and arrogance of rulers, adherence to a doctrinaire ideology, idleness, poverty and Potemkinism have been institutionalized.

In recent years, particularly since the mid-1960s when Soviet emissaries spread through Western Europe in search of technology they could buy, attention has focused on the Russians' endeavors to close their technological gap with foreign know-how. Yet not only has this been attempted during earlier stages of the Communist regime, but it is a Russian practice that dates to the sixteenth century. As long ago as 1526 Herberstein wrote that during his stay in Moscow he met "various foreign gunsmiths who cast culverins, carbines and iron balls" for the Russians. Adam Olearius, who was secretary to the Duke of Holstein's ambassador to Muscovy, wrote about the Tula mines which were established in the early seventeenth century by some German miners, sent "by his Excellence the Elector of Saxony at His Tsarist Majesty's request. Before that there were no mines in Russia . . . One and a half leagues from this mine is an iron forge, established in 1637 by a Dutch merchant. Its manager, Mr. Peter Marselis, has a special contract with the tsar and every year furnishes the Grand Prince with a number of iron bars, some hand guns and many thousands of pounds of ball."

Peter the Great employed foreigners to build his navy and canals, Catherine II, a German princess, was surrounded by foreign advisers and it was foreign capital and know-how that provided the basis for Russia's industrialization in the nineteenth century.

Yet, like the foreign computer technicians, automobile plant engineers and builders of chemical factories who come to the U.S.S.R. today, earlier travelers were surprised by the Russians' ineptness in handling new technology. In battle, wrote Herberstein, the new weapons did not help the Russians because they did not know how to apply them with the proper tactics. "They do not know when to use the large guns with which one breaks down walls, when to apply the small one whose balls put the enemy into disarray," he wrote. Three centuries later Custine remarked caustically: "Russians manifest their intelligence rather by the manner in which they use poor tools than by the care they put into the perfection of these tools. Endowed with little ingenuity, they usually lack machinery suitable for the end they wish to achieve . . ."

For hundreds of years, Russia has also tried to buy foreign goods and know-how at little or no expense to the treasury and its small reserves of foreign exchange. The mercantile acumen of the Russians is legendary and the protracted bargaining and painstaking attention to detail that precedes any contract they conclude are the nemeses of foreign merchants. In fact, it seems to be all that Western businessmen and commercial representatives talk about when they congregate in the "dollar bars" of the National and Metropol hotels at night. In 1526 Herberstein remarked: "One must be very careful with them in concluding sales and agreements. They remember precisely everything the partner promises and then compel him to keep every word. On the other hand, they do not hold to their own promises."

Indolence, filth and disorder, poor roads, shoddy workmanship, excessive bureaucracy, widespread corruption and an economy based on exhortation instead of incentives struck visitors hundreds of years ago.

Olearius complained that banquets in the Kremlin were invariably served on silver plate which had not been cleaned for years and Custine wrote that "one sees in the shadow of domestic filth a natural and deep-rooted disorder which is reminiscent of Asia."

In 1770 a French abbot and astronomer, Chappe d'Auteroche, journeyed through Russia to Siberia to observe the transit of Venus across the sun. By the time he arrived in Moscow all his sledges were broken to pieces because of the roads. Seven decades later Custine said: "At the pace one travels in Russia a carriage is soon destroyed on such roads. People break their bones and from verst to verst the bolts of the carriages fly out on all sides, the wheel rims are split, the springs burst out." Even Dumas, who tried all his life to emulate the rough-and-readiness of his Three Musketeers, found road and travel conditions a bit too strenuous for his amply padded bones and joints. Today Westerners refer to main Soviet highways such as the route from Brest-Litovsk to Moscow as "the Washboard."

Custine, undeniably the most critical and least charitable of the foreign observers, though the most applicable to contemporary conditions, devoted pages to describing the grayness and dismalness of Russian cities, "where everything was regulated as in a barracks or camp," and the shoddiness of housing. He, like countless travelers after him, was surprised by the splendor and glossiness of Russian cities and buildings from afar, their dowdiness from close up. Of Moscow he wrote: "When one approaches it for the first time toward the sunset hour when the sky is stormy, as I did, one thinks he sees a rainbow of fire hovering over the churches . . . But at three-quarters of a league from the entrance to the city the prestige vanishes . . . the disenchantment constantly increases." Of Russian construction work he said what any foreigner, studying the new high-rise apartment houses, first from a distance, then from nearby, would say today. "The appearance of certain villages surprised me. They have a real richness and even a sort of rustic elegance which is pleasing. The houses . . . appear well kept. [But] on close inspection one sees that these dwellings are really extremely poorly constructed."

Potemkinism seems to be a Russian trait that predates by centuries the birth of Prince Grigory Potemkin in 1739, whose use of false-front villages to deceive Catherine the Great gave posterity the name. Herberstein wrote that whenever foreign emissaries traveled from the border to Moscow, all the nobles and mercenaries of the territory surrounding the route were called up. Trade and craft shops were closed and the merchants driven from the market places. All were forced to assemble around the Kremlin "to impress the foreigners with the number of onlookers and to persuade him of the Grand Prince's might with their obedience. But the subjects, too, are supposed to see the might and importance of their prince through the ambassadors which powerful foreign princes send to him."

And Olearius reported that "as we drew nearer [to Moscow] various groups of well-dressed Russians rode out to meet us, swung by and went back again . . . A quarter league from the city we came upon 4,000 mounted Russians in costly dress drawn up in very fine ranks [on either side of the road]. We were obliged to pass between them." The description is similar to that of the "rent-a-crowds" which are brought by buses from various factories and dispersed along Moscow's Leninsky Prospect—the route from Vnukovo VIP airport to the Kremlin—to greet important foreign visitors and wave paper flags.

Sometime after he and the ambassador's company had been settled, Olearius described how he called upon the state chancellory. First he was kept waiting "for quite a long time together with ordinary Russians and lackeys" in the antechamber. Then he was led into the room where the senior and junior state chancellors received him. Their window frame and table were covered with fine tapestries and before the chancellor stood a large and beautiful but empty inkstand. "I was told," he wrote, "that both the tapestries and the inkstand were set in place just before my arrival and removed afterward. The chancellor's offices were usually not very tidy and perhaps that was why they had detained me [for so long in the antechamber]."

Even the types of confessions that Stalin's inquisitors forced out of their victims and the admissions of guilt for which the KGB still strives predate the construction of the Lubyanka Prison, once known as the Rossiya Insurance Company, by more than two centuries. Dr. Samuel Collins, an Englishman who served as physician to Tsar Alexis from 1660 to 1669, wrote in his book *The Present State of*

Russia in a Letter to a Friend at London that Russian judiciary proceedings "are very confused. The accused cannot be condemned, although a thousand witnesses come in against him, except he confesses the fact; and to this end they want not torments to extort confessions." Today, although only one witness would suffice to convict, the confession and admission of guilt remain the objective of police and judicial inquiry.

The importance of ideology and rote recitation of ideological platitudes is also nothing new. Olearius commented: "To teach their children fear of God the common people, especially in the countryside and villages, place them before the icons and make them bow and cross themselves and say *Gospodin* (Lord) with deep humility and reverence. Nothing is told of what it all means." Dr. Collins noted that "that priest is counted the best fellow that can mumble most in a breath." John Perry remarked that priests never preach, "for they have no skill." The main qualification for ascending to the priesthood, he wrote, was to have a good clear voice and to be able to say *"Gospodi pomilui* [God have pity]" twelve or fifteen times in the same breath.

Even the site of mass devotions—Red Square—has remained unchanged, and seventeenth-century descriptions of Palm Sunday processionals there must remind any diplomat or correspondent of the May Day and November 7 parades he has watched from virtually the same spot three centuries later. "We were allotted a wide space opposite the Kremlin gate [or approximately where GUM department store now stands]," wrote Olearius. "The Russians, more than ten thousand of whom had collected before the Kremlin, were held back so that we could see clearly. Behind us . . . stood the Persian ambassador and his suite . . . Palm Sunday celebrations are held with similar pageantry in other Russian cities where bishops or priests take the part of the Patriarch [of Moscow] and the *voevod* that of [the tsar who traditionally led the Patriarch's horse from the Spasskie Gate to St. Basil's Cathedral to emulate Christ's entry into Jerusalem].

"All during Holy Easter," he wrote, "people avidly patronized beer, mead and vodka houses. They drank so much that frequently people were seen lying here and there in the streets, and some of them had to be thrown onto wagons or sleighs by their relatives and taken home." That also sounds familiar to old Moscow hands.

The systematic rewriting of history and the transformation of erstwhile potentates into unpersons appear to be deeply rooted in Russian tradition.

Mrs. Vigor, the wife of an English diplomat, wrote in her *Letters from a Lady in Russia* in 1775 that when powerful men fall from favor, their names are never mentioned again. Their entire families are involved in their ruin, all estates are seized and they "sink to the condition of the meanest people." Custine noted that an adviser of the tsar, "who governed the empire and the emperor," had been in disfavor for two years and "for two years Russia has not heard his name spoken, this name which not long ago was on every tongue. He fell, in one day, from the highest power to the darkest obscurity. No one dares to remember him or even to believe in his existence. In Russia, the day a minister falls, his friends become deaf and blind. A man is buried as soon as he appears in disfavor. That is why Russia does not know if the minister who governed yesterday exists."

Arbitrary revision of history, to judge from Custine's observations, was as much a part of government policy in the nineteenth century as it is today. "The memory of what happened yesterday," he wrote, "is the property of the tsar. He alters the annals of the country according to his own good pleasure and dispenses each day to his people the historic truths which accord with the fiction of the moment. Thus [Kusma] Minin and [Prince Dmitry] Pozharsky, heroes [of the resistance against Poland during the Time of Troubles] forgotten for two centuries, were exhumed all of a sudden and became fashionable at the time of Napoleon's invasion for at that moment the government permitted patriotic fervor."

Foreign correspondents in Moscow today who view official secrecy concerning accidents, crime, mishaps and calamity as a typically Soviet trait could find complaints of similar obfuscation in the reports of their "colleagues" of centuries past. Thus Madame de Staël, who sought political refuge in Russia during the Napoleonic Wars, lamented the lack of frankness about the war. In Petersburg no one knew anything about what was going on at the front or around beleaguered Moscow because it was official policy to conceal the news of disasters. Said Custine: "The knowledge of figures is a privilege of the Russian police. I do not know whether exact figures reach the tsar himself, but I know that no disaster is published under his reign without his having consented to this humiliating avowal of the superiority of Providence." He described how, during a visit to Peterhof, a cloudburst descended on the Gulf of Finland and capsized numerous boats bringing guests from Petersburg to an imperial ball at the palace. The following day rumors spread through the city that 200 people had drowned. Others mentioned a figure of 1500, some said 2000. "No one," wrote Custine, "will ever know the truth and the papers will not even mention the disaster—that would distress the tsarina and imply blame to the tsar . . . Any mishap is treated here as an affair of state."

Who among the diplomats and correspondents in Moscow today has not chuckled about the manner in which *Pravda,* Tass and even radio and television newscasters list the full titles of Soviet luminaries *whenever* they mention their names in a dispatch or article? The style is something like this: "Member of the Politburo of the Communist Party of the Soviet Union and Chairman of the Council of Ministers of the U.S.S.R. Comrade Kosygin said today that . . ." This too is a practice that dates back centuries and then as now it amused and baffled foreigners. Herberstein, who could not remember all the tsar's titles, referred to such incidents by saying: "The Grand Prince (and again the boyar mentioned all his titles) . . ."

A century later Olearius also seemed to experience some difficulty in remembering all the titles. They included the mention of some thirty or more cities and provinces, all with unpronounceable names, over which the grand prince ruled. "They consider no ruler in the world comparable to theirs," wrote Olearius. "They refuse any letter addressed to his tsarist majesty if the slightest detail of his title is omitted . . ."

As long as there has been a Russia, it seems, the roads leading into it have been wider than those leading out. For over nearly half a millennium since visitors have written about this country restrictions on travel abroad for indigenes and foreign residents have struck Western observers as unique for the strictness with which they are enforced. Von Staden mentioned how he had given money, a servant and horses to another German in Moscow and directed him close to the Livonian border, from where he was able to leave the country. "In this," Von Staden wrote, "I was risking my life: for if they were caught I would have either been hanged or thrown into the river. No one is allowed out of the country without a pass or the permission of the Grand Prince."

Olearius mentioned the case of several people who obtained permission to study abroad and then immediately defected. On a number of occasions he was approached by Russian merchants and ambassadors in Holstein who asked him to instruct their sons in Latin or German. Though Olearius agreed, the youths never arrived from Russia, for their fathers had been unable to obtain exit permits for them.

Since Herberstein pioneered Western travel to Russia, a whole dossier of complaints has been amassed about bureaucratic protocol, isolation and surveillance of foreigners and attempts to quarantine the Russians from contact with travelers.

Herberstein, who seemed to have a better sense of humor than most of his successors, remarked that he "knew very well" why his escorts had quartered him "in so inhospitable an area" instead of letting him and his entourage proceed to Smolensk. They were waiting for further orders from the Kremlin and dared not allow him to travel without them. Herberstein, to test the stamina of his *pristav,* ordered his men to break camp and proceed eastward. When the escort objected, Herberstein replied: "Never before have I lived in the forests with wild animals, only in houses with human beings. The emissaries of Your Lord traveled through the lands of My King and were always put up in cities, villages and hamlets. I should be accorded the same treatment." That seemed to work. They were permitted to proceed to the next village, where, however, the escorts insisted on procuring all provisions and prevented Herberstein from having direct contact with the population. Once, when he entered a farmhouse to ask for a meal and the *pristav* objected, Herberstein threatened to beat him up.

Olearius, who described in considerable detail how his group was constantly shadowed and how everything was carefully prearranged, told of one instance in Novgorod when an old monk greeted the ambassadors with radishes, cucumbers, green peas and two wax candles and wanted to show them his church. But the armed *streltsy* (sharpshooters) accompanying the legation intervened and grumbled to the monk "that he had already allowed us to go too far." Later, when Olearius accompanied the legation on the Volga toward Persia, a similar incident occurred. They anchored overnight near the small Tartar town of Kasimovgorod, where a young Tartar prince, Res Kichi, lived with his mother and grandfather. "Our ambassadors sent him their respects and a gift of a pound of tobacco and a bottle of French brandy. He was so pleased with this that he in turn sent his greetings and hearty thanks and excused himself for being unable to entertain and honor the ambassadors in his home as he should have liked. All this was displeasing to the *voivode* [provincial governor] who did not permit foreigners to associate with him."

Then just as now vast areas of the country were closed to foreigners and visitors were obliged to follow prescribed routes. Anthony Jenkinson, one of Queen Elizabeth's ambassadors to Ivan the Terrible, revealed how he had once sent a messenger with a guide through the wilderness in search of his interpreter, who had left for Moscow four months previously and had not been heard from. Jenkinson knew and explained that it was strictly illegal to travel by indirect routes. The two were caught by a guard who would have been empowered to execute them and kill their horses. Somehow they persuaded him not to and later established contact with the ambassador again.

Unquestionably, of all the earlier visitors, Custine was most acrimonious in his comments upon Russian secrecy, surveillance and the isolation of foreigners. But his observations were also the most trenchant. Though made more than 130 year ago, they could have been written today. No book, it seems to me, is more revealing of the twentieth-century Soviet Union than this nineteenth-century classic.

"In Russia," he wrote, "secrecy presides over everything: secrecy—administrative, political, social . . . Every traveler is indiscreet, so it is necessary, as politely as possible, to keep track of the always too inquisitive foreigner lest he see things as they are—which would be the greatest of inconveniences."

Describing his arrival by ship at Kronstadt, the fortress in the bay outside Petersburg, Custine wrote of the long delays as "an army of employees" came on board: "police commissars, directors, assistant directors of the customs and finally the governor of the customs himself . . . The profusion of small superfluous precautions creates here a population of clerks. Each one of these men discharges his duties with a pedantry, a rigor, an air of importance uniquely designed to give prominence to the most obscure employment.

"At the sight of all these categories of spies who examined and questioned us, I was seized by a desire to yawn, which could easily have turned into a desire to weep, not for myself but for this people. So many precautions, considered indispensable here but completely dispensed with elsewhere, warned me that I was on the verge of entering an empire of fear; and fear like sadness is contagious."

Custine knew he was being spied upon. "Every foreigner is," he wrote. Consequently he took great precautions. His letters are laced with references about the need to hold conversations in the open, "where it is possible to talk with more safety than in one's own room." Although this technique is still employed, modern means of electronic eavesdropping such as directional microphones which can pick up conversations at great distances have made it far less reliable than it was in 1839.

Of the courier who accompanied him to Moscow, Custine said: "[He] inspires me with little confidence. Officially he is called my protector, my guide; but I see in him a disguised spy and I think that at any instant he could receive the order to declare himself constable or jailer."

Custine seemed to be most concerned for the safety of his notes and letters, because any one of them, "even one which would seem most innocent to you, would suffice to send me to Siberia." He shut himself up in his room when he wrote. When someone knocked, he removed all his papers from the desk, locked them in a drawer and pretended to have been reading. "I conceal them as if they were plans for a conspiracy," he wrote, "meanwhile awaiting an occasion when I can send them to you—a thing so difficult that I fear I shall be obliged to bring them myself . . . They know I am writing letters and holding them; they also know I never leave the city, not even for a day, without taking these mysterious papers with me in a large portfolio. They will prepare a trap for me in some forest, they will attack me, they will ransack me in order to take my letters and they will kill me in order to silence me. Such were the fears that obsessed me through the night before last."

Paranoid? Perhaps, but no different from the paranoia that affects any foreigner in Moscow after a while. And who would deny that the KGB has given them sufficient cause to feel that way?

Custine, conscious of Russian censorship, devised a variety of schemes to assure the safety of his material, from sewing them into his hatband to developing a code that only the recipient of his dispatches would understand.

Like travelers today he was baffled by the dearth of information that is available freely and officially in any other country: the exiguity of guidebooks and the superficiality of maps. "No bookshop," he said, "sells a complete index of the sights of Petersburg; furthermore, the educated people whom you question have an interest in not telling you anything . . . You have nothing to ask from Russia, not even your way, for on the Russian map of the city of Petersburg you find only the names of the principal streets." Today the most reliable maps are even less detailed. Custine said:

Russia is a country where everybody conspires to deceive the traveler. Do you know what it is to travel in Russia? For a superficial mind it is to be fed on illusions; but for one who has his eyes open and, added to a little power of observation, an independent turn of mind, it is continuous and obstinate work which consists in laboriously distinguishing, at every turn, between two nations in conflict: Russia as it is and Russia as it would like to show itself to Europe . . .

The most highly esteemed travelers are those who, the most meekly and for the longest time, allow themselves to be taken in . . . A traveler who would allow himself to be indoctrinated here by the people of the country could traverse the empire from one end to the other and return home without having seen anything but a series of façades . . .

To enter Russia you must deposit your free will along with your passport at the frontier. Would you like to see the curiosities of the palace? They will provide you with a chamberlain who will do the honors from top to bottom and by his presence, will force you to observe each thing in detail, that is to say, to see nothing except from his point of view and to admire everything without choice . . . Would you like to visit a hospital? The doctor in charge will escort you. A fortress? The governor will show it to you, or rather, politely conceal it from you. A school or any kind of public establishment? The director will be forewarned of your visit; you will find him armed and his mind well prepared to brave your examination. A building? The architect will take you over all its parts and will, himself, explain everything you have not asked in order to avoid instructing you on the things you are interested in learning . . .

The result of this oriental ceremony [which Intourist has perfected] is that to avoid making a career of seeking permissions you give up seeing many things—first advantage. Or, if your curiosity is sufficiently robust to make you persist in bothering people, you will at least be watched over in your investigations from such close range they will result in nothing. You will communicate only with the so-called heads of the so-called public

establishments and they will allow you no liberty beyond expressing . . . the admiration which is required by politeness, prudence
and gratitude . . . The observer cannot visit places or look at
anything without a guide. Never being alone he has trouble judging
for himself, which is what they want . . .

The Russia of Custine and Herberstein, of Olearius and Fletcher,
of Von Staden and Madame de Staël is almost indistinguishable from
the Russia of today. Fifty-four years of Communism has done little
to change it, though no one can deny that fifty-four years of Russian
interpretation of Communism has transformed that political and economic philosophy beyond recognition.

Repeatedly in their history the Russians endeavored to obtain the
end products of other civilizations and to circumvent the slow process
of fermentation that would lead to understanding and to social ac-
climatization. In the tenth century the princes of Kiev Rus accepted
Orthodoxy with undiscriminating ardor and without understanding
the Byzantine heritage. In the eighteenth century Peter I adopted
the language, dress and technology of Western Europe and attempted to impose them on Russia without imbuing his subjects with
the spirit of critical Western thinking and rationality. In the nineteenth century the radical intelligentsia glorified Western science and
technology without providing the basis for the free inquiry that had
made it possible. The intellectuals panegyrized Western social and
political philosophies which grew out of specifically Western conditions and had no relevance to a nation barely out of serfdom.

Isolated by the mainstream of civilization by its adhesion to the
Greek schism, by the Mongol conquest and by what became an
entirely politicized religion, Russia's real window on Europe did not
open until it was rocked by a revolution staged by exiles and cosmopolitans. The glance was a fleeting one and the blinds were drawn
shut again within a year when Lenin decided, for whatever reason,
to relocate the capital from Petrograd to the dark interior of medieval
and insular Moscow. The Byzantine rule and ritualism that followed
him with the reign of Stalin was no accident of history but the
ineluctable consequence of Russia's heritage. Today his heirs are
at the helm and they are steering Russia in the same channels of
borrowing, imitation and insulation mapped out nearly a millennium
ago by Prince Vladimir of Kiev, the founder of the Russian state.

Change over the succeeding decades and centuries has been virtually imperceptible and today the peculiarities of xenophobia, fear, arrogance, bureaucracy, ruthlessness, ineptitude and economic inadequacy which seem to some uniquely Soviet appear to me merely the result of imposing yet another borrowing—Marxism—on the Russian mind and spirit.

Change could come only after Stalin's heirs have departed and retired to the obscurity of their pensions and dachas. But even then the prospects for transformation seem unpropitious, for the legacy of a millennium is already carving the next generation in the same image.

Never will I forget what I felt while crossing the Niemen to enter Tilsit. At that moment, more than ever, I felt the Lübeck innkeeper had been right . . . I can speak, I can write what I think, I am free . . . Finally I can breathe!

Marquis de Custine, Berlin, in the
early days of October 1839

Epilogue

Exit Visa

The car wove through the swarm of lumbering trucks and Volga taxicabs and swung sharply onto Leningradsky Prospect toward Sheremetyevo airport on that afternoon of October 26, 1970. Only then did I realize that I was probably passing this way for the last time in my life. Being an expelled Moscow correspondent is nothing unique. I was merely the fourth to be declared *persona non grata* that year and a fifth was to follow my path within a few months. But to my knowledge no one has ever calculated the rate of return for such outcasts. It must be infinitesimal.

Pavel Dmitrov, the office driver, known for the "fastest right foot" in the foreign community, stepped on the accelerator as the avenue widened and within seconds he was well above the speed limit and, as usual, passing everything in sight. How often had he and I passed this way: to catch a plane, to meet a visitor, to attend planeside briefings and conferences of arriving or departing dignitaries. A burned-out *papirosa* cigarette clenched defiantly between his teeth, he raced onto the new bridge spanning the Khimkinskoye basin. Opened for traffic only six months earlier, in time for the Lenin centennial, it was already under repair and the car shook violently as it sped over the uneven surface. Soon we would pass the "tank trap monument," a cluster of oversized sawhorse barricades that marks the point of farthest advance of the Wehrmacht during World War II.

At the airport a farewell committee of other correspondents and their wives, well supplied with bottles of champagne, was already waiting. It is the custom among the foreign press corps to bid its expelled members good-bye in this fashion. How often had I been the member of such a group, never thinking that someday I too would be the focus of this attention.

This time there was no steamer trunk full of notes and books. They would follow in a few weeks when my wife had finished packing. Thus the customs check was surprisingly perfunctory. But the atmosphere was heavy with the oppressive feeling of being closely watched. Of the people in the hall, half were passengers and the remainder, it was safe to guess, were KGB agents.

When the flight was called up I moved toward passport control—the first of a series of checks that makes it impossible for anyone to leave the Soviet Union without the required documents. An iron barrier slid back and I moved into a no man's land run by border guards—a small open space facing a high-walled cubicle behind whose counter sat a grim-looking, silent soldier. As in a confessional box, one was alone. But no words were ever exchanged as the officer slowly studied the entries in the passport and visa, carefully compared the photographs with the face in front of him, then presumably checked in a thick book—which was hidden from view—to ascertain whether the suppliant was on the wanted list. The thump of a heavy rubber stamp being smashed onto the passport signaled that permission had been granted. Silently the documents were handed back and a second iron barrier leading to the departure hall slid back. The mechanism for these sliding gates is controlled from within the box.

Passport control is by no means the final check. As I passed through the others it occurred to me that the doors leading out of Russia had become narrower since I first arrived. Methodically the physical hurdles to departure have been raised as cubicles and checkpoints have been relocated to afford the authorities maximum surveillance over those who finally step aboard an outbound plane.

Just a few minutes after scheduled departure the jet taxied noisily and unsteadily toward the runway. A plump, untidy stewardess in an ill-fitting, faded blue uniform, a beehive of peroxided blond hair perched precariously atop her round head, her eyes framed by an excess of mascara, picked up a microphone in the galley.

Was it really the same one as on March 8, 1968?

"Aeroflot, the Soviet airline, welcomes you aboard our Soviet-made Tupolev-134 on its flight to Vienna," she said, this time in Russian. "On board you will find chess sets, dominoes and news-papers and magazines in many languages. Fasten your seat belts."

She came down the aisle to ascertain whether her instructions had been followed and nearly tripped over the loose carpet in the aisle. This time I did not ask for the Paris *Herald Tribune* or Vienna's *Die Presse*.

As the plane lifted off the runway and the villages of Moscow's environs shrank beneath us I had only a fleeting sense of familiarity. This was a departure unlike any other.

Slowly the kaleidoscope of the past few days' confusion—the conferences and packing, the parties, the farewells of which a number were somber and tearful, the myriad odds and ends of bureaucratic details to settle and the persistent harassment of the KGB which had outdone itself with stakeouts, shadowing and minor provocations—receded into the corners of my mind. The trap had opened and I was being hurtled back from uncertainty.

I was leaving with neither bitterness nor rancor—only a mixture of relief and sadness. The tension of working in Moscow, where a reporter's job is a twenty-four-hour, seven-day-a-week assignment, is unmatched by that of any other beat. It does not relax even when one leaves on vacation: only when one departs forever on a one-way exit visa. But in a way that probably borders on masochism I had come to love this country and its people: not only because of their generosity and spontaneity but for the suffering they have endured so long. These are qualities that far outweigh the more negative ones of indolence, apathy and sycophancy that so often taxed my patience.

And who could remain indifferent to the land—its wide expanses, its birch forests and steppes, slate gray skies, its bitter winters with their unmerciful winds and ice, its intense summers with their endless hours of daylight and the heat and dust. More Russians now live in cities than in the countryside, yet no matter how urban it may be someday, no matter how many great cities may at some future date disfigure its landscape like scars of impersonal ugliness, Russia as a whole will forever remain a vast village. And as the jet traversed a fraction of that immensity on its way toward Europe and the West, I became aware of the metamorphosis that I had undergone and began to understand the legendary Russian attachment and devotion to the *Rodina*—the motherland.

I had acquired not only many memories but also many friends. The thought of leaving them behind in that vast palisade of sorrow, desolation and oppression, of having to abandon them to an uncertain future over which neither they nor I had any control made me most disconsolate and despondent. The last meeting with Pyotr Yakir and Gyusel Amalrik's parting words—*"ya boyus, ya boyus"*—loomed hauntingly in my thoughts.

Some will say to me now, having read these many pages, that it is hypocritical of me to deny acrimony. I can only reply that I feel no rancor, but I do feel anger: at what history has done to and made of Russia.

Some will surely say that I have permitted this anger to influence my judgment and to persuade me to assess the Soviet Union more somberly and pessimistically than the facts would warrant. To them I can only answer that I am cognizant of the antithetical arguments. I will present and anticipate them—not merely for the sake of objectivity but to give myself some hope, for I would *like* to believe them.

Some Sovietologists describe what has taken place since Khrushchev's fall not as a move toward "enlightened Stalinism" but as the search for a "centralist" formula: a policy of a middle road between de- and re-Stalinization.

These observers contend, for example, that whereas a bust was raised on Stalin's grave in June 1970, the other graves in the row also have busts. To have left Stalin's unmarked and bare, particularly following the death of Voroshilov, would have been rank discrimination, because his crimes and errors notwithstanding, he was a far more important historical figure than the other men buried there. Although by that reasoning one could well ask why Khrushchev was not also buried by the wall, why he was relegated to the obscurity of a grave in Novodevichy.

The 1969 *Pravda* article that commemorated his ninetieth birthday made it clear that his excesses and mistakes are still condemned. Moreover in December 1970 his ninety-first birthday was completely ignored. One of the largest-circulation calendars for 1971 does not even mention that Stalin was born on December 21—the first time that his name has been omitted from any calendar.

Neo-Stalinist authors, editors and poets such as Shevtsov, Kochetov and Chuyev have been either silenced or strongly criticized.

In November 1970 the Chinese CP's congratulatory message to Moscow in connection with the fifty-third anniversary of the Revolution referred to the "education" of the Soviet people "by the Great Lenin and Stalin." *Pravda* published the text, omitting the words "and Stalin."

In December 1970 a new volume of memoirs by Marshal I. K. Bagramyan appeared. For the first time since his fall, Nikita Khrushchev was mentioned favorably. Describing the early months of World War II when German troops smashed toward Kiev, Bagramyan said: "Only N. S. Khrushchev did not abandon his office." Khrushchev is described as a brave political leader who maintained close liaison with the military commanders in the area and there are frequent complimentary references to him.

At the XXIVth Party Congress Brezhnev criticized *both* Khrushchev and Stalin, albeit perfunctorily. Speaking in Tbilisi on the fiftieth anniversary of Soviet power in Georgia, in May 1971, he was more critical of Stalin than he had ever been before. When he paid tribute to outstanding Georgian revolutionary leaders, he mentioned Stalin in alphabetical order almost at the end of the list.

Optimistic observers point to other developments such as a new Central Committee resolution to strengthen the role of local soviets. It provided local legislative and administrative organs with new sources of taxation and accused party organs of exercising "petty tutelage." The decree also upbraided local agencies for failing to pay proper attention to the complaints of people and for displaying a superficial attitude toward people's daily problems. Party and higher government bodies were criticized for often taking actions without consulting the councils.

Three measures were ordered which, if enacted and put into practice, will contribute appreciably to the democratization of Soviet society. First, the urban and district soviets are to receive direct taxes from enterprises situated in their territory. Second, the soviets are supposed to assume responsibility for much of the housing and public amenities presently controlled by factories and other organizations. Finally, legislation is to be drafted to codify the rights and obligations of the soviets.

It is difficult to say whether or not this March 1971 decree portends meaningful changes. The Central Committee makes many resolutions and issues numerous decrees which are then ignored and forgotten. The fact that it was made public just shortly before the XXIVth Party Congress and a few months before the nationwide election of new local soviets suggests that it too is little more than a propaganda ploy.

There are also currents of concern for legality. The Supreme Court of the U.S.S.R. has on occasion criticized the lower judiciary for excessively harsh sentences, prejudice against defendants and for placing too much trust in the investigative work of the police and the *prokuratura*. A plenary session of the Supreme Court in the autumn of 1970, for example, stressed that the high number of commutations and reversals of verdicts and sentences at the appellate level is indicative of inadequate observance of the rules of evidence by lower courts.

The bulletin of the high court referred to "many faults and serious mistakes" and to the "one-sidedness and inadequacy of the court investigation." Some judges, it said, "are guilty of prejudice and of an uncritical attitude toward the materials of the preliminary investigation . . . The verdict is often based on implausible evidence assembled in the preliminary investigation and not verified during the actual court hearing. Particularly disturbing are the cases of wrongful conviction . . . Sometimes lower courts impose severe sentences because they believe they will not be reproached for their severity. This is a mistaken view. Punishment will not achieve its purpose of education and correction unless it is just."

Soviet society, I would like to stress, is also more pluralistic and less monolithic than surface impressions sometimes indicate.

Depite the rule of a small oligarchy which imposes its will on the vast majority, the U.S.S.R. has interest and pressure groups which lobby, occasionally successfully, for their demands and points of view. There are hawks and doves, conservatives and liberals at various echelons. Evidence of their presence and their influence is difficult for outsiders to discover, largely because of the Aesopian and convoluted manner in which this ideocracy requires discussions and arguments to be conducted. But there are sufficient indications to attest to disagreements and on rare occasions the curtain of secrecy parts sufficiently to allow foreign observers to make certain assumptions. In July 1968, for example, in his annual policy statement to the Supreme Soviet, Foreign Minister Andrei Gromyko referred to "good-for-nothing theoreticians" who try to "tell us that disarmament is an illusion." He spoke of an internal, behind-the-scenes conflict between "two policies, two lines in international affairs."

Within certain limits—specifically the unwritten rule that proscribes expressing doubt or criticism of the Communist system as such, the infallibility of the party or the present leadership—the Soviet press enjoys and exercises more freedom than is generally believed. It criticizes malfeasance actively and aggressively and exposes the deficiencies and malpractices which seem to be endemic to the Soviet social system. In fact, many of the shortcomings of the Soviet economy that I have spelled out on the preceding pages are the eclectic harvest of a careful scrutiny of the Soviet press.

The optimist about the Soviet future could point to other signs as well. For one thing, dissent has brought results, albeit meager ones. The party leadership is not completely deaf to the demands of the non-conformists and there are vague but perceptible currents of democracy in the Soviet Union which raise the hope of closer adherence to "socialist legality" in the future. A new generation with different values is maturing. The revolutionary *élan* that characterized the youth of the 1920s and 1930s, the patriotic fervor that set the tone of the war years—these are gone. But there are hints of a new pragmatism. There has been a loss of control over information that can only have the effect of making Russians better informed and more aware of what is happening in the world around them. There is doubt about the future or at least skepticism about the picture of the future the party's propagandists paint. And there has been a loss of blind faith, largely because the revelations of some of Stalin's crimes, no matter how superficial and perfunctory, left a significant sector of the population doubtful of the party's infallibility.

And yet, despite such encouraging signs to which more optimistic observers point, I left the U.S.S.R. depressed and alarmed by the general direction it has taken since 1965, particularly during those years of the post-Khrushchev era when I was on the scene to observe firsthand. Of course it is not Stalin's Russia nor would I like to suggest that the retrograde swing of the pendulum will take Soviet society to those extremes of tyranny again—at least not for the foreseeable future. Despots such as Stalin, Nikolas I and Ivan the Terrible are the exceptions, not the rule, in a nation's history, and Russia, it would seem, has already experienced more than its fair share of despotism. But the general course on which Stalin's heirs have set the country allows for little optimism in predicting its future. Because I learned to love the country and its people, I wish I were wrong. I am afraid I am not.

However, there is one aspect of Soviet affairs that thus far I have hardly discussed, because I considered it tangential to the main theme of this book, and about which I am far more hopeful: the U.S.S.R.'s foreign policy.

Progress toward a relaxation of international tension, and accommodation on the basis of peaceful coexistence and peaceful competition, I believe, are not only possible but are the aims of Soviet policy.

In the decade to come economic exigencies will, I believe, persuade the Soviet Union to pursue a considerably more flexible, responsible and co-operative course in the conduct of its foreign policy than it has in the past.

Overextended and overburdened, the Soviet economy demands relief. Its foreign aid to client states runs an estimated $1.6 billion per year in addition to almost $500 million in assistance to underdeveloped countries. The U.S.S.R., with a gross national product less than half as great as that of the United States, is looking for ways to reduce that load. The Kremlin will seek to alleviate it where it can—short of jeopardizing its basic national interests, defense priorities and its role as a superpower.

Even if the state of the Soviet economy does not entitle the U.S.S.R. to superpower status, Moscow sees itself in that role and wants the perquisites that accrue to it: a far-flung navy, a network of alliances and dependencies and, above all, military parity with the United States. The Kremlin not only feels entitled to such attributes of superpowerdom but has striven assiduously for the past few years to attain them. It will, for example, no longer agree to American military superiority. These are legitimate objectives in the traditional geopolitical sense and Soviet efforts to attain them can hardly be interpreted as manifestations or expressions of exceptional aggressiveness and expansiveness.

Of course the U.S.S.R. has been expansionist and aggressive in the past, but hardly more so than any other major power, particularly the United States. I was rudely reminded of this on the morning of the invasion of Czechoslovakia when a Russian acquaintance told me sardonically that the U.S.S.R. had been asked to intervene. "The same way your government was asked to intervene in Vietnam and the Dominican Republic," he said.

The Kremlin sees Eastern Europe as its unalienable preserve and sphere of influence. As an Asian power it is naturally inclined to extend its influence on that continent and considers its main rivals there to be China, Japan and the United States. Its expansion into the Mediterranean and the Middle East is rooted in tsarist policies and aspirations and one should remember that the U.S.S.R.'s most southwesterly border is but 150 air miles from the northernmost tip of Iraq, only 250 miles from the Syrian frontier.

Soviet aims, however, are tempered by the desire to avoid a direct confrontation with the United States. The threat of such a confrontation, for example, persuaded the Soviet Union to seek to defuse the Arab-Israeli conflict. It will, most likely, induce the Kremlin to search for accommodation in other areas of potential escalation.

In Europe, particularly, the U.S.S.R. seems bent on finding some formula for *détente*. It considers the cost of maintaining a powerful military machine on its western flank intolerably high and fears that the enlargement of the Common Market and the West European community could eventually lead to its own isolation from the Continent. The Russians can be expected to work strenuously for agreements, including some form of mutual reduction of forces based on acceptance of the post-war European status quo.

Although Moscow hopes to ease the military burden on its economy and will endeavor to avoid showdowns with the United States, it is haunted by the specter of China, a fear that is visceral and irrational. Ultimately fear of China will temper and influence the Soviet desires for a limitation on the arms race, particularly controls over nuclear weapons and their delivery potential. China's future policy and behavior will have a catalytic effect on the Soviet Union's own conduct of foreign affairs.

But while I feel confident about the U.S.S.R.'s future amenability and the possibility of accommodation in foreign affairs, I have few illusions about possible amelioration of the internal situation in Russia. For many years ahead it will remain a drab, gray, bitter and backward place, steeped in an oppressive atmosphere.

Never was I more cognizant of this oppressiveness than the day on which I left Moscow for the last time. It was more than merely the sensation of brightness and light, the efficiency and superaffluence of the consumer-oriented society which overwhelmed me on my arrival at Vienna's Schwechat airport: but the unique feeling of being free again.

Within seconds I cleared passport control and as I started toward the baggage claim and customs area, the officer's *"Bitte schön, der Herr.* Welcome to Vienna" rang in my ears.

The feeling of being under surveillance, the inbred caution of whispering in public places, of not engaging in "sensitive" conversations on the telephone, of looking for hidden microphones remained with me, my wife and my son for many more months. Subconsciously perhaps we will never be free of it.

I left Russia with mixed emotions. It was good to be back in "my world." But I cannot forget the other one or what life there should teach us.

After leaving the Soviet Union in 1936, André Gide wrote: "As it always happens that we recognize the value of certain advantages only after we have lost them, there is nothing like a stay in the U.S.S.R. to help us appreciate the inappreciable liberty of thought we still enjoy in France—and sometimes abuse."

A century before him the Marquis de Custine concluded: "It is necessary to have lived in this solitude without rest, in this prison without leisure that is called Russia to be conscious of all the freedom one enjoys in the other countries of Europe, whatever form of government they may have adopted . . . When your son is discontented in France, use my formula and say to him: 'Go to Russia.'"

Select Bibliography

I made use of the following books or consider them exceptionally useful and offer them as a reading list for those interested in more detailed or specialized study.

Alliluyeva, Svetlana, *Only One Year*, Harper & Row, New York, 1969.

Amalrik, Andrei, *Involuntary Journey to Siberia*, Harper & Row, New York, 1970.

————, *Will the Soviet Union Survive Until 1984?*, Harper & Row, New York, 1970.

Berger, John, *Art and Revolution*, Weidenfeld and Nicholson, London, 1969.

Billington, James H., *The Icon and the Axe*, Alfred A. Knopf, New York, 1966.

Blake, Patricia and Hayward, Max (eds.), *Dissonant Voices in Soviet Literature*, Harper & Row, New York, 1964.

————, *Halfway to the Moon*, Holt, Rinehart & Winston, New York, 1964.

Brumberg, Abraham (ed.), *In Quest of Justice*, Praeger, New York, 1970.

Brzezinski, Zbiegnew, *The Soviet Bloc*, Harvard University Press, Cambridge, 1960 and 1967.

Campbell, Robert W., *Soviet Economic Power*, Macmillan, London, 1967.

Caroe, Olaf, *Soviet Empire: The Turks of Central Asia and Stalinism*, Second Edition, Macmillan, London, 1967.

Carr, Edward Hallett, *The Bolshevik Revolution*, Macmillan, London, 1952.

Chornovil, Vyacheslav, *The Chornovil Papers*, McGraw-Hill, Toronto, 1968.

Conolly, Violet, *Beyond the Urals*, Oxford University Press, London, 1967.

Conquest, Robert, *The Great Terror*, Macmillan, London, 1968.

Conquest, Robert (ed.), *The Politics of Ideas in the U.S.S.R.*, Bodley Head, London, 1967.

————, *Religion in the U.S.S.R.*, Praeger, New York, 1968.

————, *Soviet Nationalities Policy in Practice*, Bodley Head, London, 1967.

Crankshaw, Edward, *Khrushchev's Russia*, Penguin Books, London, 1959.

Custine, Astolphe de, *La Russie en 1839*, Librairie d'Aymot, Paris, 1846; also *Journey for Our Time*, Henry Regnery, Chicago, 1951.

Deutscher, Isaac, *Stalin*, Penguin Books, London, 1966.

————, *The Unfinished Revolution*, Oxford University Press, London, 1967.

Djilas, Milovan, *Conversations with Stalin*, Harcourt, Brace & World, New York, 1961.

————, *The New Class*, Praeger, New York, 1958.

Dumas, Alexandre, *En Russie*, Paris, 1860; also *Adventures in Czarist Russia*, Peter Owen, London, 1960.

Edie, James; Scanlan, James; Zeldin, Mary-Barbara; and Kline, George (eds.), *Russian Philosophy* (Three Volumes), Quadrangle Books, Chicago, 1965.

Fainsod, Merle, *How Russia Is Ruled*, Harvard University Press, Cambridge, 1967.

Field, Andrew (ed.), *Pages from Tarusa, New Voices in Russian Writing*, Little, Brown & Co., Boston, 1963.

Fischer, Louis, *The Life of Lenin*, Harper & Row, New York, 1964.

Frankland, Mark, *Khrushchev*, Penguin Books, London, 1966.

Garaudy, Roger, *Marxism in the Twentieth Century,* Charles Scribner's Sons, New York, 1970.

————, *The Whole Truth,* William Collins Sons, London, 1971.

Gide, André, *Return from the U.S.S.R.,* Alfred A. Knopf, New York, 1937.

Ginzburg, Evgenia S., *Into the Whirlwind,* Collins/Harvill, London, 1967.

Gitermann, Valentin, *Geschichte Russlands* (Three Volumes), Europäische Verlagsanstalt, Frankfurt, 1965.

Granick, David, *The Red Executive,* Doubleday, Garden City, New York, 1960.

Grey, Ian, *The First Fifty Years,* Hodder & Stoughton, London, 1967.

Grigorenko, Pyotr, *Der Sowjetische Zusammenbruch 1941,* Possev Verlag, Frankfurt, 1969.

Hanson, Philip, *The Consumer in Soviet Society,* Macmillan, London, 1968.

Herberstein, Sigismund zu, *Reise zu den Moskowitern, 1526,* republished Munich, 1966.

Hoetzsch, Otto, *Russland in Asien,* Deutsche Verlagsanstalt, Stuttgart, 1966.

Johnson, Priscilla, *Khrushchev and the Arts,* MIT Press, Cambridge, 1965.

Kochan, Lionel, *The Making of Modern Russia,* Pelican Books, London.

Kochan, Lionel (ed.), *The Jews in Russia Since 1917,* Oxford University Press, London, 1970.

Kuznetsov, Anatoly, *Babi Yar: A Document in the Form of a Novel,* Farrar, Straus & Giroux, New York, 1970.

Labedz, Leopold (ed.), *Solzhenitsyn, A Documentary Record,* Allen Lane the Penguin Press, London, 1970.

Labedz, Leopold and Hayward, Max (eds.), *On Trial,* Collins, London, 1967.

Litvinov, Pavel, *Dear Comrade: Pavel Litvinov and the Voices of Soviet Citizens in Dissent,* Pitman, New York, 1969.

————, *The Demonstration in Pushkin Square,* Harvill Press, London, 1969.

Marchenko, Anatoly, *My Testimony,* Dutton, New York, 1969.

Mazour, Anatole G., *The First Russian Revolution 1825,* Stanford University Press, Stanford, 1937.

Medvedev, Zhores A., *The Medvedev Papers,* Macmillan, London, 1971.

————, *The Rise and Fall of T. D. Lysenko,* Columbia University Press, New York, 1969.

Mehnert, Klaus, *Peking and Moskau,* Deutsche Verlagsanstalt, Stuttgart, 1963.

————, *Der Sowjetmensch,* Deutsche Verlagsanstalt, Stuttgart, 1958.

Mihajlov, Mihaijlo, *Moscow Summer,* Farrar, Straus & Giroux, New York, 1965.

Miller, Jack, *Life in Russia Today,* G. P. Putnam's Sons, New York, 1969.

Murarka, Dev, *The Soviet Union,* Walker & Co., New York, 1971.

Nekrasov, Viktor, *Both Sides of the Ocean,* Holt, Rinehart & Winston, New York, 1964.

Novak, Joseph, *The Future Is Ours, Comrade,* Doubleday, Garden City, New York, 1960.

Nove, Alec, *An Economic History of the U.S.S.R.,* Allen Lane the Penguin Press, London, 1969.

Observer, *Message from Moscow,* Jonathan Cape, London, 1969.

Olearius, Adam, *The Travels of Olearius in 17th Century Russia* (Translated and edited by Samuel H. Baron), Stanford University Press, Stanford, 1967.

Portisch, Hugo, *So sah ich Sibiren,* Verlag Kremayr & Scheriau, Vienna, 1967.

Post, Laurens van der, *A View of All the Russias,* Morrow, New York, 1967.

Reddaway, Peter, *Russia Uncensored,* London, 1971.

Rice, Tamara Talbot, *A Concise History of Russian Art,* Praeger, New York, 1963.

Sakharov, Andrei D., *Progress, Coexistence and Intellectual Freedom,* Norton, New York, 1968.

Salisbury, Harrison E., *War Between Russia and China,* Norton, New York, 1969.

Sartre, Jean-Paul, *The Ghost of Stalin,* George Braziller, New York, 1969.

Schapiro, Leonard, *The Communist Party of the Soviet Union,* Eyre & Spottiswoode, London, 1959.

Schapiro, Leonard and Reddaway, Peter (eds.), *Lenin the Man, the Theorist, the Leader,* Pall Mall Press, London, 1967.

Schiller, Ulrich, *Zwischen Moskau und Jakutsk,* Christian Wegner Verlag, Hamburg, 1970.

Sethe, Paul, *Russische Geschichte,* Verlag Heinrich Scheffler, Frankfurt, 1953.

Seton-Watson, Hugh, *The Russian Empire 1801–1917,* Oxford University Press, London, 1967.

Shub, Anatole, *An Empire Loses Hope,* Norton, New York, 1970.

———, *The New Russian Tragedy,* Norton, New York, 1969.

Shub, David, *Lenin, A Biography,* Doubleday, Garden City, New York, 1948.

Sjeklocha, Paul and Mead, Igor, *Unofficial Art in the Soviet Union,* University of California Press, Berkeley and Los Angeles, 1967.

Staden, Heinrich von, *The Land and Government of Muscovy,* (English translation and edited by Thomas Esper), Stanford University Press, Stanford, 1967.

Tatu, Michel, *Power in the Kremlin,* William Collins Sons, London, 1967.

Vardys, Stanley, *Lithuania Under the Soviets,* Praeger, New York, 1965.

Vladimirov, Leonid, *The Russians,* Praeger, New York, 1968.

Werth, Alexander, *Russia: Hopes and Fears,* Simon & Schuster, New York, 1969.

Whitney, Thomas P. (ed.), *The New Writing in Russia,* University of Michigan Press, Ann Arbor, 1964.

Wilson, Francesca, *Muscovy: Russia Through Foreign Eyes,* Allen & Unwin, London, 1970.

Wolfe, Bertram D., *Three Who Made a Revolution,* Thames and Hudson, London, 1956.

Yevtushenko, Yevgeny, *A Precocious Autobiography,* Dutton, New York, 1963.

INDEX